YESHUA BEN

Yeshua Ben David

Why do the Jewish people reject Jesus
as their Messiah?

WALTER RIGGANS

MARC

Crowborough

British Library Cataloguing Data
A catalogue record for this book is available
from the British Library.

ISBN 1 85424 287 3

Designed and produced by Bookprint Creative Services
P.O. Box 827, BN21 3YJ, England for
MARC an imprint of Monarch Publications,
Broadway House, The Broadway,
Crowborough, East Sussex, TN6 1HQ.
Printed in Finland.

Contents

Acknowledgements

It is my very great pleasure to acknowledge the generosity of my former colleagues at All Nations Christian College in Hertfordshire, England, and also of the College Council. They gave further evidence of their strong commitment to research and to the publication of books geared towards helping the Church to reflect more deeply on its mission and to engage more meaningfully in that mission, by allowing me to take a term's sabbatical to write this book. This was done at a time when we were experiencing a significant staff turnover, and when I myself was actually preparing to leave the college to return to full-time service in Jewish ministry. They all have my grateful thanks, and I can only hope that this book proves to be as useful as they wished it.

My thanks also go to Dr Gerald H. Anderson and the staff of the Overseas Ministries Study Center in New Haven, Connecticut, for enabling my family and myself to spend the sabbatical there. Not only do I thank them for sharing their expertise and friendship, but also for the way in which they helped me to make the best use of the resources at the Yale Divinity School and the various academic libraries in New Haven. The library staff at all of these institutions were marvellous to work with.

Considerable financial help was given to me by both ANCC and OMSC, but I am also delighted to express my gratitude to the Trustees of The Pollock Memorial Missionary Trust for their generous grant. This meant a great deal to me, since I am Scottish and a minister in the Church of

Scotland. I commend their commitment to sensitive and informed missiology.

My family and I are also grateful to Rev. Peter Rogers and his family, and to the congregation of St John's Episcopal Church in New Haven for welcoming us so warmly and caringly. Life would have been very much the poorer had it not been for them all.

Finally, I would like to express my sincere thanks to the Council members of the Church's Ministry among the Jews (CMJ), who gave me the honour of becoming the General Director of that society in the autumn of 1994. I was constantly aware of the ministry of CMJ as I wrote this book, and I dedicate it to the men and women who serve that society so faithfully and so well. May we see our future work for the Messiah being wonderfully blessed by God!

Preface

Over the past few years I have been encouraged by many Jewish believers in Jesus, and by many non-Jewish Christians, to write a book which would help them to understand better the theological, historical, and psychological reasons for the contemporary resurgence of a strong and specifically Jewish rejection of the Messiahship of Jesus. Refutations of the Gospel can be found at every turn in our societies, but *Jewish* refutationists can sound particularly threatening to Christians.

It is my pleasure to offer this small book as a first stage in my response to that encouragement. I hope that it will prove to be useful, not only as a means of providing some insight into the Jewish agenda concerning Jesus and those who accept him as Israel's Messiah, but also as a corrective to some of the misguided and inappropriate responses often given by Christians to Jewish people who make the sorts of challenges which we shall see in this book. Christians have a great deal to learn from Jewish insights, and also a great deal to repent of in terms of the awful record of Christian treatment of the Jewish people, as well as having the Gospel to share with them.

The need for a thoroughly contemporary work to examine this issue is well known by those who serve in any way in ministry to Jewish people. However, I am aware that some casual Christian readers may also be looking at this book on a shelf somewhere. Let me then try to sum up the seriousness of the task before us in a sentence or two.

Jewish refutationists, following the teaching of the rabbis, if not always in the same spirit, are not only saying that Jesus is not the Messiah, although that would be important enough to merit a response. No, they are going much further, declaring that Jesus *could not* have been Israel's true Messiah! This requires a very definite response, since it attacks the very foundations of our faith.

Christians must be able to respond to the charge of the rabbis that Jesus could not be the Messiah of Israel, because if he is not the biblically-promised Messiah of the Jewish people, then he cannot be anyone else's Christ! Of course there are those Christian theologians today who are trying to present a theory that God has two different covenant communities in his service, one covenant relationship for the Jewish people and another for everyone else. In this scenario, it would be possible to argue, as they do, that Jesus is the Christ of the Church but not the Messiah of Israel. However, evangelical and other orthodox Christians cannot accept this misreading of the biblical teaching about God's one covenant relationship with the world, through Abraham's seed, the Jewish people, and his ultimate seed, Jesus, the Messiah.[1]

I must stress that this present book is intended for use by all followers of Jesus, not just pastors, missionaries or theologians. The rabbinic denial of Jesus' credentials attacks the very foundation of our faith, and it is important that each person, whether trained in theology or not, should be able to work through the main issues and arguments. The time for a more academic treatment of the underlying issues, contexts and perspectives will come in the not too distant future, God willing. This book is not about easy Christian answers to difficult Jewish questions. It is about Jewish people, and how to help them to really meet Jesus, the Son of David.

---

[1] For a discussion of the biblical concept of covenant, see my earlier booklet, *The Biblical Basis of Covenant* (PWM Ministries, 1993).

I would be delighted to hear from anyone who has read this book and who wishes to learn more about the various issues touched on here, or who is interested in supporting, or even becoming involved in, our sensitive, informed and committed ministry among Jewish people.

I have organised this book into two sections. In Part One, we shall concentrate on the macro-issues, examining the major historical, theological and hermeneutical contexts which underlie every specific point of detail. Without a good grasp of the larger picture it is impossible to do justice to the various matters of difference between Jews and Christians concerning particular texts of the Bible, etc. But then, in Part Two, we shall focus on several particular texts and doctrines which are of fundamental importance to Christians. In this second part we shall begin to do the kind of detailed work which is also necessary in sharing the Gospel with Jewish people.

Some readers might be tempted to go directly to Part Two, because their real interest is in how Christian and Jewish theologians deal with certain thorny issues in important Messianic passages in the Bible. Let me make a plea that you resist that temptation and work through the first part of the book first. There is always a danger that studying the different possible interpretations of a text will become simply an academic exercise. This matter of the serious dispute over whether or not Jesus is the Messiah, the Son of David, is, however, a very real question which impacts on many millions of people. It is vital that we know something of the attitudes, presuppositions and goals of the two communities in conflict before we examine the more detailed matters of textual exegesis. It is too easy to find what you want to find in a text.

So let us now begin to explore the reasons for the often bitter attacks on Jesus and the New Testament which are enjoying a new vogue today in certain sections of the Jewish community.

PART ONE

*'A gentle answer turns away wrath, but a
harsh word stirs up anger.'*

I

Confident, but modest

The life and teaching of Jesus of Nazareth is not a very popular subject in most Jewish homes. In all probability, this was not the case in Jesus' own day, nor in the first generations of the birth and growth of the movement which bears his name. There can be little doubt that in those early years Jesus' parables and discourses, his opinions and decisions, his attitudes and behaviour would have been part of the conversation of the whole Jewish community, leadership and membership alike. However, centuries of bitter conflict between the communities of church and synagogue, centuries moreover in which the Jewish people were sinned against incomparably more than they sinned, produced a situation in which the synagogue was at pains to distance itself altogether from any consideration of the claims of Jesus. More than this, there was also the development in some quarters of an active strategy to categorically refute both the Messiahship of Jesus and the authority of the New Testament record of his life.[2]

The Jewish people were intent on facing up to the challenge of Jesus because of the importance to them of the issue of the Messiah. If the whole notion of a Messiah had been one which could have been jettisoned by the faithful, then that is precisely what would have happened. But belief in the reality of the Messiah and in the promise of his coming to

---

[2] I have written about this history of conflict and its effect on Jewish–Christian relations in an earlier book entitled, *The Covenant with the Jews* (Monarch Publications, 1992).

Israel is of the essence of the Jewish faith. It is the twelfth of the Thirteen Principles of Faith codified by Rabbi Moses ben Maimon in the Middle Ages and accepted as authoritative by Orthodox Jewish people till today. Here is a translation of that twelfth principle:

> I believe with complete assurance in the coming of the Messiah, and I will wait daily for his coming, even if he tarries.[3]

The question of the identity and the work of the Messiah is part of the ongoing Jewish agenda, but Jesus is not part of that agenda.

On the other hand, in recent years we have also witnessed the beginning of a brand-new type of appreciation of Jesus by Jewish scholars as he is perceived by *them* to have been in reality. This newly-found Jesus is actually being 'reclaimed' by many Jewish people from what they see as the Church's hijacking of someone who was an important pious Jew in the Galilee of the Second Temple period. He is not at all viewed as Israel's Messiah, let alone as the incarnate Son of God, but as a wandering 'Hasid' of his time, with an infectious sense of God's presence in his life, a corresponding reputation for being able to work miracles, and an unusually fine gift of teaching. This new debate about 'the real historical Jesus' is well and truly joined in our day, and is being carried out in academically rigorous ways by the people concerned, without in any sense diminishing their commitment to their own personal religious beliefs and values. Even here, therefore, the Jewish community is adamant in its insistence that the real Jesus was not the Messiah.[4]

---

[3] Rabbi Moses ben Maimon (1135–1204) inserted these Thirteen Principles of Faith as an introduction to his commentary on the Talmudic tractate, Sanhedrin. It is included in the Jewish Prayer Book to this day, and as well as being recited by Jewish people, it is sung at the close of the weekly service in a poetic version.

[4] I have written about this new quest for the historical Jesus and its implications for Jewish–Christian relations in my book entitled *Jesus Ben Joseph* (Monarch Publications, 1993).

However, in our day we are also seeing the resurgence of a specific type and style of debate which would have been better left in the past. I am speaking about a kind of forum in the Jewish community which has traditionally been given the title of 'refutation literature'. This present book has come about largely in response to repeated requests by different Christian groups to provide something like a comprehensive guide to help people to understand this particular approach, especially since it is once again becoming commonplace in our western societies. The need is there for a guide which will also help Christians to respond in appropriate ways to these charges which are made against Jesus and against the New Testament.

It goes without saying, as I have stated elsewhere and as I shall be arguing shortly, that Jewish people have every right to say 'No' to Jesus. Though at the same time it must be said, in spite of loud objections to the contrary, that Jewish people also have the right to say 'Yes' to him, to acknowledge him as their Messiah. And whereas it must be perfectly acceptable for leaders and spokespersons in the Jewish community to make clear the grounds on which they reject Jesus, is it too much to hope that we might have learned from the terrible attitudes of the past, and therefore wish to express our disagreements in tones of mutual respect? Sadly, not everyone sees it this way. Some of the shameful stratagems of earlier generations are being revived by certain Jewish leaders, who seem to endorse the attitude that the end justifies the means.

If we are not careful, then, both the Jewish and the Christian communities will be drawn back into the vulgar practice of simply trying to score points at the expense of the other. Not only that, but the game of scoring points is increasingly being played in an overtly cynical, triumphalistic and sarcastic way. I have actually had a polemicist say to me that I was only upset at this new hard-line Jewish attitude because Christians are now experiencing what they have

made the Jewish people endure for centuries. Not only is that
not true in my case, but his support of the new refutationists
reflected a terribly shallow commitment on his part to shaping a better future relationship between committed evangelical Christians and committed Jewish people.

What I intend to do in this book is to help Christians, and
especially Jewish believers in Jesus, to be able to respond
confidently and persuasively, yet with genuine respect and
modesty, to the whole range of specifically *Jewish* objections
to the New Testament revelation about Jesus. In particular, it
has, sadly, become important to respond to the fast-growing
degenerate challenge within the Jewish community, by some
of its self-appointed guardians, to the Messiahship of Jesus.
It must be said at the outset that many rabbis and other
Jewish community leaders are also embarrassed and highly
perturbed at this vulgar pseudo-scholarship. Contemporary
refutationists like Samuel Levine, Shmuel Arkush, Immanuel
Shochet and Shmuel Golding, whose names will crop up
regularly in this study, are *not* representative of the style
and behaviour of the Jewish community, but their programmes of teaching and training are finding growing audiences, especially among students and young Jewish people
generally, and their published works are readily available.
There is a danger of a kind of paralysis setting in among
Christians when rabbis or other knowledgeable Jewish people deliver strong objections to the claims of the New
Testament about Jesus and about his followers. It seems
that most Christians have an intuition that a Jewish 'No' to
Jesus is somehow more fundamental than that of anyone else,
and this intuition is surely sound. Unique among all the
religious communities, only the Jewish community can,
and does, claim *priority of revelation* over the Christian
community. In other words, the Jewish people base their
objections to the New Testament witness to Jesus on the
claim that they know better because they have known the
God of the Bible from the beginning. They were in covenant

relationship with him from the time of Abraham on, and so they, of all peoples, should know what he is really like; they, of all peoples, should understand the correct interpretation of the Hebrew Bible; they, of all peoples, should know what to expect from Israel's Messiah, etc.

It is certainly true that no-one else can lay claim to this perspective, and Christians need to take much more notice of the Jewish challenge to the Christian faith than is commonly done today. All of this is greatly compounded when a Jewish person goes on to claim, as the refutationists do, that only the Jewish people, of all peoples, are able to read and understand the Hebrew Bible properly in its original language, and therefore with its original intent. Beth Moshe, an author of one of the contemporary examples of refutationist writings, spells out this point right at the outset of her work:

> Jews know the Hebrew Bible best. Judaism is a faith built on solid Hebrew Biblical knowledge . . . It can be said that no one knows our holy revelation better than those to whom it was addressed, namely ourselves . . . Our Hebrew Bible has nothing to say about Jesus, not one thing. Christianity's use of our Bible is both their strength and their flaw. It is their strength because the Hebrew Bible is the word of God. It is their flaw because they misinterpret and misappropriate our Scriptures to support their claims.[5]

As I said at the beginning of a previous paragraph, a kind of paralysis often comes over Christians in these circumstances! In my experience, one of two attitudes tends to follow this moment of paralysis, as I have observed in both Jewish and non-Jewish believers. Some move into an attitude of *dogmatic aggression*, during which they make statements which assume a knowledge and expertise which they certainly do not possess. I can think of many conversations I have over-

---

[5] Beth Moshe, *Judaism's Truth Answers the Missionaries* (Bloch Publishing Company, NY, 1987), p 2.

heard in which the Christian has categorically denied that a Hebrew word can have the meaning which the Jewish person is claiming for it, and yet the Christian knows no Hebrew at all! I have witnessed many debates in which the Christian has seen fit to lecture the Jewish person concerning when a particular idea or liturgical practice entered the Jewish community, and yet that Christian has never engaged in personal research into the subject. At best, assuming that Christians might be right in what they are claiming, we could credit them with good secondhand knowledge, even if, as is commonly the case, the author or person who served as their source also only received the information secondhand. In this case, their confidence would really be in the person from whom they gleaned the information.

But sadly, all too often the 'knowledge' turns out to be incorrect, or flawed in some way, or even ambiguous in its interpretation. This can only lead, at best, to a kind of immediate point-scoring victory or to a stalemate in the discussion. But at worst, it leads to the experience of being accused either then and there or later, by someone who knows better, of not only ignorance but also arrogance. Such an experience is not merely embarrassing for the Christian involved, but also impairs the witness of the larger Christian community. How often have I seen this happen to enthusiastic but over-confident and dogmatic Christians!

Others react in a different way altogether to this experience of paralysis. They develop an attitude of *insecure defensiveness*, in which they assume that their own grasp of even the basics of their faith is seriously deficient. They surrender the right to any certainty and knowledge to the Jewish person with whom they are speaking, or to the Jewish community which that person represents. This is often linked to the commonly-held myth that all Jewish people know the Hebrew Bible off by heart; that they are all fluent in Hebrew; and that they all study the Talmud regularly. But even when one *does* meet such a deeply religious and knowledgeable

Jewish person, this does not mean that their interpretation of a passage in the Bible, or their presentation of the significance of a concept or the like, is necessarily correct or the only one!

What is badly needed is the discipline of the middle ground. By this I mean that Christians need to be assured that they *can* have confidence in the New Testament, in the Messiahship of Jesus, in the reality of the truth that God is Father, Son and Holy Spirit, in the atoning death and resurrection of Jesus, and also in the fact that this is all in accordance with the Hebrew Bible, in spite of the claims to the contrary from the Jewish community. But at the same time, there is no warrant for a triumphalistic attitude which despises the Jewish community's sensitivities and questions.

Christians need to be made aware that the various forms of Judaism practised today, whether in the Orthodox family of Jewish communities or in any of the others, have themselves developed a long way from the faith and practice of the Jewish people in biblical times. Judaism is not the mother of Christianity, as is too often said by people who should know better; rather, both are 'sister' faiths stemming from the same mother, but they have moved away from each other and, in their different ways, from their mother faith, over the generations. The Gospel is not believed in another guise by the Jewish people. We shall have more to say about this point later.

On the other hand, Christians need to learn that there *are* different ways to read the Hebrew Bible, ways adopted by the Jewish community; reading it in a different way need not be a sign of wickedness or ignorance; some of the fundamental doctrines of the Church are not self-evidently there in the Hebrew Bible; and the Jewish people have developed their own attitudes to Jesus, to Paul, and to basic Christian teachings and values, etc, not as a result of extensive or intensive study of the New Testament, but in the crucible of their experiences with Christians in history. The dreadful reality of Christian antisemitism is all too well known to need repeating here.[6] It is no surprise that their response has been a negative one. And so Christians need to learn modesty and humility instead of dogmatism and frustration; sensitivity and appreciation instead of ignorance and naïvety. Such a middle way requires patience and love in great measure, just as it demands a profound trust in God rather than in arguments. It is a real discipline for people to learn.[7]

In this book, then, we shall be examining several areas of study:

- The very *principles* according to which Jewish people have consistently rejected Jesus and the New Testament community
- The *methods of interpreting* the Hebrew Bible which have become standard and commonplace in the Jewish community
- The huge role played by *Christian antisemitism* in convincing the Jewish people that Jesus could not be the Messiah
- Many *specific examples* of actual areas of dispute between Jewish and Christian people regarding the correct way to read the Bible, the correct way to interpret history, the true character and characteristics of the Messiah, and the true inner nature of God, etc.

We shall also be discovering that in order to engage meaningfully in what is a robust and comprehensive dispute, simply reading a translation of the Bible at face value is

---

[6] Although I am aware of the fact that the popular spelling of the term is 'anti-semitism', it has always seemed an inappropriate spelling to me. There is no such thing as 'semitism' to be anti-, and therefore I prefer to write antisemitism as one word, expressing this anti-Christian attitude and behaviour. When quoting other people of course, I use their spelling of the word.

[7] For a modern Jewish presentation of the basic clash of theologies see the article, 'Between Christian and Jew', by Rabbi Dan Cohn-Sherbok, in *Christian Jewish Relations*, 71 (1980), pp 3–9.

not good enough. Various disciplines of study are involved in doing justice to the issues.

- *Biblical exegesis* and application play a vital part, as might be expected
- *Theological thinking* is equally important – do we know what we believe, and why?
- *Historical perspective* is a prerequisite in understanding the passion of the Jewish refutation of Jesus
- *Language issues* will also arise from time to time as we try to determine the actual meanings of words, or their possible range of meanings.

I shall be avoiding technical language as much as possible, since this book is aimed at the general reader, intelligent and committed but without specialist knowledge. However, from time to time there will be a need to deal with complex and technical matters, and I shall endeavour to present the issues and data in as reader-friendly a way as possible.

It should be clear enough by now that I am convinced of the need for Christians, and especially Jewish believers in Jesus, to be deeply committed to this process of engagement with the traditional Jewish refutations of the Gospel. The challenge is far too serious to be ignored, standing as it does head and shoulders above the challenge made by any other religious community. But as I indicated at the outset, my particular concern in writing this book is to counter, in appropriate ways, the specific kind of challenge which is being made by theologically unscrupulous Jewish writers and speakers today. If the Christian community sits back long enough in the face of some of the outrageous statements being made, then eventually the wider community, not to mention the Jewish community, will assume that the refutations are irrefutable.

We owe it to the Lord, and to our brothers and sisters in the faith, especially our Jewish brothers and sisters, to show with respect and love that in spite of all the impressive-sounding rhetoric, Jesus *is* the Messiah of Israel and the Saviour of the world, and that this is fully congruent with the faith of Israel as set out in the Hebrew Bible.

In short, it is perfectly 'Jewish' to believe in Jesus! Or, to put it another way, we can be confident that Jesus *is* the Messiah, the Son of David.

Jewish refutation of the New Testament faith has a long history, and in fact goes back to some of Jesus' own encounters with people, especially certain of the religio-political leaders within the Jewish community. A number of these confrontations are recorded for us in the gospels, as we see from these examples:

As Jesus went on from there, he saw a man named Matthew sitting at the tax collector's booth. 'Follow me,' he told him, and Matthew got up and followed him. While Jesus was having dinner at Matthew's house, many tax collectors and 'sinners' came and ate with him and his disciples. When the Pharisees saw this, they asked his disciples, 'Why does your teacher eat with tax collectors and "sinners"?' On hearing this, Jesus said, 'It is not the healthy who need a doctor, but the sick. But go and learn what this means; "I desire mercy, not sacrifice". For I have not come to call the righteous, but sinners.'[8]

While they were going out, a man who was demon-possessed and could not talk was brought to Jesus. And when the demon was driven out, the man who had been dumb spoke. The crowd was amazed and said, 'Nothing like this has ever been seen in Israel.' But the Pharisees said, 'It is by the prince of demons that he drives out demons.'[9]

The Jews answered him, 'Aren't we right in saying that you are a Samaritan and demon-possessed?' 'I am not possessed by a demon,' said Jesus, 'but I honour my Father and you dishonour me. I am not seeking glory for myself; but there is one who seeks it, and he is the judge. I tell you the truth, if anyone keeps

---

[8] Matt 9:9–13.

[9] Matt 9:32–34.

my word, he will never see death.' At this the Jews exclaimed, 'Now we know that you are demon-possessed! Abraham died and so did the prophets, and yet you say that if a man keeps your word, he will never taste death. Are you greater than our father Abraham? He died, and so did the prophets. Who do you think you are?'

Jesus replied, 'If I glorify myself, my glory means nothing. My Father, whom you claim as your God, is the one who glorifies me. Though you do not know him, I know him. If I said I did not, I would be a liar like you, but I do know him and keep his word. Your father Abraham rejoiced at the thought of seeing my day; he saw it and was glad.' 'You are not yet fifty years old,' the Jews said to him, 'and you have seen Abraham?'

'I tell you the truth,' Jesus answered, 'before Abraham was born, I am!' At this, they picked up stones to stone him, but Jesus hid himself, slipping away from the temple grounds.[10]

This kind of public dispute carried on past the time of Jesus into the life of the early Messianic Jewish communities, and we see some indication of it in the Book of Acts, where Peter, John and Stephen become involved in heated debates over the issues of who Jesus really is, what God's will is for Israel and the other nations, the means of atonement for sin, etc. Indeed we must concede that such disputes, although by no means sought by Christians, are part of the very fabric of the relationship between Christians and Jews, especially between Jewish people who believe in Jesus and other Jewish people. Strong debates between committed people are not abnormal. The fact of the matter is that we disagree passionately about some fundamentals of our respective faiths, faiths which mean everything to us. Saying this is not meant to be some form of justification for what has happened in the past, but it is a reminder that *disagreement* in and of itself is inevitable, and not necessarily a wicked matter.

---

[10] John 8:48–59.

We Christians and Jews can only seek to reconcile our differences artificially at the expense of compromising our integrity and our beliefs. The issues over which we differ could not be more fundamental, covering questions like the following:

● What are the authoritative books of the Bible?
● Is the New Testament the Word of God? Is the Talmud?
● Is the concept of the tri-unity of God a biblical concept?
● Did Jesus die on the cross as an atonement for the sins of the world?
● Has the Messiah already come, or are we still waiting?
● Is the Torah still determinative of God's will for the Jewish people?
● Does Isaiah 53 really speak about Jesus, or about the nation of Israel?
● Does the Bible teach that the Messiah will come twice, or that there will be two Messiahs?

What I am saying is that it should be possible for Jewish and Christian people to face up to the fact of these basic differences, and even to pursue a rigorous programme of debate about them, without the whole exercise degenerating, as it has done so often in the past, into showmanship, manipulation, or worse. As adults we must be able to accept the right of other people to their own beliefs, and to engage them purposefully yet respectfully. It is only when someone becomes abusive that special attention needs to be given, and that brings us once again to the purpose of this book.

Christians cannot throw any stones at the Jewish community over this matter of abusive approaches to disputes, and I could not begin to defend much of what has been said and done in the name of Jesus. Nor should it be spoken of in the past tense only, since these bad attitudes to the Jewish people and to the Jewish commitment to Judaism are still found in abundance. However, this does not mean that the contemporary attack by these Jewish refutationists should be tolerated either. I am writing this book for the vast numbers of Christians who wish to see the whole debate through to the end without fear of ridicule or manipulation. Bruce Lieske, an American Lutheran minister has put it well in his presentation of the case for *Jewish* people having this right to full and free debate about the issues:

> In our pluralistic society we hold that each person has a right to believe as he chooses, and also has the right to share his beliefs with others, as long as he does it in a loving way, without manipulation or pressure, and respects the other person even when he says 'no' to the witness.[11]

This is the way for us to move forward together. So there is no need for Christians to fear entering into debate with Jewish people over the fundamentals of our faith. Interestingly, 150 years ago a Jewish believer in Jesus, Moses Margoliouth, offered the opinion that healthy debate with the synagogue was in fact probably a sign that the Church herself was healthy!

> Jewish controversy rose and fell with the rise and fall of true Christianity. We find very little written on that subject from the 8th to the 15th century; for the Christian Church was, during that period, distracted and afflicted with intolerable corruptions.[12]

While we would have to take issue with his statement that there was little published in the way of 'controversy' in that period of 700 years, the debate was certainly not of a healthy nature. Various public disputations which the Church imposed upon the Jewish communities were symptomatic of prejudice and ignorance rather than moral and spiritual

---

[11] Bruce J. Lieske, *Witnessing to Jewish People* (revised edition, The Lutheran Church – Missouri Synod, 1984), p 3.

[12] Moses Margoliouth, *The Fundamental Principles of Modern Judaism Investigated* (Wertheim, London, 1843), p xii.

maturity. Margoliouth himself spoke about the legacy of that medieval period as being simply one of persecution, contempt and forced conversions. It is certainly a fascinating thesis that the Church only disengages from healthy debate with the Jewish community when she is weak and disobedient. Is this true of any of our Churches today?

Clemens Thoma, a Roman Catholic scholar, has also suggested that such disputes with the Jewish community are necessary for the health of the Church. He writes:

> Christian theologians would be well advised, though, to consider Jewish exceptions to their theological and Christological statements. Taken altogether, Jewish ideas are not mere negations, opposition for opposition's sake, but warnings of potential perversions of faith in the God of Israel.[13]

In other words, these writers are encouraging Christians not to be afraid, nor even to feel guilty, about the need to engage in proper dispute with Jewish people. The point remains that such dispute is 'natural'. We can learn a great deal today about how best to present the truth of the Gospel to Jewish people from the wisdom of those in previous generations who themselves engaged in the same task. However, it must also be stressed that we will learn perhaps just as much from the mistakes of the past as from the 'successes'!

As we begin to look into some specific issues and to examine some very important insights and perspectives, it is vital to emphasise that we must live our lives, and so bear our witness, in strict accordance with two fundamental biblical principles:

- Love your neighbour as yourself.
- You shall not give false testimony against your neighbour.[14]

---

[13] Clemens Thoma, *A Christian Theology of Judaism* (Paulist Press, NY, 1980), p 131.
[14] Lev 19:18; Ex 20:16.

In all of our sharing of the Gospel, whether in formal or informal settings, we must make sure that we are really listening to what is being said to us. It is of particular importance that we treat the other person with the same respect that we would like to receive, and a large part of this is making sure that we in no way misrepresent their views or arguments. Sadly, there is often all too much truth in the old caricature of Christian evangelists as people who have no real desire to listen to the other person; who insist on doing all the talking; and who try to interpret everything only through their own frames of reference, rather than letting the other people define themselves and their own beliefs. This has been especially true of much evangelism among Jewish people, leaving them with the distinct impression that Christians are simply insensitive to their sincere objections and all too often content merely to give pat answers to what are often valid and important questions. Christians would not like to be treated that way by Jewish people, and so must take to heart the biblical imperatives quoted above.

Apart from anything else, Christians need to learn that even the use of a common vocabulary does not in itself necessarily mean that people intend the same thing by the same word. This is of particular importance in Jewish–Christian debates, since such a huge percentage of the key theological terms used by both communities are held in common. But words like Messiah, salvation, sin, etc, have come to be understood in sometimes radically different ways over the centuries, and Jewish and Christian people are not always communicating when they think they are. How often have I heard Christians speaking away happily to Jewish people about the work of the Messiah, only to be staggered when they realise that whereas they were taking for granted the fact that the Messiah, whoever he is, would be a divine person, Jewish people make no such assumption – in fact the opposite! There can be no substitute for disciplined listening to the other person and to that person's community.

I hope it will not be taken as too flippant if I tell a Jewish joke at this point. I learned it from a rabbi in his sermon one Friday evening in synagogue. He was himself speaking about this very point of the need to be sensitive and attentive. The scene was medieval Europe, when the Jewish communities were suffering terribly at the hands of antisemitic Christian princes and priests. News came to a small Jewish village one day that the Pope himself was coming to supervise the total expulsion of their entire village completely out of the region. Total despair overtook everyone. There was no way that they could present a case for being left in peace with their lives and their faith, especially in the light of the Pope's personal intervention. When the terrible day came, the Pope surprised everyone, including his own retinue, by offering a glimmer of hope to the powerless Jewish community. He gave them the following challenge, which could not be refused even if the Jewish community had wished to do so. The Pope himself would engage in a public theological dispute with a representative of the Jewish community. If the Pope was victorious (and how could he lose?), then the Jewish people had to move out; but if the Jewish spokesman dared to win, then the community could stay.

The papal retinue sighed in relief, concluding that the Pope simply wanted some harmless sport before moving on. The Jewish community sighed in resignation, knowing that this was simply a way of adding public humiliation to the inevitable expulsion order. The scene was set. Things looked so bleak that no-one in the Jewish community was prepared to enter into debate with the Pope. The rabbi refused point-blank to take part. Suddenly the village fool spoke up and said that he was ready to represent the community, if that was all right with everyone else. After a moment of shock, they decided that he was as good as anyone, and besides, it was one way of laughing at the Pope as he laughed at them. When it came to the hour of the dispute the Pope imposed two conditions: in the first place, neither of them was to speak, but they were to rely entirely on non-verbal communication, and in the second place, each was allowed to make only three points. And so battle commenced.

The Pope stood up and made an exaggerated movement of his right arm away from his chest into a sweeping arc. The village fool stood up and responded by reversing the gesture and slapping his chest. The Pope staggered, and conceded defeat. He then stood up again and held out three fingers into the fool's face. His response was to hold up one finger in the Pope's face, at which the Pope once more reeled and conceded defeat. Finally, the Pope rose and set out bread and wine on a portable altar and celebrated the Eucharist. At this the fool put his hand in his pocket, pulled out an apple, and took a big bite. To the amazement of everyone present, the Pope confessed that he had been well and truly out-argued by the finest theological mind that he had ever encountered. The Jewish community was allowed to stay in their village.

On their way home to Rome, the papal retinue begged the Pope for an explanation of what had been going on! 'Well,' said the Pope, 'I began by declaring the goodness of God in that he loves all of mankind, but he responded by reminding me that the real wonder of God is that he could love even me. I continued by affirming that God is Trinity, but he rightly declared that this does not compromise his essential unity. At last I showed him the victory which we have by the grace of God, but he rebuked me in his correction that God alone has the victory, since we are still but miserable sinners.' All were agreed that this was indeed a theological *tour de force*.

Back in the village pandemonium had broken out. How had he done it? What had he said? The village fool insisted that he had no idea what had persuaded the Pope to concede defeat. But when pushed to describe the events as he had seen them, he gave the following interpretation. 'The Pope said that we all have to leave the village, but I said, "Not me!" He didn't seem to hear me, because he continued by saying that we had only three days to get out. I told him that not one of us would leave. Then I don't know what happened. He just got out his lunch, so I did too!'

This joke works on different levels. In one sense it could simply be a clever and funny joke about the pitfalls of not communicating properly when you think you are. But bearing in mind that this is a *Jewish* joke, set in the context it was, it is fairly clear that more is at stake than simply that. It is a way of trying to come out of the mind-set of the Middle Ages by ridiculing the Christian rulers who so abused their authority and overrated their knowledge and skill. I don't tell this joke lightly. It had a profound impact on me when I first heard it from that rabbi many years ago now. It helped me to see that such humour was not at all a reflection of any kind of Jewish arrogance or the like, as antisemitic people would like to present it. On the contrary, it was part of a defensive mechanism, a cathartic mechanism in fact, which helped the Jewish community to hold up its head with a right sense of dignity and affirmed the fact that the Jewish people could stand on their own feet if they were only given the chance by their Christian oppressors. We shall return to this issue later, because I believe that it is one of the most important contexts and perspectives that Christians need to take hold of if they are to respond appropriately to the worst excesses of the modern refutationists.

For the present, though, let us return to the issue of Judaism's claim to have historical and theological priority over Christianity. I have already touched upon this popular notion that Judaism is the 'mother' of Christianity. Margoliouth quotes something said to him in the early part of the last century, the essence of which has now become a commonplace in many Jewish–Christian interfaith circles:

We must still contend that if any creed has a right to pronounce a decision on the merits of religions based on Scripture, it is

Judaism – the mother is the best judge of the different characters of her daughters.[15]

Here it is then: the frequently-found designation of Judaism as the parent-faith of Christianity. This notion has been voiced throughout the generations of Jewish tradition, but it received a new lease of life in the late 1960s. It is used as an argument against the appropriateness of any evangelism among the Jewish people, since the parent-faith is assumed to be secure in God. Indeed the parent-faith is held to have bequeathed much of its own life, revelation and insights to the daughter-faith. Thus there is said to be a monumental arrogance associated with Christians who believe that they, from the child community, have the secret of life with God which they must offer back to the Jewish people, the parent community.

Significant Christian voices have been added to those who oppose and despise evangelism on this ground, including Lutherans, Presbyterians, and Roman Catholics.[16] B. Z. Sobel declared casually in his much-quoted work that 'Christianity is a child of Judaism'.[17] Other important scholars and leaders who have urged this understanding of the relationship between the two faith-communities include Balfour Brickner, Samuel Sandmel, W. D. Davies and Joseph Hertz.[18] On the other hand, there is also no shortage of scholars who reject this as simplistic and downright mislead-

---

[15] Op cit, p 34.

[16] See, for example, Harold H. Ditmanson, 'Some Theological Perspectives', in *Face To Face*, vols 3–4 (1977), pp 6–8; the 1985 Church of Scotland document entitled *Christians and Jews Today*, Appendix vii, p 54; John M. Oesterreicher, *The New Encounter Between Christians and Jews* (New York, 1986), p 136.

[17] B. Z. Sobel, *Hebrew Christianity: The Thirteenth Tribe* (John Wiley & Sons, NY, 1974), p 257.

[18] See, for example, Balfour Brickner, 'Christian Missionaries and a Jewish Response', *World-view*, May 1978, p 40; Samuel Sandmel, *We Jews And Jesus* (OUP, London, 1976), p 135; W. D. Davies, *Paul and*

ing. Noteworthy names here would include those of Jakob Jocz, James H. Charlesworth, Norman Solomon, Alan F. Segal, Leon Klenicki and Jacob Neusner.[19]

The reason for this new interest in the presentation of Judaism as the mother of Christianity is that it gives a basic motive for rejecting the suitability of the Gospel for Jewish people. If Christians wish to argue that other people need to hear and receive the Gospel, at least that can be debated; but *vis-à-vis* the Jewish people this is considered to be inappropriate. The trouble is that this notion does not survive the test of historical credibility. Both Christianity and Judaism in their various forms trace their ancestry, as it were, to the same common parent: namely the faith and the faith-community of biblical Israel. Both Judaism and Christianity have emerged and developed from the incubus of first-century Jewish life. Neither of the two communities as we know them today exist in the forms that we know they had at the time of Jesus.

Both of them have gone their separate ways, without losing touch with either their own roots or with one another. So at best, as I stated above, we could say that

---

Rabbinic Judaism (4th edition, Fortress Press, Philadelphia, 1980), p xxviii; Joseph Hertz, quoted as saying that Reform Judaism and Christianity are the two 'wayward children' of Orthodox Judaism, in W. Gunther Plaut, *The Growth of Reform Judaism* (New York, 1965), p 294.

[19]See, for example, Jakob Jocz, 'The Church of Rome and the Jews', in *The International Review of Mission*, vol 51, no 203 (1962), p 319; James H. Charlesworth (ed), *Jews and Christians. Exploring the Past, Present, and Future* (Crossroad, NY, 1990), pp 36–41, 41–43, 95; Rabbi Norman Solomon, *Division and Reconciliation* (The London Diocesan Council for Jewish–Christian Understanding, London, 1980), pp 2–3; Alan F. Segal, *Rebecca's Children: Judaism and Christianity in the Roman World* (Harvard University Press, London, 1986), pp 1–2, 179–181; Rabbi Leon Klenicki, *Jew and Christian in Conversation* (Eerdmans, Grand Rapids, MI, 1989), p 20; Jacob Neusner, *Jews and Christians. The Myth of a Common Tradition* (SCM Press, London, 1991).

Christianity and Judaism are sisters belonging to the same family. Nevertheless, this misunderstanding of the relationship between the two communities as being analogous to that of parent and child has found a ready audience in many people, Christian as well as Jewish, who want to see a moratorium on any evangelistic ministry to Jewish people, or on any active ministry in support of Jewish believers in Jesus.

One of the most eloquent expressions of this conviction that the parent faith has nothing to learn from the offspring came from the pen of Harry Austryn Wolfson, who wrote in 1925:

> Throughout the history of religious controversies between Christians and Jews in the Middle Ages Christianity was on the defensive. The Christians considered themselves called upon to prove the claims they made on behalf of Jesus by endeavouring to show that the vague prophetic promises were all fulfilled in Christ. The Jews had no counter claims to make; they simply refused to be impressed. As the historical custodians of the Bible text as well as of its manifold interpretations, the Jews looked rather amazed and at times even amused at the confidence with which the erstwhile heathen interpreted at their own pleasure the mistaken Scriptures quoted from the Vulgate. This attitude of aloofness and incredulity was sufficient to enrage even saints among Christians, for it gave them an uneasiness of feeling, deepening into fear and doubt and a general sense of discomfort, which explains much of the Christian intolerance of the Jews.[20]

Wolfson has expressed an historical truth quite accurately. Christians did experience a great feeling of frustration at the Jewish refusal to accept the force of their arguments, and they did in fact often react with a show of force against

---

[20] Harry Austryn Wolfson, from his Introduction to the 2nd edition of Joseph Jacobs: *Jesus As Others Saw Him* (Bernard G. Richards Co, Inc, NY, 1925), p vii.

Jewish people. Christians cannot, of course, ignore this kind of challenge to the integrity of their witness to Jesus. But the appropriate response is never the terrible resort to violence and intimidation which has in fact marked so much of the Christian response, but one in which Christians are able to sit down and give an honest and coherent demonstration that the Hebrew Scriptures do in fact find their ultimate fulfilment in Jesus.

The Messiahship of Jesus, contrary to the charge of those to whom Wolfson was referring, is not a Christian invention bound up with doctored versions of the Bible in foreign languages, but the actual fulfilment of the purpose of God for his people as promised in the Hebrew Bible itself, and it definitely *is* possible to defend this claim from the Scriptures and from experience. But on the other hand, this truth is certainly not self-evident, either from reading the Hebrew Bible or indeed from everyone's experience in life. What we must learn is how to defend our convictions and interpretations in the face of those Jewish refutationists who are mistaken in their dogmatism about what is or is not an acceptably Messianic view of Scripture or life.

Now having said this and stressed that the two faiths are sisters, rather than mother and daughter, it must also be pointed out that nonetheless there is still a significant sense in which the Jewish people do continue to be the people of God.[21] The New Testament makes it quite clear that somehow Jews and Christians are bound together in the purposes of God. Note that in each of the following three passages from the New Testament the relevant verbs are all in the present tense, which is to say that they are not, as some make out, just intended as descriptions of a state of affairs that existed in the time *before* Jesus.

---

[21] For a fuller discussion of this issue, paying particular attention to the principles of election and covenant in the Bible, see my two books, *God's Covenant with the Jews*, op cit; *The Biblical Basis of Covenant*, op cit.

You Samaritans worship what you do not know; we worship what we do know, for salvation is from the Jews.[22]

Theirs is the adoption as sons; theirs the divine glory, the covenants, the receiving of the law, the temple worship and promises. Theirs are the patriarchs, and from them is traced the human ancestry of Christ, who is God over all, for ever praised! Amen.[23]

As far as the Gospel is concerned, they are enemies on your account; but as far as election is concerned, they are loved on account of the patriarchs, for God's gifts and his call are irrevocable.[24]

The Jewish people *do* have some sort of priority, some kind of important continuity within God's loving purposes, notwithstanding the call and mission of the Church. This is not the place to examine what the relationship between the two is in the economy of God, rather we must be content here with affirming that there *is* an ongoing relationship. It is therefore vital that we study, and respond to, the ongoing Jewish challenges to the Gospel. There is much that we can learn, as well as all that we wish to share with the Jewish community. There will therefore be times in this book when I shall encourage Christians to acknowledge Jewish insight and perspectives, times when I shall recommend an appreciation of the ambiguous nature of many of the 'proofs' brought by either Jews or Christians to the debate, and times when I shall argue directly against the Jewish refutationist challenges.

Our confidence need not be at all shaken by rigorous dispute. It is the conviction of this writer that Jewish people need Jesus every bit as much as non-Jewish people. To put this another way, if we have nothing to say to Jewish people

---

[22] John 4:24.

[23] Rom 9:4–5.

[24] Rom 11:28–29.

about Jesus then we have nothing to say to anyone. David Harley has seen one of the most important implications of this issue very clearly:

> If the Jewish people do not need the saving knowledge of the Lord Jesus Christ, and their religious heritage is seen in itself to be fully sufficient, then a similar case can be argued, and indeed is being argued, for other people groups also, and the universal mission of the Church is called into question.[25]

Harley is unquestionably correct in this assessment. There are already many Christian voices calling for an end to any form of evangelism among people of other faiths, and not a few of them began by insisting that the *Jewish* people were exempt from the need for the Gospel. Of course the *definitive* response of the Jewish community to the question of whether or not Jewish life and the Gospel are compatible lies in the decision taken in the early period that any Jewish people who believe in Jesus are no longer to be regarded as Jewish. They are seen as apostates who have betrayed the community and who are therefore to be shunned and disowned. The very terminology used to refer to Jewish believers reflects and perpetuates this teaching that they are no longer to be considered as Jewish. Foremost among these names is *Meshumad*, derived from a biblical Hebrew root meaning 'to destroy' or 'to cut off'. The reasoning is that a Jewish person's soul is destroyed when he or she becomes a believer in Jesus, and that such people have cut themselves off from the Jewish community by this act of betrayal.

The most famous liturgical response to the continuing presence of Jewish believers in the synagogue services was the commissioning of the so-called *Birkat ha-Minim* (the

---

[25] David Harley, 'The Christian Church and the Jewish People' Paper 1 (Lectures given at Calvin Theological Seminary, USA, April 8–10, 1986), p 5.

Blessing of the Heretics) in *c* 80 CE.[26] The standard set prayer in Judaism is called the *Amidah*, meaning that it is to be said standing up. There are eighteen blessings in this prayer, thus giving it its other common name, the *Shemoneh Esrei*, meaning simply 'The Eighteen'. In fact there are now nineteen blessings in the prayer, even though it retains its original title. The added blessing, to be found as number twelve in the sequence, is actually a curse, and it was commissioned as a device to ensure that all those considered by the rabbinic leadership to be beyond the bounds of acceptable belief and practice, including Jewish believers in Jesus, would absent themselves from the synagogue community.

The earliest version of this 'blessing' which we have reads as follows:

> For the apostates let there be no hope, and may the arrogant kingdom soon be rooted out in our days, and the Nazarenes and the minim perish as in a moment and be blotted out from the Book of Life, and with the righteous may they not be inscribed. Blessed are You, O Lord, who humbles the arrogant![27]

A later, edited version of this prayer appears in most of the Jewish Prayer Books to be found in synagogues today, but even that version is expressed in the same bitter terms. The intention was either to dissuade Jewish believers from attending services, since they could hardly recite this prayer, within the central act of prayer, against themselves and their families; or it was to identify any such Jewish believers in Jesus who were hitherto unknown in a synagogue community, since they would tend to be silent during the

---

[26] Throughout this book I shall be using the abbreviations for BC and AD which are used in the Jewish context. These are CE (= AD), meaning the 'Common Era', and BCE (= BC), meaning 'Before the Common Era'. I also use the term 'Hebrew Bible' rather than the usual Christian term, Old Testament.

[27] For this text, see Solomon Schechter, 'Geniza Specimens', *Jewish Quarterly Review*, vol 10, pp 65–67.

reciting of this particular prayer. In either case, it further demonstrates the determination of the Jewish community to exclude Jewish believers.[28]

The consensus among Jewish and Christian scholars is that this 'blessing' was indeed commissioned, as the rabbinic texts suggest, around the years 80–85 CE. This, in turn, has led many to conclude that the present form of the ninth chapter of John's Gospel is later than that time, since one of its main points is that Jewish people 'were afraid of the Jews, for already the Jews had decided that anyone who acknowledged that Jesus was the Messiah would be put out of the synagogue' (John 9:22).

Now it is quite possible that it is the effect of this Jewish blessing, and the social reinforcement which would be associated with it, that John's Gospel has in mind at this point. However, it may not be this at all. There may have been a more general ground swell of opinion against these Jewish believers, and it is that which might be reflected in John 9. But even if we do wish to link the evidence of John 9 with the Birkat ha-Minim, it is not necessary to date the chapter quite so late. Surely no one would want to argue that the decision to introduce this blessing into the daily prayer service came out of a vacuum? There can be no doubt that there was considerable pressure in the Jewish community to oust the Jewish believers *before* that antagonism was institutionalised in the formal community prayer. In other words, without getting involved in the complex issue of the dating of John's Gospel, it seems to me that the ninth chapter of that gospel certainly does reflect an early reaction against the followers of Jesus.

The whole of that chapter breathes life and has all the

---

[28] Justin Martyr refers to this aspect of the liturgy in his *Dialogue with Trypho the Jew*, 16:4, as does Epiphanius (315–403 CE) in his work, *Haereses*, 24:9. See also the *Commentary on Isaiah* by St Jerome (330–410 CE), on Isa 2:18; 49:7; 54:5.

hallmarks of authentic reporting. In the context of the chapter, it is the healed man's own parents who are afraid to testify positively about Jesus for fear of the terrible consequences of excommunication from the synagogue community. Perhaps, then, this is already an example of the fulfilling of Jesus' words in Matt 10:34–39 that when he comes into a Jewish household, loyalties may very well be tested? This man's parents do not actively turn against him, but they decline to support their son in his hour of triumph and trauma. Perhaps even Jesus' words in Matt 10:16–20 are relevant here? At any rate, we know from the account in John 9 that this man who had been born blind and had then been healed by Jesus, stood up for Jesus before the religious authorities (verses 15, 17b, 25, 27, 30–33), and was driven out of the synagogue community because of it (verse 34).

It is important to point out here that such an excommunication would have been quite unbearably traumatic in Jesus' culture. The situation was not like the one which so many of us know today in the West, in which belonging to a Church is almost a luxury in the sense that if Christians fall out with someone or develop a change in their theology, etc, then they can easily leave one Church and join another. In the context of the society of Jesus' time, we are speaking about a culture which was fundamentally religious and in which the social life of the community was entirely bound up with the synagogue. Where would Jewish people go if they were forced out? No-one else in the neighbourhood would be willing to receive such people. Who would sell them their kosher food? No, this was an extremely severe punishment in that culture, and for that reason the gospels take careful note of it.

It soon became the accepted wisdom that Jewish people who called Jesus the Messiah were to be regarded as having left the Jewish community and joined the non-Jewish world in which Jesus might well be an acceptable divine figure. For vast numbers of Jewish people today this would still be the usual reaction to a Jewish person who became a believer in Jesus. To put it another way: Judaism alone is for Jews, and Christianity (as well as other faiths) is for non-Jews. In fact the Jewish novelist Philip Roth said somewhere that there is really no other single bond which unites all Jewish people in the way that this rejection of Jesus and Christianity does. Jewish believers are therefore anathema since they now belong to the Christian, which is to say gentile, world.

More than this, it is almost universally assumed in the Jewish community that Jewish believers in Jesus are merely 'rice Christians', which is to say that they merely pretend to have a real faith. The specific charge is that they either took the personal or political decision to formally join a Church by cynically pretending to have real faith so that they would be able to advance more easily in the host culture; or else they were actually exploited by Christians at a time in their lives when they were socially or economically disadvantaged and so were easily deceived and manipulated into becoming baptised church members. In either case, the 'conversion' is seen to have been for material or social advancement, rather than as a result of personal conviction about Jesus. This in turn is based on the presupposition that the person and work of Jesus could not attract Jewish people for his sake alone. It is claimed that such conviction is not possible for a Jewish person.

A sober statement to this effect comes from the pen of David Daube, a well-respected Jewish scholar:

> The majority of Jews hold that no educated Jew can become a Christian from conviction; the simple truth of Judaism seems to them so clearly superior to the irrational dogma of Christianity that no one in possession of the former could ever come genuinely to believe in the latter.[29]

---

[29] David Daube, in his Preface to Jakob Jocz, *The Jewish People and Jesus Christ* (3rd edition, Baker Book House, Grand Rapids, MI, 1979), p 1. See also pp 201–2, 224–5, 391, n 129.

Rabbi Harry Stern seems to have been one of that endangered species of Jewish leaders prepared to be honest enough *in public* to concede that there are such things as Jewish believers who follow Jesus out of a pure conviction that he is the Messiah. Let me quote something that he once wrote:

> In all fairness it must be stated that some Jews came to Christianity out of conviction, especially in days when Christianity possessed no power.[30]

These were welcome words in 1961, the more so for their rarity value. They are still to be treasured as a rare admission three decades later. Rabbi Stern serves largely as one of the exceptions which prove the rule. I hope I can be forgiven for telling at this point another joke which has come out of the Jewish community, this time from the nineteenth century. Three Jewish men who had not seen each other for many years all boarded the same train one day. After recognising each other and catching up on some family news, it became clear to them that they had all become baptised members of different Churches. The first one explained that he had converted in order to be eligible for a responsible post in a successful business firm. The second nodded in respectful sympathy, and added that he himself had converted in order to save his own growing family from the horrors of anti-semitism. After the first man murmured words of condolence and understanding, they both stared at the third man, who up till then had been silent on this matter. There was an embarrassed silence for a few moments, and then the third man said that he had become a follower of Jesus out of conviction. The other men laughed uproariously and said, 'Go tell that to the Gentiles!'

The point of this joke is the *incredulity* of the Jewish community when it hears that any Jewish person has made

---

[30] Rabbi Harry Joshua Stern, *Entrusted with Spiritual Leadership* (1961), p 62).

a positive and voluntary decision for Jesus. Some form of Judaism is seen to be the only legitimate religious faith for a Jewish person, but Messianic Judaism, the expression of faith in Jesus as lived out and understood by Jewish believers in Jesus, is ruled out of the reckoning by the Jewish community. This basic refutation of the claims of Jesus and the New Testament will come into our thinking constantly throughout this book, but we can listen now to the words of some Jewish believers in response to the charge that it is just not acceptable for *Jewish* people to believe in him. The issue hangs, they say, on whether or not Jesus is the Messiah. If not, then it would certainly be a huge mistake for the Jewish community to believe that he was their hope and the key to the authentic Jewish life. But, on the other hand:

> It follows that if Y'shua (Jesus) is the Messiah, then nothing could be more Jewish than believing in him – or more honouring to the God of Abraham, Isaac and Jacob.[31]

This is a crucial issue. It is surely Jewish to believe in the Messiah. Orthodox Jews today still recite the authoritative Thirteen Principles of the great medieval codifier Maimonides, including, as we have seen, the declaration: 'I believe with complete faith in the coming of the Messiah . . .' The question, therefore, is whether or not *Jesus* is this Jewish Messiah. If he is the Messiah, as Messianic Jews and Christians believe, then the excommunication of Jewish believers by the Jewish community on the grounds that Jewish people cannot accept him and remain Jewish, has been one of the greatest tragedies in history.

As a final point in this introductory chapter, let me say that we must be careful in our assessment of the undoubted historical fact that down through the centuries, *after the first few generations of the Church*, the vast majority of Christians have not been Jewish, and the vast majority of Jewish

---

[31] Jews for Jesus, *Questions and Answers from Jews for Jesus* (1983), p 3.

people have followed, at least nominally, some form of Judaism. The theological, psychological and sociological pressures brought to bear on Jewish people by both the Jewish and the Christian communities, for their own particular reasons, succeeded in creating a climate in which Jewish people were prevented from thinking positively about Jesus at all. However, this does not mean, as some are trying to imply, that there is a fundamental and *necessary* theological divide between Jesus and the Jewish people which endorses, as it were, the historical situation.

There are good reasons why things have worked out the way they have in life, but none of those reasons is that God is against Jewish people becoming believers in Jesus. The Churches, for their part, have let God down almost beyond belief in their treatment of Jewish people and have made it virtually impossible for Jewish people to have a positive image of Jesus. Jewish community leaders, working out of their own agenda, have also had a vested interest in keeping their people segregated from Jesus. And in the middle of all this stand the Jewish believers, bullied by both 'sides'. Today's Messianic Jewish community, however, is determined to be heard. Good biblical theology is fighting back, and I hope that this modest book will play a part in encouraging many others, especially Jewish believers, to pick up the theological gauntlet and join in the defence of our faith.

My call is for Christians to recover fully their confidence in the Gospel as the power of God for the salvation of everyone who believes: 'first for the Jew', and then also for the non-Jew. Paul opens his Roman letter with these words, and we need to take them to heart once more. This confidence which we need is not at all a cause for self-satisfaction or cheap triumphalism. It is confidence in God and the truth of the Good News of Jesus. I am reminded of the words of a first-century CE rabbi, Gamaliel, who urged his fellow-Jews to reflect in this manner:

If their purpose or activity is of human origin, it will fail. But if it is from God, you will not be able to stop these men; you will only find yourselves fighting against God.[32]

These words can also speak to us. If we believe that there is a right way to share the Good News that Jesus is the Messiah of Israel, and if we believe that it is important to share this Good News because Jesus is the one and only Messiah, then God will bless our endeavours. Confidence in the Gospel is needed in our sharing of the Gospel, but always coupled with a modest attitude to ourselves, to our own arguments and to our evidence for the truth of the Gospel.

---

[32] Acts 5:38 f.

2

Aware of the pain

It is profoundly important that Christians realise that all debate with Jewish people about Jesus is done in the context of centuries of Jewish suffering at Christian hands. Generation after generation of murderous oppression, torture, contempt and humiliation has produced a context of such pain in the Jewish communal psyche that a disinterested debate is all but impossible. But there is even more to it than this. The factor which aggravated and compounded this pain to intolerable levels was the inability of the Jewish communities to fight back. What could they do against the political, economic and military forces of the Roman Empire, or the Christian kingdoms of Christendom? As we shall see, the rules of the host community were always slanted against the Jewish people, and the resultant sense of impotence and frustration penetrated deeply into the already deeply-wounded Jewish people's soul. What we are seeing today, then, is the release of centuries of pent-up anger, frustration and pain. We know what it is like in our own personal lives. If someone or some situation intensely angers or frustrates us, yet we say nothing and bury it over an extended period of time, then if that emotion ever does break out, it is likely to do so in ways, and with words, which are not at all disciplined. We can lash out at people with our tongues and behaviour, and sometimes innocent people get caught up in it all. This can happen on the communal level too, I believe, and the Jewish people are a case in point.

Let me make it clear that I am *not* saying that the Jewish

community can be defined solely in terms of its reactions to hostilities of various sorts from the Christian world. On the contrary, the Jewish experience has also been one of immense generosity, creativity, and faithfulness to its vision of God. Nonetheless, in terms of its relationship with Christians, all the tragedies of the past centuries are as real and relevant to the Jewish people as if they had happened only yesterday. This, too, is something which we can all appreciate. It is not some form of community neurosis peculiar to the Jewish people. There are far too many examples known to us of peoples and nations being so violated by others that the memories stay on the surface. Having said this, the Jewish experience in history is worse than that of most others.

Now one of the major differences in today's western societies, compared with the situation of the past, is that the Jewish community can at last *speak out* against its treatment at the hands of Christians without fear of reprisals in the form of pogroms or the like. At last the rabbis can express their rage and their bitter disappointment at Christians, especially Christians who persist in telling them that Jesus is their promised Messiah in spite of everything. Particularly in the light of the Shoah (called the Holocaust by most Christians), this continuing determination to speak of Jesus as Israel's Messiah has proven to be just too much for many Jewish people, and they are now fighting back in ways which have never been experienced in public before.

It has become quite common nowadays, as we shall see in a later chapter, for Jewish people to use extremist, one might actually say hysterical, language, usually taken from the context of the Shoah (Holocaust), to express their contempt for all Jewish believers and Jewish evangelists. Rabbi Immanuel Shochet, for example, one of today's most active and insensitive refutationists, says this in his public lecture about Jewish believers in Jesus:

We always compare missionaries to Nazis . . . I went to the New Testament and I found there some nice juicy passages which I personally felt make Hitler's *Mein Kampf* look like a nice decent nursery rhyme.

This is crude rhetoric, designed to manipulate the emotions of his audiences, and it is easy for Christians to become very upset by it. Listen to this dreadful distortion of the truth by Beth Moshe in her determination to manipulate the emotions and psychological triggers of her audience. She knows full well that Adolf Hitler was not a Christian in world-view or practice, and yet she says:

Paul made clear that works are not part of the requirements for Christian salvation in Romans 3:28, '. . . a man is justified by faith without the deeds of the law.' This is fundamental Christianity about belief, and only belief, offering salvation . . . Let's extend this thought about Christianity's message of salvation to Adolf Hitler and the six million Jewish martyrs of the Nazi Holocaust. Picture this:- If Hitler 'believed', he is enjoying heaven's reward for believers, yet the six million Jewish human beings he so demonically tortured and murdered are in hell as nonbelievers. Is this your concept of the goodness of God? Is this your concept of heaven, filled with believers such as Hitler?[33]

It is an affront even to have to face such a rhetorical question! No wonder Christians, and especially Jewish believers, become shocked and angry. Sometimes that sense of shock leads the Christian positively to a serious investigation into the causes of that kind of Jewish insensitivity. But it is more common to find many Christians becoming angry in quite an unhelpful and sometimes even retaliatory way.

Unless Christians realise the context of pain and work with this perspective, matters will not only not improve but may

---

[33] Beth Moshe, *Judaism's Truth Answers the Missionaries*, op cit, pp 253 f.

very well deteriorate once again. It has been my unpleasant experience on many occasions to hear Christians reacting in an inappropriate, yet almost predictable way to patronising or debasing remarks about Jesus, remarks which reflect and express this new-found freedom to act on the theory that the best form of defence is attack. They do this by declaring that remarks like these prove that the old stereotypes must be true about the Jews being without respect for others and having a pathological hatred of Jesus, etc. In other words, because of their ignorance of the historical context, these Christians assume that such expressions of pent-up anger and pain reflect the best of what is typically Jewish. Nothing could be further from the truth, in my experience and study. If we were to judge one another solely on our behaviour and the words we use when we break under unbearable pressures, then there would be precious few marriages or good friendships left at the end of the day, including relationships between Christians! One of the wonderful characteristics of good friends or colleagues is that they are not only able to understand and absorb any untoward outbursts of fear or anger, etc, but actually have the generosity of spirit to *want* to do this for their friends. Friends and family are the ones who really understand and get involved in order to help. Of course there are also plenty of examples of families where relationships are not what they should be, and consequently the members of those families are not at all generous or helpful.

Now the problem in the realm of Jewish–Christian relations is that not only do Christians, in the main, not know the long and tragic story of their interrelationship, but nor is there that spirit of generosity and friendship which would look for the time and space to discover the reason for the hostility which is sometimes felt. In effect, this means that when many Christians come across what seems to be an irrational and disproportionate reaction against any sharing of the Gospel, the only frame of reference that they can think of to explain that reaction is the old stereotypical one about the Jews being misanthropes and the murderers of Jesus and the prophets before him.

This particular stereotype goes back to the opening centuries of the Common Era, being perhaps most famously expressed by Tacitus in the second century:

> Connected among themselves by the most obstinate and inflexible faith, the Jews extend their charity to all of their own persuasion, while towards the rest of mankind they nourish a sullen and inveterate hatred. Strangers are excluded from their tables. Unsociable to all others, they eat and lodge with one another only.[34]

How dreadful it is that this false and shameful accusation is still found in Christian societies. The telling truth of history is that the non-Jewish world, deeply embarrassed by its own lack of care for the disadvantaged and marginalised within its own various nations and groups, could not countenance the fact that the despised Jews, of all people, were quietly exposing that world's indifference and cruelty by their own obvious care for one another. This clear Jewish commitment to the disadvantaged was an authentic expression of the community's ethical values, rooted in the social ethic of the Hebrew Bible, and that needs to be appreciated. However, it would also be true to say that the Christian world was not likely to go out of its way to help the poor Jewish people whose plight was in large measure a result of that very world's treatment of them. So the Jewish communities *had* to look after their own – and they did so.

Although there are countless examples in history of wonderful and often sacrificial expressions of Christian love being exhibited by individuals and groups of people, nonetheless the verdict of history at many periods and in many places could be articulated in a motto to the effect that: 'Only

---

[34] Tacitus, *History*, Book 5.

the Jews look after their own.' But in their shame and twistedness, Christian (and other) antisemites distorted this virtue, and corrupted the motto into a slur by repositioning one of its words: 'The Jews only look after their own.' Therein we see the power of moving a word within a sentence! And this caricature can still be found today. I have heard it myself from many Christian *ministers* over the years, let alone from the Christian world more generally. We must develop a way of responding firmly to any undermining statements about Jesus without at the same time losing sight of the specific context which led to them, and without compromising that spirit of loving generosity which is one of the hallmarks of God himself.

Let me return for a moment to the analogy of a person who finally breaks down under extreme pressure and vents his or her frustration at a second person. Sometimes that second person could be said to 'deserve' the outburst, in the sense that he or she played a significant part in causing the situation in the first place, but often enough, it happens that someone quite outside the whole situation suffers the explosion. This latter scenario is, in a sense, much more unfortunate than the former, since the second person does not in any sense 'deserve' any such aggressive outburst. Now in the case of Jewish–Christian relations, we are looking at an analogy with the former situation, since the Christian communities do, in a real but unpopular sense, 'deserve' the aggression being directed at them. We are not receiving this highly negative reaction because of the abuse of Jewish people by another faith-community, but we are, to use a biblical metaphor, reaping what our own ancestors in the faith have sown.

I therefore want to suggest to the Christian community, and in particular to the evangelical world, that there is a real sense in which we need to be willing and prepared 'to take on the chin' some of the blows which are being aimed at us by certain of the Jewish community. True, the hard work and discipline required for this responsible attitude must be accompanied by a need to be discerning about what is actually said and done by refutationists, but we shall come to the specific issues shortly. What I simply wish to do at this point is to stress the need for Christians to acknowledge the force of what I am saying.

It is important to note at this stage the matter-of-fact response given by certain Jewish leaders who simply wish to be left alone by the Christian community, and whose reply to the invitation to become involved in a dialogue with Christians is to say, 'No! – thank you'. An important voice in this regard has been that of Eliezer Berkovits, an eminent Jewish philosopher, who wrote what has become a programmatic paper in 1966 outlining five reasons why Jewish people ought not to succumb to calls for 'fraternal dialogue' with Christians.[35] These five perspectives have proven so influential that I will outline them here for us to reflect on. The headings which I use are those given by Berkovits himself.

- *Emotional* He states that the Jewish people are not emotionally ready to enter into meaningful dialogues with a Church which has brought such unspeakable suffering on them. He goes so far as to refer to those Jewish leaders who nonetheless strongly advocate dialogue as 'either Jews without memories, or Jews for whom Judaism is exclusively a matter of public relations, or confused or spineless Jews'. In his own opinion, the Jewish people *may* be ready in 'a hundred years'.
- *Philosophical* He acknowledges, in principle, the value of interchanging ideas among different communities, but insists that there is no qualitatively superior value in any specific Jewish–Christian interchange. The Jewish community will benefit just as much from interacting with philosophers such as Sartre and Radhakrishnan as it will

---

[35] Eliezer Berkovits, 'Judaism In The Post-Christian Era', in *Judaism*, vol 15 (1966), pp 76–84.

with any Christian thinkers. He sees no special value in, or need for, dialogue with Christians.

- *Theological* Berkovits sees a purely theological dialogue between Christians and Jews as 'fruitless and pointless' because, as he sees it, a fundamental aspect of the self-definition of each consists of a *rejection* of the other. There is nothing of theological value for Judaism in Christianity apart from insights or basic teachings which were originally 'borrowed from Judaism' anyway. Even the Hebrew Bible is as much a serious area of dispute for him as it is a piece of common ground, since Christians and Jews simply do not read it the same way or through the same interpretative lens. Thus it divides every bit as much as it brings together.

- *Practical* While certain Churches (notably the Roman Catholic) are busily seeking dialogue with the various Jewish communities, they have no practical intention of compromising their conviction that they are the true repositories of all authentic revelation. What, then, will ultimately be gained from dialogue other than the satisfaction of a select few theologians? Besides which, Jewish people are by and large very happy for non-Jews to be Christians if they so wish. The Jewish people would be better occupied in concentrating on their own internal dialogues and troubles.

- *Ethical* Berkovits is especially vigorous in this section of his paper, spelling out the specific background to his first line of objection to dialogue with Christians. The impression is too easily given, he challenges, that both parties have a vested interest in working on a new relationship because there is a measure of mutuality in the responsibility for the chasm which now separates them. He continues:

This is not the case. There were no conflicts or wars. There was only unilateral oppression and persecution. We reject the idea of inter-religious understanding as immoral, because it is an attempt to whitewash a criminal past.

Berkovits' sense of trauma at the hands of Christians down the centuries is all too evident here, and in this he reflects the attitude of a considerable proportion of the Jewish people. One of his summary statements could not be more stark or moving:

> It is not a matter of whether Christianity acknowledges fragmentary truths in Judaism. All we want of Christians is that they keep their hands off us and our children!

Here, then, is one common type of reaction coming out of the anguish of the Jewish people: *let us just keep a respectful distance from each other.* Jewish people like Berkovits are simply not interested in meeting Christians in order to hammer out a carefully-researched theology. Interestingly, as we shall see later, one of the most frequently-presented arguments by those responsible for the 'Refutation Literature' is that they are doing exactly this: simply working on behalf of their people, with no intention of getting involved in disputes with Christians. They maintain that they are only writing and teaching for their own people, that they are not attacking Christianity as such at all, and that they hope Christians will also leave the Jewish community alone and forget about evangelism of any sort. I will give one example here of this type of manifesto which claims to be purely inner-Jewish and apologetic in its orientation:

> We know that Christianity is evangelical. What does disturb us, is the specific targetting of Jewish people for these proselytising advances . . . Of even greater concern is the concentration on those who for one reason or another are momentarily weak . . . We do not need to convert and we do not want to knock others' beliefs. But when we are under attack we must defend ourselves.[36]

---

[36] Rabbi Shmuel Arkush, *Operation Judaism. Fact Pack* (1986), p 3.

This, then, is a second common type of reaction coming out of the anguish of the Jewish people: *it is time to go on the offensive, even if it means being really offensive!*

Following this thought up a little bit more before moving on, it is instructive to listen to the expert opinion of Menachem Kellner, a prominent Jewish scholar of the medieval period. He presents a compelling argument to explain the phenomenon that until the fifteenth century there was precious little interest within the Jewish community in producing material which could be used in disputes against Christians, whereas in that century many of the major Jewish thinkers gave a great deal of thought to this issue. Why should this occur at that time? Kellner isolates the major factors involved in his outstanding work on the development of Jewish dogma in the Middle Ages, and concludes that the *key* factor was the terrible persecution of the Jewish community in the Iberian peninsula from 1391 to 1418, a persecution which involved not only the torture of people but also the systematic attempt to dismantle the Jewish faith itself. As Kellner puts it:

> Not only were Christians attacking Jews, but Christianity was attacking Judaism.[37]

Jewish people were forced to attend conversionary sermons in local churches, or even in their own synagogues sometimes! From time to time Christians would descend on Jewish communities with a cross in one hand and a sword in the other, offering the choice either between baptism and death, or between baptism and expulsion. In this context, the Jewish leadership felt impelled to produce theological material to combat this Christian onslaught, and also to strengthen the faith of the Jewish people who were subject to so much Christian propaganda. So, Kellner urges, the very rise of any

---

[37] Menachem Kellner, *Dogma in Medieval Jewish Thought* (The Littmann Library of Jewish Civilization, London, 1986), pp 80–82.

kind of sustained and substantial theological response to Christianity came about as a result of this pain and anguish, rather than as a result of any internal impulse to become involved in theology with Christians for the sake of it.

This has never been a case of an intellectual debate between disinterested parties. The conflict has been all too real and bloody over the centuries. And of course, true to human nature, the more that Christians tried to force Jewish people to convert, the more they resisted – and rightly so. A Jewish believer of the last century, D. S. Margoliouth, tried to get the Churches to realise this over a century ago. He spelled it out in this way:

> The persecution of the Jews has not only rendered conversion difficult by making Christianity odious, but still more by making Judaism dear.[38]

The contemporary wave of polemical material reflects a change in the mood of some Orthodox Jewish groups towards developing their apologetics in the direction of what might be called, in another type of context, pre-emptive strikes. Much of this is expressed in what passes for scholarship or serious literature, but some of it operates on another level altogether. Whereas many Christians today take great exception to this deliberate belittling of their faith, and respond by further attacking the Jewish faith and the Jewish people, my plea is that we learn to take a deep breath, accept that criticism which is fairly levelled at the Church, respond in a spirit of compassion, especially to those criticisms which might not be fair, and learn how, in this context, to make a firm defence of the Messiahship of Jesus.

---

[38] D. S. Margoliouth, *The Grounds of Jewish Opposition to Christ* (London, nd), p 7.

3

The charges of ignorance and deception

Here we come to another of the most basic and commonly-employed responses of the Jewish community in the face of increasing interest in Jesus by Jewish people. The charge, simply put, is that only Jewish people who are woefully ignorant of the richness and value of their own religious traditions and interpretations could possibly be seduced into thinking positively about the Christian faith. One of the assumptions underlying this is that *Messianic* Jewish interpretations and insights are not Jewish at all, and are therefore to be thoroughly discounted.[39] It will be worth our while spending a little time on this matter, since it is so vital in the overall Jewish–Christian dispute.

Let me cite a quotation which is typical of the many which could be brought. It is a useful quote, because a second vital issue also emerges from it, namely that the majority of Jewish people (and not a few Christians) fail to make the necessary distinction between the discrete organisation, 'Jews for Jesus', and the general population of Jewish

---

[39] Among certain groups of Jewish believers in Jesus today it makes a great deal of difference whether they are known as Jewish Christians (or Hebrew Christians) or as Messianic Jews. I have written about this important matter in my book, *God's Covenant with the Jews*, op cit. In the present book, I have decided to use the expression which is most acceptable to all, namely, 'Jewish believers in Jesus', but occasionally I will speak about Messianic Jews or Messianic Judaism as well.

believers in Jesus. The term 'Jews for Jesus' has just proved to be too popular and too convenient for most people to take the trouble to identify properly who they are talking about. In the following case, Rabbi Polish is not restricting himself to the specific organisation when he says:

> No doubt the various levels of deception involved in the Jews for Jesus movement have succeeded in confusing many Jews who are not sufficiently educated in their religious tradition or are not prepared for a more rigorous discussion of its theology.[40]

Notice the intense use of loaded language by this rabbi. It is not at all uncommon, as we shall have cause to see on many occasions, but for the moment our focus is on the issue at hand, namely whether it is true that only religiously-ignorant Jews could become believers in Jesus.

Gerald Sigal, in an immensely influential book, states categorically that refutation literature is needed as a means of 'protecting the innocent and the uninformed against aggressive missionary groups'.[41] Isaac Troki, the grandfather of all subsequent refutationists, writing in the sixteenth century, justified the need for his programmatic piece of refutation by saying it was necessary in the face of 'ignorance and growing misapprehensions' among the people.[42] Dov Aharoni Fisch laments in his conviction that the turn away from the traditional religious education offered at Orthodox *yeshivot* (religious seminaries) in favour of the modern secular university model has played a large part in

---

[40] Rabbi Daniel F. Polish, in Martin A. Cohen and Helga Croner (eds), *Christian Mission – Jewish Mission* (Paulist Press, NY, 1982), p 163.

[41] Gerald Sigal, *The Jew and the Christian Missionary* (Ktav, NY, 1981), p xv.

[42] Isaac Troki, *Faith Strengthened* (late sixteenth century). Troki, a Karaite by faith and community, wrote this work in Hebrew and gave it the title *Hizzuk Emunah*.

the current crisis, where Jewish students are easily deceived
by well-trained missionaries and Jewish believers:

> Most Jewish students do not have any background in traditional
> Judaism. Denied a yeshiva education by 'enlightened' parents
> . . . these young Jews cannot begin to cope with the attacks
> against traditional Judaism.[43]

Samuel Levine spells out this view even more clearly in the
opening sentences of the Preface to his vitriolic book:

> This book was written as a response to the many Jewish people
> that I have met who have either adopted Christianity or were
> seriously considering it. Since all of these, without exception,
> did not know the Bible or their Judaism before they were
> introduced to Christianity, they were easily manipulated by
> Christian missionaries (some of whom had converted from
> Judaism themselves).[44]

Beth Moshe adds to this argument about the need for greater
Jewish *education* to prevent Jewish people being attracted to
Christianity, an appeal for a greater sense of *warmth and
enthusiasm* within the various Jewish educational programmes. In this way, she argues, Jewish people will realise
that it is not just the Messianic Jewish groups that are excited
about their faith.

> Why are Jews being lost to Judaism? What has gone wrong? It is
> perhaps because Judaism has been lacking a spiritual spark for
> the modern generation. Its truth, offered in a vacuum of emo-
> tional feeling, has not made for religious contentment. Truth
> and religious emotion should be found together. Picture the
> Lubavich's type of religious commitment and fervor and you
> realise what Judaism is and the heights to which it rises . . . Yet,

---

[43] Dov Aharoni Fisch, *Jews for Nothing* (Feldheim, NY, 1984), pp 12–13.
[44] Samuel Levine, *You Take Jesus, I'll Take God* (Hamoroh Press, Los
Angeles, 1980), p 7. The very title of this book leaves the reader in no
doubt either about Levine's attitude towards Jesus or towards those Jewish
people who accept him as their Messiah.

your religious background may be the biggest turn-off to Judaism there is. If your Bar (Bat) Mitzvah was lacking in emotional excitement, you missed Judaism's holy breath.[45]

One might add here that Jewish ignorance, in one way or another, is regularly blamed for all that the various Orthodox establishments deem to be aberrations of the true faith and practice of Judaism (which is, of course, in each case, their own). Reform Judaism, for example, comes in for the very same attack. Let me cite a nicely-barbed instance of this which I came across recently in reading some of the onslaughts of Orthodox Jewish leaders at the turn of this century against the Reform movement. The author was referring to a classic fourteenth-century Jewish piece of refutation literature against *Christianity*, but then, after praising its content, went on to lament its ironic contemporary application to a sector of world Jewry:

> I know very well that even if we print thousands of books like this, we will not convert the Christians. Rather, I have another aim . . . to give the sons of Judah the weapons with which to defend their faith against their *Hebrew* assailants, the rabbis who preach Reform, who harm us more than the Christians. If only the pious Christians would abolish the missionaries and place Reform rabbis in their place, they could expect the speedy demise of the Jewish religion.[46]

The Orthodox Jewish defence is clear: in the modern period, the Jewish people have wandered so far away from their proper Orthodox roots and training that they are easy prey for all those aberrant Jews (like Reform and Messianic Jews) who present a compelling case for their own particular brand of heresy. This claim has by now become commonplace in

---

[45] Beth Moshe, *Judaism's Truth Answers the Missionaries*, op cit, p 256.

[46] Ephraim Deinard, commenting in 1904, as quoted by Frank Talmage, 'Christianity and the Jewish People', in *Commentary*, vol 59 (1975), p 57.

the Jewish media as well. Here are two examples from American Jewish newspapers:

> The Jews for Jesus movement has been widely denounced by both Jew and Christian alike for its cult-like, deceptive, aberrant and decidedly non-Jewish nature. The leaders of the movement have repeatedly demonstrated their lack of personal integrity and seemingly limitless capacity for deception.[47]

> Cute tracts and fellowship with music and friendly faces put many unsuspecting Jewish people at ease, and they become very receptive. The door is open to begin a cordial indoctrination of Christian fundamentalism. Many Jewish people fall victim to this missionary trap.[48]

Once again we meet the same unspoken presupposition which dominates the Jewish agenda: since, as most Jewish people believe, Jesus is not the Messiah and cannot be the Messiah, and since this is held to be so on *Jewish* grounds, then it follows that any *Jewish* person who believes that Jesus *is* the Messiah must be unaware of this Jewish counter-evidence, and so has either been deceived or manipulated. At the same time, non-Jewish people are a different case altogether, since they cannot be expected to know, and thus accept, the Jewish proofs against the Messiahship of Jesus, or to appreciate the cynical entrepreneurial skill of Paul, who engineered this whole new religion called Christianity out of the figure of Jesus.

Speaking of Paul brings us to the characteristic barb of Shmuel Golding, who seeks to ram home his message that only ignorant Jewish people could be gullible enough to

---

[47] *The Baltimore Jewish Times*, as quoted in *The Baltimore Sun*, February 3, 1986. In fact Beth Moshe actually calls the whole Messianic Jewish movement a 'subterfuge'. See her book, *Judaism's Truth Answers the Missionaries*, op cit, p 6.

[48] *The Jewish Press*, February 28, 1986.

believe in Jesus, by ridiculing *all* those who believe in Jesus as fools:

> It is not difficult to visualise the kind of people they win over by their message. Paul declares in the New Testament, 'we are fools for Christ' (1 Cor 4:10), 'I speak as a fool' (2 Cor 11:23), 'not many wise men . . . are called' (1 Cor 1:26). It seems that things today have not changed since the time of Paul.[49]

His co-labourer, Immanuel Schochet, adopts the same tone and attitude in his public lecture, and even manages to be more offensive still. He says something which will deeply offend not only Christians, but every person, Jewish and Christian, who has either suffered from emotional or psychological difficulties of some sort, or who knows someone who has. He dismisses the kind of Jewish people who might be attracted to Jesus as being deficient, emotionally or intellectually, and therefore nothing but a burden to the Jewish community. Let the Christians have all those Jewish people who are not 100 per cent productive in the Jewish community, he says, since they are worthless anyway!

> They probably have emotional problems. They're probably a bit cuckoo anyway . . . They're on drugs . . . Let them go over there. Let *them* have this refuse. Let *them* have this gutter people.

This is precisely the awful type of contemporary refutation literature to which I referred in the opening chapter of this book as particularly objectionable to both Jewish and non-Jewish believers in Jesus. Golding, for example, takes those words of Paul ridiculously out of context. Any adequate exegesis of those passages is enough to show that Paul does not mean that believers in Jesus were in any way

---

[49] Shmuel Golding, *A Counsellor's Guide* (Vikuach Ve Dusiach, Jerusalem, 1985), p 16.

deficient in their Jewishness or their common sense. He is deliberately using the rhetoric of 'wise versus foolish' in the context of establishing that no-one can say they deserve God's approval through their own merit or achievement. The key context-verse for Paul in this regard is one which Golding, of course, chooses to omit:

> For the foolishness of God is wiser than man's wisdom, and the weakness of God is stronger than man's strength.[50]

Paul himself was an especially well-educated and trained Jewish person, as he is at pains to tell his readers. Of course the refutationists dismiss this as more deception, claiming that Paul was either a Jewish ignoramus suffering from pretensions of grandeur and incomparably more successful than most, or even a non-Jew who only pretended to have a Jewish pedigree and who had no authentic Jewish theological acumen.[51]

Schochet, for his part, is a particularly poor example of Jewish leadership, since my own experience of the Jewish community is radically different from his presentation. It demonstrates a fully-committed and caring attitude towards its people, and gives the lie to his sentiment. He either believes something about the Jewish community which I think is not fair, or he is simply impervious to the implications of his words as he seeks to make cheap points at the expense of his perceived enemies. I am inclined to be generous and conclude that he is simply insensitive to the offence he is causing his own community by his rhetoric. I

---

[50] 1 Cor 1:25.

[51] Although the notion that Paul was not Jewish and had no great Jewish theological and literary skills is not given credence by serious scholars, whether Jewish or non-Jewish, it is being championed today by one British refutationist who belongs to the Reform wing of Judaism, Hyam Maccoby. See his book, *The Myth-Maker. Paul and the Invention of Christianity* (Harper & Row, NY, 1986).

cannot believe that he would actually write off the less able in the Jewish community in the way that he appears to do.

Yet another of the modern refutationists who shame the genuine searchers for truth is Samuel Levine, who has been mentioned once or twice already. He takes the approach of Golding, and writes that 'to be a Christian you must forfeit your brains'. But, he asserts, Paul discovered that even the nonsense of the New Testament message 'was good enough for the ignorant, unsophisticated pagans in his neighbourhood'.[52]

It is imcumbent upon me to state simply, and for the record, that this claim that only ignorant and deprived Jewish people accept the Gospel is categorically wrong! One can certainly understand why certain sectors of the Jewish community would wish to foster this kind of thinking, since it deflects attention away from the real issue of whether or not the New Testament claims might be right concerning God, Israel, and the world. It also serves the community by seeming to imply that Judaism, as it has developed over the generations, is itself a perfectly-sufficient antidote to the claims of the New Testament. Nonetheless, this dismissal of Jewish believers (and other interested Jewish people) as misguided, as a result of their presumed ignorance of Judaism, is in fact groundless. Apart from anything else, there are actually plenty of examples of very able Jewish scholars and leaders who have declared their faith in Jesus.

In the context of each community being determined to portray the other in as bad a light as possible, one of the most persistent *and absolutely false* stereotypes which has been created and constantly disseminated by Jewish leaders about Jewish believers is that they deliberately prey on weak, lonely, vulnerable and disadvantaged Jewish people. This unethical strategy is used by believers, so the refutationists

---

[52] Samuel Levine, *You Take Jesus, I'll Take God*, op cit, pp 64, 89.

say, in an attempt to delude these poor Jewish people with the Gospel while they are in a situation where their critical faculties are not functioning properly. The assumption is, of course, that when Jewish people are in real command of their normal critical faculties they cannot possibly be deceived into believing this nonsense about Jesus.

Beth Moshe paints a deliberate caricature of any Christians who wish to share their faith with a Jewish person, presenting such Christians as being driven by doubt and anxiety and totally unconcerned for the Jewish person as a person. Her stereotype is quite unacceptable:

> The missionary has a burning need to convert you, for he needs self-confirmation based on Judaism's destruction. When this misguided person meets with solid, sensible rejoinders, such as are pointed out in the pages of this book, he probably will not admit he is wrong or give up . . . You must understand that the missionary is a person whose power of rational reasoning likely has long since been disengaged . . . He is driven by his own need to convince you that Jesus is the Messiah . . . [53]

In the mid-1980s, the organisation known as CMJ (The Church's Ministry among the Jews) was so offended by being regularly accused, without evidence or apology, of such unethical tactics that it went so far as to publish its own Code of Practice for everyone to see. Its hands were clean, so to speak, but it had become important for the Jewish community and the media to see its policies set out in print. CMJ's integrity can be seen from the two following parts of its Code:

> We wish to affirm certain principles of right evangelism:
> To have respect for all, regardless of their views . . . To act with honesty and integrity . . . To communicate faithfully the truth of

---

[53] Beth Moshe, *Judaism's Truth Answers the Missionaries*, op cit, pp 249f.

God's saving love to sinners through the sending of his Son, the Messiah Y'shua,[54] to be our only means of atonement and righteousness . . . To be motivated by love . . . To admit our own unworthiness for the task . . . To be thoroughly acquainted with Jewish belief and custom, and able to relate sensitively and sympathetically with Jewish people . . . To understand and respond to objections to the Gospel, accepting that these must be dealt with to the satisfaction of all . . . To show clearly that Jewish people who believe in Jesus remain Jews, and are in fact fulfilled in their Jewishness . . . To be responsible and accountable in use of finance, resources and staff . . . To respond to hostility, whether physical, verbal or attitudinal, in love . . . To correct misinformation, misrepresentation or wrong accusation wherever possible.

We wish to emphasise that the following are contrary to such principles, and against the honest and open work we are engaged in:

Inviting people to events and activities under false pretences . . . Dressing up or posing as something we are not, in order to hide our true identities . . . Using illegitimate or unfair means of persuasion . . . Failing to make known the full implications and consequences of becoming a disciple of Y'shua . . . Involvement in discussion with minors (under 18 years of age) without the knowledge of parents or guardians . . . Offering any form of financial or material gain as an inducement to becoming a believer in Messiah . . . Prejudicing or vitiating the attempts of other Christians less outwardly evangelistic to build links of friendship . . . between Christians and Jews.[55]

---

[54] *Y'shua* is the Hebrew form of the name which English-speakers know by its English transliteration, Jesus. Increasingly, Jewish believers and other Christians involved with them are using this rather than any other transliterated form such as Jesu, Yesus, etc.

[55] For further discussion of the issue of deception in this context, see the paper I gave at the Fourth European Conference of the Lausanne Consultation on Jewish Evangelism in September 1992, 'Image and Reality: The Use of Jewish Symbolism'. It was published in an edited form in *Mishkan*, 19 (1993), pp 54–63.

This singling out of CMJ is not meant in any way to suggest by inference that other societies or Churches do not share the same policies. On the contrary, this kind of ethical code is practised by all the groups known to me who have a concern for Christian ministry to Jewish people.

Nonetheless, this persistent charge by Jewish leaders of deliberate deception being employed as a means of persuading those Jewish people who are least able to detect and reject it, appears regularly in the Jewish media, in articles and books, in synagogue sermons and talks and in everyday conversations. In my twenty years of hearing and reading this accusation, during which time I have repeatedly asked for evidence, not once has any evidence come my way. All that one ever receives by way of response is a vague statement to the effect that 'It's well known'. In my opinion, a great deal of both slander and libel has been committed by irresponsible people in this regard. Immanuel Schochet feels secure enough in this rhetoric to simply throw out a few statements about this in his lecture. He offers absolutely no proof for his claim that

> Over the years [they] have been able to seduce . . . thousands of Jewish kids, especially younger people. The last few years a greater effort has been made on senior citizens, especially those in old-age homes, in nursing homes.

Rabbi Shmuel Arkush, operating from Birmingham, England, produced a video in 1988 in which he proclaimed the following about the 'missionaries' and the Jewish believers whom he fights so bitterly:

> They make a point of approaching young people, those who are away from their families, taking advantage of their loneliness and possible isolation, people who are either physically or mentally disabled, people lying ill in hospital. I even know of

two cases where people have been approached on their death-beds. And of course there are the approaches to children.[56]

No attempt is made to substantiate these sweeping claims, nor to give a fair right of reply to anyone he may be ready to accuse. But this is becoming par for the course, sadly. *It is not true, let it be said once and for all, that Jewish believers, or any Christian societies which have a special ministry to Jewish people, are engaged in any kind of strategy which is aimed at the weak or vulnerable.* The accusation that it is true is a lie. If any individual person were ever shown to be involved in this kind of unethical conduct, then not only would such a person be rebuked and forbidden to engage in further actions of the same kind, but Jewish believers and evangelical societies the world over would be the first to insist upon that! There may well be mavericks out there acting on their own, but they are not accountable to any Messianic Jewish congregations or the like. *Ministry among Jewish people is not at all involved with the targetting of vulnerable or disadvantaged people.*

Another dimension about this charge of Jewish ignorance needs to be mentioned at this point. It is quite commonly claimed that Christians, well aware of the ambiguities and inconsistencies of their faith in spite of what they proclaim to others, have developed a strategy to cover up their weaknesses. This entails, so the claim goes, the use of a spiritual-sounding principle to provide shelter from moral or intellectual flaws. The principle is that faith is a gift from God, a supernatural gifting, if you like, and therefore not at all a matter of reason or common sense. It is beyond reason and common sense and requires spiritual discernment. Sigal presents this argument in his book, and then proceeds to scorn it, asking the question:

---

[56] These words are among the opening remarks of his video entitled, *Target: Jews. A Case for Concern* (Operation Judaism, Birmingham, 1988).

Is this refusal to face the biblical reality the hallmark of true faith? The missionary movement often argues that Christian faith is not a rational process by which the believer comes to a logical conclusion that Jesus is the Messiah. It is contended that Christian faith is a gift from God by which the believer receives certain spiritual truths that the non-believer is incapable of believing.[57]

Christians need to be aware of this perception by Jewish people that whenever any really difficult problem arises the believer will evade any sense of responsibility for tracing the root of the problem and seeking to solve it, by retreating behind this principle that the whole issue is beyond human understanding and can only be appreciated on a 'spiritual' level, as some sort of 'mystery'. This approach, which does reflect the position of some Christian groups, let it be said, is being presented by many of these refutationists as typical of all Christians. It is also being used to further support the claim that only ignorant and easily-deceived people are being drawn to the Gospel.

Sigal himself, for example, affirms the supernatural origin of the Hebrew Bible and the doctrine of divine revelation, but goes on to insist that in the Jewish perspective, which he sees as being in clear distinction to the Christian perspective, biblical faith 'does not preclude the proper understanding of the Scriptures'. For the Jewish community, he states, 'Biblical faith is not belief without proof, but trust without reservation.'[58]

Now that, in my opinion, is a marvellous definition of what the Hebrew Bible really means when it speaks about 'faith', and Sigal would be right to point out that all too often, especially perhaps in the Protestant world, Christians have

---

[57] Gerald Sigal, *The Jew and the Christian Missionary*, op cit, p 289. Beth Moshe ridicules this same sense of 'mystery' in her book, *Judaism's Truth Answers the Missionaries*, op cit, p 251.

[58] Op cit, pp 289f.

spoken and thought about faith in terms which are basically propositional rather than relational. The acceptance of the right creed or catechism has too often been seen as the sole test of whether or not people were to be accepted as belonging to the Christian faith. Their life of trust in God and commitment to him through Jesus was not sufficiently taken into consideration. All of this is true for many Christian groups and their attitude to their 'faith'.

However, it is certainly not true that this propositional idea of faith is typical of all Protestants, let alone all Christians. Moreover, it is a crude injustice to categorise Christians as irrational people who simply accept dogmas blindly, giving their faith no thought. There is certainly no way around the initial act of faith – trusting in the reality of the God of Israel, who is the Father of our Lord Jesus. But generally speaking, the Church has also been keen to comply with the injunction of Peter:

> Always be prepared to give an answer to everyone who asks you to give the reason for the hope that you have.[59]

Sadly, *vis-à-vis* the Jewish people, the Church has not always paid attention to the words which immediately follow these in Peter's letter. Peter goes on to say:

> But do this with gentleness and respect, keeping a clear conscience, so that those who speak maliciously against your good behaviour in Christ may be ashamed of their slander.[60]

It is imperative that anyone who wishes to engage a Jewish person in conversation about Jesus must be able to give answers to legitimate questions. At the very least, should a difficult point arise, they must be able to acknowledge their lack of a fully-considered answer and seek help from someone else. I am not recommending some programme of rote

---

[59] 1 Pet 3:15.

[60] 1 Pet 3:15f.

learning, or a school for pat answers, or the like. On the contrary, I see a real need for Churches to develop or adopt programmes concerned with good education in the Scriptures and theology for those who wish to become involved in sharing their faith with others.

There is a final issue which I would like to discuss before we close this chapter looking at the charge of Christian deception. Working on the assumption, as they do, that there can be no basis in fact for the truths of the Gospel, many of the refutationists openly charge Christians with tampering with the evidence. There can be no more fundamental attack on the Gospel than this – the accusation that either Jesus himself or his closest followers, perhaps even all of them, actually fabricated 'evidence' in the events of Jesus' life and the writing down of those events in order to 'prove' that Jesus was the Messiah. Two contemporary writers make a particular point of this *vis-à-vis* the reports of the death of Jesus in the gospels. In their opinion, Jesus purely and simply died on the cross, but the disciples just could not psychologically accept Jesus' death as the end of their hopes.

> The belief was too strong, the hurt too great, to face the terrible truth. There simply had to be an explanation, and such an explanation was found.[61]

They go on to explain how, in their view, the disciples must have stolen Jesus' body from the tomb and then combed the Hebrew Bible for verses about suffering and death which they could manipulate to make it look as if these verses were applicable to the Messiah. The next thing they had to do was to develop a novel teaching about a second life, a second coming for this Messiah who had suffered so much before dying. More will be said about this issue of the second coming of Jesus later, because it is one of the most funda-

---

[61] David Berger and Michael Wyschogrod, *Jews and 'Jewish Christianity'* (Ktav, NY, 1978), p 21.

mental issues facing Christians involved in these disputes. But the accusation of creating evidence to create a religion is extremely serious.

Here is another version of the same accusation:

> The form of demonstration peculiar to early Christianity was to build everything upon the word of the Bible, proving every statement with biblical quotations, ignoring in the process the context in which the quotation was located. This recurrent appeal to prophecy was either a so-called *vaticinium post eventum* (prophecy after the event), with the event itself inserted into the life of Jesus in order subsequently to confirm the word of the prophet, or, conversely, according to the principle *lekayyem mah shene'emar*; that is, in order to fulfil what is written, Jesus conformed his acts to prophetic statement.[62]

As I said earlier, this is about as basic a criticism as one could ever imagine. The Christian faith, like the Jewish faith, stands or falls, according to its own inner criteria, on its historical claims. If, as many Jewish commentators claim, the key historical events either did not happen, or only took place in highly manufactured and predetermined contexts, contexts over which Jesus and the disciples had complete control, then the Gospel is altogether compromised. This, of course, is their intent. They wish to present a picture of Jesus as a cynical manipulator and fraud, or as a poor Jewish man who was exploited by his friends who turned out to be cynics and frauds.

At the very best, such Jewish critics might show some compassion for the disciples, since they are simply the victims of their own profound psychological needs. But this would serve only to change the accusation from one of deliberate interference with the evidence by cynics, to one of tampering by weak and self-deluded followers of Jesus.

---

[62] Hans Joachim Schoeps, *The Jewish–Christian Argument* (3rd edition, Holt, Rinehart & Winston, NY, 1961), pp 21f.

However one reads this accusation, it remains unacceptable. Berger and Wyschogrod actually go on to make the secondary charge that because of the real truth about the death of Jesus – namely that he simply died on the cross – the early Christians knew that they had to deflect as much attention away from the life and death of the human Jesus as possible. The emphasis, therefore, was placed on the *Christ* who is in *heaven*.

> The basic structure of this . . . was to shift the function of the Messiah from a visible level, where it could be tested, to an invisible one, where it could not.[63]

Once again there is a useful lesson to be learned here by mature Christians. Whereas the ascension of Jesus is seen in wholly positive terms by Christians, it can be perceived by others as a means of escaping from the thorny issues of real everyday life here on earth. We know that Jesus is fully human as well as fully divine, and that the Kingdom of God is as much about life in this world as in the next, but the Jewish world does not appreciate that fact, by and large.

An historical overview of Jewish–Christian debates and conversations will clearly show that since Jesus is naturally seen as the real point of division between Jews and Christians, Christians have usually preferred to place all, or as much as possible, of their emphasis on Jesus. This has been so, I would argue, at the expense of a proper Christian emphasis on God the Father. As a consequence, many Jewish people have received the false impression that Christians are people who have replaced God (as they see him) by a man, Jesus. Hence the persistence of the idolatry charge against Christians, and especially against Jewish believers.

When you think about it, Jewish people who wished to learn something more about what Christians believe might understandably decide to look at one of the Christian creeds.

---

[63] Berger and Wyschogrod, op cit, p 21.

If such people turned to, say, the Apostles' Creed, which would be accepted by most Christians as a legitimate credal summary of their faith, then they might immediately be reinforced in their impression that Jesus has replaced God (the Father) in Christian theology and devotion. I will present the text of the creed here for convenience:

> I believe in God the Father almighty, creator of heaven and earth;
>
> And in Jesus Christ, His only Son, our Lord, Who was conceived by the Holy Spirit, born of the Virgin Mary, suffered under Pontius Pilate, was crucified, dead and buried. He descended to hell, on the third day rose again from the dead, ascended to heaven, sits at the right hand of God the Father almighty, thence He will come to judge the living and the dead;
>
> I believe in the Holy Spirit, the holy catholic Church, the communion of saints, the forgiveness of sins, the resurrection of the body, and the life everlasting. Amen.[64]

It is quite clear from a glance that the focus of the attention is on Jesus, the subject of the middle section of the creed. The impression could thus easily be gained on first reading that Jesus was much more important to Christians than the Father. The true situation is obviously more complex than that, but Jewish people have not always had it clearly explained to them. When a community of any sort decides that it is necessary to create a statement of policy or belief, etc, then it is only to be expected that the statement will focus particularly on the issues which provoked the controversy or confusion which led to the need for a statement in the first place. Because for the Churches the obvious issue of controversy was the person and work of Jesus, all the creeds naturally have a high degree of focus on him. It is not a mark of heretical lopsidedness.

---

[64] This translation is taken from John H. Leith, *Creeds of the Churches* (Knox Press, Richmond, Virginia, 1973).

Nonetheless, this focus on Jesus in the Church's evangelism among Jewish people, and in the credal statements of the churches, gave rise to a misapprehension among Jewish people that Jesus is more important to Christians than God himself. This in itself would make Christianity a heretical religion in Jewish eyes.

I would like to mention here that this same impression has often been given unwittingly by the editors of Christian hymnals and songbooks. Usually, there are far more hymns and songs about, and also directed to, Jesus than the corresponding number of songs about and to the Father. Recently I was at a meeting organised by a group of Jewish believers in Jesus in which we sang from a book called the *Grace and Glory Hymn Book*. This particular hymn-book was published some years ago by the 'Hebrew Christian Testimony to Israel', a society with a specific interest in Jewish evangelism, and with Jewish believers on its staff. Yet even here, insufficient attention had been paid to the impression created by a hugely marked focus on Jesus. In the index of this hymn-book there are only four songs listed under the undifferentiated heading, 'The Father'. However, the heading 'The Son' is divided into six sections, and consists of ninety-five songs![65]

Small wonder, then, that Jewish people think as they do regarding the Christian assessment of Jesus over against the Father. For many of them, all they have heard about Jesus is his divinity: how he is God among us, God incarnate, and not a mere prophet or teacher. I have met quite a few Jewish people who were completely unaware of the fact that Christians also celebrate the *humanity* of Jesus, and are keen to discover as much as possible about his Jewish life in the Galilee of Second Temple times.

There has been a great deal of misunderstanding about

---

[65] As a matter of interest, the Holy Spirit only received five songs in his section.

Jesus because of this lack of appreciation by Jewish people of the dual nature, as it were, of Jesus' life. Isaac Troki, mentioned above as the single most influential refutationist, cites as a proof that Jesus could not have been the Messiah the fact of the temptation of Jesus. On the one hand, he says, if Jesus was the Son of God that Christians believe he was, how could he have been tempted at all? And on the other hand, how are we to imagine that the Satan would have dared to try to tempt him if he were divine? Troki has not understood the full Christian teaching about Jesus.

Troki's failure has been shared by countless numbers of Jewish people, and part of it is certainly the responsibility of the Churches. Some Jewish people, knowing a bit more than others, think that we believe that Jesus was a kind of hybrid creature, half-man and half-God. This is not at all accurate. But worse still is the view of the many Jewish people whose understanding of the incarnation is that Christians believe that a man became God! It is the exact opposite which Christians believe: God became a human being. But this is how so much of our preaching has been perceived. The concept of God taking on human nature, the Word becoming flesh, is no less astonishing in its own way, but at least it is not idolatry and we do *not* worship a man who somehow became divine!

It is quite understandable why this 'over-emphasis' (as I see it) on Jesus, and especially on his divine nature, came about, and I certainly do not want to start apportioning blame or the like, but I do think that it is unfortunate. We need to learn how to explain to Jewish people that Jesus is not all there is to the Godhead, that we ourselves teach this explicitly in our doctrine of the Tri-unity of God, and that in the best Christian traditions, at least, we do not concern ourselves only with the other-worldliness of Jesus. Perhaps more of us need consciously to speak more about what the humanity of Jesus means to us when we are in conversation with Jewish people. Let me be clear in what I am saying here: I fully believe that Jesus is God incarnate, and I am certainly not suggesting any compromise on that fact. My concern is with the imbalance in our presentation of Jesus, neglecting as we often do, the fact of his full humanity.

However, to return to the basic point, we all need to learn how to respond to the charge that the life and teaching of Jesus and the early disciples, ostensibly lived out in fulfilment of promises and needs given in the Hebrew Bible, were in fact a case study in self-fulfilling prophecy. It can often be no more than a cheap argument, intended merely to dismiss someone with a sweeping gesture, as it were. But sometimes it is a serious charge, believed with all the passion that the Jewish person can summon. To be forewarned is to be forearmed. Know your Bible, and know your Lord!

In conclusion, then, let us take every opportunity which comes our way to squash once and for all this old stereotype, with its accompanying slanders, that the Gospel only appeals to the ignorant, the intellectually weak and the theologically lazy!

4

Christianity is OK for non-Jews

At this point, I would like to reflect on another of the most common claims made by refutationists in this general area of what they consider to be 'reasonable' for a Jewish person to believe. The general disclaimer is inevitably made that they are not at all attacking Christianity as such, nor are they trying to dissuade non-Jews from becoming Christians. Indeed many Jews, but not all, let it be said, regard Christianity as perhaps the best religious faith for non-Jews to hold. (The other commonly-held Jewish preference for non-Jews has traditionally been Islam.)

Generally speaking, there is a real sense of pride within the Jewish community that they do not insist that non-Jews become Jewish or practise Judaism in order to find fulfilment in life or to be assured of salvation in God. The traditional Jewish theology is that whereas Jewish people must observe the 613 commandments of God which are to be found in the Hebrew Bible, commandments given only to Israel, non-Jews need only live in accord with the seven so-called 'Laws of Noah'. These laws are derived exegetically and homiletically from the demands made by God of humanity before, and independent of, those special demands made of Israel. As far as the Jewish people are concerned, if non-Jews live righteously, that is, in accordance with these seven Noachide Laws, then they will assuredly inherit a place in the world to come.

There are some variations found in the exact number and nature of these laws in Judaism's early documents, but the consensus has developed that there are the following six prohibitions and one positive injunction.[66]

Prohibited: idolatry   *Required*: the establishment of
         blasphemy   courts of justice
         human bloodshed
         sexual immorality
         theft
         eating from a living animal

Because these laws are seen as universal in their scope and independent of any relationship with Israel or her God, people from every culture, race, nation, etc, can be called righteous if they live in accordance with these basic rules for life. This would therefore cover Christians as well. However, for quite some time there was considerable debate over the status of Christians, in the light of the first of the negative commands regarding idolatry. Many Jewish scholars were inclined to judge the trinitarian belief of the Church as polytheistic and idolatrous, thereby disqualifying Christians from the category of the righteous. However, from the late Middle Ages the Christian formulation of the tri-unity of God was accepted by many prominent Jewish scholars as a valid *non-Jewish* way of understanding the Godhead. Christians were therefore to be included among the righteous as long as they lived in accordance with the whole complement of Noachide laws.

It might be of interest to point out that part of the deliberation and decree of the great Jerusalem Council, recorded for us in Acts 15, also 'instructed' the non-Jewish believers to honour certain lifestyle codes so as to ease full fellowship with those Jewish believers who wished to maintain their strong sense of Jewish identity and lifestyle

---

[66] See Tosefta, Avodah Zarah 8:4; Sanhedrin 56a.

(see Acts 15:28–29). Do we have there a form of the Laws of Noah for the early Church?

At any rate, Judaism therefore teaches that there is no need for people to be born Jewish or to become Jewish in order to find favour with the one true God and eternal salvation. Thus the Jewish community is at pains to declare that it holds the moral high ground in this matter, setting itself over against Christianity which classically insists that people must become Christians in order to find salvation with God:

> We are the only universal religion that believes that other universal religions can coexist with us.[67]

> What is unique in Judaism and the core of its witness to other faiths is this concept of religious diversity which acknowledges the legitimacy of diverse paths to God.[68]

Rabbi Immanuel Schochet, a Canadian Orthodox rabbi who has developed an international career out of his refutationist teaching, represents a large section of the Jewish public when he teaches that all Christian evangelists are, by definition, arrogant and immoral. This is, he states, an inevitable result of the intolerance of their Christian conviction that only Christians can please God. However, his gross stereotyping of what he sees as the attitude which lies behind the desire to share the Gospel shows that he is more concerned with the scoring of debating points than with exploring the truth. In his lecture, 'Square Circles', he says at one stage that:

> The whole idea of evangelising presents something which is normally abominable . . . what does evangelising mean? Evangelising means that I am going around telling you people . . . that your religion is no good . . . that you yourself are no good . . . You aren't worth anything. You are basically an animal . . .

---

[67] Rabbi Solomon B. Freehof, in David Max Eichorn (ed), *Conversion to Judaism* (Ktav, NY, 1970), p 162.

[68] Rabbi Ben Zion Bokser, in *Judaism*, Winter 1977, p 65. See also Berger and Wyschogrod, op cit, pp 13, 61.

> So the whole idea . . . is, in principle, a totally immoral concept,
> which cannot but create . . . prejudice . . . in society.

This is a terrible caricature of what evangelical Christians believe and their attitude to people of other faiths. There are, needless to say, two sorts of Christian evangelist, just as there are two sorts of people generally when it comes to 'selling something' to other people. It does not matter whether one is talking about religion, or politics, or encyclopaedias, because the principle is the same. There are those who try to win you over to their point of view in unacceptable ways, eg the use of aggressive words or intimidating body-language, etc. This can take the form of a foot in the doorway; literature regularly stuffed into the letter-box; never keeping quiet, so that you cannot get a word into the conversation; or trying to make you feel silly or ashamed that you don't think the way the salesperson does.

These are not characteristics which are limited to Christians at all, let alone to Christian evangelists. As a matter of fact, Rabbi Schochet himself does not like to give other people a fair chance to present themselves and their own point of view! But there are Christians like this too, of course, sad though it is to admit it. Such people are not really listening to the other person; they are not sensitive to their felt needs; and they are not treating the other person with proper respect. But it is patently absurd to label all evangelists in this way. And even so, this lack of sensitivity, when it is found, never degenerates to the extent of thinking of the other person as 'an animal'. Rabbi Schochet knows this very well, but chooses to make his sensational point in order to win over his audience.

The reality of the situation concerning the lack of Jewish outreach to the non-Jewish world is also more complex than is usually conceded, needless to say, but the story of the Jewish people's once positive and indeed purposeful attitude to welcoming converts from other faiths would take too long to tell here. Suffice it to say at the moment that the present lack of an active Jewish commitment to 'evangelism' among non-Jews is more the result of the ban on such activities and attitudes by the host cultures in which the Jewish people have lived during their long period in dispersion from sovereignty in the land of Israel, than it is an inner-theological decision coming out of the inherent nature of Judaism. In a very thorough book on this subject a *Jewish* scholar, Joseph Rosenbloom, actually devotes six of his chapters to nations and tribes who converted to an active Judaism at certain conducive times and places in history![69]

One of this century's most cogent Jewish apologists, Leo Baeck, determined to draw the Jewish community's attention to the truth of this matter. He knew that it was fear of the consequences, both external and internal, that led Jewish leaders to withdraw from programmes of conversion. His conclusion is worth quoting:

> Judaism was the first religion to organize missions, and it was Jewish propaganda which prepared the ground for the diffusion of Christianity. Political rather than religious considerations put an end to Judaism's attempt to extend its realms of believers.[70]

It is therefore of considerable interest to note that in recent years, in the contemporary political climate of religious freedom, there actually has been something of a movement to reach out to the 'unchurched' non-Jews of America with a view to introducing them to the joys of Judaism. In the second half of the 1970s, an American Reform rabbi, Alexander M. Schindler, proposed a confident programme of trying to help non-Jews who had no religious affiliation to

---

[69] Joseph R. Rosenbloom, *Conversion to Judaism. From the Biblical Period to the Present* (Hebrew Union College Press, Cincinnati, 1978), chapters 17–22.

[70] Leo Baeck, *The Essence of Judaism* (Schocken Press edition, New York, 1948) p 78.

appreciate the joy and the sense of purpose of (Reform) Judaism. Many Jewish people were nervous at the possibility of an antisemitic backlash to any such programme, but an increased commitment to trying to persuade the non-Jewish spouses and potential spouses of Jewish people to convert to Judaism has been perceptible in the past decade or more. This is true in Britain as well as in America. It would seem that this has been in large part a response to the challenge by Rabbi Schindler and others to see Judaism as a religious faith and lifestyle which should be practised with pride and even shared with others, at least the spouses and potential spouses of Jewish people. But it certainly goes further than this for some Reform leaders, who wish to see more thought being given to a more general strategy of outreach.

Indeed, in October 1993 Rabbi Schindler returned to his original proposal at a meeting of the Union of American Hebrew Congregations, of which he is the President. He announced 'a $5 million program to reach out to those of our neighbours who belong to no church or no other religion'. This organisation represents 850 Reform Jewish congregations, and some 38 per cent of all American Jewish people identify themselves with the Reform movement. In an interview with the *New York Times*, Rabbi Schindler said that

> Judaism has an enormous amount of wisdom and experience to offer to our troubled world, and we Jews ought to be proud to proclaim it with fervor and with pride . . . The outreach effort should now go beyond welcoming the strangers who choose to live in our midst . . . to seek them out and invite them in.[71]

In 1987 a significant book was published in America, by a reputable publishing company, with the mildly provocative title, *Toward a Jewish America*. There was nothing mild about its sub-title, however, which read: '*A Proposal for*

---

[71] See the *New York Times* of October 24, 1993.

the Proselytizing of Gentiles'.[72] This Orthodox Jewish author suggested that it was time for the Jewish people to recover confidence in their faith and introduce Americans to the best faith available to them:

> The purpose of this book is to demonstrate that Judaism is the most appropriate religion for contemporary Americans and to promote their mass conversion to it ... I will attempt to demonstrate ... that Judaism is the better way – better in the sense of spiritual fulfilment, better in the way people see themselves and their relationship to others, and better in determining their relationship to God ... Now is the time for the proselytizing to begin.[73]

It is not true to say, then, as many Jewish people do say, that Judaism is by definition a religion which does not believe in outreach to others. There are political and social reasons why things have developed the way they have. By way of analogy, in some countries even to this day Christians are unable to be involved in any kind of outreach to their fellow-citizens. In some cases this has been the situation for generations. But it does not mean that the Christian faith is itself undisposed to evangelism. In the same way, Jewish people have been prevented for such a long time now from any open sharing of their faith with a view to winning new converts, that they actually assume that such outreach is alien to their faith, although in fact it is not.

Bearing this in mind, the claim of refutationists that Judaism is superior to Christianity because, among other things, it does not seek to convince others, is clearly not quite accurate. But having said this, in the context of this Jewish claim to be completely tolerant of Christianity, the refutationists are at pains to assure the (non-Jewish) Chris-

---

[72] Eugene Kaellis (edited by Rhonda Kaellis), *Toward a Jewish America* (The Edwin Mellen Press, Lewiston/Queenston, 1987).
[73] Ibid, pp 9, 10, 12.

tian world that their refutations are only directed at Jewish people, and only relevant for them. Moses Mocatta, who translated the work of Isaac Troki which I mentioned above, opened his translation with a Preface in which he wrote:

> As we Israelites do not seek to impose our faith on others – a practice altogether repugnant to Judaism – it is necessary to premise that the following work is intended exclusively for distribution among our Hebrew community.

Most of the famous and ground-breaking refutationists of the Middle Ages were secure in their own sense of being Jewish and did not need to denigrate Christianity in order to bolster their own sense of self-worth. There was no real identity crisis, as we know it today, since religious, cultural, linguistic and social bonds formed a powerful cohesive force within the Jewish world. Their works were actually intended to prevent Jewish people from considering the Christian faith at all seriously, rather than being in any sense public polemics. One indication of this fact is that they were often only written in Hebrew, a language inaccessible to most Christians in the Middle Ages.

Gerald Sigal opens his large book with corresponding words:

> It is not, however, the aim of this book to direct criticism at Christians who do not seek to convert Jewish people. This book has been written neither with malice nor with intent to insult either Christians or Christianity.[74]

Berger and Wyschogrod also make it clear that this perspective is important to them:

> The purpose of this booklet is . . . to explain why Jews ought

---

[74] Gerald Sigal, *The Jew and the Christian Missionary*, op cit, pp xvii–xviii. See also Rabbi Douglas S. Charing, *What You and Every Missionary to the Jews Should Know* (London, JLS Publications, 1971), p 2.

not to become Christians or Jewish Christians, but it is not directed at anyone who is not Jewish.[75]

Now when we examine this disclaimer, which at first glance looks benign and ecumenical, it does seem just a little naïve, does it not? Are we really to believe that if these refutationists succeed in their plan to discredit the character of Jesus, the character of the disciples, the integrity of the New Testament, the rootedness of basic Christian doctrines in the Hebrew Bible, and the very intelligibility of certain doctrines, all so that Jewish people will be able to see the whole thing for what it is, namely a concoction of distortions, errors and deceptions, etc, then in spite of this demolition job *non-Jews* will nevertheless be able and willing to ignore it all and base their lives on those self-same persons, events and teachings, etc? One Jewish believer has put it rather well:

> In some of the literature there is a clear insinuation that an intelligent and sensitive Jewish person given the same faith data confronting an intelligent and sensitive Gentile, cannot or may not come to the same conclusions about faith . . . Thus we face . . . a persistent refutationist belief that spiritual and theological truth can be at one and the same time totally false and unacceptable when considered by any Jew, even a non-committed Jew, but true and acceptable for a Gentile.[76]

The point is well taken. With the best will in the world, Christians cannot allow these charges which are aimed at

---

[75] Berger and Wyschogrod, op cit, p 13. I have recently re-read a classic nineteenth-century refutation, *The Restoration of Israel*, published in 1812 by Joseph Crool, and I noted there that he stresses in his opening Declaration that on no account must any Christian deduce from the work that he is 'an enemy to Christians'. The same is said at a more institutional level in the name of the National Conference of Synagogue Youth in a 1973 document entitled *The Real Messiah*, pp 7–8.

[76] Menachem Benhayim, 'The Gospel and Jewish Refutations', in *Mishkan*, 1 (1984), pp 34f. A moderated version of this position was held by the eminent and influential medieval Jewish scholar, Yehudah Halevi, whose

the very fabric of the Gospel to go unchallenged. The Good News of Jesus is not a gentile invention, nor is it the basis of life and faith only for non-Jews. We cannot accept the premise that 'Christianity is OK for Gentiles', with its hidden presupposition that it is not OK for Jewish people. Belief in Jesus is OK for everyone, including the Jewish people, since if Jesus is not the Messiah of Israel, then he cannot be anyone else's Christ (= Messiah)!

The fact of the matter is that there have been many books written by Jewish refutationists which set out to attack the Christian faith in one way or another, while at the same time playing out this 'legal fiction' game of claiming that they have no case against Christianity *per se*. Daniel Lasker, in a book devoted to medieval Jewish philosophical polemics against Christianity, actually has a section of his book in which he lists some of the most important of the works which attack Christianity in this way.[77]

More acceptable is the open honesty of Benjamin Segal, who wrote a booklet targeted at Jewish believers and Christians who wish to share their faith with Jewish people. Early on in his booklet he wrote the following acknowledgement:

> A word is due on what this booklet is not about. This is not a study in comparative religion. In no way do we intend to present a balanced comparison of Judaism and Christianity. To restate that point in a blunter, but clearer, fashion, there is neither an extensive nor a fair treatment of the Christian religion in this

---

celebrated book, *The Kuzari*, published in the twelfth century, was subtitled, *A Composition in Argumentation as Proof in the Defence of the Despised Faith*.There he says that any value in Christianity is merely an indication that it is 'a suggestion and an introduction to the anticipated Messiah', but not a religion which actually holds the truth about the Messiah in its own right. See 4:22–23. This means that there can be real value of a sort there for non-Jews, but nothing for Jewish people, who have the real thing.

[77] Daniel J. Lasker, *Jewish Philosophical Polemics Against Christianity in the Middle Ages* (Ktav, NY, 1977), pp 17–20.

work . . . The fact that no defense of Christian points of view is presented is simply the result of our purpose, the defense of the unique Jewish views.[78]

Part of the Jewish concession that Jesus and Christianity might be all right for *non-Jews* is bound up with the double dilemma which the Jewish community's leaders are facing. On the one hand, there is a profound reluctance to even countenance any further involvement between a Messiah figure and the Jewish community. Indeed there has been something of a traumatic situation within world Jewry over the past few years, with many of the followers of the late spiritual leader of the Lubavitcher movement, Rebbe Menachem Schneerson, asserting that he was in fact the long-awaited Messiah. The Orthodox Jewish world was seriously exercised over this claim, let alone the wider Jewish community, with great fear being expressed that this would only lead to yet another development of disappointment, misery, ridicule, and even persecution. Schneerson's death has devastated the Lubavitch movement.

History is full of episodes in which some Jewish person's claim to be the Messiah has resulted in awful misery for the Jewish people, and, understandably, Jewish leaders have become very reluctant to encourage Messianic speculation of any kind. But on the other hand, Jesus is here to stay on the world's stage, and it would be counter-productive, to say the least, for the Jewish community to try to remove *him* from that stage. So most Jewish leaders have settled for trying to alienate Jesus from the Jewish community, while trying to reassure Christians that it is OK for *them* to keep Jesus at the heart of their faith.

Jesus himself predicted that there would be such a history of false messiahs to trouble the Jewish people, his words being preserved for us in Matthew's Gospel:

---

[78] Benjamin J. Segal (ed), *The Missionary at the Door – Our Uniqueness* (Youth Commission, United Synagogue of America, NY, 1972), p 5.

For false messiahs and false prophets will appear and perform great signs and miracles to deceive even the elect – if that were possible. See, I have told you ahead of time.[79]

And sure enough, there have been many messianic pretenders in Israel's history. This would be a fitting subject for a book in its own right, but we have no space to devote to it here. Suffice it to say that two false messiahs are actually mentioned in the text of the New Testament itself. Gamaliel, a leading Pharisee, tells us that:

Some time ago Theudas appeared, claiming to be somebody, and about four hundred men rallied to him. He was killed, all his followers were dispersed, and it all came to nothing. After him, Judas the Galilean appeared in the days of the census and led a band of people to revolt. He too was killed, and all his followers were scattered.[80]

However, the first serious challenger *after* Jesus to the title of the Messiah arrived on the scene within a century of Jesus' own lifetime. Bar Kochba ('son of the star'), as he came to be known from the prophecy in Num 24:17, was the charismatic military leader of the second Jewish revolt against the Romans in 132–5 CE. The whole campaign was doomed from the start, and many Jews have since believed that the Roman reprisals against the Jewish people made their situation much worse than it would otherwise have been. This pattern has continued sporadically throughout history.[81]

Two points need to be stressed, therefore. First of all, Christians must realise that Jewish people today do not hear the claims about Jesus in a vacuum. Whatever transpired in the days of Jesus himself, the *present* situation is

---

[79] Matt 24:24f.

[80] Acts 5:36–37.

[81] A good book to begin with in this whole issue of Israel's false messiahs is Abba Hillel Silver, *A History of Messianic Speculation in Israel* (revised edition, Beacon Press, Boston, 1959).

that there is a certain amount of cynicism at the outset about any claim that Jesus is the only candidate for Messiah available to the Jewish community. Secondly, it is particularly important to appreciate the fact that those others who have claimed to be the Messiah have led the Jewish people into periods of profound disappointment, frustration, despair and even outright persecution. Some of those messianic pretenders even indulged in various forms of immoral behaviour. There is, therefore, something of a spiritual inertia at work within the Jewish community, serving to caution them against taking *any* claims to Messiahship seriously.

This, then, provides another necessary part of the puzzle that Christians need to be aware of as they see the Jewish community trying to reject Jesus' Messiahship, without seeming to want to jeopardise his role within (gentile) Christianity. But of course we come back once again to this basic separation in the Jewish mind between what is permissible for Jews and what is permissible for non-Jews.

The real agenda for most Jewish people is not the theology of the person of the Messiah, but the survival of the Jewish people. On the one hand, there is concern that if enough Jewish people decide to throw in their lot with Jesus, then when disappointment comes as, according to them, it will, there will be more wholesale depression and disillusionment within a Jewish community which is already in too many ways dispirited and assimilated. But on the other hand, there is the fear that the already dwindling Jewish community (becoming ever more depleted through secularisation, assimilation, and mixed marriages) will stand to make huge losses on top of everything else if enough Jewish people become thoroughly convinced that Jesus is the Messiah. This loss of Jewish people through their conviction that Jesus is the Messiah will happen, as they see it, because the Jewish community's leadership decided in the early centuries that Jewish people who believe in Jesus are no longer to be considered as being part of the Jewish community. Jewish believers are traditionally seen as having sold out to the enemy, betrayed their community, and become Gentiles.

At the very least, this surely means that Churches and Christian organisations need to affirm, loudly and publicly, that as far as they are concerned, notwithstanding the prejudices of the past, Jewish believers continue to be Jewish. Indeed this fact is a cause for celebration. Two such examples of Christian groups which have made just this kind of affirmation are the School of World Mission of Fuller Theological Seminary in California, and the Lausanne Committee Task Force on Jewish Evangelism. In 1976 the former issued a Statement which included these ground-breaking words:

> We heartily encourage Jewish believers . . . including those who call themselves Messianic Jews, Hebrew Christians and Jews for Jesus, to retain their Jewish heritage, culture, religious practices and marriage customs within the context of a sound biblical theology expressing Old and New Testament truth.

In 1983, the latter group published a similar overall Statement, choosing to open it with these words:

> We rejoice in the growing number of Jewish people who believe in Jesus as Messiah and Lord. These Jewish believers are variously known as Hebrew Christians, Jewish Christians, or Messianic Jews, depending on personal preference or the culture in which they live.

More of this kind of attitudinal change is needed within our Churches, but we shall look at this issue of Jewish identity and survival in some depth in a later chapter. Bruce Lieske highlights the dilemma well as it is perceived within the Jewish community:

> The resistance of Jews to the Gospel – once it is presented – stems from at least three reasons: sinful human nature,

theological conviction, and the fear of assimilation with consequent loss of identity with the people Israel.[82]

The blame for much of this fear must be laid at the feet of the Churches, since throughout history and right up until the present day congregations and institutions alike have insisted, working from an anti-Jewish agenda, that all Jewish believers must renounce their Jewishness and turn their back on the Jewish community. They are gradually 'gentilised' into the ways of whatever particular Church and host culture has 'adopted' them, and are thereafter forbidden to have any future contact with family or friends, except for evangelistic purposes. Therefore the Jewish community has no difficulty in finding plenty of examples from history in which Jewish believers have simply disappeared from their families and from the Jewish scene altogether.

And so the Jewish community, anxious not to offend or antagonise the Christian community, has nonetheless acted to preserve its own sense of continuity and its own survival by relegating faith in Jesus to the Christian community. Christianity is affirmed as being OK for non-Jews, but at the same time its fundamental texts and beliefs are savaged within the Jewish community. The strategy is clear and understandable, given the powerful forces at work.

However, even with all the understanding and repentance which I am asking from the Christian world, it is evident that, like it or not, these challenges to the New Testament faith by the refutationists, involving the core issues of Christian theology and devotion, *are* an attack on the heart of the Gospel. If Jesus was a charlatan, then everyone needs to know this, Jew and non-Jew alike. But, on the other hand, this means that if Jesus *is* the Messiah, then everyone needs to know this too, Jew and non-Jew alike.

---

[82] Bruce Lieske, *Witnessing to Jewish People*, op cit, p 23. See also Menachem Benhayim, 'The Gospel and Jewish Refutations', op cit, p 25.

5

The morality of being spiritual

Time and again the Bible makes it clear that, in God's eyes, spirituality and morality are inseparable. The way we live our lives is of paramount importance to God. So much is this so, that it is considered a mark of how little one knows God if one's life is morally deficient. Can there be many more serious and hard-hitting remarks in the Bible than this one from the apostle John?

> If anyone says, 'I love God,' yet hates his brother, he is a liar. For anyone who does not love his brother, whom he has seen, cannot love God, whom he has not seen. And he has given us this command: Whoever loves God must also love his brother.[83]

It is at this point that Christians have so often fallen down so badly in their witness to the Jewish people about Jesus being the Messiah. The treatment of Jewish people by those who invoked the name of Jesus and the name of the Church has been so atrocious that it would have been a miracle had the Jewish people *not* inferred that Jesus was an imposter, arguing that since his followers are patently not motivated by the love of the Messiah, then Jesus cannot be the Messiah. The fact remains that the Jewish people have judged Jesus, and continue to judge Jesus, by those who bear his name. The judgement has not proved to be positive.

The most distressing way that this will be communicated to Christian people today is undoubtedly when someone

---

[83] 1 John 4:20f.

compares the desire to share the Gospel with Jewish people to the virulent attitudes and actions of the Nazis and their collaborators during the Holocaust. The very language used can often seem hysterical in the extreme, and can leave Christians numb with pain and confusion as they reel from the shock of being called names which seem absurdly out of touch with reality. Occasionally one actually gets the impression that the extreme language is being used expressly to create that reaction. In other words, the speaker or writer is simply concerned with silencing Christians in an effort to look good. But more of that later.

Let us concentrate for a moment on this use of extremist language to hammer home the issue of Christian immorality *vis-à-vis* the Jewish people. Shmuel Golding, operating from Jerusalem, has a series of eight cassette tapes full of his teaching on how to refute missionaries. He is one of the crudest perpetrators of this use of language. Already on the first side of the first cassette he refers to evangelists as bringing 'a second holocaust', 'a massacre' and 'a pogrom' upon the Jewish people. Evangelists are even worse than the murderers of the Inquisition or the Holocaust since those people were only able to kill the body, whereas evangelists kill the very soul of the Jewish person. He calls evangelists 'today's gestapo', and refers to their meeting places as 'gas chambers for the soul'. His one aim, of course, is to shock Jewish people into an immediate emotional reaction against Christians who share their faith with Jewish people.

Perhaps he, and others, are working with the adage that 'all's fair in love and war', and they do certainly see themselves at war with Jewish believers and evangelical Christians. Perhaps the measure of our own revulsion at these descriptions of evangelists is equal to the strength of the feeling in the Jewish community against sharing the Gospel with Jewish people. Nevertheless, the language used and the attitude behind it remain offensive to Christians. Blu Greenberg, a leading Orthodox spokeswoman in

the USA, makes clever use of other Nazi-associated terminology to drive her point home. In a much-read and recom-
mended book from the mid-1980s she asks rhetorically and
very cynically:

> Would those who preach conversion for all Jews really want a
> world Judenrein, a world free of Jews? . . . the call for a kind of
> spiritual final solution?[84]

The answer to her question is, of course, a resounding 'No!',
but it does reveal once again the underlying assumption in
the Jewish community that a Jewish person who becomes a
believer in Jesus has ceased to be Jewish. Therefore, *she*
would argue, if all the world's Jewish people became believers in Jesus there would be no Jewish people left.

Overlaid on this level of argument is of course the other
issue of how the Churches have actually treated Jewish
people down the centuries. Here again the use of extremist
language serves to make the point with sharp rhetoric.
Several Christian scholars and organisations have also
begun to use this language in their determined efforts to
persuade Christians to believe that the Jewish people do
not need Jesus in their lives. Robert Everett, an influential
American Christian in the Jewish–Christian inter-faith movement, declared that

> There should be no missionary activity to the Jews. In this era
> after the Holocaust, missions to the Jews are nothing more than
> a form of spiritual genocide.[85]

The implication of this kind of statement, reinforced by the
fact that it is said by Christians as well as by Jewish people,
is that there is a necessary link between the belief that Jesus

---

[84] Blu Greenberg, in Marc H. Tanenbaum, Marvin R. Wilson and A.
James Rudin, *Evangelicals and Jews in an Age of Pluralism* (Baker
Book House, Grand Rapids, MI, 1984), p 230.
[85] Robert A. Everett, in *Christian–Jewish Relations*, vol 15, no 4 (1982), p
8.

is Israel's one and only Messiah and antisemitism. This connection is to be roundly denied and condemned. It may be true that some antisemitic people support Jewish missions, since they might welcome the false teaching that once Jewish people become Christians they cease to be Jewish, but this does not mean that the desire to share the Gospel with Jewish people is in and of itself an antisemitic attitude. Allan Brockway, however, once an experienced staff worker with the World Council of Churches, fails to appreciate this fact. He spells out his own viewpoint very clearly:

> Any Christian mission to Jews represents an anti-Judaism that, on the surface, may appear not to be anti-Semitic because it rejects hatred of, and violence against, Jews. But mission to Jews, even when it is separated from coercion ... is, by definition, anti-Judaism — and anti-Judaism, because it envisages the conversion of the Jewish people to Christianity, and thus the final disappearance of the Jewish people as such, is anti-Semitism.[86]

Time and again we notice that these two issues become intertwined in the thought and presentation of those opposed to any sort of witness to the Jewish people: that is to say, the issue of the Jewish people's treatment at the hands of Christians, and the issue of defining Jewish people who do come to believe in Jesus as being no longer Jewish, and therefore lost to their own people. But it is important for us to keep these two separate issues distinct in our minds.

The moral question has probably settled the argument for most Jewish people. A century ago, one commentator went as far as to say that in his opinion the Jewish community had been irrevocably changed by its contact with Christian contempt and persecution:

---

[86] Allan R. Brockway, 'The Jewish–Christian Agenda Today', a paper given to the Ecumenical Theological Research Fraternity in Israel, May 1, 1986, p 3.

That the Jewish heart so susceptible to love could shut itself with such stoic persistence against the self-sacrificing love of the Just One from its own midst, is a psychological puzzle which can only be explained by Israel's long history of suffering among Gentile Christians.[87]

Tragically, we see this Jewish criticism of the Gospel, which rejects it on the grounds of its poor morality, already common from the second century CE.[88] Some Jewish authors are willing to acknowledge that there is a difference between those who are truly committed to Jesus and his teachings and example, and those who are patently only nominally Christian as far as any real life-changing faith is concerned. But most are reluctant to concede this. For one thing, they say, there is just too much evidence to show that even so-called 'real Christians' have taken part in antisemitic activities; and for another thing, those Christians who belong to the same Churches as notorious antisemitic Christians did, or do, should leave those churches if they really want to dissociate themselves from the 'nominal Christians' responsible for shaming the name of Jesus.

For the most part, Jewish people see personal religious commitment as best expressed and evaluated in and through a person's religious community. It is not seen as essentially an atomistic, individualistic matter whereby each person is individually defined. Jewish people are part of the Jewish community; Muslim people are part of the Islamic community; and Christians are part of the Christian community. What is more, because of this great biblical emphasis on

---

[87] A. Furst, *Christen und Juden* (1892), p 103.

[88] For example, there is the famous early medieval Jewish work entitled the *Chronicle of Moses*, in which severe criticism is made of the Pharaoh of Moses' time, but where the clear allusion and application is to the author's own day and age, when the growing Christian community is a major problem. See O. S. Rankin, *Jewish Religious Polemic* (Edinburgh University Press, 1956), pp 3–23.

morality as a sure test of one's spirituality, an emphasis which has been signally retained in the Jewish faith, the basic test of each community is seen to be grounded upon its behaviour.

Therefore, the thinking goes, you judge Jewish communities by what their Jewish people do, and by how they behave towards other Jewish people and non-Jews as well. In the same way, you judge Christian communities by what they do and how they behave towards others. And who are the members of these various Christian communities? According to Jewish opinion, those who are baptised into membership of the various Churches are the Christian community members. Now I know that not all Christians would be happy with this definition, which returns, in part, to the issue of an individual versus a community definition of being a Christian, but that is how it is seen by most Jewish people. And if church members are judged by this criterion of how they behave towards other church members, and towards others (in this case Jewish people), then they do not come out of it very well, as a rule.

Menachem Benhayim, a Jewish believer living in Israel, writes that the distinction which evangelical Protestants usually wish to make between true believers and nominal Christians (a distinction which he himself shares) is not, however, the firm defence that they would like it to be:

> Overall, the negative image of anti-Semitic Christians, or those indifferent or immobilised in Protestant and Catholic Europe, will continue to haunt the Church for generations to come. It cannot be enough to argue that the anti-Semites or the inactive were not true Christians or were only nominal Christians. By evangelical standards many were believers, while others who helped Jews were not.[89]

---

[89] Menachem Benhayim, 'Jewish Survival', a paper delivered to the 1986 international gathering of the Lausanne Consultation on Jewish Evangelism, p 2.

Brought down to its basic message, this challenge to the Gospel is quite straightforward: Jewish people judge Jesus by the lives of the Christians they have encountered at historical moments in Jewish history. As some would word it, 'Christians have lost the moral right to tell the Jewish people how to meet, love, and serve God.'

Some refutationists turn to the New Testament itself at this point in an attempt to use the words of Jesus against himself. A favourite quotation is found in Matthew's Gospel:

> Watch out for false prophets. They come to you in sheep's clothing, but inwardly they are ferocious wolves. By their fruit you will recognise them. Do people pick grapes from thorn-bushes, or figs from thistles? Likewise every good tree bears good fruit, but a bad tree bears bad fruit. A good tree cannot bear bad fruit, and a bad tree cannot bear good fruit. Every tree that does not bear good fruit is cut down and thrown into the fire. Thus, by their fruit you will recognise them.
>
> Not everyone who says to me, 'Lord, Lord,' will enter the kingdom of heaven, but only he who does the will of my Father who is in heaven. Many will say to me on that day, 'Lord, Lord, did we not prophesy in your name, and in your name drive out demons and perform many miracles?' Then I will tell them plainly, 'I never knew you. Away from me, you evildoers!'[90]

According to Jesus' own words, so they maintain, since the Churches have shown themselves to be full of bad fruit their root must also be bad. The Jesus tree is either bad altogether, or at least sufficiently corrupt to disqualify Jesus from being the Messiah. The argument is a simple and therefore very appealing one in the Jewish community: there must be something wrong right at the heart of Christianity, or how can you explain the awful things done in its name? Christians invariably try to shrug off this charge as only proving something else which the Bible teaches consistently, namely the inher-

---

[90] Matt 7:15–23.

ent weakness and sinfulness of human nature, including the nature of the people of God.

- While not wishing in any way to contradict this explanation, I do think that we need to ensure that *our first response* to the charge that Christian antisemitism is evidence of corruption is to acknowledge the force of the charge. We are not simply speaking about some individuals who have behaved in completely unacceptable ways. Christian antisemitism has become well and truly *institutionalised* in the history of the Church. We must not make light of it, nor must we even seem to be making light of it.

- *Our second response* must be a genuine repentance from our corporate sin against the Jewish people. It is no good simply trying to distance ourselves from what others have done by claiming that we, unlike them, are the true Christians. As I have said before, this does not impress Jewish people. Indeed it is often taken as a sign of yet another moral weakness: namely, an attempt to evade the responsibility of membership in our own religious community. It is better by far to identify with the shame which membership in the Church demands from us, and within that context to express our grief that so many who call on the name of Jesus have no real relationship with him. In fact one of the marks of our day is the very increase in the number of calls from Christians to the effect that there should be wholesale repentance in the denominations and the Christian nations which have been involved or implicated in sins and crimes against the Jewish people.

- *The third appropriate response* should be a genuine commitment to a future in which the unique nature of the Jewish people will be acknowledged, respected and celebrated. This is not in any sense meant to denigrate the Church, or to set up some sort of dispensationalist schema. On the contrary. The Church is composed of both Jewish and non-Jewish believers in Jesus, and it is God's will that

'all Israel' be saved. In every generation it is the responsibility of believers, both Jewish and non-Jewish, to be
sharing the Good News of Jesus with everyone, both
Jewish and non-Jewish. So I do not subscribe to the
theology which seeks to define the uniqueness of the
Jewish people in terms of their not needing to know Jesus
as Messiah and Lord. In my reading of the Bible, Jesus is
Israel's Messiah before he is mine. Israel is still the people
chosen by God to love and serve him, and Jesus is the one
and only Messiah whom God promised to Israel. So Paul's
words are true in every generation, namely that the Gospel
is 'the power of God for the salvation of everyone who
believes: first for the Jew, then for the Gentile.'[91]

Christian behaviour towards Jewish people should be
that of respect and honour, gratitude and love. And the
Jewish community is well aware of this fact, that if the
Christian claims about Jesus were true, it would result in
this kind of behaviour. Therefore, when they have experi-
enced all the contempt and horror which they have
received at the hands of these followers of the supposed
Jewish Messiah, they have concluded, reasonably, that the
Christian faith is based on a *mistaken* identification of
Jesus with the Messiah.

It may well be that a large part of the problem lies in the
fact that for many Christians, perhaps Protestants in particular, doctrinal purity is often seen as being of more importance than moral behaviour in the definition of who really
belongs to God, who has really found salvation. What I mean
by this is that bad behaviour can so easily be written off as
something which is only to be expected, since it is merely an
expression of human sinfulness. Repentance is certainly
required, of course, but the fact of sin and the need for
repentance and forgiveness are not seen as in any way

---

[91] Rom 1:16.

disqualifications for being called a true child of God. In fact they are sometimes presented as a kind of negative proof of the Gospel, in that they lay bare before us the essential truths of the human condition which Jesus came to deal with.

On the other hand, not to believe the right things, or to believe the wrong things, is to court eternal damnation whatever one's life and behaviour towards others is like. The definition of either belonging or not belonging to the saved community, according to this type of Christian thinking, is bound up entirely with what one believes about God, especially what one believes about Jesus.

Although what one believes about God is definitely important within the Jewish community, it would also be true to say that there is not really any corresponding emphasis on doctrine, certainly not in terms of defining who is a Jew. Belonging to the Jewish community is tied up more with being born into it, with being committed to it, with fulfilling one's religious duties, and with living a godly life, than with being able to sign the dotted line on fine points of dogma. So often one hears a conversation between a Christian and a Jewish person in which there is little real communication at all about the essence of each other's faith because each is coming with such different presuppositions.

Let me mention here an unusual case study in this regard from the Middle Ages. It is a fine illustration of the way in which Christian teachings and practices were perceived by Jewish leaders, and it also has the value of probably being fresh to the great majority of the readers of this book! The context, of course, is that of the medieval Roman Catholic Church, and the specific issue in this case study is the practice of confession. Protestants should set on one side any difficulties they may have with this practice for the moment, since it is simply functioning as a means to illustrate Jewish perceptions and teachings about Christianity. After a chequered history, the practice of an annual confession to a priest was made an article of church dogma in 1215, at the Fourth Lateran Council. Failure to comply with this ruling would result in the offender being excluded from taking part in the Mass and even, in extreme cases, from Christian burial.[92] Following this new ruling, it seems that certain Christian leaders began to reproach the Jewish community for not having an analogous procedure to deal with sin in the community. This issue was taken up within a decade or so by the anonymous writer (or compiler) of a refutationist work composed in the Franco-German region of Europe. His work is known by its Hebrew title, the *Sefer Nitzahon Yashan Noshan*, and in it the Jewish people are presented with two refutations of the doctrine and practice of formal confession to a priest.

Firstly, we find there a moral and theological reason to reject it, even in the face of Christian proof-texting:

> The Christians reproach us for not practicing confession as they do. They bring a proof-text from Proverbs 28:13: 'He who conceals his transgressions will not prosper, but he who confesses and forsakes them will obtain mercy.' Answer them: On the contrary! One *should* conceal his transgressions from other men and not tell them, 'I have sinned in such-and-such a manner', lest they who hear his confession do likewise! He should, rather, confess his sins to God. For thus did David say: 'I acknowledged my sin to thee, and I did not hide my iniquity; I said "I will confess my transgressions to the Lord"; then thou didst forgive the guilt of my sin. Selah'.[93]

This would seem to cover it all. On the one hand, confession, while a thoroughly biblical practice, is to be between a person and God alone, and on the other hand, as all parents of young children know only too well, it is advisable not to

---

[92] See chapter 21 of the Council's decrees. I am indebted to Albert Ehrman for this case study. His brief presentation of it appeared in the *Journal of Jewish Studies*, vol 28, no 2 (1977), pp 194–6.

[93] *Sefer Nitzahon Yashan Noshan*, p 249.

draw attention to different forms of sin because that only serves to give people new ideas! But the author of the *Sefer Nitzahon* goes further, in order to drive home the accusation that immorality lurks at the heart of much that goes on within the Christian world.

There is an old Scottish saying that there are always two reasons for doing something: a good reason and the *real* reason! This work goes on to speak about the real reason for the development of the sacrament of confession. Since the Council of Elvira, in 300–6 CE, it was also Roman Catholic dogma that priests could not marry and had to remain celibate their whole lives. This is the necessary context for seeing the development of the dogma of confession, according to this refutationist. He continues with the casually-made assumption about priests that since they are

> exceedingly lecherous, but are forbidden by their law to take a wife, they have, therefore, come to an agreement among themselves that paramours should come to them and tell them of their adulterous affairs. Thus they learn who the adulterous wives are, and seek them out saying, 'I shall do the same!' And these wives are unable to refuse them since their lovers have already exposed them.[94]

Now one can read this and be surprised by the unjustified cynicism of the Jewish community, or one can say that there is no smoke without fire and assume that there probably were cases of this exact kind of immoral behaviour on the part of some priests, behaviour which came to the attention of the Jewish community. Even then, one can be appalled at the attitude of this rabbi who must have known that such abuses of the sacrament of confession did not at all reflect the motivation or intent of the practice within the Roman Catho-

---

[94] *Sefer Nitzahon*, op cit, p 250. The very same criticism was made by Rabbi Meir ben Shim'on in his mid thirteenth-century polemical collection, *Milhemet Mitzvah*.

lic Church. Whatever reaction one may have, it is interesting for us to note in our present context the focus on the *moral* issue which this refutationist brings alongside his theological objection to the practice of confession.

Another church practice which was severely criticised in the Jewish community was that of infant baptism. The teaching of the Roman Catholic Church that baptism brings about regeneration, or new birth into Christ, meant that infants were baptised as soon as possible in their lives, so that should they die in their infancy (a frequent occurrence in the Middle Ages), their souls would be safe in Christ. One can imagine that the Jewish community would find theological objections to this teaching, but there was a *moral* dimension highlighted in its criticism as well. Here is the challenge of Rabbi Meir ben Shim'on, writing in the mid thirteenth century in southern France:

> Consider that two children were born today – one the child of a poor Christian man . . . The father died prior to the birth of the child and his mother died during childbirth . . . neighbours nursed him graciously and piously, but he died before he was baptized. The other child was the son of a wealthy but wicked man. Because of his wealth, he found someone who baptized him. Subsequently both children died on the same day. Now tell me – what was the sin of the child of the poor man . . . so that he does not enter into paradise . . . And what was the merit of the child of the wealthy and wicked man, so that he does enter paradise?[95]

In quite typical fashion, the Jewish discussion about right theology is bound up with questions of personal and communal morality. Many Christians would also want to question the theology of the practice of confession and of

---

[95] This quote from the polemical collection, *Milhemet Mitzvah*, by Rabbi Meir ben Shim'on, was taken from the book, *Daggers of Faith. Thirteenth-Century Christian Missionizing and Jewish Response*, by Robert Chazan (University of California Press, Los Angeles, 1989), p 61.

baptismal regeneration, but there is a distinctiveness about the moral edge provided by the Jewish community's leaders. The Jewish criticism of what was seen as typical Christian immorality extended to the everyday world as well. In his famous twelfth-century polemical work, *The Book of the Covenant*, Rabbi Joseph Kimhi wrote the following sweeping condemnation of Christian life:

> Oppression and theft are not as widespread among Jews as among Christians who rob people on the highways and hang them and sometimes gouge out their eyes. You cannot establish any of these things with respect to the Jews. These Jews and Jewesses who are modest in all their deeds, raise their children, from the youngest to the oldest, in the study of the Torah. If they hear a vile word from the mouth [of a child], they beat him and chastise him so that he would no longer swear with his lips . . . Their daughters, with modesty, are not to be seen about nor found wanton like the daughters of the gentiles who go out everywhere to streetcorners . . . Are you [ie Christians] then not ashamed and embarrassed to say that you are a good people since you regularly and publicly encourage these sins . . . If they [ie, Jewish people] see their brother a captive, they ransom him; [if] naked, they clothe him and do not allow him to go about begging. They send him provisions in secret. You see with your own eyes that the Christian goes out on the highways to meet travellers – not to honor them – but to swindle them and take all their provisions from them.[96]

Christians need to appreciate that in the collective Jewish consciousness about disputations with Christians, this kind of moral argument is very much to the fore. The Christian preoccupation, as many Jewish people see it, with correct doctrine and a theologically satisfying relationship with God,

---

[96] Rabbi Joseph Kimhi, *Sefer Ha-Berit* (c 1170), 20b–21a. This translation was provided by Frank Talmage, in *The Book of the Covenant of Joseph Kimhi* (Toronto, 1979).

is viewed as of lesser (though not negligible) importance by many Jewish people.

It would also be true to say that to some extent the Jewish community is quite impatient with what it perceives as a Christian over-emphasis on personal conviction that a special word from God has been received on a matter before getting involved in anything. Where there is a need for help, so says the common Jewish wisdom, you get involved and work out the theories and theological niceties later on.

So one of the classic confrontations between even well-meaning Christians and Jewish people takes the following form. The Christian feels that the Jewish person is somewhat of a hypocrite, because it seems to the Christian that the Jewish person believes that the only really important thing in life is to do the *mitzvot*, the commandments of the Torah: to do one's duty to God and to humanity, even if one's heart and faith are not in it. No matter what your feelings or disposition may be, you do the *mitzvot*. And then you might hope and pray that at some point your heart and faith will catch up, as it were, so that your duty becomes a joy and a pleasure to you. This is what it sounds like to many Christians, and they regard it as a kind of hypocrisy, a playing-out of a part which might not reflect the existential feelings of the Jewish person at all. It might simply be automatic obedience, and to some Christian perspectives this is a decidedly inferior spirituality. Indeed it is sometimes seen as an example of an anti-spiritual attitude and life-style.

But on the other hand, the Jewish person is also tempted to regard Christians as being hypocritical in their lives. A common Jewish perception of what, in particular, evangelicals believe is that the only really important thing in life is to have one's heart right with God and to be personally at peace with him. All else is of secondary importance. Now this might actually mean that a Christian will delay becoming involved in some humanitarian project, such as famine relief, or even decline altogether to become involved, because he or she does not feel a direct call from God to do so. Or perhaps because other groups are involved in the same humanitarian project, groups which the Christian does not approve of, such as a secular humanist association. And in the meantime, people are suffering. This smacks of the worst kind of hypocrisy to Jewish people: talking and praying a great deal, but letting people suffer in the name of one's own peace of mind.

This is, then, yet another dimension to the complex issue of the debate between Christians and Jews over the relationship between morality and spirituality. There have, of course, always been problems of immorality in the Churches, as we see even right at the inception of the Jesus movement. The New Testament does not seek to hide these problems from us. It is a little amusing, and also a little irritating, to listen to some refutationists quoting the New Testament as though they had discovered some dark secret known only to an ecclesiastical élite within Christendom. I am speaking about honest passages such as the following:

> It is actually reported that there is sexual immorality among you, and of a kind that does not occur even among pagans: A man has his father's wife. And you are proud! Shouldn't you rather have been filled with grief and have put out of your fellowship the man who did this?[97]

> My brothers, as believers in our glorious Lord Jesus Christ, don't show favouritism. Suppose a man comes into your meeting wearing a gold ring and fine clothes, and a poor man in shabby clothes also comes in. If you pay special attention to the man wearing fine clothes and say, 'Here's a good seat for you,' but say to the poor man, 'You stand there' or 'Sit on the floor by my feet,' have you not discriminated among yourselves and become judges with evil thoughts?[98]

---

[97] 1 Cor 5:1f.

[98] Jas 2:1–4.

> We hear that some among you are idle. They are not busy; they are busybodies. Such people we command and urge in the Lord Jesus Christ to settle down and earn the bread they eat.[99]

Whereas some refutationists like to mock the Churches with these passages, claiming that they prove that the very fabric of the Christian faith is corrupt, this weapon actually turns out to be a two-edged sword. Yes, it is true that in a sense there would be no epistles in the New Testament had it not been for the *problems* in the early churches, but in the same way, how many of the prophetic books of the Hebrew Bible would there be if it had not been for similar moral and spiritual problems? Does this mean that there is something fundamentally flawed about God's covenant relationship with Israel, or with the Torah? No religious Jewish person would agree to that interpretation of Israel's life with God, so how valid is it as an interpretation of the Church's life with God? This point needs to be made very clearly.

Consider also the honesty of the Hebrew Bible when it deals with its foundational characters, let alone with the people as a whole:

> Now there was a famine in the land, and Abram went down to Egypt to live there for a while because the famine was severe. As he was about to enter Egypt, he said to his wife Sarai, 'I know what a beautiful woman you are. When the Egyptians see you, they will say, "This is his wife." Then they will kill me but will let you live. Say you are my sister, so that I will be treated well for your sake and my life will be spared because of you.'
>
> When Abram came to Egypt, the Egyptians saw that she was a very beautiful woman. And when Pharaoh's officials saw her, they praised her to Pharaoh, and she was taken into his palace. He treated Abram well for her sake, and Abram acquired sheep and cattle, male and female donkeys, menservants and maidservants, and camels.

---

[99] 1 Thess 3:11f.

But the Lord inflicted serious diseases on Pharaoh and his household because of Abram's wife Sarai. So Pharaoh summoned Abram. 'What have you done to me?' he said. 'Why didn't you tell me she was your wife? Why did you say, "She is my sister", so that I took her to be my wife? Now then, here is your wife. Take her and go!' Then Pharaoh gave orders about Abram to his men, and they sent him on his way, with his wife and everything he had.[100]

Abram is not roundly condemned and dismissed from Jewish significance by the rabbis because of this incident, although his weakness and humanity are acknowledged and explored. But I hope that I am not being unfair if I suppose that had this incident been recorded of, say, Peter or Paul in the pages of the New Testament, then some of the refutationists would have made a very great deal of it as evidence of the impossibility of Jesus being the Messiah. It is vital that we appreciate the distinction between God's committed relationship to us and our flawed response to him. The latter, while extremely serious, does not cast doubt upon the former. A second famous example of a Jewish leader behaving in an unacceptable manner is King David's actions concerning Bathsheba:

One evening David got up from his bed and walked around on the roof of the palace. From the roof he saw a woman bathing. The woman was very beautiful, and David sent someone to find out about her. The man said, 'Isn't this Bathsheba, the daughter of Eliam and the wife of Uriah the Hittite?' Then David sent messengers to get her. She came to him, and he slept with her . . . Then she went back home. The woman conceived and sent word to David, saying, 'I am pregnant.' . . . In the morning David wrote a message to Joab and sent it with Uriah. In it he wrote, 'Put Uriah in the front line where the fighting is fiercest. Then withdraw from him so that he will be struck down and die.' . . . When Uriah's wife heard that her husband was dead,

---

[100] Gen 12:10–20.

she mourned for him. After the time of mourning was over, David had her brought to his house, and she became his wife, and bore him a son. But the thing David had done displeased the Lord.[101]

Are we to argue that since King David was himself the head of the Messianic line, then the whole Messianic enterprise is fatally flawed as a result of David's behaviour? Again, the Jewish refutationists would resist that interpretation quite forcefully. And rightly so. As for passages which criticise the Jewish community as a whole for their behaviour and beliefs, their number is of course vast. Here is a typical judgement from God voiced by one of the prophets:

Hear, O heavens! Listen, O earth!
For the LORD has spoken:
'I reared children and brought them up,
but they have rebelled against me.
The ox knows his master,
the donkey his owner's manger,
but Israel does not know,
my people do not understand.'
Ah, sinful nation,
a people loaded with guilt,
a brood of evildoers,
children given to corruption.
They have forsaken the LORD;
they have spurned the Holy One of Israel
and turned their backs on him.[102]

No-one in the Bible, whether hero or commoner, whether in the Hebrew Bible or the New Testament, can lay claim to spiritual or moral perfection, with the exception of Jesus himself. The Bible makes no effort to conceal this fact, but rather seems at pains to stress it. So we return to the issue at hand: does the Church's history of sin, especially directed

---

[101] 2 Sam 11:2–5, 14–15, 26–27.
[102] Isa 1:2–4.

against the Jewish people, merit going beyond a condemnation of Christians to the conclusion that it amounts to a disqualification of Jesus' own Messiahship? The answer really has to be 'No', but having said that, the full blast of the Jewish condemnation of so much Christian behaviour, especially antisemitism, has to be faced by Christians. We *have* betrayed our Lord.

Let me close this chapter by drawing out something of the broader implications of the debate. There are many voices telling us today that as a result of this terribly distorted picture of Jesus which has been presented to the Jewish people for so long, the only proper response is for Christians to call a moratorium on each and every attempt to share the Gospel with Jewish people. In short, the argument is that we have lost the moral right to be evangelists among Jewish people. We must not simply dismiss this idea out of hand, without giving it a second thought. In my opinion, any Christians who do not take the time to look behind this call for a cessation of witness to Jewish people, and who therefore never learn the full implications of the awful story of Christian antisemitism, have perhaps indeed lost the moral right to witness to Jewish people about the glory of Jesus.

And when you do begin to appreciate what has been done to Jewish people in the name of Jesus, then it is impossible not to be filled with shame and fear. And only then, I believe, can God really use you to be an effective witness to the Jewish community. To withdraw from any sort of active witness because of that history, however, would only be one possible strategy. There is another strategy which I think is more appropriate to the Gospel message: the proper response to a distorted presentation of Jesus as Israel's Messiah is not a retreat from any presentation of him as the Messiah, but a corrected and faithful presentation of Jesus as Israel's Messiah! We are still under the mandate to show Jewish people the love of their Messiah for them, even though that task is perhaps harder now than it has ever been.

Can anyone be at all surprised that in the face of the Churches' treatment of Jewish people they themselves want nothing to do with Jesus as their Messiah? Some Christians, though, almost beyond belief, do seem to be surprised and want to jettison the Jewish people to history, arguing that God himself has surely finished with them by now. Not at all! Listen to the words of Paul, echoing down the centuries and calling out to us:

> Again I ask: Did they stumble so as to fall beyond recovery? Not at all! Rather, because of their transgression, salvation has come to the Gentiles to make Israel envious. But if their transgression means riches for the world, and their loss means riches for the Gentiles, how much greater riches will their fullness bring![103]

It is a mountain of a task, in the shadow of the Holocaust, for Christians to live and witness in such a way that they will make Jewish people actually jealous of their relationship with Israel's own Messiah. But that is the task before us. Relegating Jesus to the status of just a good charismatic teacher, or agreeing to alienate him from the Jewish world so that he becomes a foundational person just for non-Jews, is not the way to accomplish this call from God. Rather, our task is to find the way to maintain a testimony, by *both* authentic life *and* explicit word, to the Messiah of Israel and the Saviour of the world, Jesus of Nazareth.

---

[103] Rom 11:11f.

6

Frustration

This will prove to be one of the key words in any analysis of the situation between Christians and Jews. For different reasons, each community struggles with enormous frustration as it attempts to relate to the other. At the most basic level, Christians have agonised from the very beginning of the life of the Jesus movement over the question of why the Jewish people did not become followers of Jesus *en masse*. Early on there arose a pernicious theory that it was because of a particular and pathological blindness on their part to the spiritual truths of God. This theory is far from dead today in some quarters of the Church. Rather quickly a 'teaching of contempt' was developed regarding the Jewish people. A favourite text which was used against them was the following one from Amos:

> Hear this word the LORD has spoken against you, O people of Israel – against the whole family I brought up out of Egypt:
> 'You only have I chosen of all the families of the earth; therefore I will punish you for all your sins.'[104]

The Jewish refusal to accept Jesus as Israel's promised Messiah was seen as evidence that they were an especially wicked and ungrateful people. They were regarded as coming under the most severe judgement of God for having rejected the Messiah. In the spirit of the Amos text given above, it was argued that all the other peoples of the earth at

---

[104] Amos 3:1–2.

least had the excuse of not actually expecting a 'messiah', and therefore must be judged more leniently. But the Jewish people were the very ones to whom the promises had been given, and so they would be punished most severely of all.

However, it did not end there. If that had been all there was to it, then the Christian contempt for the Jewish people could have been uncomplicated and relatively contained. But it frustrated the Christian leadership intensely that for all their preaching about how wonderful and clear the plan of God was from the very beginning, the Jewish people refused to co-operate by agreeing to the Christian interpretation of the Hebrew Bible! As David Berger puts it:

> Christians were genuinely puzzled at the Jewish failure to accept the overwhelming array of scriptural arguments which they had marshalled.[105]

To the Church's shame, her response did not stop at puzzlement, but developed into a strong reactive aggression. Michael Wyschogrod traces the history of a specifically Christian antisemitism to this theological tension:

> Christian anti-Semitism is a function of a certain kind of Christian self-confidence. If one believes with unquestioning conviction that Jesus was the saviour who died for the sins of the world, then it becomes a source of serious concern and irritation that he was not so recognized by his own people.[106]

What seems to have particularly aggravated the frustration of Christian leaders was the way in which *pagan* writers and leaders used the fact of the Jewish rejection of Jesus as Messiah in their own polemics against Christianity. The line of argument is simplicity itself: if this Gospel about Jesus being the long-promised Messiah is true, as you say,

---

[105] David Berger, *The Jewish-Christian Debate in the High Middle Ages* (JPSA, Philadelphia, 1979), p 11.
[106] Michael Wyschogrod, 'The Future of Jewish–Christian Relations', in *Face to Face* (Winter/Spring 1976), p 19.

then why is it that God's own people, those in covenant relationship with him, those who were actively awaiting the advent of this very Messiah, have not recognised and embraced this brother of theirs, Jesus of Nazareth? What do they know that we do not? What are you not telling us? Why should we commit our lives to him if they refuse to?[107]

As a matter of interest, this type of reasoning is still heard from time to time, as can be seen in the reports of missionaries in different parts of the world. It is an intelligent question! Michael Wyschogrod is right in saying that this became a source of terrible frustration in the Christian world. It was considered to be bad enough that the Jewish people themselves chose not to believe in Jesus, but it was altogether intolerable that their unbelief should hinder others from coming into the Kingdom of God! To grasp this context is to begin to understand the specific nature of the *Christian* frustration at the continuing presence of Judaism as a world faith.

All the world faiths are in disagreement with one another at some level, and there is, so to speak, a market-place of ideas out there. People can easily point to role models who have chosen to become members of faiths other than Christianity as reasons for themselves preferring that other faith. Recent celebrated instances of this would include the singer Cat Stevens and the boxer Cassius Clay, both of whom became Muslims. But only Judaism can and does claim to be the true fulfilment of the religious tradition which Christianity itself claims to represent in today's world. Judaism can be an embarrassment and an irritant to a degree unattainable by any other faith, because only Judaism is bound up with the *self-definition* of Christianity. And Christians have responded to this irritation from time to time with vicious reprisals.

---

[107] Two early instances of this debate taking place can be found in the following works: *Contra Celsum* 7:18, by Origen, and *Against the Galileans* 253b, 238b, 320b, by Julian the Apostate.

Now what about the attitudes to Jesus within today's Jewish community? By and large, it seems that most Jewish people and families have not given Jesus or the New Testament much thought at all. Their frustration and bitter resentment at what has happened to them in his name has led to what some refer to as 'a conspiracy of silence'. Jesus has been largely boycotted. Consequently, many Jewish people are genuinely ignorant about him, about his life and teachings, about his essential Jewishness. Traditionally, when he is referred to at all, it is by the phrase, 'that man', or 'the hanged one'. His name is not to be mentioned for fear of giving the impression that he is worthy of a personal mention in a Jewish home.[108]

In the event that he has to be referred to by name, the Jewish leadership quickly decided on a name which would seem to be acceptable to outsiders but which would actually have a hidden message of contempt. Jesus' Hebrew name was a diminutive version of the Hebrew name Y'hoshua (Joshua). The diminutive form, which was common enough in Jesus' time and place, was Y'shua (Jesus). But it seems very likely that there was a dialectical variation of the spelling and pronunciation of this name in the Galilee region, namely, Yeshu. Both forms would have been acceptable at one time. However, the Jewish establishment quickly discovered that the second of these forms suited its own purposes perfectly, and this led to the exclusive use of the form Yeshu in Jewish tradition. It is the form used by Israelis in the State of Israel today.[109]

---

[108] For the names and terms given to Jesus in the Jewish community, see Jakob Jocz, op cit, p 59, and my own book, *Jesus Ben Joseph*, op cit, chapter 6.

[109] For a good presentation of the basic issues surrounding the forms of Jesus' name in his own time and place, see John P. Meier, *A Marginal Jew. Rethinking the Historical Jesus* (Doubleday, NY, 1991), pp 205–8. He does not, however, mention the later use made of the form of that name by the rabbinic authorities.

But it is never used by Jewish believers themselves, since they are well aware of the hidden meaning behind the seemingly harmless use of the variant spelling. The rabbis discovered that if you use the variant spelling, which employs only three letters of the Hebrew alphabet, in contra-distinction to the four letters of the fuller form, then you can turn the name Yeshu into a subtle acronym meaning, 'May his name and memory be blotted out!'[110] In other words, while seeming only to say his name, you can actually be passing a value judgement on him as well.

The three words are: *Y*imach   = May it be blotted out
                  *Sh*emo   = His name
                  *U*zikhrono = And his memory

My experience in the State of Israel today has been that whereas most Israelis refer to Jesus as 'Yeshu', by and large they have no idea of the ideological substratum to the choice of this form of the name. They are genuinely surprised when you inform them of its second meaning and urge them to use the fuller name, Y'shua. This ignorance of the struggle is probably characteristic of the younger generations of Jewish people the world over, who use Yeshu as the name for Jesus thinking that it is the only version of his name in Hebrew.

Although the situation is definitely changing in our generation, with increasing numbers of Jewish people, especially students, doing incomparably more reading and thinking about Jesus than any generation for an extremely long time, the fact remains that Jesus has not been an acceptable topic of conversation in most Jewish homes or study programmes. When we remember the formally-staged public disputes of the Middle Ages and beyond, then we are duty-

---

[110] For good discussions of the issues here see Joseph Klausner, *Jesus of Nazareth, his life, times, and teaching* (English translation, George Allen & Unwin, London, 1925), p 229; Hugh J. Schonfield, *According to the Hebrews* (Duckworth, London, 1937), p 221.

bound, as I mentioned in an earlier chapter, to acknowledge
that the Jewish representatives were *compelled* by the Christian political and ecclesiological authorities to participate.
The agenda was always set by the Christian camp, so that
the Jewish representatives were always on the defensive,
answering the question, 'Why do you not believe such-and-
such?' They soon came to dread these disputes, since they
knew that whatever happened in the debating arena, the
neighbouring Jewish communities would all suffer the consequences, whether under the banner of triumphalist zeal or
bitter reprisal. Frank Talmage quotes a thirteenth-century
rabbi on this matter:

> If the Jew be victorious, he will provoke wrath upon himself for
> belittling and refuting their faith. But if he is defeated and
> shamed, and if on his account and through ignorance truth is
> silenced, his punishment is twofold.[111]

One example of the outcome of such an enforced disputation
is that which followed the most famous of them all, the 1263
Barcelona Disputation, in which the Jewish community was
represented by the magisterial figure of Rabbi Moses ben
Nachman. The rabbi actually 'won' the debate against his
opponent, himself a Jewish person who had 'converted' and
become a baptised member of the Church. The rabbi had
taken the precaution of requesting from the Christian king,
James of Aragon, who himself presided over the affair,
permission to exercise complete freedom of speech. The
king, who was deeply impressed by Rabbi Nachman, agreed
to this. And so the rabbi presented his case with consummate
skill and carried the day.

Soon afterwards, under pressure from some Jewish quarters, he actually published an account of the proceedings, but
this was adjudged by the church authorities to be offensive

---

[111] Frank Talmage, quoting Rabbi Solomon ben Moses, in *Commentary* (February 1975), p 57.

and seditious. He had been granted full freedom of expression within the debate itself, so they argued, but this did not protect him from prosecution for committing to public scrutiny a written record of the Church's defeat. This was too dangerous to allow, as it could influence others who read it and reflected on the rabbi's points. Under excessive pressure from the Church, which King James could not afford to antagonise too far, the king agreed to the order to have this account of the disputation burned. In addition, Rabbi Nachman himself was exiled for two years. And then, when this period of exile was almost over, Pope Clement IV intervened personally and had the expulsion order extended to exile for life.

Herein lies the root of one of the Jewish community's greatest frustrations with the Christian community. Now, as then, Jewish people have no desire to become involved in public debates of any kind with Christians. The vast majority of Jewish people simply want to be left alone to live in peace with their neighbours, whoever they are. Most of the rabbis and community leaders whom I have met are weary of the constant desire by Christians to engage them in debates about theology, and are also highly embarrassed by the type of material being put out by the professional 'anti-missionaries' in the name of the Jewish community.

Of course both communities experience immense frustration when they find both themselves and their faith being misrepresented by the other. It was in fact the sustained efforts of certain contemporary Jewish refutationists to thus misrepresent and ridicule the Christian faith which led to the request for this present book!

But Christians cannot throw stones at the Jewish community in this matter. Sad to relate, much of the Christian refutationist material *vis-à-vis* the Jewish faith, especially from the lips and pens of many 'converts' from Judaism, has been misrepresentative and/or presented in a biased manner and/or generally done in an insensitive way. Even if Christians are sure that they are speaking the truth on a certain matter, indeed especially at such times, then they are quite explicitly commanded in Scripture to speak that truth in *love*.[112] Unfortunately, there seems to be a universal human drive to show the superiority of one's own beliefs or values, etc, by trying to belittle and degrade those of others. This often involves a cynical attempt merely to score points at the other person's expense by the power of rhetoric and personality.

Both Christians and Jews are guilty of this attitude and behaviour, though in the *public* arena the Jewish people have been sinned against far more than they have sinned. Sigal summarises it like this:

> The driving force behind the missionary movement's efforts against Judaism is the conviction that the validity of Christianity requires the withering away of ancient Jewish practice and belief . . . To accomplish this end, missionaries must undermine the foundation of Judaism.[113]

There is a sense in which there will inevitably be fundamental conflict between the teachings of Christianity and Judaism. There are some incompatible differences between them concerning the nature of God, etc. So in one sense, by definition, both faiths are undermining the other. But this is something quite different from trying to belittle and even misrepresent the other faith and those who adhere to it. And this is the real cause of anger and frustration. Christians have made a science out of ridiculing and demeaning the Midrashim and the Talmud, etc. Few things could be more guaranteed to upset any religious community than having their source documents and their most valued insights abused in this fashion.

And of course it is not difficult to discover why the worst

---

[112] Eph 4:15.

[113] Gerald Sigal, *The Jew and the Christian Missionary*, op cit, p xvi.

culprits in this strategy of misrepresentation were the Jewish 'converts' to Christianity. They, more than any other Christians, felt that they had to prove their loyalty to their new faith-community. The suspicion of Jewish people and all things Jewish had become so ingrained in the Churches that many Jewish converts felt the need to 'expose' some terrible truth about their former religion in order to prove the genuineness of their conversion. So they made things up, or deliberately twisted the interpretation of certain doctrines and practices, etc, all to ingratiate themselves with their new masters in the Church.

This situation was complicated by two other factors. On the one hand, Christian leaders knew full well that vast numbers of Jewish people went through the motions of a genuine 'conversion' in order to escape death or exile, or in order to achieve the hope of some advancement in (Christian) society. It is for this reason that I am placing the word 'convert' within quotation marks in this section. Without any doubt, it was such false converts who were callous enough to abuse their former community in an attempt to convince the ecclesiastical authorities that they were in fact genuinely converted to the Christian faith. We must remember that contempt for the Jewish people and for their religious culture was a characteristic of much of Christian history, and so it was expected that Jewish people who became Christians would be rejoicing at being rescued not only from sin, but also from the Jewish world. It is also important to remember that Jewish people who converted were no longer considered by the Church, let alone by the Synagogue, to be Jewish.

A wonderfully sarcastic Jewish joke captures this situation very well. A Jewish family 'converts' under the guidance of the local priest who baptises them. As he sprinkles them with water he repeats over and over again, 'You are no longer Jewish – you are Christian!' A few weeks later the priest receives word from one of his gentile parishioners that the family deceived him. They only converted to receive temporal benefits from the Church, and in reality they are continuing to live as Jews. The priest makes up his mind to test the family on the following Sabbath evening.

On the Friday night, he goes to their home, looks through a crack in the curtain, and sees them eating chicken, a traditional Jewish dish on Friday night. Furious, he bursts through the door and accuses the father of deception and heresy. 'But what have I done?' asks the father. 'You know that Catholics only eat fish on a Friday,' shouts the priest. 'But Father, this *is* fish.' 'No it's not, it's chicken.' 'No, it is fish all right.' 'Don't try to fool me. I know chicken when I see and smell it.'

'Father,' the father continues, 'I admit that this *was* chicken when I bought it this morning, but I brought it right home, sprinkled it liberally with water, and called out for all to hear, "You are not a chicken – you are a fish!"'

No great commentary is really necessary to explain the joke. It clearly expresses the contempt which the Jewish community had for the church leaders and the Jewish people who displayed their lack of integrity (and intelligence?) by accepting a formal conversion ritual without any substratum of real conviction.

There is another bitter-sweet Jewish joke which captures the sad hypocrisy at the heart of all this so well that I want to include it here. It is a story of two Jewish men who are completely impoverished. They have no money at all, and the time has come to pay the bills and also the interest on money already borrowed. Each is at his wits' end. As they are walking along together they stop outside a church and exchange meaningful looks. One of them says, 'No matter if I and my whole family starve to death, I will not convert to Christianity in order to get money.' His friend, however, says that he is so desperate that he *will* do it. So he goes into the church while the first Jewish man waits outside full of trepidation.

Four hours later, the friend emerges from the church

wearing new clothes, looking well-fed, and even placing a wallet in his jacket pocket. The first Jew asks nervously, 'Well, did you get it?' To which the other one answers, 'You Jews are all the same. All you think about is money!'

In the joke, the integrity is all with the Jewish man who refused to go through the motions for personal and social advancement, even though he remained poor. The Jewish man who sold out to the church is doubly despised: firstly for selling out at all, and then secondly for the way he turned on his former friend. And so it was seen to be in real life too. These 'converts' sold out their families and friends in this double fashion. No wonder then that the favourite Jewish term for 'converts', even including all those Jewish believers who have had a genuine experience of God in the person of Jesus, is 'traitor'.

All Jewish people who profess faith in Jesus, whatever the reality of that profession, are tarred with the same brush.

But the second complication in the life of these so-called 'converts', alluded to in the chicken/fish joke above, was the fact that during the very traumatic years of the Inquisition in the Iberian peninsula, thousands of Jewish people went through the formalities of a conversion to Christianity but actually intended to practise their Judaism secretly, while maintaining the pretence of living Christian lives. The Church was well aware of this, and some of the worst excesses of the Inquisition were exhibited in the attempts of the Church to root out these '*marranos*', as they were called. Once again, some false converts who nevertheless wanted to live as Christians, particularly if they wanted to gain some elevation in the Church, tried to establish the fact that they were not this type of *marrano* by informing on *marranos* known to them and establishing their contempt for Judaism through shedding light on what they presented as the dreadful nature of Jewish faith and life.

One of the most influential post-Enlightenment Christian refutationist books has been that of Alexander McCaul, a brilliant scholar who served with the London Jews Society in the last century. His work, entitled *The Old Paths*, is still very much in use in some mission circles. He was completely determined to exalt Christianity at the expense of Judaism, to expose what he called 'the utter inadequacy of Judaism', and to show that there is absolute disparity between rabbinic Judaism and the teaching of the Hebrew Bible. However, he asserted, Christianity and the Church are in full continuity with God's revelation from the beginning. After more than 650 pages of argument, McCaul concludes not only with these very points, but also with the statement that the men who formulated and developed modern Judaism were wicked and thoroughly undeserving of any merit, and their insights and contributions are therefore totally devoid of value.

This attitude is patently unfair and unacceptable, proving to be an embarrassment even for many Christians who are convinced that Judaism is not a salvific faith apart from belief in Jesus. It was a book whose tone alone was guaranteed to upset even those Jewish people who were well able to cope theologically with the basic disagreements between Jews and Christians. Here is a typical piece of McCaul's rhetoric and generalisation:

> If there be one sign of true religion more satisfactory than another, it is the placing of holiness of heart and life as the first great requisite, at the same time that it does not undervalue any of God's commandments. Now this mark Christianity has, and Judaism wants.[114]

This determination to show the other 'side' in as negative a light as possible has been one of the sad characteristics of the Jewish–Christian dispute over the generations. It would be a major breakthrough if both could agree to judge the other, if

---

[114] Alexander McCaul, *The Old Paths, or, A Comparison of the Principles and Doctrines of Modern Judaism with the Religion of Moses and the Prophets* (London Societies House, London, 1837), p 652.

judging there must be, by the *best* which the other has to offer, rather than by the worst. There are, thankfully, some precedents for this in our shared history. In the tenth century, one of Judaism's greatest representatives, known as Sa'adia Gaon, showed this spirit in a discussion of the Christian doctrine of the Tri-unity of God:

> When I present this refutation I do not have in mind the uneducated among them who profess only a gross corporeal Trinity. For I would not have my book occupy itself with answering such people, since that answer must be quite clear and the task simple. It is rather my intention to reply to the learned who maintain that they adopted their belief in the Trinity as a result of rational speculation and subtle understanding.[115]

This passage does not mean that Sa'adia was displaying contempt for the common people. The point is that he was writing a response to the doctrine itself, not to the range of understandings of it by all sorts of people, and so he decided to judge it by the understanding offered by those Christian theologians who were best able to present it in its orthodox form. This kind of attitude should be a model for us all. If we wish to question the Jewish concept of the two moral inclinations within each person, for example, then we should make sure that we base our questions on the doctrine as it is expressed in the consensus of orthodox teaching, rather than as it is held by some Jewish person or group we may have come across, who may not stand in the mainstream at all.

At the other end of the spectrum from Sa'adia Gaon, we have the type of judgements represented by the collection of crude stories and calumnies brought together in the early Middle Ages in the Jewish book known as *Toldot Yeshu*,

---

[115] Sa'adia Gaon, *Emunot ve-Deot*, 933 (translated by S. Rosenblatt, 1948), p 103.

the 'History of Jesus'. Here, for example, we find stories purporting to show that Jesus' mother was actually an adultress and that Jesus was therefore just a common bastard child:

> I found a genealogical scroll in Jerusalem and in it was written, ' "A certain man" is the bastard son of a married woman.'[116]

There are stories about how Jesus was an unscrupulous sorcerer who stole the secret of God's holy and personal name from the temple and used it to do his miracles and claim divinity; there are accounts of what was really supposed to have happened at the resurrection of Jesus; some versions tell that Joseph actually raped Mary and then deserted her to look after Jesus by herself; etc.[117]

What I will do now is quote extensively from one chapter of the *Toldot Yeshu* in which Jesus' power to do miracles is explained in such a way as to 'expose' him, according to their plan, not only as a charlatan, but as a blasphemer and an enemy of God. As we look at this section, note that no attempt is made to deny Jesus' power to perform miracles! The strategy was to invent a story about the *source* of that power. I imagine that this was for two reasons. On the one hand, there had been too many witnesses to the miracles of Jesus for there to be any hope of trying to suppress the evidence, and besides, his contemporary followers also had the reputation for special healing power. But on the other hand, it suited the Jewish authorities just as well, if not better, to use Jesus' means of acquiring his power as a

---

[116] Many of the episodes in the book are taken from passages in the Talmud, and this is one such passage. It comes from Yebamot, 49b. Origen responds to this very charge in *Contra Celsum*, 1:46. For the whole issue, see Travers R. Herford, *Christianity in Talmud and Midrash* (Ktav, NY, 1903), *passim*.

[117] For a good introductory discussion of the *Toldot* see Jakob Jocz, op cit, pp 60–64.

means to *disgrace* him and his followers in the eyes of the Jewish people.

And in the temple was the foundation-stone . . . and on it were graven the letters of the Ineffable Name. And whosoever learned them could do whatsoever he would. But whereas the wise men feared that the young men of Israel would learn them, and thereby destroy the world, they took steps that it should not be possible to learn them. Dogs of brass were bound to two pillars of iron at the gate of the place of burnt-offerings, so that whosoever entered and learned the letters, as soon as he went forth the dogs bayed at him: if he then looked at them the letters went forth from his mind.

Then came Jesus and learned them, and wrote upon parchment and cut open his thigh and laid the parchment with those letters therein; so that the cutting of his flesh pained him not. And he restored the flesh to its place. And as he went forth the dogs of the pillars bayed at him, and the letters went forth from his mind. He went into his house, and cut into his flesh with a knife, and lifted out the writing and learnt the letters. Then went he forth and gathered together three hundred and ten of the young men of Israel.

He saith unto them, See ye them which say concerning me, [a bastard and son of a woman in her separation]; they desire greatness for themselves and seek to exercise lordship in Israel. Have ye not seen that all the prophets prophesied concerning the Messiah of God, and I am the Messiah. And concerning me Isaiah prophesied, and said, Behold, the virgin shall conceive, and bear a son, and shall call his name Immanuel. And, again, David my ancestor prophesied concerning me, and said, The Lord said unto me, Thou art my son; this day have I begotten thee. He begat me without a male lying with (my mother); yet they call me a bastard. And again he prophesied, Why do the heathen rage, and the people imagine a vain thing? The kings of the earth set themselves, and the rulers take counsel together, against the Lord, and against his anointed.

I am the Messiah, and them that withstand me are the children of whoredoms, for so saith the scripture, For they be the children of whoredoms.

Then answered him the young men, If thou art the Messiah, show unto us a sign. He saith unto them, What sign seek ye of me that I should do for you? Straightway they brought unto him a lame man, that never yet had stood upon his feet. He spake over him the letters, and he rose up upon his feet. In that hour they all worshipped him, and said, This is the Messiah. Again he performed for them another sign. They brought unto him a leper, and he spake over him the letters, and he was healed. There joined themselves unto him the insurgents of his people.[118]

Several points deserve to be highlighted after this section of text. It gives a good sample of the kind of material to be found in the whole work, although it is more subdued than certain of the passages! So let us note the following points:

- As I mentioned before quoting the chapter, the author/ editor casts no doubt at all upon Jesus' power to perform miracles.
- The power to perform miracles is said to be bound up with the power of God's own name, not at all in Jesus' own person or abilities. In this account, God did not graciously decide to share his power with Jesus, but rather the power was stolen from God.
- Jesus is said to have devised a premeditated plan to steal this power from God, and to have succeeded in his plan.
- The original number of the followers of Jesus is said to have been 310. I believe that this number was chosen because it happens to be the numerical equivalent of the Hebrew word '*req*', which means 'empty'. In Hebrew, the letters of the alphabet also function as the numbers, so that every combination of letters could be either a word or a large number or, of course, both. The number value of the three letters which make up the word for 'empty' is 310.

---

[118] This is chapter two of the *Toldot Yeshu*, as translated by Hugh J. Schonfield, *According to the Hebrews* (Duckworth, London, 1937), pp 39–41.

Hence, what seems to the non-Jewish reader a number picked out of a hat is actually conveying a coded message to the Jewish readership. This kind of interpretative method is very common in Jewish religious exegesis and homiletics, and Jewish people to this day are very familiar with it.

- Note also that it was only the 'young men' and the trouble makers who were said to be deceived by Jesus. The older and therefore 'wise men' knew better. These young men were deceived by Jesus' power to do miracles, since they were not wise enough, in the view of the author/editor, to know that power in itself is not enough to prove one's Messianic credentials. The older and wiser men would have reflected on the words of Moses:

> If a prophet, or one who foretells by dreams, appears among you and announces to you a miraculous sign or wonder, and if the sign or wonder of which he has spoken takes place, and he says, 'Let us follow other gods . . . and worship them,' you must not listen to the words of that prophet or dreamer. The LORD your God is testing you to find out whether you love him with all your heart and with all your soul . . . That prophet or dreamer must be put to death, because he preached rebellion against the LORD your God . . .

- Note that the accusation of Jesus' illegitimate birth is reflected in this source.
- Finally, note that the author/editor is well aware of the early believers' use of certain biblical passages as Messianic proof-texts for the authenticity of Jesus' claims.

In connection with this matter of Jewish knowledge of the classic prophetic passages being used by believers, let me mention that in my opinion the person responsible for the account of how Jesus smuggled the name of God out of the temple by hiding it in his thigh based his bizarre story on some awareness of a verse in the last book of the New Testament. In Rev 19:12 we are told that Jesus has written on himself a name 'that no-one but he himself knows'. This is a clear allusion to the divine personal name of God, the correct pronunciation and meaning of which had been lost to the Jewish people by Jesus' time. This is the name which is referred to in the *Toldot Yeshu* story.

Then in verse 16, a climactic point in that triumphant chapter of Revelation, it is said of Jesus that:

> On his robe and on his thigh he has this name written: King of kings and Lord of lords.

I think that Jewish people were aware of this passage through their disputes with believers, so that the idea that Jesus' *thigh* played a significant part in his story was based on a corrupt attempt to reinterpret the New Testament message.

There is much to be learned, then, from an examination of these accounts of the life of Jesus and his followers. They are not, to be sure, a reliable source of information about Jesus or his disciples, but they have an important role to play, nonetheless. We find revealed here a whole world of reaction to the rise of the Christian community. As has been emphasised in a previous chapter, it is vital that Christians appreciate that a basic context for this kind of Jewish writing and teaching was the sense of impotent frustration and pain with which the Jewish community was struggling *vis-à-vis* the Christian community. Ridiculing and dismissing Jesus and his Jewish followers in this manner was the only way in which the Jewish community could 'fight back' against Christianity. We must certainly be determined to correct the errors and to challenge those who are deliberately perpetuating these terrible stories, but we must do so in a spirit of compassion and understanding.

An example of someone who is unfortunately intent on keeping the dispute at a confrontational and vulgar level, pretending to scholarship and integrity but simply interested in scoring cheap points, is Shmuel Golding. Golding, a self-styled rabbi and a supposed convert to Judaism from the highest ranks of evangelical Christianity, if we are to believe his own testimony of himself, lives and works in Jerusalem. He conducts workshops and seminars, publishes a magazine, and has produced a manual of 'proofs' against the Gospel.

As an example of his attitude and technique, let me give his use of a text in Isaiah. He makes a point of using, and indeed reintroducing, with approval and enthusiasm, an interpretation supplied in a 1420 polemical document by Rabbi Yomtob Lipmann Muhlhausen. The verse in question is Isa 5:18: 'Woe to those who draw sin along with cords of deceit.' Golding follows Muhlhausen in saying that this is a prophecy of the ringing of church bells! These bells, so they claim, are calling Christians into idolatrous worship. Exasperation threatens to overcome sensitive Christians at this point, even though they know that this is a pathological reaction to a life of persecution, and even though they know that Christians cannot throw stones at the Jewish community, since there are plenty of instances of the same attitude being shown by Christians against Jews. How then, if at all, can we escape from this terrible impasse of frustration?

Let me mention one further source of frustration within the evangelical Protestant world. There is a charge which is often heard that Jewish people do not differentiate enough between different Christian groups when they are making criticisms. This is not the same issue as that of including nominal Christians along with committed Christian people, though there is often some overlap between the two issues. As Eugene Fisher once said in an important article:

> What was, and is, missing in much of the Jewish understanding of Christianity, is a sense of the complexity of Christian belief, the variety of practice, and the nuances and historical contexts which alone can give flesh to the bare bones of doctrine.[119]

---

[119] Eugene Fisher, 'Typical Jewish Misunderstandings of Christianity', in *Judaism*, vol 22, no 1 (Winter 1973), p 23.

In particular we find evangelical Protestants being associated with Roman Catholic beliefs and practices. Much of the traditional Jewish rejection of Christianity found in the classic works by refutationists involves reactions against teachings and practices which do not reflect evangelical Protestantism. Included here would be the following: an objection to the perception that Christians virtually divinise Mary, the mother of Jesus; an objection to the teaching that the bread and wine of Holy Communion literally become the body and blood of Jesus; an objection to the concept of papal infallibility, based on the conviction that only the biblical prophets could ever speak with absolute truth.

Protestants will complain that they too reject these and other teachings and practices of other Churches. Moreover, they will usually plead that whatever the dreadful rhetoric of Martin Luther against the Jewish people and religion in the latter part of his career, the actual persecution of Jews by Christians is really a matter for the conscience of Roman Catholics (Church Fathers, the Crusades, Adolph Hitler himself, etc) and the Russian Orthodox Church (the pogroms in Eastern Europe). We shall look more closely at the role of Luther and the Reformation Churches in a later chapter.

Now there is a great deal of historical naïvety in all of this, not to mention a self-centred desire to be seen as guiltless, but nonetheless there is perhaps something of a case to be made, as long as it is borne in mind that one can only speak about *relative* guilt. Because the fact remains that all our Churches are guilty to some degree, Protestants included.

Let us pause for a moment on this question of relative guilt. It is undoubtedly frustrating to feel that you are not being listened to because you are being tarred with someone else's brush. Many Christians today really *are* expressing genuine shame at what has been done, and are initiating services of repentance within their church families. Just as Christians surely need to learn the complexity of modern

Judaism, so too do Jewish people need to learn the complex nature of the Christian family.

Of course there is one area in which much of the Jewish leadership is very well aware of the broad spectrum of Christian belief, and indeed is happy to exploit it. One of the characteristics of modern refutation literature is the use being made by Jewish leaders of 'liberal', and sometimes quite radical, Christian scholars to represent modern Christian thought. These Christian scholars are people of integrity who sincerely hold to their beliefs, but it would not be fair to suggest that they speak for the majority of Christians. Using them as if they were representative of the 'orthodox' Christian faith is again an exercise in misrepresentation. The point is, of course, that their ideas suit the Jewish perspective incomparably more than the orthodox evangelical Christian faith does.

Eugene Borowitz is one Jewish scholar who is keen to exploit the more amenable theology of certain contemporary, but unrepresentative, Christian scholars. He criticises Jewish thinkers for not being aware of this new resource:

> When modern Jewish thinkers have sought to contrast their faith with that of Christians, their treatments of the other religion seem tendentious and subjective. Instead of facing up to the highly variegated and richly nuanced christologies of their Christian analogues they have preferred to deal with a popular image of their own creation.[120]

Borowitz goes on to discuss two modern Jewish philosophers who, in his opinion, made this mistake of not debating with the proper modern type of Christian theologian or philosopher. These two men were Hermann Cohen and Leo Baeck, both of whom he says

---

[120] Eugene B. Borowitz, *Contemporary Christologies. A Jewish Response* (Paulist Press, NY, 1980), p 4. See also Rabbi Henry Siegman, writing in *Judaism* (Winter 1971), pp 98f.

taught a modernist, German, liberal interpretation of their faith but rejected the idea that Christianity might have an equal right to a neo-Kantian interpretation. That would have compromised their polemic agenda. Surely their confrontation with Christianity would have been more significant had they argued with their modernizing Christian equivalents.[121]

What this all boils down to is that when it suits their purposes, Jewish refutationists will cite liberal Christian thinkers against the orthodox Christian position, regarding any issue of belief or practice. In effect, we will often find ourselves involved in an inner-Christian theological debate as we engage in a Christian–Jewish debate. In times past, Jewish writers might have felt themselves restricted to the use of liberal Jewish thinkers. One such hero was Rabbi Isaac Mayer Wise, who emigrated to the USA from Bohemia in 1846 and became one of the first rabbis there to publicly criticise Christianity on general theological grounds, let alone specifically Jewish ones. In 1883 he wrote an immensely popular polemical work, entitled, *Judaism and Christianity*, which turned out to be one of the mildest in a series of such works. Here are some representative quotes which show his antagonism to *any* kind of supernaturalist religion, including Orthodox Judaism. Wise was definitely a 'liberal' Jewish thinker.

> All so-called lives of Christ or biographies of Jesus are works of fiction, erected by imagination on the shifting foundation of meager and unreliable records. There are very few passages in the gospels which can stand the rigid application of honest criticism.[122]

> Those who expect us to believe in revelation . . . and then want

---

[121] Borowitz, op cit, pp 5f.

[122] Rabbi Isaac Mayer Wise, *Martyrdom of Jesus of Nazareth* (The Bloch Publishing & Printing Company, Chicago, 1888), p 132.

us to believe another number of miracles . . . evidently ask too much of the reasoning man.[123]

Neither the Christian nor the Jew can be willing to admit that the pretensions to supernatural communication of both the apostles and the rabbis are correct.[124]

The New Testament is the fulfilment and continuation of the Old, by the grace of the church and the book-binder.[125]

Christianity can never become the religion of all mankind because its teachings are contrary to the common sense of man.[126]

It will come as no surprise to the contemporary reader that Jewish people delighted in having Wise as an authority whom they could use against Christians. But nowadays one is much more likely to find liberal Christians being quoted, since refutationists consider it to be a basic tactic of warfare, I suppose, to try to divide 'the enemy'. Here is a good example of a quote from a Christian leader, cited in a Jewish refutationist manual of some twenty years ago:

Jews and Christians both have vocations from God. We are God's people, and not two people . . . Our analysis assumes that these [missionary] activities are wrong.[127]

Other favourite Christian writers include Rosemary R. Ruether who says, for example, that Christians must accept

---

[123] Rabbi Isaac Mayer Wise, *Judaism and Christianity* (The Bloch Publishing & Printing Company, Cincinnati, 1883), p 24.

[124] Rabbi Isaac Mayer Wise, *Origin of Christianity* (The Bloch Publishing & Printing Company, Cincinnati, 1868), p 49.

[125] Rabbi Isaac Mayer Wise, *A Defense of Judaism versus Proselytizing Christianity* (The Bloch Publishing & Printing Company, Chicago, 1889), p 106.

[126] Ibid, p 127.

[127] Archbishop Fulton J. Sheen, quoted by Rabbi Benjamin J. Segal, *The Missionary at the Door – Our Uniqueness*, op cit, p 42.

the Jewish rejection of the Messiahship of Jesus, and come to terms with the

> inescapable fact that the messianic age has not come . . . in what sense is Jesus the Christ? . . . we must say that he is not yet the Christ.[128]

Another favourite is A. Roy Eckardt who goes so far as to say that

> Jewish non-acceptance of Jesus as Messiah remains among the most sublime and heroic instances of Israel's faithfulness to her Covenant with God.[129]

Of course there are other major theological debates within the Christian world today which have nothing to do with the specific Christian–Jewish agenda, regarding such issues as the Virgin Birth of Jesus, the Resurrection of Jesus, the Second Coming of Jesus. These debates are also used by Jewish refutationists to cast doubt upon the evangelical Christian position. In fact Dan Cohn-Sherbok perceptively notes that some of this contemporary inner-Christian debate reads like the kind of material we are used to dealing with in the earlier Jewish–Christian disputes. He cites as an example the huge furore over the publication of the book of Christian theology, *The Myth of God Incarnate*, which led, among other things, to the publication of the response volume of Christian theology, *The Truth of God Incarnate*. He summarises the Jewish position in the light of this inner-Christian debate:

> Our main concern is . . . with the issues . . . Were the early Christians mistaken in ascribing deity to Jesus? Has the Church

---

[128] Rosemary R. Ruether, 'An Invitation to Jewish-Christian Dialogue. In What Sense Can We Say That Jesus Was "The Christ"?', *The Ecumenist*, X, 2:17, pp 17–22. 1987.

[129] A. Roy Eckardt, contributing to Richard W. Rousseau (ed), *Christianity and Judaism. The Deepening Dialogue*, p 33.

been guilty of idolatry ever since? What actually is the New Testament evidence? Is it reliable?[130]

Cohn-Sherbok also draws our attention to the fact that many Jewish thinkers are now being attracted to work with the so-called 'liberation theologians' in the Christian family. In particular, they are keen to engage in dialogue with those theologians who seem to have moved some distance away from the mainstream evangelical camp.

> This movement attempts to use the insights of Marxist social criticism to forge a new vision of the Christian message. Most important for Jewish–Christian encounter, liberation theologians have gone back to their Jewish roots in the Old Testament . . . Although Jews cannot accept any christological doctrines embedded in the exposition of this message, they can recognize much common ground . . . The vision of Jesus as a prophet of Israel calling the people back to true worship of God is at the heart of Christian liberation theology . . . Such a conception of Jesus should enable both Jews and Christians to set aside previous christological barriers to interfaith dialogue and concentrate on a shared prophetic vision.[131]

We therefore need to learn to anticipate this use of amenable 'liberal' Christian thought by Jewish people, and thereby avoid the frustration which it can otherwise bring. This is certainly not to say that western evangelicals have nothing to learn from these other theological perspectives. To the contrary, I believe that there is a great deal to be learned from the liberation theologies of different cultures and social groups. But by and large, Jewish refutationists are not interested in this inner-Christian dialogue; their concern is simply to exploit the challenges to certain traditional evangelical perspectives.

---

[130] Rabbi Dan Cohn-Sherbok, art cit, p 6. See also his use of John Hick's work in his book cited in the following note, p 6.

[131] Rabbi Dan Cohn-Sherbok: *On Earth as it is in Heaven* (Orbis Books, NY, 1987), pp 7, 11, 51.

It should also serve as a warning to *Christians* against using any Jewish sources which happen to suit their agenda without first checking whether or not those sources reflect mainstream voices within Judaism, or merely some lone voices in the Jewish spectrum of beliefs. We should not be doing to our neighbour what we would not like our neighbour to be doing to us!

And now let me close this chapter with a final Jewish frustration. It comes about as a result of the different attitudes to the process of 'conversion' in the two communities. Traditionally speaking, it is extremely difficult for a non-Jewish person to become a Jew. In the Orthodox world of today it is still a very lengthy and grudging business. At least a year would be required of a potential convert, with testing periods of much longer being quite common in certain countries or regions. The Beth Din, or Ruling Council, of Great Britain has the reputation in the Jewish world for being one of the strictest of all. The whole process is designed to be a severe test of the motives of the potential convert for wanting to become Jewish, and many people, including sincere candidates for conversion, give up in frustration long before the process is complete. It can be a very much easier process in the Progressive Jewish communities, but nonetheless the complexity and length of the process is known by all Jews.

The potential convert is enrolled in a programme of study which is quite exacting, and in a set of relationships with Jewish people where he or she is able to learn the practicalities of Jewish worship and lifestyle while being monitored at the same time.

What many Jewish people simply cannot understand is the ease with which a Jewish person can 'become a Christian'. It seems to happen overnight, or in a matter of days or weeks. There is often no kind of programme of study apart from reading the Bible for oneself. The new convert is pronounced to be a Christian and baptised in no time, and *then* is expected to get involved in regular worship and Bible study. To a Jewish person this all too easily smacks of both insincerity and superficiality.

The legacy of past ages, when many Jewish people did in fact 'convert' for expediency's sake, is still very much a part of contemporary Jewish suspicion about Jewish believers. It is spelled out here:

> Jews who speak to fellow Jews attracted to Christianity find it hard to believe that such Jewish Christians are sincere. The reason for this is simple. For many centuries many Jews who converted to Christianity did so out of motives of self-interest rather than religious sincerity ... and Jews resented such conversions of convenience ... Gradually, this attitude became deeply ingrained in the Jewish mind, and as a result many Jews find it hard to believe that a Jew who embraces Christianity can be sincere.[132]

Even Jewish people who speak disparagingly about the excessive caution and reluctance of the Orthodox Jewish leadership in accepting converts to Judaism regard the Christian conversion process as little more than an emotion-based experience. Where is the intellectual rigour? Can we be sure that sufficient care is taken to weed out those with motives of self-interest? This can be a real concern for the family of a new Jewish believer struggling with the acceptance of his or her coming to faith in Jesus.

There is, then, a lot of frustration awaiting us if we are not prepared for the complex nature of ministry to Jewish people. As we continue in this book to explore the major issues involved in becoming better prepared, it is time to begin to look at specific issues and strategies in the long history of Jewish–Christian disputation. I hope that this book will serve to inspire creative thought and action on behalf of many

---

[132] Berger and Wyschogrod, op cit, p 13.

Christians, particularly Jewish believers, who have the desire to become involved with Jewish people in helping them come to faith in Jesus, the Son of David – the Messiah.

7

Hermeneutics and ambiguity

Hermeneutics is the name given to the branch of theology which is concerned with how we interpret texts. It is the science, as some would say, or the craft, as others would prefer, of interpretation. Of course everyone has a system of sorts when it comes to reading and working with the text of the Bible, even if they are not consciously aware of it. No one comes to the Bible without assumptions of one sort or another. To say this is not to prejudice the issue of whether the Bible is the Word of God, but simply to make the point that when the Bible is opened, different people, different denominations within the Church and different Christian schools of thought will often understand what they read in different ways. Sometimes the differences may seem to be of relatively little importance, but sometimes they have significant implications. Just opening the Bible and looking at the words on the page will not make it evident whose interpretation is right. We have to listen to all sides of the argument and decide in the context of our discussions which seems to be the best interpretation.

Before we are able to look at any other issue in this book, then, we must face the fact that the traditional Jewish and Christian understandings of the Bible, and the traditional methods of interpreting the Bible, are quite different. Not only that, but there is a further complication that neither of the two hermeneutical systems is self-evidently true. Both are the result of faith-commitments. Therefore there is a sense in which there will always be some ambiguity about the conclusions drawn, at least as far as the one community hears the interpretation of the other. Readers of this book who wish to familiarise themselves with the science or craft of hermeneutics in either of the two communities will find plenty of help in the standard textbooks, but our present task is simply to highlight some of the commonest areas of dispute between them when it comes to the issue of whether or not Jesus is the Messiah.

I propose to deal with this under three broad headings:

- The Jewishness of the New Testament writings, and appropriate methods of interpretation
- The meaning of the claim that the Hebrew Bible is 'fulfilled' in the New Testament
- The role of the Septuagint (LXX) in the whole issue.

It will become quite clear what many of the specific interpretative principles are and how they are applied, when we come in Part Two of the book to examine Jewish and Christian interpretations of selected passages in the Hebrew Bible. We shall, in fact, be looking at a large number of disputed passages in the course of this book, but my purpose at this stage is simply to set out these three macro-level issues, since they are so important in the whole debate.

The New Testament is Jewish

Traditionally, and certainly since the time of Isaac Troki, Jewish critics of the New Testament have chosen to ignore the fact, or have remained ignorant of the fact, that the New Testament is a collection of *Jewish* pieces of religious literature. Even although it is more than likely that Luke, responsible for the Book of Acts as well as his own gospel, was not Jewish, it is also probable that he was himself one of the 'God-fearers' whom he mentions in Acts from time to time. In other words he lived his life around the synagogue community and shared the spirituality and morality of the

Jewish community. He was not an out-and-out Gentile by any means, and even his Greek has all the resonances of the Septuagint, the *Jewish* Greek version of the Hebrew Bible. The point which I wish to make here is that when one is seeking to interpret the gospels or other parts of the New Testament, one must apply the appropriate literary, historical, cultural and religious tools.

We know that the gospels are not 'histories' in the twentieth-century European sense of the word, just as we know that the opening chapters of Genesis are not an astrophysics manual, but they *are* historical accounts in keeping with the best traditions of writing history in that time and place. In fact we need to go one step further and affirm that the New Testament documents were written in the way that *Jewish* people of that time and place would have written them. They are every bit as much a product of the distinctively Jewish culture within the world as the documents of the Hebrew Bible. Jewish people either do not appreciate this fact because they have never read the New Testament and heard it presented in a fair light, or, if they are aware of this fact, they choose to disregard it when it suits them.

The Jewish community has been berating Christians for centuries now (and with full justification) for the sin of not trying to appreciate the Jewish religious sources (Mishnah, Talmud, Midrashim) in their own right. It is certainly true that antisemites have found a happy hunting-ground in this profound and difficult literature for their own preconceived and prejudiced notions of what Jewish people are like, and have used quotations out of context to ridicule and condemn Judaism. Just as one evaluates poetry in a different way from scientific textbooks, or folk music from grand opera, so too one must judge religious texts by their own canons of interpretation. And just as Christians rightly object when people take biblical texts out of context, so too should rabbinic texts only be studied in context. Therefore the rabbis have had every right to be indignant when, for example, Christians who know nothing about the way in which the Talmud teaches, have proceeded to interpret it quite out of context, and in misrepresentative ways.

But sauce for the goose is sauce for the gander. The New Testament should also be interpreted in its proper context. This means using *Jewish* canons of interpretation *from the New Testament period*. What often happens is that a Jewish person will be at pains to point out that one must not take the theological expressions of the rabbis literally when one reads a midrashic comment on a biblical text, or when one reads Talmudic discussions about points of doctrine; but then the very same person will insist on always approaching the words of Jesus or Paul in a quite literal fashion. This is certainly not acceptable. Open-minded Jewish people who are knowledgeable about their religious sources will soon recognise the Jewishness of the New Testament, should they make the effort to read it. Furthermore, they will appreciate at once that Jewish canons of interpretation are the appropriate ones.[133]

A leading *Jewish* scholar of our own time, Jacob Neusner, has pointed out the unacceptable bias in the Jewish community's criticism of the Christian community's reading of the New Testament texts. He realises that sauce for the goose must be sauce for the gander:

The apologetic claim of Judaism in its modern and contemporary formulation . . . has rested upon the allegation that Judaism sets forth the real, the historical meaning of the scriptures of ancient Israel, and Christianity, self-evidently, does not. That is to say, no one can imagine Isaiah really had the Virgin Mary in mind when he spoke of the virgin or the young woman who would conceive; or that Isaiah spoke of Jesus Christ when he prophesied about the suffering servant . . . The beam in the hermeneutical eye of Judaism, of course, is the Judaic herme-

---

[133] This whole issue forms a major part of my book, *Jesus Ben Joseph*, op cit.

neutic supplied by the Midrash compilations of ancient times, which impart to the scriptures of ancient Israel a rich and contemporary meaning, no more the plain sense of the ancient writers than the Christian one of Matthew.[134]

Neusner is no special friend of Jewish believers and he is not writing these words to encourage the Christian interpretation of the Messianic prophecies, but his sense of the rightness of fair play in the hermeneutical debate is nonetheless appreciated.

What is more, the Jewish community of today is not at all the same as that of Jesus' time and place, nor even as that which produced the great Jewish works of faith. We must also insist that western Jewish readers of today need to read the texts of the New Testament through the eyes, as it were, of first-century Jews, not as European or North American Jewish people at the end of the twentieth century. The rules and assumptions were different then. Christians often pick up a copy of some piece of rabbinic literature and come away with the impression that there are no rules at all governing the way that texts are related to one another, but there definitely are rules which govern how texts are to be legitimately related to one another. There are in fact a few different sets of hermeneutical principles, but I will give the simplest and best-known of them here, so that Christian readers can gain some useful idea of the rules which govern Jewish religious textual study.

The so-called 'Seven Principles of Hillel' are inseparably linked with the name of a contemporary, roughly speaking, of Jesus, one of Judaism's most revered sages. Here we have a series of rules which seek to set parameters for any acceptable exercise in biblical (or other) exegesis and expo-

---

[134] Jacob Neusner, *Jews and Christians: The Myth of a Common Tradition* (SCM Press, London, 1991), p 119.

sition. Some, if not all, of these principles would have been operative in the time of Jesus.

1 *Qal va-Homer*. This Hebrew phrase means that it is legitimate to make inferences in Scripture from less important cases to more important cases, and vice versa.
2 *Gezerah Shavah*. This means that it is also legitimate to make inferences by analogy between, say, two laws in different contexts but with key words which are identical or similar.
3 *Binyan 'av Mikkatuv 'ehad*. This means that when you have a number of passages linked by a common phrase, or the like, the principal passage imparts a common character to them all, and applications of something found in only one of them can be made to any of them.
4 *Binyan 'av Mishshene Ketuvim*. This is simply a modification of the third rule when it is based on only two passages.
5 *Klal u-Frat u-Frat u-Klal*. This means that it is legitimate to extrapolate particular instances from general passages, and vice versa.
6 *Ketotse bo be-Maqom 'aher*. This is a principle which authorises the hermeneutic of letting any one biblical passage be interpreted by any other.
7 *Davar ha-Lamed Me'inyano*. This principle states that it is legitimate to deduce the meaning of a passage from its context.[135]

Looking at this from another point of view altogether, there are four dimensions, one might say, of interpreting the Scriptures within Jewish tradition. These are known by the mnemonic Hebrew word, '*Pardes*' which means 'an orchard'. This symbol of rich and sustaining fruit refers, via its four consonants, to four types of interpretative principle:

---

[135] I am indebted for this particular version of the Principles of Hillel to Hermann L. Strack, *Introduction to the Talmud and Midrash* (JPSA, Philadelphia, 1931), pp 93f.

P'shat: This means the primary sense of the text, its plain and simple meaning.

Remez: This means a hint, or an allusion, based on the assumption that Scripture often leads us to indirect implications and applications.

D'rash: This refers to various homiletical interpretations which are based on imaginative ways of associating passages with one another (see Hillel's rules above for a set of principles governing this use of associative interpretation).

Sod: This is a word denoting a secret or a mystery, and so is used for allegorical or mystical interpretations of a text.[136]

We have no reason to doubt that Jesus, Peter, Paul, etc, employed these and/or similar principles in their own teaching from the Hebrew Bible. This is one of the acid tests of their Jewishness. These principles are certainly not known to western Christians today, but that is not the issue. Arnold Fruchtenbaum, a leading Jewish believer in the USA, emphasises this point that the New Testament must be assessed in accordance with the appropriate *Jewish* hermeneutical rules in order to do full justice to it:

> Jesus is all too often judged by twentieth-century Judaism rather than first-century Judaism or Biblical Judaism . . . Judaism today is too fragmented with messianic views ranging from 'He will come' to 'What Messiah? There will be no Messiah.' The fact is that most Jews today do not believe in any Messiah at all. The real issue is, is Jesus the Messiah of *Old Testament* Judaism?[137]

To date, probably the most valuable modern book written to help Christians respond to the Jewish refutationist challenges has been that of Arthur Lukyn Williams in his rebuttal of

---

[136] For a good introduction to Pardes see Bernard M. Casper, *An Introduction to Jewish Bible Commentary* (Thomas Yoseloff, NY, 1960), chapter 5.

[137] Arnold Fruchtenbaum, *Jesus was a Jew* (Broadman Press, Nashville, 1974), p 89.

Isaac Troki. Williams concludes with a very interesting list of what he calls the first three chief lessons to be learned in this endeavour. These lessons are to be passed on to Jews and Christians alike, he says.

a) The New Testament writings are not 'elaborate and scholarly disquisitions', but words for everyday life and faith which are applicable to everyone, and intended to be comprehensible to everyone.

b) The basic goal of the New Testament is not to convert non-believers, but to encourage and instruct those who have given their lives over to serving God in Christ. Therefore we should not be looking for self-evident proofs of any kind that somehow make the Gospel irresistible.

c) The New Testament's way of handling texts from the Hebrew Bible, of asking and answering questions, of presenting truths about God, etc, must be judged by Jewish people in accordance with the midrashic standards of its day.[138]

There are some classic modern works which have been available to Christians and Jews for some time which help to show just how wonderfully well the New Testament does fit into its Jewish world. And of course we can go one stage behind this and discover the Jewishness of Jesus himself and his followers.[139] This is no longer in any doubt by the Jewish scholars who specialise in this area.[140] Of course there are still some hard-line reactionaries who wish to preserve the old barriers between Jesus and his Jewishness, but modern scholarship will not permit this.

What this all boils down to is that if a Jewish person says to you that the New Testament is just not acceptable to the

---

[138] A. Lukyn Williams, *A Manual of Christian Evidences for Jewish People* (two volumes, vol 2, SPCK, London, 1919), pp 181–182.

[139] Readers are advised to turn to the following works for enlightenment: C. G. Montefiore, *Rabbinic Literature and Gospel Teachings* (Ktav, NY, 1930); *The Synoptic Gospels* (2 volumes, Ktav, NY, 1968).

[140] I have dealt with this matter in the book, *Jesus Ben Joseph*, op cit.

Jewish community because it is not Jewish, then you are perfectly entitled, indeed duty-bound, to decline to accept that argument. Rather than becoming defensive, ask the person by what criteria he or she is judging the New Testament to be non-Jewish. Try to ascertain how familiar the person is with the language and thought of the Jewish religious literature of the period of Jesus. Along with this, of course, goes the necessity of some serious reading in the Jewish sources yourself, familiarising yourself with the kinds of reasoning used, the ways in which biblical passages are interpreted and applied, etc. A whole new world is waiting to be discovered by Christians – a world familiar to Jesus, James, Peter and Paul.[141]

The Hebrew Bible and the New Testament

The gospels are constantly appealing to the text of the Hebrew Bible as they speak about Jesus 'fulfilling' the promises to Israel and the requirements from Israel, both given by God. This is evidently a matter of fundamental importance. Matthew in particular speaks about 'fulfilment' coming with Jesus (see 1:22; 2:15, 23; 4:14; 8:17; 12:17; 13:35; 21:4; 27:35; John 19:24 has a similar expression), but all the gospels are concerned to show that Jesus' life and ministry was in keeping with what was 'written' (see Matt 26:24; Mark 1:2; 7:6; 9:13; 14:21; Luke 2:23; 3:4; John 12:14). Christians have never lost sight of the importance of this concept of fulfilment in seeking to present the Jewishness of Jesus' Messiahship. Sometimes, however, Christians can give Jewish people the impression that when they speak about Jesus 'fulfilling' the promises of God concerning the Messiah which are found in the Hebrew Bible, what they mean is that there was a crystal-clear blueprint lying there in

---

[141] For a good introduction to the traditional Jewish principles of exegesis, see Hermann L. Strack, *Introduction to the Talmud and Midrash*, op cit.

its pages which precisely and without ambiguity defined Jesus. Perhaps there are Christians who actually do believe this! All that Jesus had to do, they seem to believe, was simply to walk on to the stage of history and pick up the blueprint; and all that Israel had to do was to look, in order to see the obvious match-up between the blueprint and Jesus. This way of understanding the concept of fulfilment is, in my view, quite mistaken and, among other things, leads to a severe, and I believe incorrect, judgement of Peter in the well-known incident near Caesarea Philippi:

> When Jesus came to the region of Caesarea Philippi, he asked his disciples, 'Who do people say the Son of Man is?' They replied, 'Some say John the Baptist; others say Elijah; and still others, Jeremiah or one of the prophets.' 'But what about you?' he asked. 'Who do you say I am?' Simon Peter answered, 'You are the Messiah, the Son of the living God.'
>
> Jesus replied, 'Blessed are you, Simon son of Jonah, for this was not revealed to you by man, but by my Father in heaven. And I tell you that you are Peter, and on this rock I will build my church, and the gates of Hades will not overcome it . . .
>
> From that time on Jesus began to explain to his disciples that he must go to Jerusalem and suffer many things at the hands of the elders, chief priests and teachers of the law, and that he must be killed and on the third day be raised to life. Peter took him aside and began to rebuke him. 'Never, Lord!' he said. 'This shall never happen to you!' Jesus turned and said to Peter, 'Get behind me, Satan! You are a stumbling block to me; you do not have in mind the things of God, but the things of men.'[142]

I do not believe that Jesus is accusing Peter of being singularly wicked. Rather, Peter is suffering from the terrible condition of ignorance, and that can be a dangerous condition, one which Satan is well able to exploit to his own advantage. How could Peter be so right one day and then so wrong the next? The answer, I believe, lies in the fact

---

[142] Matt 16:13–18, 21–23.

that there was *no* obvious blueprint for him or any other Jewish person to pick up concerning the Messiah. There is ambiguity at every turn when we examine the text of the Hebrew Bible, whether it be for times and seasons or for exact definitions and implications.

Peter intuited quite rightly, with the inspiration of God's own Spirit, that Jesus was much more than most people were making of him. Those who thought that he might be Elijah were close, since the Jewish tradition was (and still is) that Elijah would return to Israel as a forerunner of the Messiah when the time came for the Messiah to come.[143] But Peter knew, somehow, that Jesus was in fact the Messiah himself, even though this did not quite match up with what so many Jewish people were anticipating from the presence of the Messiah in their midst at such a time of Roman oppression and persecution. But here, in my opinion, is the nub of the matter: Peter was trying to make sense of what he believed, sensed, intuited to be the case concerning Jesus. There were no passages which neatly spelled out the whole plan for him.

And then Jesus took everyone by surprise by teaching them that not only was he the promised King Messiah, sent to rule over Israel, but he was also the Suffering Servant spoken about by Isaiah. Peter was just not prepared for this. Notice how four different 'biblical personalities' are brought together in this intense interchange between Jesus and Peter: the Son of Man, the Messiah, the Son of God, and the Suffering Servant. Though the last is not named as such here, it is clear that Jesus is referring to that biblical figure. *Jesus* was the one who connected all of these biblical personalities together into the one Personality – himself. This was not a typical Jewish concept at all. If Christians try to read the Hebrew Bible from an outsider's perspective, as it were, then they will see that it would have been far from

---

[143] This is based on a Messianic interpretation of Mal 4: 5–6.

self-evident to Peter, or any of his contemporaries, that all of these figures were in fact one and the same person.

Many readers will be aware of the point I am about to make, but it must be made nonetheless. Jewish tradition in Jesus' day, and right through to our own day, taught and teaches that the Messiah is to be simply a human being. Granted that he will be empowered by God to a degree never before known by any person and that therefore he will be capable of things which would be impossible for others, it is still maintained that he is himself not at all a divine figure. Berger and Wyschogrod make much of this point in their book:

> Judaism never understood the Messiah to be anything more than a human being chosen by God to bring the era of peace and love foretold by the prophets of Israel . . . The prohibition against idolatry . . . is one of the most severe in Judaism. According to Jewish law, there are only three transgressions which are so severe that when faced with a choice of transgressing or death, the Jew is commanded to sacrifice his life rather than transgress. One of these is idolatry. It is therefore important for Jews to know that a Jew who believes that Jesus was God . . . commits idolatry as defined by Jewish law.[144]

Note the use of emotional blackmail in this 'friendly warning' to Jewish people who are thinking seriously about Jesus as the divine Son of God! Again we observe the use of this kind of manipulation by those who accuse believers in Jesus of that unethical practice.[145] However, the point which I wish to emphasise at this moment is that it was also Jesus who actually brought into conscious debate the very notion that the Messiah was to be a divine figure. We cannot really

---

[144] David Berger and Michael Wyschogrod, *Jews and 'Jewish Christianity'*, op cit, pp 24, 32.

[145] The very same type of emotional blackmail is used by Beth Moshe, *Judaism's Truth Answers the Missionaries*, op cit, p 255.

condemn Peter for not being able to cross all the T's and dot all the I's.

Let me repeat this point: there is no self-evident blueprint in the Hebrew Bible which can be said to unambiguously point to Jesus. Only *after* one has come to believe that Jesus is the Messiah, and more specifically the kind of Messiah that he is, does it all begin to make sense and hang together. Jesus, to put it another way, is greater than the sum of the parts found in the Hebrew Bible. He is not predictable in any precise sense at all, and cannot be put into a box as if we know everything there is to know about him. He is unique, sharing in the sovereignty of the Godhead and in the sovereign freedom of the Godhead. Even once the step of faith to follow Jesus is made, he still manages to surprise his people, as countless testimonies could prove. God's ways are not our ways, and his thoughts are not our thoughts – even when we are Christians!

This is not at all to say that the personality, character and mission of Jesus cannot be found in the Hebrew Bible, or cannot be reconciled with everything we read in the Hebrew Bible. It is to say, quite specifically and in Orthodox Christian fashion, that there was no clear blueprint to be found in the Hebrew Bible; he could not (and cannot) be constructed by human reason and wisdom alone. No one in Israel had control over the Messiah, not even in the sense of being able to predict exactly what he would be like. No matter how much study of the Scripture one does, there is no alternative to making a commitment of *faith* at some stage or another, asking God for further personal revelation and confirmation.

Again, this is not to say that the whole enterprise is irrational and based purely on emotion or emotionalism. But it is a recognition of the fact that people are not like mathematical problems – you cannot predict a person's personality, attitudes, or behaviour from what other people have written about him or her. The fact of the matter is that all the geniuses of history, let alone Jesus, have in some sense or another transcended the factors that we can account for in their lives and background. At the end of the day no-one can fully 'explain' the Galileos, the da Vincis, the Einsteins, the Beethovens, etc. How much less chance is there, then, of explaining or predicting the person and work of Jesus! His transcendent freedom cannot be taken away from him, even with the Hebrew Bible in your hand. Not until Jesus actually came did we really know who and what the Messiah would be!

What I have presented here, I believe to be true, even though it sounds a little uncomfortable at first to some Christians. It demands a strong and confident faith to acknowledge this point. However, it can also be made to sound hollow and defeatist by someone who wishes to make it come over that way, and several Jewish refutation-ists are keen to do just that. Berger and Wyschogrod believe that Christians exploit this lack of a blueprint to manipulate texts to mean what they want them to mean. They accuse Christians of taking 'rare, isolated, difficult passages' in the Bible, passages which stand apart from the general thrust of its teaching, in order to find 'proof-texts' for obscure beliefs.[146] They go on to state that many Christian scholars also concede that these classic Messianic proof-texts are difficult to interpret with any real certainty, and then ridicule the dimension of faith by ironically declaring that they 'can only be discerned by someone who already knows them to be true'.[147]

Of course Berger and Wyschogrod fail to mention that the methods of exegesis found in the New Testament are fully consonant with those found in other Jewish material of the period. Lukyn Williams had said it simply and well:

Christian Jews only carried on the methods of Biblical inter-

---

[146] Berger and Wyschogrod, op cit, p 35.
[147] Op cit, p 36.

pretation which they had used before their conversion, and Gentile Christians naturally followed suit.[148]

This language of 'Christian Jews' is not the terminology which we would use nowadays, but the point is clear. The way in which those first generations of believers related both their experience of and conviction about reality to their foundational texts was no different from the way in which the proto-rabbis and the rabbis after them did the same. This hermeneutical procedure is quite acceptable to Berger and Wyschogrod in rabbinic literature, of course, but they do not want their readers to make the connection between the methods of the rabbis and those of the central characters and authors of the New Testament. Of course very few Christians today are aware of the Jewish context of the hermeneutics of the New Testament either.

Christians from different cultures and denominations have developed and defended their own canons of interpretation, particularly with regard to the proper way to relate the two biblical Testaments to one another. There are several favourite methods of interpretation of 'how the New Testament fulfils the Old' that we find in use by Christians, and each of these is keenly disputed by Jewish audiences. We shall have cause to examine all of these in the course of this book. The five commonest models would probably be the following:

1 The simple performance of something which was promised generations beforehand (eg, Mic 5:2, and Jesus being born in Bethlehem);

2 The 'fullest fulfilment' of a prophecy which had a double fulfilment (eg, Isa 7:14, which would have had some sort of relevance for King Ahaz and his people at the time, but

---

[148] A. Lukyn Williams, *Adversus Judaeos* (CUP, London, 1935), p 17. On this point see also Jacob Jocz, *The Jewish People and Jesus Christ* (third edition, Baker Book House, Grand Rapids, MI, 1979), pp 206–9.

which received its ultimate fulfilment in Jesus' virgin birth);

3 Typology, in which real historical people or events are held to embody principles which can be re-embodied, as it were, in later, more significant people or events (eg, the temple in Jerusalem as a type pointing to Jesus);

4 Allegory, where there is no historical correspondence at all, just a conviction that when something is spoken about there is really a deeper message being given about something else altogether, known only to those who have the key to such knowledge (eg, the scarlet thread of Josh 2:17–21 being taken in 1 Clement 12:7, an early Christian document, as a prefiguration of the saving blood of Jesus);

5 Christophanies, defined by one believer as

those unsought, intermittent and temporary, visible and audible manifestations of God the Son in human form, by which God communicated something to certain conscious human beings on earth prior to the birth of Jesus Christ.[149]

The most commonly-cited cases of Christophanies are Gen 18:1–33; 19:1–22; and Judg 13:2–22.

Not surprisingly, these models of Christian fulfilment are not accepted by Jewish people, and are rejected primarily on the grounds that there is no warrant within the Hebrew Bible itself for interpreting its texts in these ways. They are all seen as later Christian rules for 'eisegesis', which means reading into texts what you want to find, rather than proper 'exegesis', which means unpacking texts to find what is really there waiting for you.

It should be quite clear by now just how fundamental an issue this is. No matter how simple or how sophisticated a doctrine or a concept is, until it is acknowledged that the

---

[149] James A. Borland: *Christ in the Old Testament* (Moody Press, Chicago, 1978), p 10.

hermeneutical principles used to establish its truth according to the Bible are bona fide *Jewish* ones, many (perhaps most) Jewish people will feel justified in ignoring the argument or conclusion of the New Testament. When we turn in Part Two to specific passages in the Bible, we shall see how this clash of principles works out in practice.

The role of the Septuagint (LXX)

This may be an area of study which is completely new to many readers, but it is an indispensable one for anyone who wishes to engage in Jewish–Christian debate. Around the middle of the third century BCE, the Jewish communities which were living outside the land of Israel succeeded in having their need for a version of the Hebrew Bible in their own first language officially recognised and sanctioned by the leadership in Jerusalem. Hebrew was not a dead language by any means, but it was not the everyday language of these Jewish people. We must also bear in mind that in those days, as today, there were more Jewish people living outside the land of Israel than there were inside its borders. Their common language was Greek, this being a legacy of the Hellenistic empire which dominated the known world.

A great deal of modern *pseudo-scholarship* is trying to persuade people that 'Greek' automatically means non-Jewish, or even anti-Jewish. This is simply not true. It is evident that there was a real danger of assimilation of Jewish people to non-Jewish ways of thinking and acting resulting from their constant exposure to the Hellenistic world-view. Indeed there were Jewish groups which constantly warned their people about this danger. However, the use of the Greek language itself was assuredly not a sign that the writer or speaker was not Jewish. One of Rabbi Immanuel Schochet's forays into pseudo-scholarship involves this very issue of the Jewishness or otherwise of Jewish texts written in Greek. He says in one place in his lecture:

Matthew, Mark, Luke did not know Hebrew. How do I know that? Very simple. Proof in the New Testament. In the whole New Testament there's only one passage that's written in Hebrew.

Schochet's sole intention is to have his listeners go home with the impression that even if Jesus' first followers were Jewish, then they were ignoramuses of the highest order, not even knowing Hebrew and therefore not able to assess Jesus' religious credentials sufficiently well. But this is a flagrant misrepresentation of the social and intellectual reality of the Jewish world of the time of the Second Temple. Greek-language Gospels do not mean a non-Jewish Gospel!

There are, in fact, a growing number of scholars, Jewish ones among them, who believe that there may well have been an original Hebrew 'Life of Jesus', produced in Palestine for the believers there but subsequently translated into Greek for the congregations in the Greek-speaking Jewish Diaspora. At any rate, the fact that our canonical gospels are in Greek in no way discredits them from being Jewish documents, and it certainly does not mean that the original gospel-writers did not know Hebrew. As it turns out, Paul's letters are all written in excellent Greek, but there is no serious doubt that he could have written them in fluent Hebrew had the occasion demanded it. He wrote in Greek to communicate most easily with Jewish as well as non-Jewish believers in the Diaspora.

Be all this as it may, the diaspora Jewish communities requested, and received, an official Greek translation of the Hebrew Bible around 250 BCE.[150] This was a Jewish translation authorised by Jewish leaders and intended for Jewish people. It therefore existed, and was in use, for some 250

---

[150] This translation, known as the Septuagint, from a word for seventy which reflects a legend about the number of translators, is often referred to by the Latin numeral for seventy, namely LXX.

years before the birth of Jesus and some 300 years before Paul's first New Testament letter.

As far as the Jewish community is concerned, however, there is, if I might be allowed the metaphor, a Christian fly in the Jewish ointment. The LXX evidently became the favoured version of the Hebrew Bible in the nascent Church. Initially this was because the first generations of Jewish believers in places like Corinth and Ephesus, etc, were part of this diaspora Jewish community which spoke Greek and needed the LXX in the first place. Then, as increasing numbers of non-Jewish people became believers in Jesus, Greek had to become the language of the mixed fellowships, since most of these non-Jews did not know Hebrew and those 'God-fearers' who knew some did not know it fluently.

The short story is that as the LXX grew in popularity among the churches, the Jewish community leaders decided to withdraw from using it. They preferred to work only from the Hebrew in their disputes with these Jewish believers and their non-Jewish converts. This process of withdrawal was so successful that the only full early manuscripts we have of the LXX have been preserved by *Christian* monastic and scholarly communities. The Jewish people therefore no longer trust the versions of the LXX which are available to us, suspecting the early Church of tampering with the text over the years in order to produce a translation which matches its own needs and militates against traditional Jewish understandings of the Hebrew text.

How would one test this hypothesis that the text of the LXX has been tampered with? At this stage it is necessary to point out that there are in fact many places where the text of the LXX is in clear disagreement with the authorised Hebrew text, known as the Masoretic text, of the Hebrew Bible. This Masoretic text takes its name from a Hebrew word meaning 'tradition', and it reflects the official version of the text which the rabbinic community considered to be the authentic, traditional text from the beginning. Having said that, it must be borne in mind that this authentic version of the text was compiled and authorised only in the eighth to tenth centuries CE! The accepted tradition is that it nevertheless reflects faithfully the authentic original text, and it has become the authorised Hebrew version for both the Synagogue and the Church.

Therefore, as far as the rabbis are concerned, if there are places where the LXX disagrees with the Masoretic version, the latter, being the official text, is accepted and the LXX texts are simply regarded as bad translations or even perhaps deliberate alterations. This, of course, is often the accusation of the Jewish refutationists, claiming that the LXX was originally trustworthy but the Christian monks and theologians in the early centuries of the Church made deliberate alterations for their own purposes.

The common wisdom used to be that the LXX was indeed a translation of the Hebrew texts which lay behind, and in faithful continuity with, the much later Masoretic text. However, it is now seen as much more likely that the LXX was the result of translations of different families of Hebrew texts altogether. There were in fact several different families of Hebrew text which were used and preserved by different Jewish groups, and a major motivation for the 'Orthodox' leadership commissioning the Masoretic text in the early Middle Ages was to standardise one authoritative text which could be used to define which Jewish groups were 'orthodox' and which were 'heretical'.

In modern Christian translations of the Bible into the world's languages, this principle of always according final authority to the Masoretic version of the text is not automatically followed. I point this out not only because it is true and important in itself, but also because it is used by Jewish refutationists to establish what they refer to as the ongoing compromising of the 'original' text (meaning the Masoretic text) by Christians. This in turn is taken as evidence that

Christians cannot be trusted to maintain the integrity of God's Word. Let me give an example of this preference for the LXX over the Hebrew to illustrate this point. The illustration is taken from the New International Version of the Bible, although others could equally well be used. This is one of the growing number of modern translations which gives footnotes to its readers, and constantly refers to the discrepancies between the ancient versions and the Masoretic text.

In the wonderful twenty-eighth chapter of Job, which speaks about the futility of ever trying to master wisdom apart from a surrender to the Lordship of God, we find one verse (verse 11) which reads in the Hebrew:

He dams up the sources of the rivers and brings hidden things to light.

Since the whole context of this chapter is about humanity seeking, exploring and rooting around in its search for wisdom, the NIV translators decided that it was incongruent to find here a verb which means the opposite of digging and delving, namely, 'to dam up'. And so they turned to the LXX to see what light it might shed on the subject. The LXX, followed by others, actually has here a verb meaning 'to search', and so the NIV translators decided to accept that as being the more likely original word. There is a corresponding footnote to the text for all to see. A casual reading of the footnotes in these various translations will show just how prevalent this practice of preferring the LXX has become in much Christian tradition. I feel obliged to add here that in the case of Job 28:11, the Hebrew verb makes perfect sense to me, so that there is no need to make recourse to the LXX. In verses 9 and 10 Job has described, in striking poetic form, the thoroughness of this search for wisdom in which the searcher even checks inside and underneath the mountains, as it were, just in case the secret is hidden in some deep cave covered over by a mountain. What would make greater sense, then, than to follow this poetic description by another, in which the searcher thinks that another clever place to hide a secret treasure would be under a flowing river, since no one could look there? And therefore the searcher dams up the river in order to expose the dry river-bed to his explorative digging!

And so we continue with our discussion of the importance of the LXX in Jewish and Christian history. I might mention here that certain Jewish circles in the second century CE were so intent on eliminating the LXX from the Jewish world because of its status in the Churches, and yet so aware of the need for a Greek translation for their own people, that they commissioned a Greek convert to Judaism, Aquila, to render a wholly new translation from the Hebrew original. His attempt at a highly literal version was sanctioned for Jewish use but never became popular, since the Greek was somewhat artificial and rough. Nevertheless, the point is reinforced about the need felt within the *Jewish* diaspora community for a *Greek* version of the Bible.

Now why should this be of such great importance for Christians today? Simply put, Christians cannot ignore the importance of the LXX because the New Testament itself is so profoundly influenced by it. The New Testament documents are all written in Greek and actually owe a very great deal to the influence of the LXX on the early communities of believers, both Jewish and non-Jewish. Although we must restate that this fact does not thereby disqualify the New Testament from being considered a bona fide Jewish document, it is this link between the LXX and the New Testament which is the major reason for the Jewish community's own boycotting of the LXX. But just to say this is not enough. We need to look at some of the statistics which give an idea of the strength of the relationship between the LXX and the New Testament.

There are about 275 New Testament passages which are regarded by scholars as being quotations from, or allusions to, passages in the Hebrew Bible. One major textbook has analysed the complex relationship in this way:

a) *Passages where the Hebrew text and the LXX agree, and the New Testament quotes accordingly.* This accounts for only 53 of the passages, which is to say less than 20 per cent of them.
b) *Passages where the LXX disagrees with the Hebrew text, and the New Testament prefers the Hebrew.* There are only 10 such cases, amounting to some 4 per cent.
c) *Passages where the LXX disagrees with the Hebrew text, and the New Testament prefers the LXX.* This happens 37 times, i.e. 14 per cent, significantly more often than the preference for the Hebrew text.
d) *Passages where the LXX disagrees with the Hebrew text, and the New Testament differs from both.* This accounts for 99 of the references, or 36 per cent, easily the largest of the five categories. What is this saying to us about the use of the Bible in the early communities of believers?
e) *Passages where the LXX and the Hebrew text agree, but the New Testament differs from both.* Perhaps surprisingly, there are 76 such references, which is to say some 27 per cent, making this the second largest of the categories.[151]

Now these figures represent the research and organisation of one scholar, and others would have slightly different breakdown statistics, but the major point remains the same. The New Testament is heavily influenced by, and perhaps even to some extent dependent on, the LXX. This in turn, as I have said, reflects the fact that the LXX was the version of the Bible which was used by the diaspora churches. Jewish scholarship also knows its importance for Jewish studies, and in fact some of the world's leading LXX experts today

---

[151] These statistics are taken from Robert Horton Gundry, *The Use of the Old Testament in Matthew's Gospel* (Brill, Leiden, 1967).

are Jewish, but by and large the Jewish community is ignorant of the provenance of the LXX and dismisses it as 'the Bible of the Christians'.

Aggravating the situation are the further facts that the actual ordering of the books of the Hebrew Bible is different in the LXX: the LXX texts include the so-called apocryphal books; and there are some differences in the context of the books, eg, the LXX of 1 Kings contains some verses not found in the Hebrew text. How this all came about is a very complex issue. The various complex historical and technical issues need not concern us in this book. We shall have reason to look at key passages of dispute in Part Two, but suffice it to note here that, for example, in the debate over the correct interpretation and translation of the Hebrew word in Isa 7:14 which is rendered either as 'virgin' or as 'young woman', the role of the LXX is vital. In this example, Christians cite as solid evidence for their interpretation of the disputed Hebrew word the fact that the LXX uses the Greek word for a virgin to translate the controversial Hebrew word in Isaiah's text. This shows, they say, that the Jewish community of the third century BCE knew the meaning of the Hebrew to be just that. However, many Jewish refutationists are simply content to dismiss the LXX evidence, claiming that the Christians inserted that word there to *create* the evidence which they so badly needed. This should give a good idea of the importance of the role of the LXX in the hermeneutical debate between Jews and Christians.

These three macro-level issues are therefore of paramount importance to us as we begin to come to terms with the complexities involved in Jewish–Christian dialogue about hermeneutics. Seeking to establish a point from the interpretation of a passage in the Bible will be a difficult endeavour, not as a result of any wilful obstructionism by a Jewish person, but as a result of centuries of entrenched hermeneutical positions. Christians and Jews just do not always speak the same language, even when it seems on the surface that they do. So at the end of this first of two chapters on the issue of hermeneutics, we can say that one of the most fundamental areas of study which Christians need to get involved with, if they are to engage fruitfully in the Jewish–Christian debate, is precisely this one of biblical hermeneutics. Our differences make all the difference in the world!

8

Jewish identity and survival

For most Jewish people *this* is the really important issue, not
the debate over doctrinal exactness or the search for exegetical clarity. From the second century CE, if not earlier, both
Synagogue and Church have been telling Jewish believers in
Jesus that they are no longer Jewish and can no longer
consider themselves to be Jewish. Both communities have
been following their own distinctive agendas, of course, but
the final message has been the same. Because of this, Jewish
believers often suffer a terrible identity crisis when they
accept Jesus as their Messiah, and indeed large numbers of
Jewish people who have become convinced that Jesus is the
Messiah have actually declined to take the final step of open
commitment to him for this very fear of losing their Jewish
identity. Few issues, then, are of this level of significance.

The Churches have been adamant in insisting that Jewish
people who accept Jesus as Messiah and Lord have 'become
Christians', and have 'converted' from being Jewish. This
has been a direct reflection of the antisemitism and anti-
Judaism which has disfigured and shamed the history of
the Churches from close to the beginning of the movement.
Such Jewish 'converts' have been forbidden to use their
Hebrew names, or to give Hebrew names to their children;
they have been forbidden to circumcise their sons; they have
been forbidden to celebrate the biblical and Jewish festivals,
especially the Sabbath and Passover; they have even been
forced to eat pork and other foods which Jewish people do
not eat, in order to prove their liberation from the Law. In

short, Jewish converts have not been given the freedom to maintain a Jewish home and family life, with the consequent result that, in most cases, within a generation or two the family or the single person has ended up living like the non-Jews in the Christian community.

On the one hand, the Jewish community has simply watched this attitude and behaviour, and has noted carefully that Jewish people who convert to Christianity invariably end up living as non-Jews, and are thereby lost to the Jewish community.

But on the other hand, they have also taken their own initiative in excluding all converts, whether genuine believers or not, from their own community. Jewish people are told that to believe in Jesus is to have changed religions. Furthermore, it is to have changed communities altogether, leaving one whole cultural milieu for another. Not only that, but it is to join the camp of the worst enemy of the Jewish people, and it is therefore also an act of treason, betraying the memory of the countless faithful Jewish people who went to their deaths as martyrs rather than sell their souls to the Christian torturers of their children. There can be no greater sin, according to the refutationists, than becoming a Christian.

It is important that Christians realise that this 'anti-conversion' pressure is not just applied to Jewish individuals who might be thinking seriously about Jesus, in the hope that they as individuals will therefore be persuaded not to go any further by the cost, or penalty, of being cast out of their families, neighbourhoods and community. The envisaged threat to the survival of the whole Jewish people and the historic Jewish faith is also spelled out to Jewish people who are giving Jesus some serious consideration. In other words, there is a two-pronged attack on Jewish people who are thinking about becoming followers of Jesus:

a) An attempt to frighten them with the threat of complete social banishment.
b) An attempt to heap guilt on them for contributing to the demise of the Jewish people and their culture.

Because the Jewish population is seen as shrinking, due to the effects of ongoing secularism and assimilation, a continued low reproduction rate, and an increase in the numbers of Jewish people marrying outside the Jewish community, etc, Jewish leaders are describing the possibility of Jewish people becoming Christians in any significant numbers as just one more threat to the viability of the Jewish people.

This anxious concern for the survival of the Jewish people has taken on a radically new sense of urgency since the Holocaust, as can well be appreciated. Very many Jewish people are unable to advance beyond the psychological and emotional barrier which that indescribable horror has created, as are not a few Christians. I spend a great deal of my own time trying to help Christians to realise the need to be silent and to spend a good deal of time listening and endeavouring to understand the impact of this terrible reality and ongoing threat on Jewish people. John Edwards gives wise counsel in his book on Jewish–Christian relations of an age past, counsel which reflects his familiarity with the issues:

> It is important for the non-Jewish reader to remember, at all times, that any consideration by Jews of the Jewish role in European history in earlier periods is likely today to be, to a greater or lesser extent, consciously or unconsciously, governed by the experience, either personal or vicarious, of the Shoah, or Holocaust. Thus the history of Jews in Catholic Europe in the sixteenth and seventeenth centuries is liable to be seen by Jewish commentators in a more defensive way than might have been the case before 1900, or even before 1939. The policies of Gentile governments will be judged by their

willingness or otherwise to grant to Jews life itself . . . [152]

Christians must learn to appreciate the pain and the anxiety which lie behind this tendency to filter everything which touches Jewish life through an analysis of its implications for *Jewish survival* in the modern world. Now it is true that even some Jewish commentators think that the Jewish community is reacting out of irrational fear when it speaks about the number of Messianic Jews being a significant threat to the numerical survival of the Jewish people. Stuart Charmé, for example, writes:

> In the face of intermarriage rates that are approaching 50%, Messianic Judaism is a statistically minor problem.[153]

Nat Kameny, the chairman of the Anti-Defamation League's National Program Committee in the 1970s, agreed with this assessment:

> While conversion attempts among Jewish youth are obviously a matter of considerable concern, Christian evangelicals constitute no real threat to Jewish survival.[154]

Others express shock at the ignorance, as they see it, of those Jewish leaders who fail to grasp the serious nature of the present situation in world Jewry. One leader stated bluntly:

> I don't think the rabbis really understand what's going on here. This is nothing less than a threat to the existence of the Jewish people. It is an attempt at spiritual genocide.[155]

---

[152] John Edwards, *The Jews in Christian Europe 1400–1700* (London, Routledge, 1988), p 5.

[153] Stuart L. Charmé, 'Heretics, Infidels and Apostates: Menace, Problem or Symptom?', *Judaism* (Winter, 1987), pp 30f.

[154] Nat Kameny, 'ADL Survey Shows Cultists Falling in Conversion Efforts', *Sentinal*, March 24, 1977, p 6.

[155] Quoted by Michael Masch, 'Their Mission: Converting Jews', *Philadelphia Jewish Exponent*, vol 171, no 5 (1982), p 45. See also, Stanley N. Rosenbaum, 'Jews for Jesus: Causes and Treatment', *Midstream*, vol 31, no 10 (1985), p 11.

The fact that this debate is taking place at all within the Jewish world is evidence enough that the reality of the presence of Jewish believers in Jesus has tapped into that deep-seated sense of insecurity which Jewish people share in the light of their experience in history. And once again we see the presupposition that Jewish people who become Christians are no longer considered to be Jews. Thus Rabbi Golding, for instance, declares most emphatically that Jews who believe in Jesus are no longer Jewish, and in fact lose all chance of redemption, whether as Jews or as Christians. Rabbi Arkush, in a recent publication, says this:

> The greatest cause of anguish is the myth that one can become a better, fulfilled Jew by accepting Jesus of Nazareth as the Messiah . . . to convert to Christianity is an act of treachery, and . . . Jewish–Christianity is an impossibility.[156]

This is certainly the received wisdom of the Jewish establishment and the general Jewish public. But having said this, it must be pointed out that there is a range of reactions to Jewish believers within the Jewish community. Some Orthodox families still go through the traditional ritual of a symbolic funeral for the person who has so betrayed the family name and religion. Many will cut the person out of the family will. Some take an oath never to mention the person again, and he or she will often be ostracised from all family occasions, whether informal meals at the parents' home or family weddings, etc. Just as typically, today one will also find that others take a more liberal and casual view and simply voice their incredulity and disappointment from time to time, while keeping an arms-length relationship with the person.

In 1976 David Harley conducted a survey of Jewish believers in Britain in which one of his areas of interest was this very one of family and social attitudes to the new-

---

[156] Rabbi Shmuel Arkush, *Operation Judaism. Fact Pack* (1986), p 3.

found faith of the Jewish believer. In a few of the cases he reviewed, the family did regard the new believer as dead, and even held symbolic funeral ceremonies. In 50 per cent of the cases examined, these Jewish believers were evicted from the family home, although most of them were eventually reconciled, at least in part. The time which elapsed between alienation and reconciliation was often many years. Sadly, for 15 per cent of these believers there had been no reconciliation. Harley comments on this group:

> They were forced to leave home and are still separated from their family. These are those who have suffered most in the cause of following Christ. In one case the grandchildren were cut out of the will.[157]

The social ostracism of Jewish believers even extends to the refusal of many authorities to grant them the right to be buried in a Jewish cemetery. Here are the words of one leading Jewish academic:

> A defector from the faith, who adopts another religion without compulsion, is not to be permitted burial in a Jewish cemetery, and is not to be mourned at all. The realization that all privileges and honors of the Jewish people will not be accorded the apostate may serve as a deterrent to those considering such action.[158]

This is the social reality of the situation. Historically, the pattern is clear to see: the overwhelming majority of Jewish people who have ever lived have followed a form of Judaism which rejects Jesus' Messiahship, and the overwhelming majority of Christians who have ever lived have not been Jewish. Of course in the first few generations of the Jesus movement the vast majority of its members were Jewish, and

---

[157] David Harley, *Areas of Jewish Response* (Private publication, 1976), p 9.

[158] Maurice Lamm, *The Jewish Way in Death and Mourning* (Ktav, NY, 1969), p 83.

there has always been a significant Jewish presence within the Church, despite the antisemitism which took root early on. The trouble is that the Jewish leadership translates this historical and social reality into *theological* inevitability, claiming that it proves that, by definition, Judaism (without Jesus) is for Jews and Christianity is for non-Jews (if they choose it or are born into it).

It proves no such thing, of course. The truth of the matter is that both the Synagogue and the Church *imposed* definitions and sanctions on Jewish people which had neither biblical nor theological warrant, and which led to the historical situation in which Jewish people and Christianity were seen as mutually exclusive terms. It is a theological and moral lie of the highest magnitude, but it has been told so confidently for so long and by so many people, that most people seem to have come to believe it. This has then led to a situation in which there has been virtually no possibility of any open and fair assessment of the status and role of Jewish believers in Jesus.

Jewish believers are adamant that they have not ceased being Jewish, and this emerges clearly from their statements about the use of the word 'conversion' when applied to them. Here are a couple of representative quotes from leading spokesmen:

> A Jew . . . is not converted in the ordinary sense of the term. He does not turn around or change direction. On the contrary, he proceeds in the same direction; he advances in faith from the Old Testament to the New Testament.[159]

> Don't call me a converted Jew. I never converted from being Jewish, but I was converted from sin – and being Jewish was never a sin![160]

---

[159] Arthur W. Kac, *The Messiahship of Jesus*, op cit, p 99.

[160] Moishe Rosen, quoted in *The Hebrew Christian*, vol 55, no 1 (1982), p 13.

These kinds of convictions reflect the depth of the commitment to Jewish identity and survival which is in fact a characteristic of the contemporary Messianic Jewish movement, as it is usually called. Jewish believers are also ashamed of those Jewish people who 'convert' in order to turn their backs on their Jewish roots. Jakob Jocz wrote:

> A Jew who accepts baptism with a view to losing his identity is not a Hebrew Christian, though he may be a Christian . . . a Jew who accepts baptism without conviction is not a Hebrew Christian, but a renegade.[161]

These are powerful words, and they are to the credit of those Jewish believers who identify with them. This affirmation of Jewishness is often accompanied by the testimony that since becoming believers in Jesus Jewish people have come to identify incomparably more with their Jewish roots and heritage than ever before. For example, in David Harley's survey of British Jewish believers, mentioned above, he found that this was claimed in almost every case.

Typical statements included: 'I feel 100% Jewish since I have accepted the Messiah'; 'I feel a closer and stronger allegiance to the Jewish people'; 'I am not now ashamed to be Jewish'; 'I am more proud of my Jewishness and more conscious of it'.[162]

The inner-Jewish debate about the proper definition of 'Who is a Jew?' goes on furiously even today. It is a particularly difficult problem for the Jewish people to resolve, and Jewish believers are caught up in the midst of it.

---

[161] Jakob Jocz, *The Jewish People and Jesus Christ*, op cit, p 230.

[162] David Harley, *Areas of Jewish Response*, op cit, pp 10–11. Similar convictions are found in the testimonies collected by Arthur W. Kac, *The Messiahship of Jesus*, op cit, pp 140–1; Eliezer Maas, *Stand Firm. A Survival Guide for the New Jewish Believer* (Lansing, IL, 1990), p 22; Robert I. Winer, *The Calling: The History of the Messianic Jewish Alliance of America, 1915–1990* (Wynnewood, PA, 1990), p 46.

- *There is a biological definition available.* If your mother was Jewish, then so are you. Even here, though, there is serious disagreement, with Progressive Jews accepting either the mother or the father as a legitimate and legitimating Jewish parent. In any event, this would be the definition of a Jew which would come first to the lips of most Jewish people. The other definitions would be regarded as refinements or further definitions of this basic context.

- *There is a religious definition available.* To be a Jew you must also be a religiously observant Jew. You must keep the Torah. If you were born as a non-Jew, then your conversion to Orthodox Judaism is essentially that – a conversion which is largely concerned with learning to live and believe in an Orthodox Jewish way. At least the Orthodox Jewish community would see it this way. Other Jewish people, perhaps the majority today, would question the definition of 'religious' before agreeing to this definition, or would reject the definition altogether.

  However, it is probably safe to say that most Jewish people would agree at least to this, that conversion by a Jewish person to any other religion than Judaism would constitute a violation of the definition of a Jew.

- *There is a social–cultural definition available.* This definition states that if you are seriously involved in the social and communal life of the Jewish community, then you are acceptably Jewish. Commitment to world Jewry as a unique and important civilisation within the overall family of world civilisations is regarded as the essential evidence of Jewishness. This would perfectly suit the attitudes of both Reconstructionist and many 'secularised' Jewish people.

- *There is a Zionist definition available too.* According to this definition, the only Jews worthy of the name are those who are, at the very least, actively dedicated to the Zionist cause, but preferably living out the Zionist cause in the

State of Israel. It is a definition most classically associated with the name and influence of David Ben-Gurion, Israel's first prime minister. To serve in the Israeli armed forces, to pay one's taxes to the State, and to play an active part in the process of really establishing the State of Israel in its historic homeland – these would be seen as sufficient evidence of being an acceptable Jewish person for many Israelis at least.

Where then, if at all, do Jewish believers fit into this complex debate? Let us imagine someone whose parents are both undeniably Jewish. In other words, let us assume that the first of the four types of definition listed above presents no difficulty. But the second type of definition brings an immediate problem. Jewish believers are not regarded as being Jewish *religiously*. Now this is, to say the least, a contentious issue today. In the Talmud it is clearly stated that 'an Israelite, though he sin, remains an Israelite'.[163] This is the *halakhah* – the religious law. Jewish believers are in the process of trying to argue that even though the Jewish establishment sees them as heinous sinners, this Talmudic ruling nevertheless decrees that they are still to be regarded and treated as *Jewish* sinners. This has been conceded by some significant Jewish leaders, even within the Orthodox community, but not by most.

The *Encyclopaedia Judaica*, in an article on 'Apostasy', and in the context of a discussion about the controversy surrounding Jewish believers in Jesus, offers this summary:

> Prevailing halakhic opinion throughout the ages has always considered the apostate a Jew for all purposes of obligations, ties, and possibilities given to a Jew, but denied him some specific legal rights, in particular in the economic sphere, and in the performance of certain honorary symbolic acts.[164]

---

[163] Sanhedrin 44a.

[164] *Encyclopaedia Judaica*, vol 3 (1972), p 210.

Of course social attitudes are often different from the normative teaching, and it would be true to say that genuine Jewish believers, like all Jewish 'converts', have been and often still are ostracised by the community at every level. The above article does in fact go on to say:

> Jewish society regarded the apostate . . . as 'dead', as proscribed from the Jewish community, considering him the very essence of desertion and treason.[165]

Nonetheless, I hope that the significance of the difference is clear between being thought of as a *dead* Jew and being thought of as a *former* Jew. Some important lobbying is being considered by certain leading Jewish believers, in Israel and elsewhere, to achieve at least this as a short-term goal: to be accepted under the label of sinners and heretics, as long as they are seen as *Jewish* sinners and heretics! This would be seen by many Jewish believers as a definite step in the right direction after so many generations of the out-and-out denial of their very existence.

The State of Israel, because of its central place in the heart of the Jewish people, has played a significant part in this debate in recent years due to its stand on this issue of the Jewish identity, or otherwise, of Jewish believers in Jesus. Citizens of the State of Israel. including Messianic Jews, are allowed to believe whatever they wish about God as far as the Israeli courts are concerned. But there is a point of contention concerning those Jewish people from outside Israel who wish to emigrate there and become full Israeli citizens. A fundamental dimension of the Zionist dream was to create a Jewish State where all Jews in the world would be welcome, and where they could find safe haven. The new State's leaders therefore worked to produce legislation to enable any Jewish person to come to Israel and become a citizen of the Jewish State *by right* – simply by being Jewish,

---

[165] Ibid.

or by being the child or even the grandchild of someone who was Jewish.

Two laws became the basis of all the subsequent legislation on this matter: the Law of Return (1950) and the Nationality Law (1952). Our immediate concern is with the first of these. David Ben-Gurion introduced it to the Israeli parliament with these famous words:

> This law lays down not that the State accords the right of settlement to Jews abroad, but that this right is inherent in every Jew by virtue of his being a Jew if it but be his will to take part in settling the land.[166]

All Jewish people were thus given the right to emigrate to Israel. But what about those Jewish people who believe in Jesus? They are not to be allowed to share in this automatic right. Stated briefly, the legal authorities in Israel, mindful of the policy of following legal precedent as all legal authorities are, have consistently decided that the Jewish man in the street would not accept as Jewish any Jewish person who became a believer in Jesus. In other words we are back to the judgement that to believe in Jesus is to be non-Jewish. Therefore such believers cannot be recognised as having the right to automatic Israeli citizenship, because they are not in fact Jewish.

The legal precedent which is being followed in this case is that of Orthodox Jewish religious tradition. There is growing evidence that the average Israeli citizen is more open-minded about this than the Orthodox are prepared to admit, but the law remains that Jewish believers in Jesus are *a priori* to be considered ineligible for citizenship under the Law of Return. The Law of Return (as well as the Population Registration Law) was amended in 1970 in a way which

---

[166] The full quote is given in the *Encyclopaedia Judaica*, vol 10 (1972), p 1486.

tried to embody in law the religious bias of the religious establishment. Section 4B of the Law then became:

> In regards to this Law a Jew is one who was born of a Jewish mother, or converted to Judaism, and has not converted to another religion.

The focus had become quite clear: if a Jewish person becomes a believer in Jesus, has he or she converted to Christianity? The authorities say that indeed they have, irrespective of whether or not they have officially joined a church community or signed a credal statement, etc. Of course Jewish believers respond by saying that if Jesus is Israel's Messiah, then nothing could be more *Jewish* than believing in him. In other words, they have not 'changed their religion'. And so the process of challenging this ruling goes on in the courts of Israel. There have been several celebrated test cases involving Jewish believers, from Oswald Rufeisen (Brother Daniel) in the 1950s and Esther Dorflinger in the 1970s to Gary and Shirley Beresford, and others, in the 1990s.[167]

If and when the day comes when Jewish believers in Jesus are accepted as Jewish by those who administer the Law of Return in Israel, then a giant stride forward will have been achieved. There is nothing more sensitive in the Jewish community than the interrelated issues of Jewish identity and Jewish survival. These questions matter to all Jewish people, operating on visceral and psychological levels throughout the Jewish world. The niceties of correct exegetical techniques in biblical studies, or of appropriate com-

---

[167] For useful information and comment on these and other cases, see Nechama Tec, *In the Lion's Den. The Life of Oswald Rufeisen* (OUP, 1991); Arthur Kac, *The Messiahship of Jesus*, op cit, pp 136–9; *Mishkan*, 10 (1989), pp 79–90; *The LCJE Bulletin*, 20 (1990), 'An Open Letter to the Supreme Court of Israel', *The Jerusalem Post, International Edition*, May 5, 1990, p 4. I am preparing a full article on this whole issue to be published in the near future.

parative studies in kabbalistic and Christian theological studies, etc, do not, as a rule, make the same difference to Jewish people. Christians *must* come to appreciate the importance of this matter in the Jewish community. It is vital to appreciate this so that the Jewish people may be better understood for their own sake, and it is also crucial to an understanding of the issues and the emotions underlying the agenda of the refutationists.

As a final note in this chapter, I would like to refer the reader to the discussion in an earlier book of mine of the different nuances regarding the value and meaning of Jewishness in the lives of Jewish believers.[168] To be sure, it is important for all the various groups in our day that their Jewishness is acknowledged and honoured, although that acknowledgement was not always so fiercely fought for. But even today, there are differences among the congregations and fellowships as to the correct meaning of the term 'Jewishness' and the suitability of much of what has become traditional Jewish custom and practice for the life of Jewish followers of Jesus. The affirmation of their Jewish identity has become firmly established on their agenda, even though there may continue to be points of difference for some time to come.

The Christian world must be helped to appreciate all that is at stake in this determination by the Messianic Jewish community to be accepted as Jewish. It is an identity matter for each of them, of course. But it goes far beyond this. It affects their family and community life; it affects relationships with the larger beloved Jewish community; and it has a direct impact on the way in which Jewish people who are attracted to Jesus weigh up the consequences of considering him to be their Messiah.

This issue, then, is of fundamental importance in the

---

[168] *God's Covenant with the Jews*, op cit, chapter 7.

dispute between the Jewish and Christian communities, impacting directly on the Messianic Jewish community. We will do well to keep it in the forefront of our minds throughout the rest of this book.

9

Grandfather Troki and his sons and heirs

Isaac Troki has been mentioned a few times in this book already, but I want to devote a little bit of time to an overview of his contribution to the refutation literature. He is, without any possibility of contradiction, the grandfather of contemporary refutationist teaching. His book, entitled *Hizzuk Emunah*, meaning *Faith Strengthened*, was written about 1593 and provided both inspiration and argumentation for each succeeding generation of rabbis. In spite of the fact that he was a Karaite, ie, a member of a movement which is often labelled as one of the major Jewish schisms, the rabbis, operating on the time-honoured principle that the enemy of my enemy is my friend, overlooked their antipathy to Karaites and adopted his large-scale polemic against Christianity as their own. It was, quite simply, the best available to them. Many Jewish people today are unaware of the fact that Troki was not Jewish, a tribute to his status and role within their community.

Troki was definitely not the first person to present distinctively Jewish (or Karaite) arguments against Christian doctrines and interpretations of biblical texts. However, he really was the first to produce a systematic rebuttal of the Christian faith in a working manual intended for use by those who were seeking either to engage Christians in debate or, more likely, to prevent their own people from being attracted to Christianity. We shall look at eight of his arguments to disprove the Christian claims about Jesus, arguments which are still used today, with or without acknowledgement, by rabbis and others the world over. Readers who have never heard of Troki will doubtless recognise some of his arguments, perhaps even verbatim in some cases!

Troki says Jesus was too self-effacing to be Israel's Messiah. He just could not make sense of Matt 20:28, for example: 'The Son of Man did not come to be served, but to serve, and to give his life as a ransom for many'. Jesus spent too much time in the wrong company for him to be the glorious King of Israel. Jesus, Troki says, did not exhibit the dominant personality which was to be expected of the Ruler who had come to claim power and glory. He did not behave like a king should. He did not fit Troki's concept of the fulfiller of passages such as Zech 9:10 or Dan 7:17.

Christians classically respond to this by saying that it simply represents a conflict of ideas about what true greatness is in God's eyes. Furthermore, they claim, Jesus the Messiah will receive all the honour and glory which is his due when he returns to effect the Last Judgement and bring about the eschatalogical consummation of the universe. Franz Delitzsch, one of the most able modern Christian Hebraists and scholars of Jewish theology, responded that just as God was the King of Israel before Sinai, but in one sense only became so when Israel accepted him as king with the words 'we will hear and obey', so too Jesus is already the Messianic King of Israel, but in another sense will only become that grand and glorious king when Israel finally accepts and worships him.[169]

How would *you* respond to this argument?

Troki says that the true Messiah will establish a single kingdom upon earth. He takes as his basic text the words of Dan 2:44, which say that 'the God of heaven will set up a

---

[169] Franz Delitzsch, *Messianic Prophecies* (T & T Clark, Edinburgh, 1880), ad loc.

kingdom that will never be destroyed, nor will it be left to another people. It will crush all those kingdoms and bring them to an end, but it will itself endure forever.' Patently, he asserts, Jesus did not do this. He is not at all impressed by talk of a spiritual kingdom which unites all who believe in Jesus, but insists that the Hebrew Bible is speaking about a public and political kingdom, discernible to all peoples.

The Church has responded with the proclamation that nonetheless it *is* a spiritual kingdom which God has instituted in Jesus, and that Jesus is reigning even now at the right hand of the Father in heaven. When Jesus returns in glory, *then* will be the time to establish the indisputable public dominion of God on earth. Jesus speaks of this at several points, for example in Matt 25:34 and John 18:36–37 (see Rev 19:16). And of course at the very heart of the Christian faith is this creative tension between the truth that the Kingdom of God has already come (Luke 10:9; Matt 12:28), the truth that it is still growing to fullness (Matt 13:31–32), and the truth that it is still to come in the future (Luke 22:29–30; Matt 25:31). God has not finished his work in and through Jesus yet!

How would *you* respond to this argument?

Troki says that the true Messiah will make idolatry a thing of the past. He refers to passages such as Isa 45:23; Zeph 3:9; Zech 8:23; 14:9, and the following important one from Isa 2:12–18: 'The LORD Almighty has a day in store for all the proud and lofty . . . the LORD alone will be exalted in that day, and the idols will totally disappear.' He does not accept that Christianity is a thoroughly monotheistic faith, itself helping to bring about that day as more and more idolatrous people become Christians. He prefers to see Christianity as a subtle attempt by an idolatrous faith to appear monotheistic.

Once again Christians appeal to the Second Coming of Jesus as the great event which will usher in the time when this goal of liberating the world from idolatries of every kind will be completely accomplished. This is anchored to Paul's words in 1 Cor 15:24, where he refers to the future consummation of history, and proclaims: 'Then the end will come, when he hands over the kingdom to God the Father after he has destroyed all dominion, authority and power.'

How would *you* respond to this argument?

Troki says that the true Messiah will rid the world of sin, once and for all. He quotes passages such as Jer 3:17; 50:20; Deut 30:6; Isa 60:21; Zeph 3:13; Ezek 36:25–27; 37:23–24, as *all* relating to the Messianic Age. He is not amenable to the obvious criticism that Jer 50:20 relates God's forgiveness to a remnant only, and so might be more clearly restricted in its efficacy than he wants. Nor does he accept the criticism that only the Ezekiel passages are actually regarded as Messianic prophecies by both Jewish and Christian scholarly consensus.

At any rate, the Church has traditionally responded to this challenge by stating its belief that the key to this sinless future is true contrition, confession and repentance. This is still not in evidence as a characteristic of either the Jewish people or the so-called Christian nations, let alone the rest of the world, and it is out of the question to expect the Messiah to simply wave a magic wand or the like, to bypass the ways of God and transform people in an instant.

Furthermore, Christians have argued, the last passage selected by Troki is expressly linked to acceptance of the Messiah, and since Jesus is the Messiah and the Jewish people have not accepted him as their Messiah, how then could there yet be an eradication of sin?

Finally, the Church has again appealed to the Second Coming of Jesus for the ultimate defeat of sin and death.

How would *you* respond to this argument?

Troki, arguing from a literal perspective, says that the true Messiah really will reconcile nature to itself. He quotes Isa

65:25; Ezek 34:25, 28; Hos 2:18; and the famous passage, Isa 11:6–9, about the wolf and the lamb becoming friends, etc, as non-negotiable public signs of the coming of the Messianic kingdom. Troki is not always literal in his hermeneutics, but in this polemic against Christianity it suits him. In other words, he is not prepared to see these verses simply as poetic expressions of the point already highlighted, namely that the Messiah will usher in an age of peace in the world. He demands a literal fulfilment.

However, many (most?) Christians have insisted that the poetic or symbolic interpretation *is* the correct interpretation of these passages and those others like them. It would be true to say that most Jewish commentators understand them symbolically as well. The considerable authority of Maimonides is given to the figurative interpretation, as we see in this statement:

> Let no one imagine that in the days of Messiah anything in the course of nature will be altered . . . Isaiah's words, 'And the wolf shall dwell with the lamb' are a parable and figure of speech.[170]

On the other hand, there *are* Christians in the church family who do take these passages literally, and who accept a symbolic application of the promise only in this interim period, postponing the literal fulfilment of the passages until the return of Jesus to set up his millenial kingdom.

How would *you* respond to this argument?

Troki says that the shekhinah (ie, the glorious presence of God) will return to Israel when the true Messiah comes. Here he quotes Ezek 37:26–28; Joel 2:27; 3:17, 21. It was glaringly and painfully apparent in Troki's time, and has been ever since, that Israel is not yet filled with the great and glorious presence of God. (However, this is not to

---

[170] Rabbi Moses Maimonides, *Hilkoth Melachim*, xii, 1.

say, as some Christians have said, that there is absolutely nothing of the glory and presence of God with the Jewish people.) According to Troki, the Messiah cannot have come if the Jewish people are still in a despised state in the world.

Christians respond by affirming that the active presence of God did indeed come to Israel as a result of the life and ministry of Jesus. This all took place at the Jewish feast of Shavuot (Pentecost), which followed after the Passover season when Jesus experienced death, resurrection and ascension to heaven. The Holy Spirit who descended on the Jewish people in Jerusalem at Pentecost was the expected shekhinah of God. What is more, Christians say, some three thousand or so Jewish people became followers of Jesus that day because when the Holy Spirit entered their lives they came to appreciate that he was the Messiah (Acts 2:1–41).

How would *you* respond to this argument?

Troki says that the true Messiah will build the New Temple when he comes. He relies for this teaching on Ezek 37:26–28 and chapters 40–48, of course, but Isa 2:2–3 is also in his mind. Troki held fast to the prevailing opinion that the extended period of time without the temple, and therefore without the possibility of animal sacrifice and the atonement brought by it, was part and parcel of the punishment decreed by God for his people's sins. But God's purpose was to restore this sacrificial system when the time for Israel's full forgiveness and restoration came, and the Messiah was sent. Therefore no temple, no Messiah.

Christians have responded to this charge on two quite different levels. In the first place, probably all Christians would argue that Jesus himself is the fulfilment of all that the temple represents in Israel's life. If you like, the temple was but a type of Jesus, pointing to him, speaking as it does of the active presence of God with his people; of the need for confession, repentance and atonement; of the possibility of the forgiveness of God; of the need for mediation; and of the glory and majesty of God. Jesus is seen as the real Temple of God on earth, representing in the fullest manner possible all these temple associations. Jesus' own words are often quoted here from Matt 12:6: 'I tell you that one greater than the temple is here.' As the Letter to the Hebrews describes him, Jesus is the 'once and for all' sacrifice for our sins.

The key to understanding these temple prophecies, so it is argued, is a spiritual one, not a literal one. There will be no return to the sacrificing of animals in a Jerusalem temple, because of this 'once and for all' sacrificial death of Jesus. There will be no more need for symbolic representations of the active presence of God with his people when Jesus, the Messiah, returns to live on earth himself.

However, there are some Christians, largely in dispensationalist churches and groups, who wish to maintain that notwithstanding all that has been said in the above two paragraphs, the closing chapters of Ezekiel are actually speaking about a physical temple which will indeed be built either just before or just after Jesus' return in glory. At that point all of Troki's hopes will be fulfilled.

How would *you* respond to this argument?

Troki says that the dead will be raised to life when the true Messiah comes.   In defence of this he quotes Deut 32:39; Dan 12:1–2; and the marvellous Isa 26:19, which says: 'But your dead will live; their bodies will rise. You who dwell in the dust, wake up and shout for joy. Your dew is like the dew of the morning; the earth will give birth to her dead.'

Once again the Church has traditionally replied that this promise will be wonderfully fulfilled at the return of Jesus, when at the Last Judgement all the dead will rise to life to receive their verdicts and their final destinations.

I do wonder, though, why more has not been made by believers of the Messianic sign recorded for us in Matt 27:52–53, where we are informed that when Jesus was crucified, 'the tombs broke open and the bodies of many holy people who had died were raised to life. They came out of the tombs, and after Jesus' resurrection they went into the holy city and appeared to many people.' This was surely a Messianic sign of some significance, relating to those very prophecies highlighted by Troki!

How would *you* respond to this argument?

These, then, have been eight very typical refutationist arguments. They typify the approach of Troki himself, but their real importance lies in the fact that these arguments, and the many like them, have informed the Jewish community as a whole. One constantly comes across them in Jewish books, magazine articles, sermons and conversations.

Most importantly, however, two overwhelmingly serious challenges to the Messiahship of Jesus have become part of the Jewish refutationist armoury since the days of Troki and his own critical analysis of the Christian faith. It is well known that they dominate the agenda, and surface in all the literature, the lectures and all the conversations. We must turn to these now.

Jesus did not bring peace to Israel or to the world

Without doubt, this is the commonest challenge of them all. It is found on the lips of Jewish next-door neighbours as well as of rabbis and academics. Troki berates the Church for claiming that Isa 9:6b gives the names of the Messiah, and yet treating superficially the fact that therefore the Messiah must be the 'Prince of Peace'. Why, he asks, does the Church continue to ignore the fact that there has been no peace since the coming of Jesus into the world? Not only is the world at war with itself, and not only are Jewish people far from being at peace in the world, but even the very Churches, those bodies of Christians who are the very disciples of Jesus, are constantly fighting with one another. The English judge, Lord Hewart, once made a rightly celebrated remark when he said:

> It is not merely of some importance, but it is of fundamental importance, that justice should not only be done, but should manifestly and undoubtedly be seen to be done.[171]

The Jewish tradition has insisted that the same attitude be taken to the establishment of Messianic peace on earth. Rabbi Randall Falk expressed it well in a recent book which he co-wrote with a Christian scholar:

> It is important to recognize that the disagreement about Jesus as Christ is not over what Jesus taught or did, but rather about what did not occur during his lifetime.[172]

Many verses apart from Isa 9:6b about the promise of peace in the Messianic Age are quoted by Troki and others, including Isa 2:4; 11:6–9; Zech 9:10; and Mal 4:6 (which is 3:24 in the Hebrew). Isa 25:8 is also cited to include in the dispute the promise of the peace of freedom from all pain and suffering. The force of this challenge is one to which Christians must face up.

Troki, and those following him, also denigrate Jesus as being sometimes too aggressive in his words and manner to be the Prince of Peace. Sigal, in his work referred to earlier, admits that humanly-speaking, we often distinguish between the sometimes regrettable need for the use of aggression or violence, and the violence which is simply an expression of evil, so that some might say that aggressive acts or speech by Jesus need not be a sign of evil or maladjustment.[173] But Sigal proceeds to assert that as far as the Jewish Messiah is

---

[171] Lord Hewart, R v Sussex Justices (1923) 1KB 259.

[172] He wrote this in the book, *Jews and Christians. A Troubled Family* (Abingdon Press, Nashville, 1990), which he wrote with Walter Harrelson, p 105.

[173] Gerald Sigal, *The Jew and the Christian Missionary*, op cit, p 207.

concerned, he must be free not only from evil, but also from *any* kind of violence. This is the case, he insists, because the Messiah must fulfil not only Isa 9:6b, but also Isa 53:9b, which teaches that this 'suffering servant' will be buried with the wicked even though 'he had done no violence'.[174]

The charge, then, as it is usually brought, is that Jesus is disqualified from being the Messiah not because he was an evil man, but because he was not a true man of peace; because he did not instil peace in his followers; and because he did not bring peace to the world. However, there are other voices that wish to go further than this and seek to demonstrate that Jesus was an unacceptable man of violence. Many verses are quoted to try to show that Jesus was actually a man of aggressive and divisive personality. The favourite text of the refutationists is one which we shall look at in some detail in a moment.

Before we do that, however, I would like to suggest that readers of this book also spend some time examining the following additional texts which we do not have the space to deal with. Bear in mind throughout that your main task is twofold: to try to see why Jewish refutationists interpret these passages as evidence against Jesus' claim to be the Prince of Peace; and to try to respond to that (mis)interpretation in an appropriate way. Here are the texts for private study:

Matthew 21:12; 21:18–22; Luke 12:49–53; 19:27

Disputes over the claim of Jesus to be the Prince of Peace have gone on incessantly. One celebrated interchange took place in the Netherlands in 1686, when a learned and cultured Jewish man, Isaac Orobio de Castro, engaged an Arminian Christian, Philipp van Limborch, in a relatively

---

[174] Ibid.

civilised and amiable debate. The substance of this debate was edited and published shortly afterwards.[175] There are basically three letters by Orobio and three replies by Limborch. In 1.7 and 17, Orobio draws attention to this departure from the ways of peace, as he sees it, in Jesus' life, and then in 111.4 he concludes that the fragmentary nature of the Church, in which each part claims to be the sole bearer of the image of Christ, is the final proof that Jesus did not bring the promised peace which would unite the world. Orobio's argument is often quoted by others.

Christians continue to argue that Jesus did bring peace, if you know where to look for it, and Jewish people still claim that the state of the world belies this argument. Christians quote Jesus' words about peace in passages like John 14:27 and 16:33. In the former passage Jesus says, 'Peace I leave with you; my peace I give you.' He then goes on to alert us to the fact that this will not satisfy the casual glance of the world, since he is not giving the kind of peace that the world thinks it needs. In the latter passage Jesus promises that this peace will be an inner reality for those who trust him, although the overall context is that of a world which is still in conflict.

Christians also insist that the peace of God is not possible for those who do not repent and turn their lives around to live in accordance with the will of God. This is played down by many refutationists, who prefer to speak rhetorically about the Messianic age as being one where God brings peace as a pure *gift* to Israel and the world. However, this theological conviction that peace will not be given with the wave of a celestial wand is altogether part of traditional Jewish theology too, and the refutationists are simply ignoring their own best traditions. This is not a case of saying that somehow people must *earn* the peace of God, but it is an acknowl-

---

[175] *De veritate religionis christianae; amica collatio cum eruditio Judaeo*, 1687.

edgement of the biblical truth that without genuine faith and repentance the promises of God can never be fully realised.

Immanuel Schochet stresses this point in his short study on the Jewish commitment to the coming of the Messiah. In the following quotation, he uses two Hebrew words in transliteration: *mitzvot* is the term for commandments, and *teshuvah* means repentance.

> There are a number of ways conducive to hasten the Messianic redemption . . . these involve the observance of some special mitzvot which constitute comprehensive principles of the Torah . . . First and foremost among these mitzvot is the principle of teshuvah . . . 'When you return unto God, your God, and will listen to His voice . . . God, your God, will return your captivity and have compassion upon you, and He will restore and gather you from all the nations to which God, your God, has dispersed you' (Deut 30:2ff.) . . . What then is delaying the redemption? The lack of teshuvah.[176]

Christians proclaim that this repentance must be done in the name of Jesus, who has already brought peace to those who call on his name, whereas Jewish people generally proclaim that the repentance and the peace claimed by Christians are often conspicuous by their absence. The whole dilemma was neatly summed up by the Jewish philosopher Martin Buber, who put it like this:

> The Jew is to the Christian the incomprehensibly obdurate man who will not see what has happened; and the Christian is to the Jew the reckless man who, in an unredeemed world, affirms that its redemption is accomplished.[177]

A justifiable generalisation would be to say that in Jewish tradition, as it has developed down the generations, the focus

---

[176] Jacob Immanuel Schochet, *Mashiach. The Principle of Mashiach and the Messianic Era in Jewish Law and Tradition* (SIE, NY, 1991), pp 41f.
[177] Martin Buber, *Mamre. Essays in Religion* (translated by Greta Hort, 1946), p 31. See also Borowitz, *Contemporary Christologies*, op cit, p 4.

of thought has become this Messianic Era of peace and justice, rather than the person of the Messiah himself. Once more we can note how Berger and Wyschogrod stress this point:

> In other words, the only way to define 'the Messiah' is as the king who will rule during what we call the Messianic age. The central criterion for evaluating a Messiah must therefore be a single question: Has the Messianic age come? It is only in terms of this question that 'the Messiah' means anything.[178]

With all this in mind, what we must do now is spend some time looking at the most (mis)quoted of these New Testament passages which are held to disqualify Jesus' Messianic claim, endeavouring to discover the true meaning of Jesus' words. The passage is Matt 10:34–36, and I shall quote it here in full for ease of reference. Jesus is speaking to his disciples:

> Do not suppose that I have come to bring peace to the earth. I did not come to bring peace, but a sword. For I have come to turn a man against his father, a daughter against her mother, a daughter-in-law against her mother-in-law – a man's enemies will be the members of his own household.[179]

At first glance this passage could easily look as if Jesus is indeed preparing his followers for a life of violence, a life dedicated to breaking up families and dissolving the fabric of society. This is certainly how it is interpreted and presented by Jewish refutationists who are keen to show Jesus in such an unfavourable light. Rabbi Dan Cohn-Sherbok, who is by no means an active polemicist, also illustrates this disregard for proper context in his book on liberation theology, where he cites as an objection to Jesus,

---

[178] Berger and Wyschogrod, op cit, p 19.

[179] Jesus is building here on the important passage, Mic 7:6.

his admonition to break all human ties: 'Whoever of you does not renounce all that he has cannot be my disciple' (Lk 14:33) . . . Similarly, he declared: 'Call no man your father on earth, for you have one Father, who is in heaven' (Mt 23:9). In contrast to these views, Judaism asserted that persons could not live a full life unless they were members of a family and were well integrated into the larger community. The renunciation of family bonds was regarded as a travesty of the created order.[180]

As we shall see shortly, rabbinic literature actually has plenty of examples which give the lie to Cohn-Sherbok's rather shallow analysis here. We read that, in some respects at least, a Jewish man's rabbi or master is more important to him than his own biological father, and that he should be prepared to put his rabbi first. Not only that, but of course the whole community at Qumran, on the shores of the Dead Sea, stressed the need for a withdrawal from not only the wider world but also from the larger Jewish world. There was a kind of associate membership for certain families, but full participation and membership were only for those devout Jews who were prepared to sacrifice a 'normal Jewish life' for life in the community there.

There certainly *is* a Jewish context in which to see the call of Jesus for a radical lifestyle. But this is all actually a little academic in the sense that Jesus was *not* calling here for his disciples to leave or diminish happy homes. The view that Jesus is intent on breaking up Jewish families is only possible if one settles for a first, and superficial, glance at this passage. Not surprisingly, a number of refutationists settle for exactly that! Speaking about the situations which sometimes do occur, when families react badly to the news that someone has become attracted to Jesus, Beth Moshe writes concerning the Christian who shares his or her faith with a Jewish person:

---

[180] Dan Cohn-Sherbok, *On Earth as it is in Heaven*, op cit, pp 17f.

Isn't he asking you to break the commandment of honoring father and mother? The missionary does not care what he leaves in the wake of his attempt to capture the soul of a son or daughter. Great unhappiness and mental anguish result because of apostasy. If this is the peace Christianity offers, it seems to be only for the convert, not for his family which is left in torment.[181]

This all-too-typical rhetoric is exposed for the malicious nonsense it is by any proper examination of the context of Jesus' words, and by any proper consideration of the cirumstances in which families and friends sometimes become disjointed or alienated. Look at the immediate context of these words in Jesus' long commissioning speech to his disciples, and you will find that he has just finished cautioning them with this statement (verses 17–23):

Be on your guard against men; they will hand you over to the local councils and flog you in their synagogues . . . Brother will betray brother to death, and a father his child; children will rebel against their parents and have them put to death. All men will hate you because of me, but he who stands firm to the end will be saved. When you are persecuted in one place, flee to another.

What Jesus is really saying, then, is that when Jewish people become believers in Jesus they will end up as *victims* of aggression. They will *suffer* the violence, not perpetrate it! Jesus is being entirely realistic, and cautioning his followers to be equally realistic. Those who devote their lives to Jesus will become radically different from the others in their families and synagogues, and this situation will produce friction, not because the believers want the friction but because the other people cannot tolerate this witness to the true Messiah among them. He is warning his people about

---

181 Beth Moshe, *Judaism's Truth Answers the Missionaries*, op cit, p 252.

the cost of discipleship, not arming them for an onslaught upon their erstwhile friends and family.[182]

In other words, this passage is not a disqualification of Jesus from being the Messianic Prince of Peace. On the contrary, it is evidence that Jesus was preparing his disciples for real life in the Messianic Age. And what is more, this could not be more in keeping with the rabbinic traditions about the way people would turn upon the true believers in the Messianic Age! The rabbis also interpreted the Mic 7:6 verse as a word about the undermining of Jewish loyalties at the time of the coming of the Messiah, when people will prefer their own ways to those of God.

> In the footsteps of the Messiah insolence will increase and honour dwindle . . . a son will revile his father, a daughter will rise against her mother, a daughter-in-law against her mother-in-law, and a man's enemies will be the members of his household.[183]

> In the generation when Messiah comes . . . daughters will rise up against their mothers, and daughters-in-law against their mothers-in-law.[184]

Both the rabbis and Jesus are saying to their people: 'Don't be naïve. The coming of the Messiah brings conflict as well as peace. There will be struggle for a while, perhaps even martyrdom, for the sake of the Kingdom.'

---

[182] Christians for whom this has actually been a personal experience, whatever their cultural background, might benefit from reading D. A. Carson's 1987 book, *When Jesus Confronts the World*. Chapter six is particularly appropriate, since it deals with the verses in Matthew 10 which we are presently studying. That chapter is entitled, 'The Divisiveness of Jesus', and in it Carson gently leads the reader into an exploration of the implications of seeing Jesus as a radical challenger of the world's values.

[183] Talmud, Sotah 49b.

[184] Talmud, Sanhedrin 97a. See also, in the pseudepigraphal literature, *Jubilees* 23:16, 19.

As a matter of interest, even the words of Jesus in Matt 10:37–42, immediately following on from the controversial passage, also match exactly the perspective of the rabbis. As I mentioned above, there are passages which declare that one's religious teacher and his needs can come before that of one's own parents if there is a clash of loyalties.[185] So even these further severe-sounding words of Jesus are not at all 'un-Jewish'.

Jesus is not contradicting in any way his teaching about the peace which trust in him brings to a person, and can bring to whole communities. He is honestly describing some of the implications of faith in him. The very same kind of phenomenon is also observable within the Orthodox Jewish world today, as Sigal and others know only too well, although they are hardly likely to draw attention to it. Many examples could be cited from recent years of secularised, highly-assimilated Jewish people who have had some sort of transforming experience and become Orthodox Jews in their beliefs and lifestyle. Their new way of life, their new beliefs and their new set of values often do not meet with approval and acceptance by their families and friends; indeed not always by their spouses either.

Here are some quotes from one of the definitive studies to be made on this phenomenon, by a leading *Jewish* sociologist, Janet Aviad.[186] Her book analyses the impact of this return to Orthodoxy by these Jewish people who are known as *ba'alei teshuvah*, a Hebrew phrase designating those Jews who have taken the step of repentance and committed themselves to an Orthodox life and faith.

> Relations between parents and children are upset on several grounds. A baal teshuvah finds it difficult to eat in the home

---

[185] See, in the Talmud, Yebamot 5b, and in the Mishnah, Baba Metzia 2:11.

[186] Janet Aviad, *Return to Judaism. Religious Renewal in Israel* (The University of Chicago Press, 1983).

of his parents who do not observe the dietary laws of Judaism. He finds it difficult to spend the Sabbath and holidays with his parents who violate the religious prescriptions regarding their observance. In most cases, baalei teshuvah moved out of the homes of their parents and set up their own apartments.[187]

Would Orthodox rabbis and other spokespersons want to argue that the Torah itself must now be disqualified from being an authentic gift from God, etc, because observing it can break up Jewish homes? Of course not! They would claim that this is, tragically, an almost predictable consequence of the modern situation where so many Jewish people prefer to go their own way rather than God's way. Such Jewish people will always oppose the witness to the God of Israel which *ba'alei teshuvah* bring with them. The Torah is not corrupt, they will say, just because conflict often comes in its wake in these circumstances.

Quite so. And Christians maintain that Jesus is not corrupt just because conflict often comes in his wake in circumstances where a Jewish person discovers that Jesus is the Messiah. Peace with God, and peace to accept oneself as a child of God, are not inconsequential results of a relationship with Jesus, either, as some refutationists try to make out. These people are so intent on stressing that public political peace is the only acceptable fulfilment of all the biblical promises, that they belittle the life-transforming peace which believers in Jesus experience. It is worth emphasising here that this experience of peace is real, invaluable and a definite part of the promised new life which God wishes to give to his people.

However, it is nonetheless true that the Bible does also promise more than this. The full-blown Messianic Age will be one in which there is peace in the whole of life, the public arena as well as the personal world of believers. Christians

---

[187] Ibid, pp 116, 117.

proclaim that this life of peace will become a reality in the world when Jesus returns, specifically after he has defeated the enemies of God in the final battle. The traditional Jewish view is that the Messiah will only come the one time, and that peace in the public arena will be part and parcel of life in the days of the Messiah. Jewish people therefore question why there should be so much war and conflict in the world if the Messiah has already come, and Christians need to be able to discuss this point honestly and confidently.

How would *you* respond to this argument?

The doctrine of the second coming of Jesus is nothing but an escape clause for defeated Christians

Here is the second of the two dominant criticisms made about Jesus' life and ministry. It should have become quite obvious from the overview of the Christian responses to Troki's eight points, and especially from our discussion of whether or not Jesus is the Prince of Peace, that time and again the Christian response to Jewish challenges is to refer to the paradox of the 'now-but-not-yet' theology of the Kingdom of God. In other words, not all of Jesus' ministry was accomplished in his thirty or so years of life on earth. The Kingdom of God most certainly came in an unprecedented way with him, but not until his return will his full ministry be complete. Jesus is, at present, waiting to return to bring about the consummation of all history.

Thereby, it seems to Jewish people, difficulties of every sort are simply avoided by the facile claim that they will be explained or put right when Jesus returns. Thus no possibility exists for a *historical* discrediting of Jesus, since Christians simply refuse to take actual history seriously, preferring to hide in the safety of an unexplored and untested future hope. Put crudely, Jewish people see the Christian doctrine of the Second Coming of Jesus as no more than an escape hatch for those times when Christians find that their theological position is indefensible.

In my opinion this is a charge which has not been taken nearly seriously enough by Christians. It is surely a perfectly understandable point of view. How would Christians react to a new religious movement, say an off-shoot from Christianity, which had what seemed like several unsurmountable theological problems in its claims, but whose adherents kept saying that they were waiting for a 'Master' to come who would miraculously make everything clear? It does not take an extraordinary amount of cynicism to imagine Christians saying that the whole thing was a 'cop-out' to escape accountability in the face of historical and theological reality.

Here is an example from the Middle Ages of a sarcastic Jewish challenge to this cardinal Christian doctrine:

> Why is his chariot so long in coming
> To deliver them that put their trust in him?
> And why are the steps of his course so slow
> When he has paid for his brethren the redemption price?[188]

This has in its favour at least a certain poetic flair, and an invitation to respond with civility. A contemporary example is typically crude. This comes from the pen of Mordecai Alfandari, an active refutationist in Jerusalem. In one of his tracts, devoted to this subject, he writes:

> The only way the Church can explain it all is that Jesus is going to 'finish the job' at his second coming (a statement of faith, not fact) . . . They will tell you that you have to take it 'on faith'. 'Faith' is wishful thinking, not FACT! Only FACTS can save mankind and redeem the world.[189]

Alfandari knows that faith is not the same thing as wishful

---

[188] *Memoir of the Book of Nizzahon of Rabbi Lipmann*, IV, lines 7–10, *c* 1401.
[189] Mordecai Alfandari, *Is Jesus Coming Again?*, a tract with no date, but written in the 1980s.

thinking, and he knows that there is a great value placed on faith within his own Orthodox Jewish world-view, but it happens to suit him in this piece of polemic to ridicule the notion of faith. Christians will also respond that as far as they are concerned the return of Jesus *is* a fact – albeit one which is yet to be realised in real history. Presumably even Alfandari would also believe it to be a 'fact' that God will fulfil all his eschatalogical promises one day in the future.

Nevertheless, the force of the Jewish frustration at this Christian belief is an important issue for us. Christians need to do considerably more homework on the basis of this belief in the Bible, and on the difference between what the Bible calls Messianic hope and what might legitimately be described as a flight from responsibility by certain Christians in the face of difficult arguments or evidence.

I can well remember a rabbi in Tiberias, Israel, saying to me that if Christians wished to believe such a far-fetched doctrine, then that was alright by him, but what he was not prepared to allow was the claim by the Church that this doctrine was rooted, like all its other dogmas, in the very text of the Hebrew Bible. This was a distinctly New Testament and Christian doctrine as far as he was concerned, with no basis in the Hebrew Bible. Therefore *Jewish* people could not begin to consider that there might be some truth in it.

Here are some words from a popular 1975 Jewish book, relevant to our subject:

> Judaism does not believe that Jesus was the Messiah because he did not fulfill any Messianic prophecies. For Christians a second coming is necessary so that Jesus can fulfill the Messianic prophecies which he did not fulfill. Jewishly speaking, there is no problem, since the Jews never had reason to believe that Jesus was the Messiah, and the Bible never mentioned a second Messianic coming.[190]

---

[190] Dennis Prager and Joseph Telushkin, *Eight Questions People Ask About Judaism* (Tze Ulmad Press, Simi Valley, CA, 1975), p 81.

As early as Justin Martyr's *Dialogue with Trypho* in the second century CE, we have evidence of the importance of this teaching about two advents of the Messiah, as well as evidence of the fact that the Jewish community did not accept this teaching. Justin wrote:

> For they do not understand what is shown by all these words, that two advents of his have been announced; one in which he has been proclaimed as liable to suffering, and without glory, and without honour, and crucified; and the second, in which he will come with glory from the heavens . . . [191]

The Jewish people still do not understand. Some Christians have also begun to square up to the work involved in this area, and one Christian scholar, thinking about the doctrine of the Parousia, that is to say the Second Coming or Appearance of Jesus, went so far as to write this:

> If Jesus took over the conception of a Parousia from current Jewish teaching, we must inquire where exactly this doctrine is to be found in pre-Christian literature. It is certainly absent from the Old Testament, the most important source for the teaching of Jesus.[192]

Now this opinion begs a few questions, not the least of which concerns whether or not Jesus himself might have legitimately introduced original teaching to Israel. Nevertheless, the statement that this doctrine has no exegetical grounding in the Hebrew Bible will come as a shock to many (probably most) Christians. Surely it *is* there in the Hebrew Bible, simply waiting for Jesus or the New Testament writers to draw attention to it and elucidate it?

John Fischer, a leading American Messianic Jewish writer, speaks very honestly to this issue. He responds to the Jewish charge that there is no unambiguous teaching to be found in

---

[191] *Dialogue*, op cit, 110.2. See the whole section 110–11.

[192] T. Francis Glasson, *The Second Advent* (1945), p 13.

the Hebrew Bible about the Messiah coming on two different occasions by agreeing that this is true.[193] The key matter in this case is the attitude towards *ambiguous* evidence. Fischer goes on to say that even the rabbis acknowledge that something has to be done with the complex passages which speak now of suffering and now of glorious victory in the life of the Messiah. Fischer is satisfied that the New Testament teaching about the Messiah coming twice is fully consonant with the witness of the Hebrew Bible, but in the nature of things, he agrees that the same texts could be read in a different way.

The Essenes, a radical Jewish religious movement which arose some generations before the birth of Jesus, and which remained contemporary with him, interpreted the two types of Messianic passages as actually referring to two different Messianic figures. The first Messiah, the son of Aaron, would be a priestly warrior who would suffer and eventually be killed in his service of Israel in the last days and the last wars. At that point, the second Messiah, the son of David, a royal figure, would take centre stage, leading Israel to triumph and glory over all her enemies.[194] In this way, the two types of Messianic text found in the Hebrew Bible, some focusing on suffering and death (albeit in a glorious fashion) and others celebrating triumph and joy, are explained as referring to two different people.

This suffering Messiah, known in different communities as the Messiah ben Joseph or the Messiah ben Ephraim, will be the commander-in-chief of Israel's forces during the wars of the Messianic era. After some initial victories he will be killed in a great battle in which Israel itself is then defeated by Gog and Magog. At that point the Davidic Messiah will be

---

[193] John Fischer, *The Olive Tree Connection* (IVP, Leicester, 1983), p 174.

[194] See the discussions in the following material from the Dead Sea Scrolls: *Cairo-Damascus Document* 12:22–13:1; 14:9; 20:1; *Scroll of Discipline* 9:11.

raised up by God to take his place, and some texts even state that the Davidic Messiah will signal his glorious reign by bringing the first Messiah back to life.

In other Jewish texts, this Messianic figure is simply said to be descended from the tribe of Levi, again in distinction from the Davidic Messiah who will be from the tribe of Judah.[195] Neither of the two sources which have been referred to so far (ie, the Qumran Essenes and the pseudepigraphal writings) became authoritative in Orthodox Jewish tradition, but the point I wish to make is that by the time of Jesus' birth the Jewish people were clearly already trying to make sense of the two types of text which they accepted as being Messianic.

There is also a discussion among the rabbis in the Talmud about two corresponding Messiahs, one called the 'son of Joseph' and the other called the 'son of David'. This is important, since it shows that this concept of a suffering and dying Messiah survived within Judaism until long after the time of Jesus and, moreover, that it did find supporters within what became normative Jewish theological circles. In the context of discussions about the range of meanings of the words in Zech 12:12, 'And the land shall mourn . . . ', we find the following section:

> What is the reason of this mourning? Rabbi Dosa and the rabbis differ about it. Rabbi Dosa says: 'On account of the Messiah who will be slain'. But the rabbis say: 'On account of the Evil Inclination which will be killed.'[196]

So we see that there was a difference of opinion among the rabbis themselves, but that some of them certainly inter-

---

[195] See in the pseudepigraphical book, *The Testaments of the Twelve Patriarchs*, 'The Testament of Reuben' 6:5–12; 'The Testament of Levi' 18:2–4; 'The Testament of Judah' 21:1–15; 'The Testament of Naphtali' 5:1–3.

[196] Babylonian Talmud, Sukkah 52a.

preted these words as referring to the death of the Messiah. The section continues:

> The rabbis have taught that the Holy One, blessed be He, will say to the Messiah ben David (may he soon be revealed in our days): 'Ask anything of Me, and I shall give it to you . . . ' And when he sees that the Messiah ben Joseph is slain, he will say to Him: 'Sovereign of the world! I ask nothing from You except life!'[197]

The notion that the Messiah would die, and yet that he would lead Israel into final triumph, is also found in the great collection of midrashim, where it is related by analogy to the disappearance of Moses before the people of Israel reached the Promised Land.[198] This double-Messiah teaching eventually became so typical of Jewish theology that at the end of his exhaustive study of the teaching of the masters of medieval Jewish theology on the subject of the Messiah, the Jewish scholar Joseph Sarachek could say:

> They all take for granted the appearance of the Ephraimitic [i.e. the priestly] Messiah who will be slain in battle after a brief and impetuous career.[199]

This method of interpreting the texts is still taken for granted by most of the Jewish people today who have given any real thought to the issue. It is certainly taught in many synagogues and Jewish seminaries. In fact this different way of interpreting the relevant texts, either by having two different Messianic figures, each with a distinct role and destiny, or by having one Messiah who comes twice on to the stage of history, is often singled out by authors as one of the dis-

---

[197] Ibid. For a helpful selection of translated texts on this theme carrying on into the medieval period, see Raphael Patai, *The Messiah Texts* (Wayne State University Press, Detroit, 1979), pp 65–70.

[198] See Numbers Rabbah 11:2.

[199] Joseph Sarachek, *The Doctrine of the Messiah in Medieval Jewish Literature* (Jewish Theological Seminary of America, NY, 1932), p 309.

tinctive and classic differences between Jews and Christians when it comes to Messianic theology. It is presented as a given that here is an issue where Jews and Christians just do not, and cannot, agree.

This drawing of a sharp distinction between the ways that the Jewish and Christian communities deal with the two types of description of the life and work of the Messiah is fair enough up to a point, but there is another, suppressed, theology to be found within Judaism on this matter. Belief in the coming of two different Messiahs is not the only theological stance which Jewish people have taken. Indeed there are texts which definitely speak of the Messiah suffering for the sins of Israel. Here are some extraordinary words about the Messiah, named Ephraim in this source, from a medieval collection of comments on biblical and theological matters:

[At the time of the Messiah's creation], the Holy One, blessed be He, will tell him in detail what will befall him: There are souls that have been put away with thee under My throne, and it is their sins which will bend thee down under a yoke of iron and make thee like a calf whose eyes grow dim with suffering, and will choke thy spirit as with a yoke; because of the sins of these souls thy tongue will cleave to the roof of thy mouth. Art thou willing to endure such things?

The Messiah will ask the Holy One, blessed be He: Will my suffering last many years?

The Holy One, blessed be He, will reply: Upon thy life and the life of My head, it is a period of seven years which I have decreed for thee. But if thy soul is sad at the prospect of thy suffering, I shall at this moment banish these sinful souls.

The Messiah will say: Master of the universe, with joy in my soul and gladness in my heart I take this suffering upon myself, provided that not one person in Israel perish . . . [200]

In this complicated text, the Messiah is spoken of under

---

[200] Pesikta Rabbati, Piksa 36:1 (translated by William G. Braude, Yale University Press, New Haven, 1968), vol 2, pp 678–9.

two names, both as Ephraim and as the son of David. Reading the whole section through, the impression gained is that the Messiah has two distinct dimensions to his life and ministry, almost like two personalities. For example, in the second part of this Piksa, we read:

> During the ordeal of the son of David, the Holy One, blessed be He, will say to him: Ephraim, My true Messiah, long ago, ever since the six days of creation, thou didst take this ordeal upon thyself.[201]

There is no teaching here about the Messiah coming twice to his people, but even this teaching is found in one old liturgical text. John Fischer quotes part of an ancient Yom Kippur musaf prayer from the prayer book known to us as *Oz Milifnei Bereshit*, a prayer which says, in part:

> The Messiah our righteousness has turned from us. We are alarmed, we have no one to justify us. Our sins and the yoke of our transgressions he bore. He was bruised for our iniquities. He carried on his shoulders our sins. With his stripes we are healed. Almighty God, hasten the day that he might come to us anew; that we might hear from Mount Lebanon a second time through the Messiah, who is called Yenon.[202]

Note how Isa 52:13–53:12 is being used with respect to the Messiah, in spite of the claims of refutationists that this never happened in the Jewish community. Note again, germane to our present discussion, how two advents of this Messianic figure are implied. Perhaps, then, the concept of two advents is not so un-Jewish as many Jewish people wish to make out? Here is another suggestive passage to this effect, this time from the midrash on the Book of Numbers:

> Like the first redeemer so will the final redeemer be. The first

---

[201] Pesikta Rabbati, Piksa 36:2. See also Piksa 37:1.

[202] Fischer, op cit, p 179. The name 'Yenon' comes from the Hebrew text of Ps 72:17.

redeemer was Moses, who appeared to them and then disappeared. For he (the Messiah) will disappear from their sight and will then again appear to them.[203]

But there might well be a good deal more evidence that there was an early Jewish concept of the Messiah coming to Israel, leaving for a heavenly realm, and then returning to Israel in the last days. Jesus may not in fact have introduced a totally unheard-of Jewish concept to his disciples at all. In 1987, a significant gathering of renowned Jewish and Christian scholars took place in Philadelphia, and in 1990 the papers presented at that gathering were edited by James Charlesworth and published. Charlesworth, in a discussion of the criteria for deciding whether an early text is Jewish or Christian in origin, said at one point:

> We used to have a very clear paradigm: if we found a passage that talked about the Messiah returning to earth, it was clearly Christian because it must be referring to the parousia of Jesus. Some Jewish documents give me the impression we have clear evidence of a belief that the Messiah was with Adam in paradise, that he was then hidden, and that he would return to the earth . . . In other words, if we find a passage referring to 'the return' of the Messiah on earth, we can no longer say it must be Christian.[204]

Charlesworth is a professor of New Testament at Princeton University and an academic theologian who is highly respected by Jewish as well as Christian scholars. Therefore his words are especially important in this debate. He cites *2 Baruch* 30:1 as one such text which suggests a Jewish matrix for the concept of a returning Messiah. This pseudepigraphical work is certainly a Jewish piece, and the particular verse in question was translated by R. H. Charles as follows:

---

[203] Numbers Rabbah 11:2.

[204] James H. Charlesworth (ed), *Jews and Christians. Exploring the Past, Present, and Future* (Crossroad, NY, 1990), p 59.

And it shall come to pass after these things, when the time of the advent of the Messiah is fulfilled, that He shall return in glory.[205]

Charlesworth is properly cautious about this verse and its implications, but he also rightly draws the academic theological world's attention to the fact that things are not nearly as cut and dried as students perhaps learned some years ago, or as theologians perhaps would like them to be. The concept of the Messiah coming twice to Israel and to the world may very well have been acceptably Jewish in Jesus' day. It might be the case that the Jewish establishment deliberately steered their community away from that concept as part of their programme of alienating the nascent Church from its authentic roots, and alienating potential believers in Jesus from Christian theology.

More work needs to be done on this little-explored aspect of Jewish theology and liturgy. There are certainly many New Testament passages which speak about the return of Jesus, and systematic theologians are able to find enough text there for the doctrine.[206] But the key dispute with Jewish people, as we noted above, is whether the roots of this doctrine are already there in the Hebrew Bible, or whether it is a later innovation, and not therefore relevant to, and certainly not binding upon, Jewish people.

The Church says that the doctrine is assuredly rooted in the Hebrew Bible, citing passages like Isa 49:7; 52:13–53:12; Zech 12:8–10. The Jewish people respond that there is nothing explicit there about two Messianic advents separated by two millennia. At best, they say, it could be speaking about one man's lifetime of mixed fortunes. There is

---

[205] R. H. Charles (ed), *The Apocrypha and Pseudepigrapha of the Old Testament in English* (Clarendon Press, Oxford, 1913), vol 2, p 498.

[206] See for example, Matt 19:28; 24:29–31; 1 Cor 15:20–28; 2 Thess 1:5–10; 2:1–4; Heb 9:27–28; Rev 20:4–6.

certainly nothing to compare with the explicit nature of the New Testament passages.

Sadly, I have been able to find precious little by way of an attempt to deal with this issue in either the standard Christian works of systematic theology or the material being produced by Messianic Jewish writers. Is it at all a 'reasonable' result of an exegetical study of the relevant passages in the Hebrew Bible to conclude that they *are* speaking of two advents for the Messiah? Or is it altogether a New Testament doctrine (which might be quite acceptable, of course), and therefore one which can only be found in the Hebrew Bible with Christian hindsight, as it were?

As an example of an important Christian study of the doctrine of the Second Coming, let me mention A. L. Moore's 1966 book devoted to this subject. He spends an entire chapter looking at 'The Background of the New Testament Expectation', in which he offers a very general overview of the central concept of the sovereign rule of God in the Hebrew Bible, followed by a sketch of the eschatological interests and teachings of the various intertestamental Jewish groups. He then includes a mention of the rabbinic writings as well. At no point, however, does he actually address the issue of the root of the idea of the Messiah coming on two distinct occasions, let alone provide the basis of a coherent means of interpreting such texts in the Hebrew Bible as might be deemed relevant to this question. Not only is this so, but a perusal of his page of contents indicates that the final contribution of his book is an 'Index of Biblical References', whereas what one actually finds upon turning there is a 'Select Index of New Testament References'. He has nothing to say about this vexed question of the exegetical base in the *Hebrew Bible* of such an important Christian doctrine. And in this he is typical. The Hebrew Bible is there for general material regarding the eschatological hope of Israel for the Messiah to come to redeem the world, but the precise issue of whether this Messiah will come once, completing the work given to him by God the Father, or twice, with two distinct phases in his life and work, is ignored.

If I may now mention Arthur Kac, a man who is without doubt one of the most able thinkers in the modern Messianic Jewish movement, even he represents the common approach to the problem in that he simply states that the belief in two advents is fully biblical, and then moves on to other matters. In his book on Jesus' Messianic credentials he merely comments at one point that

> a careful analysis of the Messianic portions of the Old Testament will show that we do not have two different Messianic personalities but rather two aspects of the Messianic mission of one and the same Person.[207]

Merely repeating something does not make it true, even when the belief is shared by the people who are reading the words. This kind of rhetoric may satisfy some of the faithful, but it will never do as an argument in debate with Jewish people. So much hangs on such a little-understood doctrine. Small wonder that it comes under such attack from Jewish people.

A final point to be made is an obvious one. The Jewish community wants to know what evidence there is that *Jesus* fulfils this image of a Messiah who will come twice, even if it is conceded for the sake of argument that the Messiah might indeed come twice. Trypho said it plainly enough in his dialogue with Justin Martyr:

> Granting that even all this that you say is true, both that Christ was prophesied as about to be liable to suffering . . . and after his first advent . . . he was to come in glory . . . yet prove that this is he [ie, Jesus] about whom all this was prophesied.[208]

How would *you* respond to this argument?

---

[207] Arthur W. Kac, *The Messiahship of Jesus*, op cit, p 271.

[208] *Dialogue*, op cit, 36.1. See also 39.7.

In many respects the world has changed altogether from the time of Troki in the sixteenth century, but as we have seen from this short chapter, in the matter of Jewish challenges to the integrity of the Gospel, very little has changed. Grandfather Troki's influence is as strong as if he were only two generations away from us.

It is now time to look in greater detail at the long story of Jewish–Christian polemic and counter-polemic. How has the history of disputations affected the two communities, and in particular the Jewish community?

IO

The legacy of disputations

Having taken a look in the previous chapter at the kinds of challenges which are brought against the Messiahship of Jesus, it would be good to pause for a moment to rehearse the story of the public disputes between Christians and Jews, and to try to sense something of the impact this legacy has had on both communities. They were often little more than barely-disguised trials, and the Jewish representatives were constantly reminded that they were on the outside, merely a tolerated minority. As late as 1933, a date which causes a shudder among us, a German Protestant theologian, Karl Ludwig Schmidt, in debate with the Jewish philosopher Martin Buber, expressed this same attitude when he wrote:

> The evangelical theologian who has to talk to you, must talk to you as a member of the Church of Jesus Christ, must endeavour to talk in a manner that will convey the message of the Church to Jewry. He must do this even if you would not have invited him to do so. The assertion of a mission to you may have a somewhat bitter taste as if intending an attack; but such an attack precisely involves caring about you as Jews – so that you may live with us as our brethren in our German fatherland as throughout the world.[209]

It is profoundly distressing to read these words in the realisation that they were written at the start of the period of Hitler's rise to power in Germany. But the words have a

---

[209] Karl Ludwig Schmidt, *Theologische Blaetter*, 12 (1933), p 258.

pedigree which goes way back into history, and which is inextricably linked to the Churches' attitude to, and treatment of, Jewish people. Summoning Jewish leaders for public disputes was just one expression of the Church's frustration and contempt.

Serious conversations and public debates about Jesus were certainly taking place in the formative centuries of the two communities, as we can see not only from the direct evidence of the New Testament but also indirectly, as it were, from the rabbinic literature.[210] We actually have a fascinating glimpse of the different experiences and expertise of the rabbis in Palestine and Babylon in Roman times regarding these serious disputes with *Jewish* believers in their respective regions. There were many more Jewish believers living in Palestine at that period, and so there were significantly more opportunities for, and indeed much more need for, a sustained apologetic. We actually have a record that word had reached Palestine that some Jewish believers had come off rather well in conversation with some Babylonian rabbis. Rabbi Abbahu, a Palestinian rabbi, comments, by way of explanation, to a number of Jewish believers with whom he is in conversation:

> We who are living with you regard it as our task to study [Scripture] thoroughly. They [in Babylon] are not so well versed in it.[211]

This aside in the Talmud reveals that such discussions about the meaning of the Messianic promises and prophecies in the Hebrew Bible, etc, were probably quite common in Palestine as the new Jesus movement grew in strength and confidence. But the earliest dispute of which we have hard evidence,

---

[210] See, for example, Sifre Deuteronomy 87–91; Ecclesiastes Rabbah 1:8; 2:1; Song of Songs Rabbah 7:13; Jerusalem Talmud, Berachot 9:1; 12d–13b.

[211] Talmud, Avodah Zarah 4a.

albeit only from the Christian perspective, comes from around 160 CE. It is keenly debated among scholars today whether this actually does represent a real debate, or whether it was just a rhetorical way for the Christian to write a piece which set out to dismantle Jewish objections to the Gospel. Whatever the case may be, it certainly gives us valuable insight into the kind of arguments being used by Christians in the second century. If we adopt what would be a generous position, then it also shows us the kind of arguments which the Jewish community was using at that period. But if we prefer a more cautious approach, doubting that a Christian document would be completely faithful to the perspectives and insights of the 'opposition', then we can at least say that it tells us something about how Christians perceived and presented what the Jewish community was saying in the second century. Even this would be valuable to us.

The work we are talking about is Justin Martyr's famous *Dialogue with Trypho the Jew*. As this was written around 160 CE, it is important to note that this places it in the aftermath of the unsuccessful Bar Kochba revolt, in which the Roman legions brutally defeated the Jewish forces which were seeking to liberate their country and people from Roman oppression. It is an especially significant campaign for our purposes, since the Jewish leader of this nationalist revolt was actually hailed as the Messiah sent by God to spearhead Israel's redemption, by no less a figure than Rabbi Akiva, one of Israel's most respected teachers. This must have been a time, then, when there was some considerable debate among the Jewish people as a whole, let alone with Jewish believers specifically, about who the Messiah really was and his personal identity and mission. It is much the same now, as we noted in an earlier chapter, with the current controversy over the claim by many Lubavitsch Jews that their leader, Rabbi Schneerson, was the Messiah. The Christian faith was still an unprotected and persecuted religion at the time of this writing, and this too is a significant context for

Justin's Dialogue. He does in fact speak of the persecution of Christians in this document, and actually includes Jewish people among those who were persecuting believers. The tone of the whole piece is quite sharp. Justin asserts that the suffering of the Jewish people at the hands of the Roman powers has happened

> rightly and well. For you slew the Just One and his prophets before him, and now you reject, and, as far as you can, dishonour those who hope in him . . . cursing in your synagogues those who believe in Christ.[212]

Note that Justin is focusing here on Jewish believers, those who were still at that time seeking to remain within the synagogue community. Justin also claims that the real spiritual meaning of the text of the Hebrew Bible can only be discerned when it is read christocentrically, and he provides examples of passages with their 'proper' interpretation.[213] Trypho, who is the Jewish 'partner' in this formal Dialogue and may well be based on the Jewish scholar Rabbi Tarphon, responds to this charge in what has also become a classic way:

> Why do you select for quotation only such parts as you choose out of the sayings of the prophets, and make no mention of those [that do not fit]?[214]

Trypho attacks the worship of Jesus in the Christian community, and goes as far as to say:

> It were better for you to continue to hold the philosophy of Plato or of some learned man . . . but when you forsook God, and

---

[212] Justin Martyr, *Dialogue with Trypho the Jew*, 16.2–4.

[213] An important early collection of such passages and interpretations, as used by Christians in disputes with Jewish people, is that composed by Cyprian, and known as the *Testimoniorum libri adversus Judaeos*.

[214] Justin Martyr, op cit, 27.1.

placed your hope on a man, what kind of salvation yet remains for you?[215]

This rebuke is immediately followed by a plea to Jewish believers to repent before it is too late:

> First be circumcised, then . . . keep the Sabbath and the Feasts and God's New Moons, and, in short, do all the things that are written in the Law, and then perchance you will find mercy from God.[216]

We see Trypho attacking the doctrine of the Tri-unity of God in classic Jewish fashion, that is, on the grounds of general religious reason as well as on the grounds of it being a form of idolatry:

> For your assertion that this Christ existed, and was God, before all ages, then that he was even born and became man and suffered, and that he is not man by origin, seems to me to be not only strange, but even foolish.[217]

The climax of Trypho's presentation lies in the by now standard claim that Christianity might be fine for non-Jews, but Jewish people are not free to accept Jesus as Messiah and Lord:

> Let him be recognised by you Gentiles as Lord and Christ and God, as the Scriptures signify, seeing also that you have all acquired the name of Christians from him. But as for us, who are worshippers of God, who made even him, we do not need to confess him or worship him.[218]

Thus we see something of what was probably a typical Jewish–Christian dispute from the mid-second century CE. Another Christian writer who holds a key position in our knowledge of these first serious debates is Origen (*c* 185–254

---

[215] Op cit, 8.3.

[216] Op cit, 8.4.

[217] Op cit, 48.1. Cf 38.1.

[218] Op cit, 64.

CE). He was one of the most influential of the early Church Fathers, and he lived in Palestine soon after the Mishnah was committed to writing. This meant that he was even more able to further his study of the religious traditions of the Jewish people, especially as he spent a great deal of his time with the Jewish scholars among whom he lived. There was a good tradition of stable Jewish life and scholarship at Caesarea, on the Mediterranean coast, so Origen settled there and also established a vital Christian intellectual centre there.

Unfortunately, although there are several clear references in Origen's writings to disputations with rabbis and others, we have no actual record of any such debate.[219] He evidently engaged in much christological exegesis of texts from the Hebrew Bible, as was typical of his day, focusing on the authority of the Sinai laws as revelation of God's character and purposes; on the nature of God's covenant commitment to Israel in the light of the coming of Jesus; and on the person and work of the Messiah. His really lasting contribution, though, was his insistence that only Christians have the proper hermeneutic for understanding the Hebrew Bible, since only they are able to penetrate to the deep meanings of the texts, aided by the Holy Spirit of God. Jesus, the incarnate Word of God, is the indispensable key to unlock the Word of God which is the Bible. Therefore it is hardly surprising, says Origen, that Jewish people cannot appreciate the true nature of Jesus, or the Church, or the New Testament, since they do not properly understand their own Scriptures.[220]

---

[219] For an excellent treatment of this matter, see N. R. M. de Lange, *Origen and the Jews* (CUP, 1976).

[220] See his *Homilies on Leviticus*, 13.1; *Homilies on Isaiah*, 6.6; *Homilies on Exodus*, 12.1. This has become one of the classic Christian charges against Jewish religious consciousness, linked with the biblical allusion to the 'veil' over the eyes of the Jewish people. Favourite passages from the Bible which are commonly used in association with this charge include Isa 6:9–10 (especially in the LXX version); 2 Cor 3:7–18; Heb 8:4–6.

It is clear that Origen participated willingly and vigorously in these various disputations with Jewish scholars in Palestine. What is also clear is that on occasion he resolutely and robustly defended the Jewish people in the face of less than cordial attacks by pagan critics.[221] Putting this into its full context, it is not quite as surprising as it may sound, since we are still speaking about a period when both Christianity and Judaism were under fierce attack by aggressive pagan religions. Origen knows that in order to combat the accusation that Christianity is just a new and superficial cult, he has to demonstrate that, apart from anything else, Christianity is as old as Judaism itself and is the proper fulfilment of the prophecies of the biblical prophets. Many of the challenges to Jewish beliefs were indirect challenges to Christian beliefs too, and so Origen is keen to do battle with these pagan philosophers and practitioners.

It becomes a moot point, then, and one which occupies scholars to this day, as to the extent of Origen's respect for the Jewish faith and people. Was he defending them, or simply engaging in a self-serving act of theologising? In either case, there are certainly precious few models in history like his, of Christians and Jews actually standing together to fight against the common enemy of paganism. It is only really in our own day that we see this type of active co-operation back on the agenda, as Jews and Christians call for co-operation in combating the common enemy of a dominant and creeping secularism.

We should also note that Origen is familiar with some of the scurrilous tales about Jesus which are found in the Talmud and which later surface in the *Toldot Yeshu*, the medieval collection we looked at in an earlier chapter. He is also well aware of the infamous Birkat ha-Minim, the

---

[221] This counter-challenge to the pagan philosophers is best seen in Origen's seminal work, *Contra Celsum*. This was probably written in 248 CE. See chapter 6 of the book by de Lange mentioned above.

controversial 'blessing' in the synagogue service which was intended to help to identify and oust Jewish believers from the synagogue community.[222]

When we turn to Jewish sources for the first centuries CE, we find that very little is recorded there about disputes with Christians, whether Jewish or not. There are several reasons for this:

- in general, references to Jesus and to Christians, especially Jewish believers, were clearly suppressed by the Jewish authorities with the aim of giving the impression that, to the Jewish community at least, it was all insignificant;
- a further reason for this reluctance to have such discussions in their literature was the desire to prevent their young men from becoming too aware of, and intrigued by, this belief in the Messiahship of Jesus;
- there was also a fear among many that there might be reprisals from the Christian political authorities if any references to Jesus or Christians were not seen as positive; it was therefore easier to keep references to a bare minimum and to disguise any such references as much as possible;
- perhaps, finally, it was also the case that since Judaism was altogether in a state of creative flux after the loss of its temple base in 70 CE, and since the rabbis did not know whether or not this Messianic faith in Jesus would endure, there was no desire to embody what might prove to be only interim disputes between the communities in a permanent religious record.

Whatever the interplay of reasons, there are only scattered references of any sort in the Jewish sources, and these are not

---

[222] *Homilies on the Psalms*, Psalm 37, 2.8. See also Justin Martyr's references to this, a century or so earlier, in his *Dialogue*, op cit, 16, 47, 93, 96, 107, 117, 137.

at all easy to interpret with any historical precision.[223] For instance, there is an account that 'Yeshu ha-Notsri' (Jesus of Nazareth) 'burned his food in public'. This metaphor is saying that he became a heretic and an apostate, causing public scandal and demoralisation.[224] Only from the end of the Tannaitic period do we find a rabbi, Eliezer ha-Kappar, accusing Jesus of exalting himself as a god, and this presumably reflects something of the growing disputes between the Jewish community and the consolidating churches.[225] From the third century on, we have Amoraim who are said to have been known for their involvement in disputes of various sorts with Christians. Some of these famous named scholars were Joshua ben Levi, Bar Kappara, Hoshaiah, Abbahu, Simlai and Idi.[226] Rabbi Abbahu says the following when discussing the issue of Jesus' divinity:

> If someone will tell you, 'I am God', he is a liar; 'I am the son of man', his end is that he will regret it; 'I am going to heaven', he says this but he will not fulfil it.

Here we have a clear rejection of the possibility of Jesus being divine and, further, a word of condemnation on him for daring to state or imply it. Thereafter, from the fourth century onwards, the strength and range of the Jewish

---

[223] Readers are advised to work through the book, *Christianity in Talmud and Midrash*, op cit, by R. Travers Herford, for help in this technical process.

[224] Sanhedrin 103a. Other texts tend to suggest that this metaphor carries with it the implication that he led others astray with him: see Sanhedrin 43a; 107b; Sotah 47b.

[225] Yalkut Shim'oni 765, 66, relating to Num 23:7.

[226] Berachot 7a; Shemot Rabbah 29:4; Jerusalem Talmud, Shabbat 6a; Bereshit Rabbah 1:1; Jerusalem Talmud, Ta'anit 65b; Shemot Rabbah 29:5; Jerusalem Talmud, Berachot 9:1; Bereshit Rabbah 9; Sanhedrin 38b; Yalkut Shemot 359. A summary of the calumnies of Jesus can be found in Jocz, op cit, pp 57–60.

challenges to Jesus increase markedly. Judah bar Shalom, a fourth-century sage, taught:

> When God said to Moses, 'Write!', Moses also requested that the Mishnah should be given in writing. But God anticipated that the Gentiles would translate the Torah, read it in Greek, and say, 'We are Israel, and we are the children of God, and henceforth, the scales are balanced.' God said to the Gentiles, 'You say that you are my children. I only know that those who possess my secret writings are my children.' And what are these writings? The Mishnah.[227]

We note in passing here the casual dismissal of the Septuagint as a Gentile translation of the Hebrew Bible. As we have seen, this was not actually the case, but it has become a commonplace misapprehension within the Jewish community. The dispute has evidently broadened to embrace the two fundamental hermeneutical contexts:

a) What is the true Word of God?
b) Who are the true people of God, able to recognise the true God at work in the world and in the Scriptures?

In the fourth century, relationships generally became much more bitter and recriminatory after Christianity became the official religion of the Roman empire. Judaism and the Jewish people were subjected to fierce attacks by John Chrysostom and other Church Fathers, not least because many Christians were evidently full of respect for the Jewish people. However, in spite of this, ordinary Christians still maintained a great deal of respect for Jewish values and for interpretations of certain biblical principles, and this enflamed the preachers even more. The *systematic* teaching of contempt for Judaism and the Jewish people began. Although not much has been preserved in any detail, we do have some evidence in remarks and notes found in certain

---

[227] Tanhuma Va-Yera 5.

works about disputes in the fifth to the tenth centuries. The really terrible story, of course, is some of the actions carried out against Jewish people in this period. How many Christians know the story of a Jewish merchant, Priscus, who resisted the pressures to convert to Christianity and was subsequently murdered on his way to synagogue one Sabbath by a Jewish 'convert' to Christianity?[228]

And yet this was only one part of the story. At the same time as the above type of incident was being perpetrated and often going uninvestigated, let alone unpunished, Eugene Fisher can draw our attention to the fact that:

> Pope Gregory I in the late sixth century established the norms that were to guide canon law regarding the Jews during the Middle Ages: no forced conversion of Jews, no disruption of Jewish worship, charity in practice. Throughout this period, until at least the turn of the first millenium, relations were marked by frequent and largely friendly contacts. As late as the ninth and tenth centuries, for example, we still find bishops complaining that too many of their flocks are going to the rabbis rather than the priests for blessings.[229]

Sadly, however, a rather limited number of the public disputations of the period seem to have shared this ethos of respect. But to give an example of a disputation carried out in a courteous, open and fair manner, we can note one that was organised in 1090 or thereabouts by Gilbert Crispin, a disciple of St Anselm and Abbot of Westminster. No name has been preserved for us for the Jewish speaker, who came from Mainz in Germany, but his major point was one which we have already rehearsed, namely that the troubled state of

---

[228] The story is recounted by Bishop Gregory of Tours in the *Historiarum libri decem*. The incident took place in Paris, in 581 CE.

[229] Eugene Fisher, in *Christian Jewish Relations*, vol 18, no 3 (1985), p 13.

the world was proof enough that Jesus was not the promised Messiah.[230]

The age of the bitter, specific works of refutation had not yet really dawned in the Jewish world. It is significant to note that the first Jewish works to contain serious refutations of Christian teachings were in fact biblical commentaries, for example those of Rashi (1035–1105), not distinct books of polemic at all.[231] It is only as we enter the violent twelfth century that, under terrible pressure from the Church's crusading spirit and actions, Jewish leaders felt the impetus to produce works to combat the aggressive and triumphalistic spirit and teachings of the Church.

From then on, a recurring event in the Jewish world was the publication and circulation among the Jewish communities of polemical anti-Christian treatises. These were often given the generic title of a *Nizzahon*, a Hebrew word meaning a 'victory'.[232] The Jewish communities were never going to be able to resist the military might of the Christian forces, or the mob riots of the Christian peasants, but they could win

---

[230] This disputation was written up in a report from Crispin to Anselm, named *Gisleberti Crispini Disputatio Judei et Christiani*. An edited version of it was published in 1956 by B. Blumenkranz.

[231] See the fine article by Erwin I. J. Rosenthal, 'Anti-Christian Polemic in Medieval Bible Commentaries', *Journal of Jewish Studes*, vol 11, nos 3 and 4 (1960), pp 115–35.

[232] This, in fact, became no more than a technical name for a disputational polemic. See O. S. Rankin, *Jewish Religious Polemic*, op cit, pp 49f. The most important such polemics of the twelfth to the seventeenth centuries are the following: *Milhamot Adonai*, by Jacob ben Ruben (1170); *Sefer ha-Brit*, by Joseph Kimchi (1170); *Even Bohan*, by Isaac Shaprut (1380); *Al Tehi Ka-avotekha*, by Profiat Duran (1396); *Kelimmat ha-Goyim*, by Profiat Duran (1397); *Nizzahon*, by Rabbi Lipmann (c 1401–1405); *Bittul Ikkere ha-Notsrim*, by Hasdai Crescas (1410); *Ezer ha-Da'at*, by Isaac Pulgar (1420); *Nizzahon*, by Yomtov Lipmann Mulhausen (1420); *Hizzuk Emunah*, by Isaac ben Abraham Troki (1593); *Magen wa-Herev*, by Leon de Modena (1630); and *Vindiciae Judaeorum*, by Manasseh ben Israel (1656).

'moral victories', as they saw it, by demonstrating to themselves that these Christians were following a false god and
inferior values. Surely God would some day grant to Israel
the final 'victory' over these enemies? Joseph Kimhi, for
instance, attacked the Christian lifestyle as proof that Christians were not inspired by God to follow Jesus:

> You cannot claim that you are circumcised in heart, for he who
> . . . murders and whores and robs and molests people, ridicules
> them and behaves like a brigand, is uncircumcised both in heart
> and body. For you will not find a Jew whom they [ie, the Jews]
> will hang, neither will they gouge out his eyes, nor will they
> mutilate one of his members for any transgression that he may
> have committed.[233]

An anonymous twelfth-century work focused on the venera-
tion of Mary and the saints in the Roman Catholic Church, a
criticism which became very common.[234] In the first of the
two late fourteenth-century works by Profiat Duran mentioned in note 232, he claims that the Christian faith is
simply irrational, and he is heavily critical of what he sees
as the Christian reliance on 'feelings' and 'faith alone'. In his
second work he turned his attention to exposing what he
called the inaccuracies and contradictions in the New Testament, as well as poor Christian translations and understandings of the Hebrew Bible.

At the turn of the sixteenth century, Abraham Farissol
argued strongly in his work that Jesus of Nazareth might
very well be the way to the God of Israel for non-Jews, but
only that.[235] Much later in the century, a doctor in Constantinople closely argued the case that only the *Hebrew* text of
the Hebrew Bible could legitimately be used in any sort of

---

[233] Joseph Kimhi, *Sefer ha-Brit* (1170), 26b.
[234] *The Old Nizzahon* (late twelfth century), 128–32.
[235] Abraham Farissol, *Magen Abraham* (*c* 1500), 38.

proof-texting exercise.[236] This has become a standard argument, of course, and one which Christians must take very seriously, in my view.

So there is a substantial amount of written work from the latter part of the Middle Ages to the dawn of the modern period, and this material is considered to be definitive in the religious Jewish world, having been written by the giants of halakhic and exegetical scholarship. Very little of substance has been added in the work of modern refutationists, since they naturally rely on this authoritative tradition. This is why it is so important to read the medieval material. But of course this material, which was being written by Jewish scholars for Jewish people, was probably quite different from the attitude taken in confrontations with Christians. These public disputations had a massive impact on the Jewish tradition as well, setting the tone and supplying the material for most of what has happened since. In our own day, as I have pointed out more than once, the very same material is still being used, although the tone of the presentation has changed completely.

For interest's sake, here are some of the most significant and influential disputes from the twelfth to the eighteenth centuries.[237]

Paris. In 1240, the French king, Louis IX, called a disputation to take place in front of the high French clergy, and various state dignitaries. It lasted three days in the June of that year. The Christian protagonist was an infamous Jewish

---

[236] Abraham Ibn Migash, *Kevod Elohim* (1585), *passim*.

[237] The three which are usually singled out by authors for discussion are those which took place at Paris, Barcelona and Tortosa. For specific discussion of these three, see Hyam Maccoby, *Judaism on Trial* (1982); Hans Joachim Schoeps, *The Jewish–Christian Argument*, op cit; Oscar Skarsaune, 'The Jewish–Christian Dialogue in Ancient and Modern Times', *Mishkan*, no 3 (1985), pp 14–27.

'convert' called Nicolas Donin, and the chief Jewish defendant was Rabbi Yehiel ben Joseph. Donin petitioned the king to direct that the dispute focus on the Talmud, which he did, and Donin proceeded to make thirty-five attacks on its spiritual and moral integrity, as it were. Ben Joseph acquitted himself rather well, but he could not prevent the foregone conclusion of the Christian court that the Talmud was an obstruction to the Gospel. Donin was deemed by the Church to have ably demonstrated his case that the Talmud was not part of God's Law, but rather contained blasphemies against Christianity and a great deal of nonsense. Shortly afterwards, twenty-four wagonloads of copies of the Talmud were confiscated and burned in the city square.[238]

Cluny. In 1254, the Abbot of Cluny engaged in a celebrated debate with Nathan ben Joseph Official, who wrote an influential refutation of the classic christological passages in the Hebrew Bible, a work known as *Yosef ha-Mekanne*. The result of this disputation could perhaps best be described as an honourable draw. In fact there was a second, minor, disputation that same year in Cluny. This was in part a consequence of the former one, but there was no honour involved on the Christian bench, indeed the Jewish participant was actually killed by a Christian knight for speaking openly about his objections to the Gospel.

Barcelona. In 1263 Rabbi Moses Nachmanides was compelled by King James of Aragon, at the initiative of a notorious Jewish 'convert' Pablo Christiani, to debate three questions in a public court. The three questions were:

---

[238] The basis of these notions was a condemnation of the Talmud in 1233 by Pope Gregory IX. For the text of this influential ruling, see Solomon Grayzel, *The Church and the Jews in the Thirteenth Century* (Philadelphia, JPSA, 1933), p 241, n 96.

a) Has the promised Messiah already come, or not?

b) Was the promised Messiah to be divine, or not?

c) Was the promised Messiah to die as the atonement for the sin of the world, or not?

Christiani was confident that he had a tactic which would demonstrate once and for all the clear superiority of Christianity over Judaism. He worked from the text of the Talmud whenever he had the opportunity. To be able to prove one's own case from the distinctive texts of the opposition would be a strategic *tour de force*, as Christiani knew well, and this was precisely his boast – that he could actually prove the truth of Christianity from the very pages of the Talmud. However, he had met more than his match in Nachmanides, who was superbly gifted both in temperament and in the appropriate apologetic skills. He answered all three questions in the negative, exposed the shallow nature of Christiani's grasp of Jewish theology and even dared, ironically, to flaunt the rise of Islam over Christianity in certain parts of the world as possible evidence of Islam's superiority over Christianity. In strict terms, he 'won' the dispute and everyone at the court knew it.

As a result, Nachmanides was eventually banished for life from his home country of Spain. The Pope himself brought his influence to bear on this situation, so outraged was the Church at losing this much-advertised and prestigious dispute. He left for Palestine, and arrived there in 1267, to live out his days in the land of Israel. There were three further significant outcomes of the dispute: Nachmanides himself published an account of the whole affair, serving as an inspiration to the Jewish communities (in fact this was a major factor in the decision of the authorities to exile him); the tactic of using Jewish materials to demonstrate the truth of the Gospel was maintained in an effort to justify the principle, even though Pablo Christiani had been less than successful in implementing that principle (this was done in an important book of 1280 by Raymond Martini called *Pugio Fidei*); a Papal Bull, *Turbato Corde*, was later issued as a rationale and license for burning the Talmud and prosecuting suspected 'Judaisers'.

Tortosa. Once again the initiative was taken by a Jewish 'convert', Joshua Lorki, who took the Christian name Geronimo de Sante-Fe. In 1413–14 this major disputation took place before Pope Benedict XIII, who presided over the proceedings. It lasted twenty months and involved sixty-nine sessions! Although the Jewish representation was headed at first by Don Vidal Ben-Benveniste Ibn Labi, it was an eminent Jewish scholar Joseph Albo who really emerged to represent the Jewish case. He was incensed when he realised that this disputation was in fact little more than a pseudo-trial, ranging over the various Christian doctrines and the gamut of anti-Jewish feelings held by the Christians involved.

Many forced conversions and mob riots against Jewish communities followed the completion of the disputation. Another significant outcome was the issuing of another Papal Bull in 1415 which forbade the study of the Talmud.

Rimini. There was a relatively urbane debate in 1447 between several Jewish scholars and one Giannozzo Manetti. The by-now-standard arguments were brought out on both sides, and nothing remarkable transpired.

Rome. A Franciscan friar, John of Capistrano, who was without doubt a man who harboured profound and active antisemitic feelings, organised a public disputation in 1450. It resulted in an embattled draw but in 1455, still angry at the relative success of the Jewish representative, another friar, Calixtus, instigated riots against the Jewish communities in the region.

Kamienec and Lvov.   In 1757 and 1759 a two-part disputation took place between leaders of Polish Jewry on the one hand, and Jacob Frank and his followers on the other. Frank is an extremely interesting person. He was a Polish devotee of the false Messiah, Shabbetai Tzvi, who actually converted to Islam at one point in his career. Frank followed suit and also converted. When he came under threat from the Jewish community he appealed for protection to the Roman Catholic Church. The Bishop of Kamienec granted this, considering that Frank's movement might well be ripe for conversion at last to the 'true faith'. Frank was 'earnestly encouraged' to debate with the local rabbis in what amounted to an anti-Talmudic protest, and indeed after both disputes many Talmuds were seized and burned.

The sixteenth century also saw the birth of the Reformation, of course, and the rise of the Protestant Churches. Born with them was a reawakening of the impulse to be involved in mission to the world, and this very definitely included a profound desire to witness to the Jewish people about the Messiahship of Jesus. The major factors which led to the strong focus on this witness to Jewish people were the passionate concern for knowing the original languages and cultural contexts of the biblical Testaments, including the Hebrew Bible; a related deep desire to recover the God-givenness of Israelite life and culture; a rediscovery of the important role of the Jewish people in the eschatalogical prophecies in the Hebrew Bible; the impact of the Jewish refutations against the Messiahship of Jesus; and the excitement engendered by the thought that it might now be possible to lead the Jewish nation, *en masse*, to faith in Jesus.

The idealism of Luther himself, and others after him, turned soon enough, tragically, into frustration and rage at the 'determined unbelief' of the Jewish people. Luther's conviction that the Jewish people would quickly turn to faith in Jesus when they were approached in the correct manner and with the right understanding of the Christian faith, was discredited when there was no such mass turning to the new Churches. Shameful things were said by Luther (and others) when he realised that the Jewish people were intent on keeping their own faith intact. Since that time, even though the Protestant Churches, as a rule, have not been as guilty of overt violence against Jewish people as have the Roman Catholic Church and the Orthodox Churches of eastern Europe, their hands are not clean. And certainly as we turn to the twentieth-century Nazi atrocities against the Jewish people, we see a strong appeal being made by Hitler and his top aides to the invective of Luther, as well as to the attitude of other historical church leaders.

Besides all of this, the Jewish people soon saw that they were still basically serving as pawns in Luther's strategy for engineering the return of Christ and the end of the world, and of course they naturally resented what they saw to be a self-serving and patronising Christian theology. We may note, however, that this theology was to play an increasing role in the modern era.

When we come forward to the modern era, that is, into the nineteenth century, we find that in western societies, particularly in Britain and America, the Jewish people were being granted more and more freedom and respect. Public burnings of the Talmud, etc, were not acceptable. But we also find that there was a surge in Jewish refutationist publications, particularly in America. The *theological* reason for this was the rise of a second wave of enthusiastic and confident missionary zeal among Protestants, coupled with a strong interest in the teaching of the New Testament about Christ's thousand-year reign on earth. Although there was a considerable range of views on the various details of the return and millenarian reign of Christ, all of those who were committed to seeing it come about in their generation, and there were many, agreed that somehow the Jewish people had a significant role to play.

Conversionist sermons were preached and published, and whole mission societies devoted to Jewish ministry were established. According to W. T. Gidney, twenty-eight Jewish missions were founded between 1809 and 1896![239] This time, the Jewish community not only felt obliged to respond, but also found that it was in a social context where a confident response was actually possible. Once again, the Jewish people saw themselves and their purpose in life being defined by Christians, but in this case they determined to speak out more boldly than they had in earlier generations. Once again, their leaders cried, Christians spoke as if they were concerned for the Jewish people, whereas their sole concern was the fulfilment of their own theological agenda.[240]

The overall legacy of this history of refutation, particularly the history of public disputations, has been negative in the extreme, as can readily be appreciated from even this brief overview. The polemics and counter-polemics have instilled in the Jewish community a wariness of any sort of public debate with Christians. They have also hardened the Jewish community against what have become the standard Christian arguments for the integrity of the Gospel. Moreover, these disputations have provided the Jewish community with its perception of the Jewish convert to Christianity as an enemy of the Jewish people, keen to misrepresent the Jewish people in order to promote personal acceptance within the Christian community. They have convinced the Jewish people that there is a hidden and cruel agenda behind every Christian invitation to a serious conversation.

Christians, on the other hand, tend to have knowledge neither about these events themselves, nor about their sig-

---

[239] W. T. Gidney, *The Jews and their Evangelization*, Appendix A (Student Volunteer Missionary Union, London, 1907), pp 120f.

[240] For this nineteenth-century explosion of Jewish works on Jesus and Christianity see my book, *Jesus Ben Joseph*, op cit, chapters 7 and 8.

nificance. I have often taken part in conversations in which Christians have barely been able to disguise their irritation at Jewish people for wanting to refer to medieval events and personalities. These Christians want everything to happen within the existential present, so that what may or may not have taken place in the past is dismissed as irrelevant and a distraction from the real business at hand. Jewish sensitivities are quite different, however, and all contemporary debates are seen as continuations of the historical process. This perspective needs to be learned and appreciated by Christians who wish to be involved in meaningful Jewish–Christian dialogue of any sort.

After this short historical chapter, we need to return to an analysis of the macro-level theological issues, to make sure that we are quite aware of the current, active Jewish philosophical/theological agenda. We shall find, however, that this agenda is still dealing with the very fabric of the legacy of centuries of dispute.

11

Hermeneutics and ambiguity revisited

Throughout the Middle Ages and up to the dawn of the modern era there were three areas of fundamental disagreement, philosophically-speaking, between the Christian and the Jewish communities. We have referred to each of these in this book at different times, but we shall now attempt to analyse them more maturely, now that we are more aware of the broader perspectives and larger contexts. These three fundamental areas were (and are):

- the correct way to read the text of Scripture
- the correct way to read the events of history
- the correct way to relate reason and experience to faith.

We shall look at each of these areas of conflict in turn. They are certainly all basic issues, and anyone who has had any serious conversations with Jewish people will recognise them as very much at the forefront of the contemporary scene.

Reading scripture: text and meaning

As we have seen, there was considerable disagreement over the correct methods of interpreting the texts of the Hebrew Bible. These differences of opinion concerning the proper hermeneutic also extended to the New Testament and the Talmud (as well as the other rabbinic works), which is hardly surprising. The New Testament and the Talmud are the authoritative 'lenses' through which the two communities look at and interpret the Hebrew Bible. Christians claim that the Hebrew Bible cannot be properly understood apart from the New Testament, and Jewish people claim that the Hebrew Bible has no independent existence apart from the Oral Torah.

Both communities – and this is very important indeed – agree that the Hebrew Bible cannot stand on its own within the community of faith which regards it as part of its divine revelation. The difference between the two lies in the choice of texts which are believed to faithfully exegete and expound the Hebrew Bible. To put it another way, each community acknowledges the need for a lens through which to see the Hebrew Bible in complete focus: for the Christians, this lens is the New Testament, and for the Jews, it is the Oral Torah. Both communities therefore constantly quote from their other authoritative texts in the hermeneutical debates while at the same time concentrating on the text which they have in common. It is basically in the message of their *common* Scripture that Christians and Jews seek both to establish their own beliefs and also to refute those of the other.

On one level the issue was textual, pure and simple. The Synagogue accepted only the Masoretic Hebrew text as authoritative, while the western Church not only accepted the Greek LXX as inspired and trustworthy, but also used the Latin translation of the Bible, the so-called Vulgate, as its basic biblical text. We saw above how the readings of the Hebrew and the LXX do not always agree, and the same is true if we compare the Hebrew with the Vulgate. This is especially significant for some passages considered by Christians as of paramount importance regarding the life and ministry of the Messiah, eg, Ps 110:1; Dan 9:24; Ps 22:16.[241] As a result of these and other discrepancies regarding the true nature of the biblical text, what we might expect

---

[241] For a discussion of this point, see Daniel J. Lasker, *Jewish Philosophical Polemics against Christianity in the Middle Ages*, op cit, pp 173f.

to find is indeed what we do find: each community accused the other of tampering with the text.

The Vulgate was largely the work of an outstanding biblical scholar called Jerome, who was fully aware of the fact that any good translation of the Bible would have to be based on the original text. To this end he studied Hebrew, living in Bethlehem as he learned and translated. However, even he had to bow to official pressure from the church authorities, and the influence of the LXX on the final work is unmistakable. Troki comments on the Church's Bible in this fashion:

> We know well that Jerome has made a practice of accommodating Scripture to the notions of his own creed.[242]

Profiat Duran, mentioned above, calls Jerome 'the corrupter', and Abraham Farissol, whom we also noted earlier, devotes a whole chapter in his work to what he calls Jerome's inadequate and erroneous translations. To this very day the perception in the Jewish community is that Christian Bibles, even those Hebrew versions of the Hebrew Bible which have been produced by Christian publishing houses, are not the same as Jewish Bibles, and are not at all to be trusted. How many times have I had to wait until a Jewish person has found a Hebrew Bible published by a *Jewish* publishing house before we could agree that something which I said was in the original text, was indeed in the original text! Copies of the Hebrew Bible which are published (and distributed to theological students, for instance) by Christian Bible translation agencies will not be acceptable to many Jewish people, so ingrained is this distrust of the Christian text. It would certainly be wiser to buy a copy of the Hebrew Bible published by a Jewish publisher, and this would relate to translations as well as to Hebrew versions.

---

[242] *Faith Strengthened*, op cit, 1:21.

On another level, the textual issue concerned the definition of what was to be regarded as the text of the Word of God. Neither Jews nor Christians were prepared to examine a text in the Hebrew Bible without seeing it in its wider perspective, and this included not only the rest of the Hebrew Bible but also the second part of their respective 'canons'. Is the New Testament to be accepted as an indispensable part of God's revelation, and therefore relevant to questions about the meaning of passages in the Hebrew Bible? Is the Talmud (and other works, such as the midrashim) to be so accepted?

We have already noted that the precise meaning of words and phrases was often a crucial issue, and both communities insisted that their 'lens-text', to coin a phrase, whether the New Testament or the Talmud, gave the correct interpretation. From the Christian perspective, this was beautifully summed up by Martin Luther in the first quarter of the sixteenth century. We shall look at his words in a moment, but I want first to preface them by introducing and quoting a quite remarkable passage from the Talmud.

In this passage, some rabbis are reflecting on the implications of the fact that God has chosen to entrust the Jewish people with the words of the Torah. God's revealed word is to be the standard by which everything else is judged. After all, that is precisely what the 'canon' of Scripture means. Apart from anything else, this means that if someone comes along at any time and claims to have knowledge of God and his ways at the level of 'revelation', then even that person, with his or her knowledge, is to be judged in the light of the already-given Torah. It cannot be superseded or abrogated.

The New Testament shares the same concern, of course. Life is full of people who claim to be speaking in the name of God, and it is of the utmost importance that a faith-community which believes that God speaks to his people should have criteria for deciding what is authentic and what is not. This is a major part of the background to Paul's insistence that

If anyone speaks in a tongue, two – or at the most three – should speak, one at a time, and someone must interpret. If there is no interpreter, the speaker should keep quiet in the church and speak to himself and God.[243]

The Church must be able to understand clearly what is being offered in the name of God so that it can decide, in accordance with the revealed word of God, whether it is to be received. Paul says that the same holds for the claim to have a prophetic word from God. Such words are not to be accepted at face value, but tested. As Paul sums it up for us: 'The spirits of prophets are subject to the control of prophets.'[244]

It is not insignificant that the New Testament actually closes with words about this very issue. It is a matter of supreme concern to Christians (as to Jewish people) that the fundamental revelation of God given in the word of God should be clearly and precisely defined. And of course it says at the end of the Book of Revelation:

I warn everyone who hears the words of the prophecy of this book: If anyone adds anything to them, God will add to him the plagues described in this book. And if anyone takes words away from this book of prophecy, God will take away from him his share in the tree of life and in the holy city, which are described in this book.[245]

There is no doubting the fundamental importance of establishing the firm text of Scripture, nor can there be any doubt that this written text was regarded as having priority over any subsequent claims to revelation. This whole issue is presented in a particularly attractive and didactic way in the Talmud passage which I wish to quote now:

On a certain occasion R. Eliezer used all possible arguments to

---

[243] 1 Cor 14:27f.
[244] 1 Cor 14:29–32.
[245] Rev 22:18f.

substantiate his opinion, but the Rabbis did not accept it. He said, 'If I am right, may this carob tree move a hundred yards from its place.' It did so . . . They said, 'From a tree no proof can be brought.' Then he said, 'May the canal prove it.' The water of the canal flowed backwards. They said, 'Water cannot prove anything.' Then he said, 'May the walls of this House of Study prove it.' Then the walls of the house bent inwards, as if they were about to fall. But R. Joshua rebuked the walls, and said to them, 'If the learned dispute about the Halakah [the rule, the Law], what has that to do with you?' So, to honour R. Joshua, the walls did not fall down, but to honour R. Eliezer, they did not become quite straight again. Then R. Eliezer said, 'If I am right, let the heavens prove it.' Then a heavenly voice said, 'What have you against R. Eliezer? The Halakah is always with him [his view is always right].' Then R. Joshua got up and said, 'It is not in heaven' (Deut 30:12). What did he mean by this? R. Joshua said, 'The Law was given us from Sinai. We pay no attention to a heavenly voice . . . '[246]

What is being said in this wonderful passage is that no-one, no matter how well-respected he or she may be as a scholar and religious leader, is to be allowed to appeal to miracles or visions, etc, rather than to the revealed and accepted words of revelation, when it comes to establishing right doctrine or practice.

Whether Martin Luther knew this passage I'm not sure, but there is something of an echo of it in the way he expressed his conviction that the New Testament was the definitive lens by which to understand correctly the words of the Torah. In a discussion of the correct interpretation of Isa 7:14, where one of the points at issue is the translation of a Hebrew word which might mean 'virgin' and might only mean 'young woman', whether virgin or not, Luther defers to Matthew's quotation and translation of the word in his gospel. Matthew's text has the Greek word for a virgin (*parthenos*),

---

[246] Baba Metzia' 59b, as quoted in C. G. Montefiore and H. Loewe (eds), *A Rabbinic Anthology* (Schocken Books, NY, 1938), ad loc.

and this settles the matter for Luther. It opens up the wider issue of trustworthy interpretations, however, and Luther uses this Isaianic text as a case study. He says that we can be confident that

> Isaiah interpreted '*alma*' as 'virgin'. We can believe him [Matthew] more than all the world, particularly the Jews. And if an angel were to speak from heaven: 'It does not mean virgin' – we would not believe this. For God, the Holy Spirit, goes through St. Matthew and Luke, and speaks . . . [247]

Here we have a delightful analogue to the Talmudic passage. Luther, representing a consensus within Christendom at this point, is asserting that the New Testament witness to the meaning of the Hebrew Bible is always to be accepted as the correct witness. No other interpretation or claim to a revealed and inspired truth is to be entertained.

Jews and Christians, then, in their own ways, both saw themselves as people of the Book. Neither of the communities, however, was really willing to respect, let alone to accept, the distinctive and definitive text of the other.

The Jewish community simply denigrated the New Testament, with some rabbinic wits going so far as to create a popular pun on the Greek word for 'good news', which is *evangelion*. This is, of course, the word which gives the English language the term 'evangelism'. So whereas the Christian community took a stand on the *evangelion*, the Jewish community came to refer to it, using Hebrew words which sounded like it, as the *aven gillayon* or the *avon gillayon*. The first of these phrases means 'a lie of blank paper', while the second one means 'sinfulness of blank paper'.[248] Origen records that in the second century CE the denigration of the New Testament as worthless Christian

---

[247] Martin Luther, *WA* 11 (1523), 321, 18–26.

[248] This pun is actually found as early as the Talmud. See Tosefta Shabbat 13:5; Shabbat 116a.

propaganda was already common in the Jewish community.[249]

For their part, Christians mercilessly attacked the Talmud as a source of blasphemous teaching, alien to the spirit and intention of the Hebrew Bible.[250] All the same, as we have seen, this did not prevent some Christian polemicists from trying to use it in a tactical fashion to confirm Christian teaching about Jesus' divinity, the Tri-unity of God, etc.[251]

The basic problem, then, is that Jews and Christians share a common bedrock of revelation, the Hebrew Bible, but then differ entirely as to the second and more definitive part of their accepted revealed text. Neither community can authentically suspend their commitment to the second text when they read and study the Hebrew Bible, and so appeals to 'the Word of God' will always involve some controversy. On top of this we have the second problem that each community has more than its share of adherents who love to ridicule and denigrate the 'lens-text' of the other community.

This second, and vexed problem is one which lies at the heart of the strained relationship between Christians and Jews. One of the factors which aggravates the whole situation is the ignorance which each community has of the other's 'lens-text'. My constant plea is that Christians spend some quality time reading and studying the rabbinic texts, trying to understand what they are really doing, and that

---

[249] Origen, *Contra Celsum* 1.28, 32.

[250] One example of a passage taken to be blasphemously anti-Christian was Avodah Zarah 2:1. Justin Martyr refers to this issue in his *Dialogue*, op cit, 16–17. As a matter of interest, in the Paris disputation of 1240 which has already been mentioned, Yehiel ben Joseph responded to this particular accusation by declaring that the idolaters and the Jesus mentioned in that actual Talmudic text were not Christians and Jesus of Nazareth, but another group altogether. See Lasker, op cit, pp 175–6.

[251] With respect to Jesus' Messiahship, a favourite passage was Sanhedrin 97a–b; 98a.

Jewish people do the same with the New Testament. Is this too much to ask?

The third whole area of dispute within this issue of reading the text properly was, of course, the correct way to interpret the text once it was agreed upon. In our previous chapter on hermeneutics we looked at the traditional Jewish system called *Pardes*, and the richness of interpretation which was available to the Jewish exegete, but when it came down to it, the real dispute between Jews and Christians was usually over whether a text should be read literally or allegorically (figuratively, as it was called in the Middle Ages). By and large, the Christian polemicists tended to favour the figurative approach to the texts which they considered important in debates with Jewish people. Accordingly, we find Jewish community leaders often stressing the priority of a literal approach.

But as a matter of fact, it is well known that the rabbis were masters at using both forms of interpretation when it suited them, as indeed were the Christian theologians. Here is a revealing piece of 'dialogue' between a Jewish believer and a rabbinic Jew in Rabbi Meir ben Simon's famous twelfth-century work, *The Book of the Covenant*. Note that the one who believes in Jesus is the one who is called here a *min*, a heretic/sectarian, this being a term we looked at in an earlier chapter of this book. And note also that the rabbinic Jew is called a *ma'amin*, this being a Hebrew word for a faithful believer, and ironically (deliberately so) the term generally used by Jewish believers of themselves!

> The min said: You understand most of the Torah literally, while we understand it figuratively. Your whole reading of the Bible is erroneous for you resemble him who gnaws at the bone, while we [suck at] the marrow within. You are like the beast that eats the chaff, while we [eat] the wheat.
>
> The ma'amin said: Tell me. When the Holy One, blessed be He, gave the Torah to Moses who taught it to Israel, did he understand it figuratively or not? If you say that he did not

understand it figuratively but literally and taught it so to Israel, then Israel is not to be held accountable in this matter. If you say that he understood it figuratively, why did he not teach it to Israel figuratively? For that matter, why did the prophets who came after him not do so? . . . Know that the fact is that the Torah is not [to be taken] altogether literally or altogether figuratively.[252]

We shall see in Part Two of this book how the two communities moved between the literal and the allegorical in their treatment of key texts *vis-à-vis* one another. Quite often the strategy which was chosen to win an argument involved the suppression of interpretations not known to the other community, and there was usually more freedom of interpretation within each of the two communities of scholars than was allowed to be expressed in the specific context of public disputations with one another. This is still the case, of course.

Reading history: events and meaning

The second area of fundamental disagreement was over the correct way to interpret historical events and trends. Both faith-communities are based on the premise that theirs is a historical faith, which is to say that God acts and makes himself known through the medium of real life, of historical reality. Therefore both of them are particularly sensitive, if not downright vulnerable, to what happens in history. Both the Jewish and the Christian traditions affirm that you cannot build acceptable theology on a faulty reading of history. One of the basic Christian polemical arguments was that history itself had shown conclusively that the Jewish people were under the condemnation of God. The Roman destruction of Jerusalem and the temple; the exile and thorough demoralisation of the Jewish people; and the ascendancy of the

---

[252] Rabbi Meir ben Simon, *Sefer Ha-Berit*, op cit, 25b–26a.

Christian faith, were all part of a historic package signalling God's final pronouncement of judgement on the Jewish people. They had finally disobeyed God in an unforgivable way by rejecting his Son and handing him over to the Roman authorities to be executed. In short, they were getting what they deserved.[253] Above all, this interpretation of the history of the Jewish people, whereby their impotence and shame were viewed as a certain proof of God's rejection, was the legacy of St. Augustine. He argued persuasively against the policies of inflicting violence on the Jewish people, of driving them out of Christian lands, or of forcing them to convert to Christianity. His theological rationale was that the very presence of a defeated, demoralised and subservient Jewish community in Christian lands would act as a permanent teaching aid for the Church in its battles against all sorts of heretics and blasphemers.

F. E. Talmage summarises the situation in this way:

> As medieval Jewish polemicists complain, all prophecies of redemption and consolation were applied to Christians; all prophecies of chastisement to the Jews. The Jews were entitled only to divine wrath but not to divine love . . . The Jews were typified by Cain, who murdered the Just One, and were therefore condemned to wander the earth forever. Their sole value lay in the fact that their very destitution was proof of the truth of Christianity.[254]

How did the Jewish leadership respond to this charge? On

---

[253] This argument is already found in Justin's *Dialogue with Trypho the Jew*, 16:2–4 and *The Epistle of Barnabas*, also second century CE, ch 16. At the other end of the historical spectrum, as recently as 1895 a distinguished Anglican scholar, A. Lukyn Williams, published a whole tract on this reading of history. It was published by the Religious Tract Society, and entitled, *The Jews in their Present Condition. Witnesses to the Bible*.

[254] F. E. Talmage, *Disputation and Dialogue*, op cit, p 6. For an assessment of Augustine himself, see Edward H. Flannery, *The Anguish of the Jews* (revised edition, Paulist Press, NY, 1985), pp 52–5.

one level, there were four responses to which the Jewish people resorted:

Christians might be deceiving themselves, but they were not deceiving God or the Jewish people. On the one hand, the Christians were persecuting the Jewish people mercilessly, and ensuring that their lot in life was miserable and degrading, while on the other hand they were claiming that the miserable and degrading lot of the Jewish people must be the result of God's rejection of them! The Christian communities' consistent and persistent policies (from the early fourth century) of abusing their new political, economic and social power in order to oppress Jewish people, was a case study in the art of creating self-fulfilling prophecy. It was simply not acceptable to persecute Jewish people and then claim that their persecution was proof of their unrighteousness. More to the point was the unrighteousness of the *Christians* who were involved in such programmes of torture and degradation. The real lesson of history was how corrupt the Church had become in such a short space of time!

Christians were also deceiving themselves if they failed to face up to the reality of the total world situation as one of continuing and constant warfare and strife. We have looked at this argument in some detail in an earlier chapter. Christians could only claim their victory in history as a proof of their theological legitimacy and spiritual authority if the whole of historical life was seen to be as God intended it to be. Only the Messianic Kingdom would last for ever. But, the Jewish leaders said, there was too much evidence that the Messianic Kingdom of peace had not yet come, and so the Christian empire (Christendom), at present so dominant, especially regarding the Jewish people, was essentially no different from any of the other powerful empires in Israel's past. It was, like them, seemingly invincible in its subjugation of Israel, yet, like them, it would only last for a definable historical period before being subdued by God. Christendom might well be the most powerful force yet to come against the Jewish people, but it too would fall in God's good time.

In the light of the phenomenal rise to power of the Islamic religion, Christians would be guilty of an embarrassing degree of self-deception if they maintained their theology of history. Did the sudden appearance and growth of Islam, and the success of its mission in the east and North Africa mean, if there was any consistency at all in Christian theology, that God had now rejected the Church in favour of the House of Islam?[255] Rabbi Meir ben Simon, whose work we looked at earlier, took a bold line when he put forward this argument. Referring to the fact that Jewish people were living, in certain places and in large numbers, under Islamic as well as under Christian rule, he wrote:

> For behold the Muslims rule in portions of the world as do the Christians, and we are in exile under their control . . . Indeed it seems fitting to say that . . . God sent us into exile among these two people, so that neither might have a claim against us in this regard.[256]

Rabbi Meir is cleverly playing the Christian and the Muslim theologians against one another. If either of them seeks to claim theological justification from their historical domination of the Jewish people (and others), then each has to account for the 'equal' success of the other!

These Christians who were claiming, vis-à-vis *the Jewish people, that an impotent and despised status in life was*

---

[255] For these arguments, see Jacob Neusner, *Aphrahat and Judaism* (Brill, Leiden, 1971), pp 97–110; Justin's *Dialogue*, op cit, 34; 110; and the works mentioned above by Yom Tov Lipmann Mulhausen and Abraham Farissol.

[256] *Milhemet Mitzvah*, quoted from p 64 of Robert Chazan, *Daggers of Faith*, op cit.

evidence of the loss of God's favour, were indulging in what might be called 'selective memory', since they themselves were descended from Christian communities who had suffered comparable exile and persecution. And yet in *that* situation the claim had been, and continued to be, that such suffering was proof of God's election and favour, not of his wrath and rejection, and so it was therefore something for Christians to glory in. A favourite text to justify this positive view of Christian suffering was John 15:18–19, where Jesus said:

> If the world hates you, keep in mind that it hated me first. If you belonged to the world, it would love you as its own. As it is, you do not belong to the world, but I have chosen you out of the world. That is why the world hates you.

Now, the Jewish people said, the theology underlying that word from Jesus could be applied just as well to God's choice of Israel. Christians were acting without integrity when they interpreted their own suffering in one way and the suffering of the Jewish people in the opposite way. This was especially so when it was the Christians who were causing most of the Jewish suffering! The real lesson of history was how the self-serving theology of the Church prevented the sauce for the Christian goose being sauce for the Jewish gander.

These four arguments, then, were employed by Jewish leaders in their rebuttal of the Christian claim that history itself, when read properly, was a proof of God's abandonment of the Jewish people and his election of the Christian Church in its place. But this was only one level of the Jewish people's response.

On another level altogether, Jewish leaders affirmed God's continuing covenant relationship with them at the same time as confessing that they nevertheless did deserve punishment and discipline from God for their sins. They did not try either to deny or minimise the terrible condition of the Jewish communities around the world. Instead, they spoke about this life of humiliation in exile as something which God has prophesied in the Hebrew Bible would happen to Israel if she did not walk in his ways. However, in speaking about the prophetic warning that Israel's sins would lead to such a life of degradation, they did not include in the list of sins the sin of rejecting Jesus or the Church. Exile and persecution were severe disciplines from God, and much, if not most, of God's blessing on Israel was being withheld by God on account of her transgression of his moral and spiritual laws.[257]

But the withholding of blessing is not at all the same thing as rejection and abandonment, and Israel had not been rejected by God, the rabbis insisted. Through all her punishment she knew that she was still the object of God's love and election, and would one day be restored to a full and healthy relationship with God. There is a beautiful sentiment expressed in the Jerusalem Talmud:

> Men commonly acknowledge only rich relatives, denying the poor; but even in its deepest humiliation God calls Israel brother and friend.[258]

The Jewish people admitted that sin lay behind their exile, basing themselves on texts like Lev 26:44 and Deut 28:64. What they rejected was the idea that the specific sin which had led to their exile was the refusal to accept Jesus of Nazareth as their Messiah. The Jewish people were outraged and offended that these Christians, who were the perpetrators of such terrible acts towards other human beings, should see themselves as the chosen instruments of God's righteous purposes. Some rabbis even tried to rationalise the Exile to

---

[257] Verses which were taken to be God's foretelling of this period of exile and subjugation include Lev 26:33; Deut 28:49; 32:21.

[258] Berachot 13b.

some extent by suggesting that it was the providential love of God which had led to the scattering of Israel over the face of the earth, otherwise the Christian communities would have had them all in one place and destroyed them.[259] Christians were seen as villains within the world's rebellion against God, not at all as God's chosen instruments and replacements for the Jewish people.

One of the commonest Christian claims was that the temple had been destroyed in 70 CE as a sign that God had rejected those who had rejected the Messiah. This fundamental charge had to be carefully addressed by the Jewish community, and indeed we find no less than eight nuanced reasons in the Talmud which give the rabbinic explanation of the fall of the temple at that time:

> The Jewish people habitually profaned the Sabbath
> They failed to recite the Shema' as they should
> They neglected Torah education for their children
> They forgot to fear the power and influence of evil
> They generally disrupted moral values
> They failed to admonish each other when necessary
> They denigrated the scribes
> Men of real faith had disappeared from Israel's life.[260]

In this way they explained the cause of the fall of Jerusalem and, as it were, justified God's actions. It is expressed just as explicitly in the daily liturgy of the Orthodox Jewish community:

> On account of our sins we have been driven from our land and have entered upon misery. We have been banished from our soil because of the hand which was stretched out against Your sanctuary.

Some rabbis, reflecting on the precedent recorded in Isa

---

[259] See Pesahim 87b.
[260] Shabbat 119b.

10:5–19, where the Assyrian empire is used by God as a tool
for dealing with Israel, suggested that perhaps the very same
reason lay behind God's use of the nations to punish contemporary Israel for her sins. Rabbi Yose ben Halafta, *c* 160
CE, said as much in a comment on Gen 27:40:

> When you (ie, Edom) see that your brother (ie, Israel) is shaking
> off the yoke of the Torah, then inflict religious persecution on
> him and exercise dominion over him.[261]

Of course this punishment by God was not seen as God's last
word to Israel. Restoration is also promised, as the rabbis
constantly pointed out.[262] Two great examples of the confidence of the rabbis that God would restore Israel to glory
and vindication are found in Talmudic stories about the faith
of Rabbi Akiba. Let us read these stories now, and learn
about one of the ways in which faith works:

> Once R. Gamaliel, R. Elazar, R. Joshua and R. Akiba were
> journeying, and they heard the tumult of the city of Rome
> from afar, and the first three wept, but Akiba laughed. They
> said, 'Why do you laugh?' He said, 'Why do you weep?' They
> said, 'These heathen, who pray and burn incense to idols, dwell
> in peace and security, whereas in our case the House, which was
> the footstool of our God's feet, is burnt with fire; how should we
> not weep?' He replied, 'That is why I laugh: if this is the lot of
> those who transgress His will, how much more glorious shall be
> the lot of those who perform His will.'
>
> Again, on another occasion, they were going to Jerusalem,
> and when they came to Mount Scopus, they rent their clothes.
> And when they came to the Temple-mount, they saw a fox
> coming out of the Holy of Holies. Then the first three wept,
> but Akiba laughed. They said, 'Why do you laugh?' He said,
> 'Why do you weep?' They said, 'In and out of the place of
> which it is said, "The foreigner that comes near to it shall be put

---

[261] Bereshit Rabbah 67.

[262] Favourite verses which speak of God's intention to restore Israel
include Ps 85:12; Isa 2:2–3; Jer 31:31–34; 10:10; 16:19f.

to death'', now foxes run (Lam 5:18; Num 1:51). How should we not weep?' He said, 'That is why I laugh, for it says, "I will take unto me faithful witnesses, Uriah the priest, and Zechariah the son of Jeberechiah'' (Isa 8:2). How came Uriah and Zechariah together? Uriah lived during the first Temple and Zechariah during the second. But the Scriptures made the prophecy of Zechariah dependent upon the prophecy of Uriah. For Uriah said, "Zion shall be ploughed as a field, and Jerusalem shall become heaps'' (Mic 3:12 and Jer 26:18–20), and Zechariah said, "Yet again shall the streets of Jerusalem be full of boys and girls playing in its streets'' (Zech 8:5). If Uriah's prophecy had not been fulfilled, I might fear that Zechariah's prophecy would not be fulfilled, but now that Uriah's prophecy has been fulfilled, it is certain that Zechariah's prophecy will also be fulfilled.' Then they said to him, 'Verily, Akiba, you have comforted us.'[263]

These wonderful stories capture beautifully for us this conviction within the Jewish community that severe though the punishment upon Israel was, it was not God's last word to her.

There was (and still is!) a serious debate, however, as to whether the restoration was dependent on Israel's prior repentance, or whether national restoration would come as a gracious gift from God, in the manner of Israel's initial election, with Israel's repentance following in the wake of this wonderful manifestation of God's mercy. We see this latter view, that God would restore Israel *before* there was any wholesale repentance, expressed in a midrash on the Psalms:

> Not because of your righteousness or the uprightness of your hearts are you going in to possess the land (Deut 9:5). Neither have I done this for the sake of Abraham, Isaac, and Jacob. Why, then? For the sake of my great name.[264]

What was more, the rabbis claimed, this restoration, when it

---

[263] Makkot 24b.

[264] Midrash Tehillim on Ps 107:1.

came, would prove once and for all that God had not rejected
Israel and that Jesus was not the redeemer, since God himself
would come as Israel's saviour and redeemer. This conviction that God himself is the paradigmatic redeemer of Israel
is celebrated annually at the festival of Passover, when, at the
appropriate part of the recounting of the story of the deliverance from Egypt, it is emphasised that God himself was
Israel's redeemer:

> 'And the Lord brought us forth out of Egypt': not by the hands
> of an angel, and not by the hands of a seraph, and not by the
> hands of a messenger, but the Holy One, blessed be he, himself,
> in his own glory and in his own person. As it is said: 'For I will
> go through the land of Egypt in that night, and will smite all the
> first-born in the land of Egypt, both man and beast; and against
> all the gods of Egypt I will execute judgements: I am the Lord'
> (Exod 12:12).

Just so will it be in the great Exodus to come, said Rabbi
Yohannan bar Nappaha (a sage from the third century CE),
when Israel is delivered from her enemies once and for all:

> After the slavery in Egypt came the deliverance through Moses;
> after the slavery in Babylon came the deliverance through
> Daniel. Then came the persecutions by Elam, Media and Per-
> sia, and deliverance through Mordecai and Esther. Then slavery
> under Greece, and deliverance through the Hasmonaeans and
> their sons. Then they came into the Roman captivity. Then the
> Israelites said, 'We are tired of being delivered and subjugated,
> delivered and again subjugated. We want no more deliverance
> at the hands of men. Deliverance comes only from God.'[265]

The inclusion of the Exodus from Egypt as an example of
deliverance at the hands of a human being is not meant to be
in conflict with the Passover theology, but is just a way of
highlighting the fact that the final deliverance of Israel will
make all the others seem trifling in comparison. The Jewish

---

[265] Midrash Tehillim on Ps 36:10.

people, then, were full of hope, in spite of the circumstances of everyday life. In fact, in the tenth century CE Sa'adia Gaon turned the traditional Christian teaching on its head, arguing that, if anything, the enduring faith of the Jewish people in their desperate situation was a proof of the reality of their ongoing living covenant bond with God. He contrasted this Jewish constancy with the sinful behaviour of the other nations, Christians included:

> The Almighty has exalted the nations, and yet they do not believe in Him, so that the argument is destroyed; the Israelites He has humbled, and yet they do not renounce His Torah, so that the truth is plainly on their side.[266]

At this deeper level, then, the Jewish people acknowledged their plight and were aware of the need for a theology of history which would account for the dreadful life of Israel in the world. The Christian claim that the destitute nature of the existence of the Jewish people was a major proof that God had abandoned them, was roundly condemned and refuted by the Jewish leadership. In their response, they argued that it was merely the realisation of the punishment which God had warned them would come if they persisted in their contempt for the Torah. This debate about the correct way to interpret history, like the first debate mentioned in this chapter regarding the correct way to interpret Scripture, still goes on today.

Reading life: reason and revelation

The third classic area of hermeneutical disagreement between Christians and Jews was over the right interplay between the acceptance of supernatural revelation from God, on the one hand, and the legitimate use of rational and experiential criteria, on the other. If we imagine a

---

[266] *Emunot ve-De'ot* III, 44. See also Judah Halevi, *The Kuzari* (c 1140) I:113.

continuum which shows the options in this debate, then at one end of the continuum would be those who say that the only authentic position for the believer to hold is that of blind faith. According to this position, which is actually held by some people, the mind and all other aspects of human endeavour and experience are not only inappropriate to spiritual affairs but positively harmful. At the other end of the continuum would be those who insist that authentic human life must be based on empirically-established and rationally-explained principles. Belief in a supernatural God who intervenes in human history, and whose will is always to be obeyed, is not an acceptable option for these people.

Most people fall somewhere between the two extremes on this continuum. Of course it must be said that both the Jewish and Christian communities have members who tend towards one or the other of these two extremes, as well as members who live with the tension of working with some combination of the two dimensions of life. Believers are constantly working with an interplay between revelation on the one hand and the need for common sense and discernment on the other.

In the disputations, however, there was a definite tendency among the Jewish protagonists to present a more rational approach to the issues. For example, it was commonly objected that it is irrational and contrary to good sense and the laws of logic to believe that God became a human being in the person of Jesus. God is spirit, the rabbis insisted, and cannot be flesh at one and the same time. God is holy, they proclaimed, and cannot be tainted by birth from the body of a sinful woman. Christian theologians, as a rule, argued that faith ultimately transcends philosophical reasoning, whereas, again as a rule, the Jewish theologians responded that even theological dogma must be seen to make sense, and must be seen to be subject to philosophical integrity and reasoning.

In the twelfth century, one of Judaism's most influential

polemicists, Bahya ibn Paquda, wrote the following programmatic words:

> Instruction based on tradition must necessarily precede knowledge obtained by the exercise of reason, inasmuch as learners must necessarily rely on what they are taught before they can obtain independent knowledge; yet it would show want of zeal for anyone to rely on tradition alone who can obtain certainty by the method of rational demonstration.[267]

Ibn Paquda is saying here that a faith which depends solely on spiritual tradition and revealed truths is appropriate for those who are spiritually immature. However, a mark of maturity is the commitment to rational thought as a means of establishing the truth of the revealed truths.

In Judah Halevi's celebrated twelfth-century account of the conversion of the entire Khazar kingdom to Judaism in the early Middle Ages, he presents a highly dramatic scenario in which the king listens to representatives of the Christian, Jewish and Muslim faiths, as well as to a 'philosopher'. Halevi does not miss the opportunity to have this pagan king spot the *rational* flaw at the heart of the Christian faith. This becomes one of the reasons that he finally chooses the Jewish faith as the best of them all. After the Christian has explained his creed to the king, the king replies:

> I see here no logical conclusion . . . nay, logic rejects most of what thou sayest . . . As for me, I cannot accept these things, because they come upon me suddenly not having grown up in them. My duty is to investigate further.[268]

The king is effectively saying that only someone brought up in the Christian faith could accept all the doctrines within Christianity which are contrary to reason. This neatly sums up a common Jewish attitude to Christianity which is found

---

[267] Bahya ibn Paquda, *Duties of the Heart* (ed Hyamson, NY, 1925), 1, p 10.

[268] Judah Halevi, *The Kuzari* I,5 (trans Hirschfield, NY, 1964), p 42.

to this day. Isaac Troki, whose work we have examined earlier, argued that the irrational Christian doctrines were simply the anachronistic and dangerous remnants of the pagan beliefs which these non-Jewish Christian peoples had held before their conversion to Christianity.

The following is a good example of a Jewish plea for rationality being made in response to the Christian doctrine of the Incarnation. Note again the opinion that only indoctrination in the Christian dogmas could explain a rational person's adherence to them. It comes from the 1263 Barcelona disputation, during which Nachmanides said to King James:

> And you, our Lord and King, are a Christian . . . and all your days you have listened to priests . . . and they have filled your brain and the marrow of your bones with this doctrine, and you have believed it out of habit. Of a certainty, the doctrine which you believe and which is a dogma of your faith cannot be accepted by reason . . . That the Creator of heaven and earth . . . should withdraw into the womb of a certain Jewess . . . neither the mind of a Jew nor of any man will sustain this.[269]

Some seventy years earlier, Maimonides had actually stated that, in accordance with good philosophical principles, principles which he saw as compatible with God's own 'mind', there were some things that even God – notwithstanding his omnipotence – could not do.

> Thus, for example, the coming together of contraries at the same instant and at the same place, and the transmutation of substances (I mean the transformation of a substance into an accident and of an accident into a substance) . . . belong to the class of the impossible, according to all men of speculation. Likewise, that God should bring into existence someone like Himself, or should annihilate Himself, or should become a body, or should change – all of these things belong to the class

---

[269] Quoted in *Sefer ha-Brit*, ed Frank Talmage, op cit, pp 71–9.

of the impossible; and the power to do any of these things cannot be attributed to God.[270]

The fundamental distinction was made between what Jewish philosophers called 'logical impossibilities', which are held to be impossible even for God, because they would contradict his own inner nature, and 'natural impossibilities', which are possible only for God, should he will, since they merely involve the suspension of rules which exist only for the created universe and are not at all binding on the transcendent Creator himself. Into the second classification, then, come the biblical miracles like the ten plagues in Egypt or the healing of Naaman or the raising of the Shunammite woman's son to life. But into the first classification would come the notions of the Incarnation, the Trinity, transubstantiation, etc.

This emphasis on the 'reasonableness' of Judaism *vis-à-vis* Christianity became an important hallmark of Jewish refutationist thinking. Moses Mendelssohn, one of the leading lights of the Jewish Enlightenment in eighteenth-century Europe, called upon this very tradition of criticism in his rejection of Christianity as a viable option for the 'modern Jew'. In a letter to a Christian prince, he wrote:

> And I must confess that the doctrines I have just listed [Trinity, Incarnation, passion, gratification of first person of Deity by suffering of second person] strike me as an outright contradiction of the fundamental principles of reason. I simply cannot harmonize them with anything that reason and cogitation have taught me about the nature and attributes of the Deity.[271]

If I may sum it up in this way: Jewish philosophers argued that there were philosophical truths which should be believed because humanity's rational faculty, given by God himself,

---

[270] Moses Maimonides, *Guide for the Perplexed* (1190), III:15

[271] This letter is quoted in part by Daniel J. Lasker, *Jewish Philosophical Polemics against Christianity in the Middle Ages* (Ktav, NY, 1977), p 38.

dictated it; there were also truths taught by Judaism which should be believed because, although they were based on a belief in divine revelation and the trustworthiness of the Jewish traditions, they were in harmony with, and stood the test of, the power of reason; but then there were all the Christian doctrines and beliefs which were unacceptable because they flew in the face of all philosophical reason. This dispute over the right use of human reason is the one least discussed in most of the modern and popular treatments of the Jewish–Christian relationship, but it is an extremely important one, and, like the disputes over the use of Scripture and the use of history, is still very much a live issue today.

Let me close this exploration into the importance of human reason in Jewish philosophical polemics by quoting Beth Moshe, whose 1987 book had as one of its basic premises:

> Christianity's faith cannot be accepted by any Jew who is even slightly knowledgeable of the Hebrew Scriptures and who uses his reasoning ability. As God created our minds, He expects us to use our reasoning together with our faith. Faith is not a substitute for reason, but a development from it and alongside it.[272]

These, then, were the three basic areas of disagreement, philosophically-speaking, between the two communities right up to the arrival of the eighteenth century and the European Enlightenment. The Jewish community experienced its own version of the Enlightenment in the wake of the larger intellectual and cultural revolution in Europe, and combined with the Emancipation of the Jewish people, this meant that with the coming of the nineteenth century everything was in a state of flux and development. Massive changes came about in both the Christian and the Jewish worlds. Religion *per se* was losing its all-powerful hold over people in the western world, and orthodox believers

---

[272] Beth Moshe, *Judaism's Truth Answers the Missionaries*, op cit, p 2.

within the Jewish and Christian communities were bitterly grieving over the rise of what is today commonly known as 'secular humanism'.[273]

One of the major social changes was that Jewish people were free to turn their backs on their Jewish faith and religious heritage, to become baptised members of Churches, and to live as Christians in their Christian society. Many Jewish people, particularly in the nineteenth century, took advantage of this very fact in an attempt to be accepted into the greater society, to be admitted to working positions in professions hitherto closed to them, and to be received into the institutions of higher education, etc. Interestingly enough, though, there was always a steady trickle of non-Jews who chose to convert to Judaism, even in those heady days when the reverse process was a significant phenomenon, and when becoming a Jew was invariably considered to be not only a grave family scandal but also social suicide. That such conversions to Judaism did take place from the eighteenth century, however, is demonstrated by a retort given by Moses Mendelssohn to Johann Caspar Lavater in 1769. Mendelssohn had been pressured into a public debate where much was being made of the rapidly increasing numbers of Jewish people who were converting to the Christian faith. Mendelssohn replied at one point that because the social and economic advantages of conversion are always with the person who converts to the host community's dominant religion, then

> A single Christian who agrees to be circumcised proves more for Judaism than a hundred Jews who agree to be baptised prove for the truth of Christianity.[274]

Mendelssohn marks a watershed in the history of Jewish–

---

[273] For the effects of the Enlightenment and Emancipation, see my *Jesus Ben Joseph*, op cit, chapter 7.
[274] Moses Mendelssohn, *Collected Works* 7.

Christian debate, since he was the leading liberal Jewish intellectual involved in the enterprise at a time when the Jewish community itself was undergoing the trauma of the growing power of the modernist challenge to Orthodoxy. He himself was convinced that the essence of Judaism could be reduced to certain reasonable and wise principles and insights about life, and he also believed that the Jewish people would come to accept this new and better formulation of its religion. He was equally sure that Christianity could be similarly reduced, but he feared that for most Christians their faith was inextricably bound up with an inappropriate and stubborn supernaturalism. In a letter to Elkan Herz, dated 23rd July 1771, he wrote:

> We have no doctrines of faith which go against reason, or go beyond it. We add nothing more to natural religion than commandments, ordinances, and precepts, but the basic principles of belief of our religion rest upon the foundation of reason; they are in agreement with the results of study in all areas without any contradiction or conflict.

Mendelssohn, and those of the same liberal persuasion (Christians as well as Jews, let it be noted), were committed to liberating their religious traditions, as they saw it, from the fetters of their old dogmas and superstitions. Mendelssohn was drawn to Christian Deists and Unitarians, whom he said had the right kind of attitudes and beliefs for Christians to have. He sought, and received, their support in calling doctrines like the Tri-unity of the Godhead or the vicarious atoning death of Jesus 'human additions' to the essential faith. It must be said, of course, to complete the picture, that he also spoke out against Orthodox Jewish supernaturalism. He had no time for the desire of the Orthodox to see the temple rebuilt and sacrifices reinstituted in Jerusalem, and he spoke against their belief that the Oral Torah was given by God to Moses at Sinai. Mendelssohn represented the new liberal thinking in Jewry which had its analogues in the new liberal Christian world.

The modern age of the radical questioning of revelation and supernaturalism had begun, and nothing has been the same since for either Jews or Christians. But the most notable aspect of the modern development, in terms of the ongoing Jewish–Christian dispute, has been the consolidation of the third of the three main areas of controversy which we have dealt with in this chapter. There has been a steady progression of emphasis on the need for a critical evaluation of faith and reason, including, of course, a critique of the relative intelligibility of the dogmas of the Jewish and Christian communities.

The western Jewish community has grown in confidence in the modern era, convinced that it clearly holds the superior philosophical and intellectual position when compared with Christianity. A number of Jewish thinkers have spoken in the following way when comparing Judaism and Christianity with paganism:

• Judaism represents the high ground of reason and humanity;
• Paganism represents the base and merely natural tendencies of human nature;
• Christianity occupies some middle ground between the two, owing its rational element to its Jewish roots, but always tending to paganism when it forgets those roots and parameters, as it does from time to time.

In fact it is not uncommon to find Jewish authors expressing the opinion that the corrupt and tragic tendency to forget, perhaps even to actively forsake, the good Jewish roots of the Christian faith began in some way with Jesus himself. Paul Goodman, for example, wrote the following at the start of this century:

It is the Jewish view that Jesus added no important original element to the religious and moral assets which had been accumulated by the Jewish prophets and sages, and that he has certainly been the more or less direct cause of lowering the pure and lofty ideas about God and man current in Judaism.[275]

This particular assessment of Christianity, as derivative from Judaism, indebted to Judaism for its healthier and more rational insights, but tragically errant in its ways and goals, was established in the twentieth-century Jewish mind by another deeply influential Jewish philosopher, Leo Baeck. He presented Judaism as a textbook *classical* religion: forward-looking, this-worldly, and actively involved in caring for the world. Christianity, on the other hand, he saw as a textbook *romantic* religion: gazing backwards at a golden age, other-worldly, and passive in the face of the world's everyday needs.[276] Judaism, he argued, is more in touch with the realities of life, and better integrates by far the whole of human life – theological, philosophical, psychological and sociological.

In our modern period there has been a growing momentum to help Jewish people to rediscover confidence in their own faith. In this new age of intellectual and social freedom, it is presented as a Jewish duty to speak out in a loud voice about the importance of Judaism. Two seminal Jewish thinkers must be mentioned at this point. Alfred Gottschalk mentions them both as he sets out the context in this way:

During this century of unparalleled mass murder of Jews, two or three divergences from that path have taken place. I mean by these, intense dialogues between individual Christians and Jews which pointed to the potential for meaningful interfaith discussion. The exchange of letters between Franz Rosenzweig and Eugene Rosenstock-Huessey is one such example, as is the

---

[275] Paul Goodman, *The Synagogue and the Church* (Routledge, London, 1908), p 233.

[276] Leo Baeck, *Judaism and Christianity* (1958).

interfaith dialogue between Martin Buber and the Protestant theologian, Karl Ludwig Schmidt, held in Stuttgart on 4th January 1933, just two weeks before the Nazi seizure of power.[277]

Rosenzweig, who came very close to becoming a baptised Christian, accelerated the confident movement within Jewry to emphasise Judaism's strengths, without, as he hoped, in any way debasing the faith or contribution of the Christian world. He spoke of Judaism as being like fire, with Christianity as the flames of the fire; and as being Life with God, with Christianity being the way to this God for non-Jews. Rosenzweig's point, which has since become a commonplace in much of the Jewish–Christian dialogue literature, was that the Jewish people already have a secure covenant relationship with God and are not in need of any other way. It is *non-Jews* who need a covenant of their own, and this is what Jesus came to establish for them, he says. Here is his famous exposition of Jesus' words, 'No one comes to the Father except through me' (John 14:6b):

> No one comes to the Father except through him (ie, Jesus). No one comes to the Father – but the situation is different when one need no longer come to the Father, because he is already with Him. That is the case with the nation of Israel. The development of Judaism passes by Jesus, to whom the heathen say 'Lord', and through whom they 'come to the Father'; it does not pass through him.[278]

Buber developed this momentum of Jewish confidence in itself still further, and argued eloquently for a new relationship of respect and appreciation between the two faith communities. Christianity, though, as he noted often, does not lack a sense of its own worth, so it is the Jewish people

---

[277] Alfred Gottschalk, in *Christian Jewish Relations*, vol 18, no 3 (1985), p 15.

[278] Franz Rosenzweig, *Der Stern der Erlosung*, book 3 (1921), p 73.

who have to learn real self-respect. The Jewish people need to rediscover the truth of their prior knowledge of, and prior relationship to, the God of Israel, that is, the only true God.

12

Summary

Our western society is one which is pressing for a commitment to a kind of pluralism and a kind of religious dialogue which are opposed to any form of evangelism. Messianic Jews, therefore, and evangelicals who are involved in Jewish ministry, are frequently stereotyped as being intolerant, insensitive and prisoners of the bad theology of previous generations. Some leading Christian theologians and church leaders are actually casting doubt on whether it is correct to say at all that Jesus is Israel's promised Messiah. Both Christian and Jewish spokespersons are labelling those involved in Jewish ministry as antisemitic, tearing at the very fabric of the Jewish religious experience. The big question facing us is whether we can respond to all this and defend our conviction about Jesus' Messiahship, while convincing our opponents that our theology is biblically sound and that we will not commit the antisemitic sins of so many of our fathers.

Ours is also a society in which personal and community assertiveness are being highly valued. Part of the Jewish expression of this is the increase in the volume and intensity of refutationist materials and lectures. The identity and integrity of Jesus and his disciples, let alone of all the countless Christians who have followed, are being debased and ridiculed as the Jewish community comes to terms with its new freedoms and responsibilities in modern life. How, then, can Messianic Jews and evangelicals who are involved in Jewish ministry respond to all this? Can we defend both the Messianic identity and also the spiritual and moral integrity of Jesus and his disciples? Can we demonstrate the authentic Jewishness of being a Messianic Jew, while at the same time convincing our opponents that we will not commit the antisemitic sins of so many of our fathers?

Is it in fact still possible to defend the authentic Messiahship of Jesus and the Jewishness of the New Testament revelation about Jesus in the face of today's insistent propaganda to the contrary which is being disseminated by these refutationists?

I hope that this book will help to show that it is indeed possible to maintain an evangelical witness to the Jewish community about Jesus as their Messiah and Lord while at the same time behaving with respect and generosity of spirit. But it is far from easy. We are not simply speaking about a group of people who have said 'No' to Jesus, but we are involved in a fundamental dispute with Jesus' own family and people, and they are the very ones who are rejecting his claim to Messiahship. Whenever there is a serious family dispute, there is always some set of specific reasons for it, and the modern Jewish predisposition to reject even an open consideration of Jesus' credentials for being their long-awaited Messiah is no different.

The French people have a proverb, 'Tout comprendre, c'est tout pardonner', which means 'To understand everything is to be able to forgive everything'. In other words, we often become angry or frustrated at someone for an attitude or behaviour pattern which they exhibit, whereas, if we only knew enough about their own personal history or psychological profile, etc, we would understand the forces which drive them and therefore be able to show compassion, generosity of spirit, and forgiveness. Now I do not suggest that this will always be the case, and it must certainly not be used to condone unacceptable attitudes or behaviour, but a great deal of wisdom lies behind this proverb, I believe.

In the hope that this book has already demonstrated that I

am not an intolerant, insensitive or naïve person when it comes to relationships with Jewish people, I would like to suggest that this proverb has some relevance for Christians who come across refutationist material which disturbs them. I do not mean by this that the awful experiences of the Jewish people at the hands of Christians in Christian lands can be shrugged off by Christians by simply resorting to a proverb. What I am saying is that knowledge of the experiences and memories of the Jewish people will help to prevent another cycle of frustration, anger and confrontation. How many times have I met Christians preparing for Jewish ministry, whose motivation is seriously compromised by a certain anger and frustration caused by contact with material which ridicules or otherwise distorts the Gospel! My plea throughout this book has been that Christians take the time and the effort to learn about the Jewish story.

There are specific reasons for the Jewish people's refusal to listen to the Gospel, and to understand their story is to experience the transformation of any feelings of frustration into a feeling of shame, a conviction of the need for repentance, and an attitude of humility. It is to realise what some people have even called the 'inevitability' of the Jewish rejection of the Gospel. To ignore this story and to resist an appropriately modest (though confident) ministry is to act as if relating to Jewish people could be done in a vacuum. This is not only ridiculous, it is also an insult. To love our Jewish neighbours as ourselves demands of us that we do everything in our power to understand them, so that we can relate to them as real human beings like ourselves.

What, then, have we learned, as we have gone through the first part of this book, that will help us in this task? Let me group the major points as follows.

Christians must relate to Jewish people in a completely different way from the way in which they relate to any other people. Jewish people claim priority over Christians as regards a living relationship with God, familiarity with the Hebrew Bible, knowledge of the Messiah, etc. In large measure Christians must agree to this and seek to learn from the Jewish people as well as to share the Gospel with them. God's covenant with the Jewish people has not been revoked. But the other side of this is the fact that Jewish people often sound irritated at Christians for thinking that they might have a distinctive contribution to make to the issue of the identity of the Messiah. Christians are often made to feel like upstart younger brothers presuming to teach their elder brothers about their common Father, and yet those who know Jesus to be the Messiah *do* have a distinctive and needed message to share with the Jewish people. Christians should not be ashamed of the Gospel.

While endeavouring to understand the perspective of this covenant-people who are, in one sense at least, older in the faith than they are, Christians should take seriously the serious questions put to them by the Jewish community. I have met too many evangelists in my time who actually refuse to take questions seriously, referring to them merely as attempts to draw attention away from the real issues (namely the ones which the evangelist claims to understand). Yes, there will always be a measure of rhetorical manœuvring when people from two different persuasions are trying to persuade one another, but at heart, the Jewish refutation of Jesus is based on real issues. There is much homework to be done!

As we have noted, most people in the Jewish community are actually content, as it were, to let the younger brother go his own way. They are happy for non-Jews to be Christian, as long as Christianity is seen to be a separate religion from Judaism. The spokespersons for world Jewry are generally intent only on trying to prevent *Jewish* people from becoming followers of Jesus. It is the lively existence of Jewish believers in Jesus which is the real problem and embarrassment for them (as for certain Christians too). This determined strategy of restricting faith in the Messiahship of Jesus to non-Jews cannot be allowed to succeed. The Jewish claim to priority in understanding the true nature of the Messiah must not be allowed to ride roughshod over the counter-claim of the Messianic Jewish community that Jewish believers in Jesus have indeed found Israel's promised Messiah.

Christians, therefore, should show real respect when listening to the perspectives and the objections of the Jewish community, and should temper their own confidence with modesty. However, this does not mean accepting teaching which is at variance with the New Testament message about Jesus and the movement of people who believe in him. In particular, the teaching that the Christian faith was actually founded on a Messianic fallacy, resulting from the need for a psychological compensation for the death of Jesus must be energetically resisted.

Listening to one another, and really communicating with one another, are more important than mere proclamation. Serious differences between Jews and Christians on fundamental matters of theology and philosophy are to be expected. There is no virtue in crying, 'Peace, Peace', when there is no peace, nor should Christians feel that disagreement is in itself something deplorable. Christians, and especially evangelicals, need to rediscover the responsibility of involvement in dialogues of every sort with Jewish people. What is important is that any disagreements should be expressed in a spirit of respect and generosity. The key commandment from God in this context is: 'Love your neighbour as yourself', one indispensable element of which is expressed in another commandment: 'You shall not give false testimony against your neighbour'. Mutual misrepresentation, often quite deliberate, has constantly bedevilled the relationship between Jews and Christians and, although it is a sin in itself, it has also led to the further sins of spiralling antagonism and resentment. Christians must speak the *truth* about Jewish people and about Judaism, and must do so in love.

Christians must never be allowed to forget that it was the Church's frustration at the Jewish refusal to accept the Church's message which played a major part in the creation of the specifically Christian antisemitism which has plagued all relationships with the Jewish people. Strong differences of opinion can never again be allowed to degenerate into contempt and violent aggression.

On another level, it needs to be remembered that just because Jews and Christians may be using the same words, this does not necessarily mean that the same meanings are being either intended, assumed or communicated. Care has to be taken to make sure that what is being heard by one party is what the other party was intending to say. To press ahead in any discussion without this sensitivity to the nuances of language and to the distinct development of ideas within Jewry and Christendom, is to invite frustration and exasperation. Key terms such as salvation, sin, Messiah etc, mean significantly different things within the current overall theological frameworks of the two faith-communities.

One of the concerns we noted in particular was that the Jewish community has failed by and large to appreciate the centrality of God the Father to Christian theology, as a result of the Christian emphasis, for good reason, on Jesus, God the Son. What Christians have thought they were communicating about Jesus as the *Mediator* between the Father and humanity has not been what Jewish people have been hearing. Another important area of confusion which we looked at is the nature of the process known as conversion. We need to listen very carefully to one another on this matter. Christians must take pains to ensure that Jewish people realise that becoming a believer in Jesus is not a superficial infatuation, and that relatively swift processes of commitment and baptism are really not the result of some form of cultic entrapment.

Pain and suffering are the context of the Jewish involvement in today's refutations, rather than an intellectual commitment to theological discussions with evangelical Christians and Messianic Jews. Christians simply must come to terms with the anguish and the bitter anger which lie behind so much of what is said about Jesus and Christianity by Jewish refutationists. It may yet be quite some time before Jewish people are able to debate the question of the Messiahship of Jesus on the kind of *relatively* 'rational' theological basis which Christians seem to desire. When Christians and Jews talk about whether or not Jesus is the way to find peace with God, then these conversations are not simply passionate because each party cares about theology, but because the Jewish people have suffered so dreadfully in the past as a result of such conversations and disputes.

The Jewish community is no longer obliged to be pathologically defensive about its beliefs and values, and it is determined to move on to the offensive, even if sometimes its statements might seem somewhat offensive! It is insistent that it has seen the last of its involvement in those public disputes which were engineered to produce a 'no-win' situation for the Jewish participants, and which predetermined that the Jewish people would be on the defensive throughout. Thank God that the Church has been stripped of that kind of power to make Jewish people cower! But we are now reaping what our fathers sowed.

At the same time, this legacy of disputes has left the Jewish community deeply suspicious of any attempt by evangelicals, and particularly by Jewish believers in Jesus, to engage its members in theological debates of any kind. Put simply, the Jewish community still fears a hidden agenda. For this reason, very few evangelicals are invited to participate in inter-faith dialogue groups, although these groups usually refer to themselves as representing 'Christian' theology, as if they could speak for the whole Church without an evangelical voice!

The heart of this Jewish challenge to Christians, though, coming out of the experience of pain and persecution, is not one of petulant rivalry for power, but a profound conviction within the Jewish community that Christianity has proven itself to be bankrupt *vis-à-vis* Judaism because its morality has given the lie to its spirituality. Had Christianity been a religion with cruelty and exploitation as its self-styled foundational values, then that had been another story altogether. But Christianity declares itself to be the religion *par excellence* of love and forgiveness. What is more, Christians claim to worship and adore the God of Israel, the God of the Jewish people, and yet have despised the Jewish people themselves. Therefore Christianity is seen to be condemned by its own profession of faith and love.

The central and non-negotiable concern of most Jewish people is for the survival, and indeed the flourishing, of the Jewish people per se. The idea of 'conversion to Christianity' carries distinct overtones to Jewish people of leaving the Jewish community and joining the non-Jewish world of history and culture. It is most assuredly not seen as simply individuals exercising their freedom of choice for their own lives. It has massive implications for the health, identity and survival of the whole Jewish community. This Jewish perspective needs to be well and truly grasped by Christians in the West. Christians who are citizens of Muslim or African countries, for example, will appreciate and share this concern for the community. A person's identity is seen as entirely bound up with the identity of the whole community. This means that, for example, to be thrown out of the community is like a death sentence in many cultures.

Western, evangelical Protestants tend to be the worst at appreciating the community dimension of religious faith, so caught up are they in their own cultural world, in which religion and public life have been separated, and in which there is so much stress on the rights and importance of 'the individual'. The 'personal' cost of discipleship for someone who is part of such a community-oriented culture is high when that commitment to Jesus results in ostracism from their community. Of course there are many examples of modern Jewish people who have become as individualistic as the next (non-Jewish) person, but the traditional association of belief in Jesus with *alienation* from the Jewish community is still strong within that community.

Conversion, then, is perceived by Jewish people as a weakening of strength and vitality of the Jewish community. Jewish believers are defined in Jewish tradition as being no longer part of the Jewish community, so that one of the most important issues on the agenda of Jewish–Christian discussions today, as far as evangelicals are concerned, is the rehabilitation of Jewish believers within the Jewish fold.

It is within this context that Christians need to realise the significance of baptism for Jewish believers in Jesus. One of the central teachings in the Churches about baptism is that at baptism people become part of the universal Church. For most Churches this is symbolised and actualised in the baptised people becoming members of the specific church community which has administered their baptism. In other words, being baptised by a Church and joining that Church are very often inseparable parts of the same overall event.

Therefore, in Jewish eyes, if there is, in effect, a formal moment when a Jewish person leaves the Jewish community and enters the non-Jewish world, it is the moment of baptism. This is seen as the point of no return. Up until that point, the Jewish person can, with *relative* ease, renounce the Christian faith and return to the Jewish community. However, once that baptism has taken place, everything is considerably more difficult for any Jewish person who thereafter wishes to return to Judaism and the Jewish community. For this reason, baptism is a more serious issue for Jewish believers (and new Christians in other cultures too) than it is for a typical, nominally Christian westerner who comes to a real faith in Jesus. Sensitivity is therefore called for in this matter as well.

There is a Jewish self-defence mechanism which both pities and despises Jewish believers in Jesus, in an attempt to protect the image of Judaism-without-Jesus as the only proper Judaism. In a way this is, of course, simply a common human reaction, not at all peculiar to the Jewish people. When there is a disruption in our relationships with one another, whether on the personal, communal, or national level, then we have a natural tendency to blame the other party or parties concerned.

The Jewish community defines Jewish believers in Jesus as having left the Jewish community, as no longer, therefore, to be considered as Jewish, and as having brought this dreadful shame upon themselves. The declaration by the Jewish community to the effect that this person is no longer to be considered as Jewish is interpreted as the necessary response to that person's prior declaration that he or she has decided to leave the Jewish community. This act of excommunication is accompanied by one of two different attitudes. The more severe of these attitudes regards the Jewish believer as a traitor who has not only knowingly gone out from the mother faith and community, but who has actually *abandoned* or *deserted* that faith and community at a time of great need and in a hostile environment. The less severe, but no less discriminatory attitude looks with pity on these people who are seen to be clearly deficient in their knowledge of the infinite riches and possibilities of Judaism; deficient, therefore, in the resources with which to combat the missionary menace; and ultimately deficient in the power to recognise and resist the deceptive ploys of the missionaries.

Either way, any Christians who wish to share their conviction with a Jewish person that Jesus is Israel's Messiah, are assumed to be unscrupulous and deceptive, and the possibility that any intelligent, well-adjusted, Jewishly-aware Jewish person might become a believer in Jesus from conviction is dismissed out of hand. Since Christians are held to be aware of the impossibility of a mature and knowledgeable Jewish person coming to faith in Jesus, it then follows that Christians who are involved in Jewish ministry are knowingly manipulative.

These charges are deeply offensive to Jewish believers, and to all Christians involved in Jewish ministry. However, history does give us enough examples of exploitative missionaries and clergy and Jewish pseudo-converts to Christianity who turned nastily on their former Jewish communities, to provide the Jewish community today with the precedents which it wants to justify its attitudes. Christians, therefore, need to learn how to respond to these charges, and to the presuppositions which lie behind them, without rancour or despair.

Genuine inter-faith dialogue, and a practical commitment to a society in which each person is valued and respected irrespective of his or her beliefs, must be part of the evangelical agenda. Jewish leaders are proceeding apace today in their efforts to portray Judaism as an example of the kind of tolerant and pluralist-friendly religion which our societies need as we come into the twenty-first century CE. Alongside this, many of the refutationists are equally keen to portray Christianity as intolerant of the claims of other faiths, and as likely to foster social unease and prejudice with its missionary programmes. Christians must square up to this challenge.

On the one hand, we do wish to maintain our witness to Jesus as the only way to the Father and to eternal life, but at the same time we also wish to promote and live a life of respect and good-neighbourliness with people of all faiths in our societies. Evangelicals are as committed to loving their neighbours as themselves in a pluralistic society as any other person. Sadly, however, there is a common perception in the world that evangelical Christians are less likely to be really accepting of others than many other groups. Let us make sure that in our desire to share the Gospel with others we do not reinforce that image!

We also need to be aware of the fact that Jewish leaders are forming friendships and working relationships with those Christians who themselves take strong exception to the evangelical position on many central doctrines and values. This is especially true when it comes to the issue of whether or not Jewish people need to accept that Jesus is their Messiah and Lord. Not surprisingly, evangelical Christians are being confronted by the statements made by Christian opponents of Jewish ministry, and these so-called 'radical' theologians are being held up as the acceptable face and voice of Christianity. Knee-jerk reactions to this, whereby it is dismissed as 'typical liberal nonsense', as I heard a young Christian student in training for the ministry say recently, will not do. The Christian theologians who are opposing Jewish ministry are doing so as a result of their own deeply-held convictions, and we must treat them with the same respect that we would like to see from them. Once again we remind ourselves of the commandments from God that we love our neighbour as ourselves, and that we do not give false testimony against our neighbour.

Although there are obviously a number of factors which are involved in the development of this so-called 'liberal theology', and although I do not share this theology, it must be said that these Christian theologians have usually done a great deal of homework on this whole area of Jewish–Christian relations, often more than most evangelicals. They are themselves only reflecting on, and agonising over, the anguish and the shame which any knowledge of the Christian persecution of the Jewish people brings.

What these non-evangelicals often do not appreciate, however, and indeed sometimes try to deny, is that those evangelicals who are involved in Jewish ministry, and Jewish believers in Jesus, are every bit as ashamed of what has been done in the name of Jesus; are every bit as committed to leading the Church to repentance for this; are every bit as involved in trying to combat antisemitism and ensure a future where Jewish people will be perfectly secure, and part of the creative fabric of society; and are every bit as passionate about the State of Israel, as these other Christians are. We need to get that message across!

It would also be a constructive development if those Jews and Christians who serve as executive officers of the various inter-faith groups and fellowships would consider inviting evangelicals and Jewish believers to become members of those groups and fellowships. In this way, the standard mutual relationships of stereotype and marginalisation could gradually be overcome, as people got to know each other. It really has become tiresome to be excluded from these groups which claim to represent integrity and dialogue, yet which persist in violating one of their own cardinal doctrines by regularly debating the issues and personalities of mission and Messianic Judaism, while denying Messianic Jews and those Christians who are involved in Jewish ministry the right to be members of the group and to define themselves.

Messianic Jews and evangelicals involved in Jewish ministry are not permitted to represent themselves, even although they are frequently on the agenda. Of course there will sometimes be a token invitation to speak to some committee or other about a specific matter, but this is not at all the same as membership and full participation. Most of these modern dialogue groups prefer to impose their own definitions, and then condemn those people and the integrity of their beliefs as a result of those imposed definitions. What is rather amusing is that they then proceed to accuse others of a lack of integrity!

Two specific charges are brought by the Jewish community as evidence which disqualifies Jesus from being the Mes-

siah. The two most commonly found and over-arching criticisms of the claim that Jesus is Israel's Messiah, are, firstly, the accusation that he failed completely to bring God's *shalom* (peace) into the world; and, secondly, that Christians deal with this (as with other insuperable problems) in a cavalier fashion, by resorting to the appeal that all will be put right and explained in the eschatalogical future.

Once again I issue an appeal for serious homework to be done by Christians on both of these matters. Is it possible to respond in any other than an individualistic and pietistic way to the first of these charges? Is it possible to find a solid exegetical base in the Hebrew Bible for the teaching that the Messiah will come twice to Israel and the world? The answer to both of the questions is a confident, but modest, 'Yes', even although it is a more hard-won 'Yes' than many Christians realise or wish to acknowledge. The Jewish teaching that there are two Messiahs, while not accepted by all Jewish people, is sufficiently pervasive and influential to merit serious investigation, so that Christians are able to engage this alternative Messianic theology with intelligence and conviction.

Ambiguity in life and in the meaning of biblical texts is not a disaster, but pretending to have absolute knowledge about the meaning of everything in life is probably a sin. I must finally remind us of the field of research which so many Christians would rather avoid altogether, namely an investigation into the different, sometimes radically different, methods of interpretation commonly used by Jews and Christians. We differ on the selection of what we consider to be the Word of God; on the correct hermeneutical principles to be brought to bear on the Word of God once we have identified and defined it; on the Jewishness of the New Testament, especially in connection with its close relationship to the Septuagint; on the compatibility of the life and teaching of

Jesus with the promises in the Hebrew Bible about the one who was to come; on the appropriate reading of history, and what is to be considered significant in that history, especially concerning the issues of power and vulnerability; and on the degree to which our fundamental convictions about God should be 'rational', in the sense of being accountable at the bar of western, post-Enlightenment reason.

There is no way around this need for patient, generous and humble learning about what has now become a rich and authoritative set of traditional Jewish ways of 'reading' life and the Hebrew Bible. If only Christians could realise what a stimulating and enriching experience this learning is! It will not lead to a weakening of one's conviction about Jesus, but will rather enable a fuller and more mature grasp of the central issues and a deeper commitment to Jesus. Those who follow Jesus have nothing to fear from an honest investigation into his Messiahship and the implications of following him. When people differ as much as Jews and Christians do on so many fundamental issues which have to do with interpreting life, history and sacred texts held in common, then there is a moral imperative to investigate those differences honestly, and to ensure that ambiguous texts, or events which can be read in more than one way, etc, are acknowledged to be so. Faith is about trusting God in an ambiguous and vulnerable world, and Christians and Jews alike should resist the temptation, to which both have been guilty of succumbing, of trying to create objective certainties where none exist. Christians have nothing to fear from an honest admission of ambiguity in life.

Here, then, are some of the fundamental issues and concerns which I have tried to highlight so far in this book. Without some familiarity and sympathy with them, very little is likely to be achieved. An immediate call for detailed exegesis of Messianic prophecies in the Hebrew Bible, for example, in an attempt to bypass this kind of study, which is the action of many evangelicals, will not prove profitable. The Jewish–Christian relationship, like all relationships, needs to be carefully worked at if it is to be fruitful.

In the second part of this book, by way of introduction to the complexities of rigorous Bible study involving Jews and Christians, we shall proceed to look at five specific texts in the Hebrew Bible, all of which are claimed by Christians to be Messianic prophecies fulfilled in Jesus. As a major part of this, we shall examine some of the specific areas of conflict between Jews and Christians concerning the correct interpretation of these and other disputed Messianic texts. We are now much better prepared for such an exploration.

PART TWO

*'A man finds joy in giving an apt reply – and
how good is a timely word!'*

PART TWO

Introduction

There are five crucial passages in the Hebrew Bible which will receive our attention in this part of the book. They are all famous Messianic texts in the Church, and have therefore all been treated to extensive consideration by the Jewish community as well, because of this fact. The five texts to be explored are:

Genesis 3:15   Genesis 49:10
Isaiah 7:14   Isaiah 9:5–6   Psalm 22:17

We shall devote a chapter to each passage, in the course of which we shall deal seriously with its historical, biblical and theological contexts; we shall look at its traditional christological interpretation; we shall examine the traditional Jewish interpretations, as well as their refutations of the christological interpretation; and then we shall suggest some appropriate responses to the Jewish objections.

If this sounds somewhat pedantic, then my only justification for working in this way is that the matter is often so complex that a clear and methodical path is necessary to make sure that we are disciplined in what we are doing. By necessity, we shall from time to time be involved in various disciplines of study: *historical and sociological*, as we try to comprehend the real-life factors which would be relevant to an understanding of what a passage meant to the people who originally received a prophetic word; *theological*, as we try to fit the passage into a coherent understanding of the context of both the whole of Scripture, and also of the revealed will and character of the God of Israel; *linguistic*, as we try to discover what particular words and phrases meant in particular times and places.

Sometimes the discussion will have to become a little technical, as for example when we are discussing the range of meanings for the Hebrew word found in Isa 7:14, and translated in many Bibles as 'virgin'. But I shall endeavour to keep the technical material to a minimum, and to explain it all in non-technical language as we move along. Those with some facility in Hebrew, Greek, the history of Israel, etc, will immediately grasp the issues and be able to go beyond the information given in this book, but others, who cannot use the information in this way, will still be able to follow the arguments given here. Bear in mind, however, that this book is not a commentary on the Bible, so that we shall not be analysing all the relevant matters of translation, interpretation and application. Each reader is therefore strongly encouraged to pursue an independent exegesis of the passages highlighted here should he or she wish to thoroughly investigate the overall issues. Our interest in this book is specifically in the way in which the Jewish community has rejected the Messianic significance of these passages *vis-à-vis* Jesus. I do not claim to have even answered every relevant question, but I do intend to cover all the major issues in a responsible and creative way.

13

The first Gospel message? Genesis 3:15

Is this *really* the first prophecy in the Hebrew Bible about the coming of the Messiah? From the second century CE, if not before, the Church has consistently proclaimed that this verse in the middle of the curse on the serpent contains the first prophetic reference to the Gospel, and early on even gave it the Latin title of *proto-evangelium*, meaning 'first gospel'. An important early Church Father who championed this view was Irenaeus.[281] It is considered to be the first word in Scripture about the coming to earth and victory of Jesus, the Messiah. Some Christians, particularly in the Roman Catholic Church, have even claimed to discern a reference to Mary and a hint of the virgin birth in this verse.[282] Many Christians, on the other hand, give little thought to this particular verse except at Christmas time, when it is often included in the traditional services of lessons and carols.

The Synagogue denies that there is any possible reference to Jesus in this verse. Or, to be more accurate, although there is evidence of a Messianic interpretation of this verse in the older Jewish translations, the Synagogue has attempted, since the high Middle Ages, to marginalise any attempt to see Messianic importance in these words.

The verse itself reads as follows:

---

[281] See his *Adversus Haereses* (*Against Heresies*), 390–1.

[282] See, for example, the footnote given in the 1973 edition of the Roman Catholic translation of the Bible, known as the Jerusalem Bible.

And I will put enmity between you and the woman, and between your seed and hers; he (it) will crush your head, and you will strike his (its) heel.

First of all we must examine the context of these words as we begin to determine their meaning. The verse is, of course, part of the Genesis account of the Fall of humanity into a state of self-centred rebellion against God. In verses 1–5 of the chapter, the serpent challenges the will and the word of God, and Eve is tempted to listen to him. In verse 6 both Adam and Eve succumb to the temptation to become their own master and mistress, and we see the resultant guilt and shame in verses 7–8. God confronts them in verses 9–13, pronounces judgement in verses 14–19, yet nevertheless provides them with protection in verses 20–21. Then God banishes Adam and Eve from the Garden of Eden to prevent them from eating the fruit of the tree of life (another punishment?), as we see in verses 22–24.

One further important context for this verse is the fact that it is not quoted in the New Testament. How significant are we to judge this fact, given the importance which many Christians claim for this first Gospel message? Personally, I use the rule of thumb that we must be cautious about prophecies which are not acknowledged to be such in the New Testament itself. But on the other hand, it could well be that this verse is being alluded to in 1 Cor 15:22–25, and it seems likely that it was in the mind of the author of the Book of Revelation as he wrote Rev 12:1–13:1. What is more, I am convinced that Paul had the whole context of Genesis 3 in mind when he related this verse to Christians (not Jesus, take note) in Rom 16:18–20. Here are those significant Pauline words, echoing, as they do, the words and realities of Genesis 3:

For such people are not serving our Lord Christ, but their own appetites. By smooth talk and flattery they deceive the minds of naïve people. Everyone has heard about your obedience, so I am full of joy over you; but I want you to be wise about what is good, and innocent about what is evil. The God of peace will soon crush Satan under your feet. The grace of our Lord Jesus be with you.

So the New Testament does give even the cautious person enough encouragement to explore this verse a little further.

There are three classic methods of interpretation of this text to be found in the Jewish and the Christian communities.

The naturalistic interpretation

According to this understanding, the passage is merely speaking about the natural conflict which exists between serpents (perhaps, some say, representing all the other 'natural' enemies of humanity, or inspirers of fear) and people. It is seen to be a text which sets out the cause of our universal phobias and instincts. Quite a few Jewish commentators have adopted this view.

In 1985 a new English translation of the Hebrew Bible was made for English-speaking Jewish communities around the world. It translates our verse as follows:

> I will put enmity
> Between you and the woman,
> And between your offspring and hers;
> They shall strike at your head,
> And you shall strike at their heel.[283]

Nahum Sarna, one of the most respected contemporary Jewish commentators on the Pentateuch, wrote the official commentary on Genesis in a one-volume book based upon this 1985 translation and published a few years later. Of our verse he wrote:

---

[283] *TANAKH. A New Translation of the Holy Scriptures According to the Traditional Hebrew Text* (The Jewish Publication Society, Philadelphia, 1985).

This curse seeks to explain the natural revulsion of humans for the serpent.[284]

There is no hint given by Sarna in his comments on the passage that there might be a symbolic moral dimension to these enigmatic words, let alone a Messianic one. He was evidently keen to revive the naturalistic interpretation. Whether this was for its own sake or in order to deflect attention away from Messianic speculation about the verse, we do not know.

The symbolic interpretation

For those who adopt this view, the passage is speaking about the universal struggle between good and evil which exists within each of our cultures. The seed of the woman is taken to represent righteous people, while the seed of the serpent 'naturally' represents wicked people. A number of both Jewish and Christian scholars have supported this interpretation, including Keil and Delitzsch whose Christian commentaries are very popular among Jewish believers, since they take the Jewish traditions seriously and knowledgeably.

A verse from the New Testament which is often quoted as justification of this interpretation is John 8:44, in which Jesus says the following to those Jewish people with whom he is then in dispute:

> You belong to your father, the devil, and you want to carry out your father's desire. He was a murderer from the beginning, not holding to the truth, for there is no truth in him. When he lies, he speaks his native language, for he is a liar and the father of lies.

Jesus is responding here to these people's own claim that, 'The only Father we have is God himself' (verse 41). Jesus makes the counter-statement that he comes from God, but

---

[284] Nahum M. Sarna, in *The JPS Torah Commentary* (The Jewish Publication Society, Philadelphia, 1989), p 27.

that they belong to the enemy camp (verses 42–47). And so the supporters of the symbolic interpretation of Gen 3:15 understand Jesus to be affirming the appropriateness of this symbolic division of humanity, including the Jewish people, into two groups, the righteous and the wicked.

There is, according to some modern Jewish interpreters, an early Jewish example of this understanding in the Targum literature. The Targums were the Aramaic-translation commentaries on the Hebrew Bible formed from the collections of oral interpretations given in the synagogues by skilled translators. In the same way that many diaspora Jewish people needed the LXX for a fluent understanding of the old Hebrew texts of the Bible, since their natural daily language was Greek, just so did many Jewish people in the land of Israel value an Aramaic version of their Bible, since Aramaic was their language of communication in the Near East. In one of the Targums, our verse is dealt with in this fashion:

> When the sons of the woman keep the commandments of the Torah, they shall be ready to smite you on your head; but when they forsake the commandments of the Torah, you will be ready to smite them on their heels, though for them there shall be healing, and for you there shall not be healing, and though they will make peace in the end, in the days of King Messiah.[285]

In this case the symbolism is directed specifically towards the Jewish people, contrasting those who keep God's commandments with those who do not. There is also a Messianic dimension to the discussion, as we see, but only in the sense that a full return to harmony among the Jewish people will not be at all possible until the Messiah comes! This is not a

---

[285] Targum Pseudo-Jonathan, ad loc. Dating this document is not easy, and the interpretations will predate their collection and committal to writing anyway, but this certainly reflects an interpretation from the first or second centuries CE.

self-consciously Messianic interpretation. The seed of the serpent will have a limited power over those Jews who try to live outside of the will of God, whereas the righteous Jews will have a life of victory over him. It is very important to note the conviction expressed here that the negative efforts of the serpent will never be fatal, since there is healing available for the Jewish people, whereas there will be a final defeat of the serpent at some stage. The great Genesis Midrash spells this out even more clearly when it says that in the Messianic Age there will come this time of healing for all except the serpent.[286]

There are a number of Christian scholars who also favour a more general interpretation of this verse over one which sees it referring specifically to the Messiah. For one thing, they claim, this would be too early for there to be such a promise of the Messiah, since the Bible has not even reached the stage of Abrahamic history, and therefore has not begun to document the movement towards the fulfilment of God's promise to Abraham at his election by God (Gen 12:1–3). For another thing, they cite Rom 16:20a as evidence that Paul himself understood this verse as referring not to Jesus, but to the ultimate victory of the community of Christians over Satan.

John Calvin was certainly attracted to this interpretation of the verse as referring to the victory of the Church, albeit by the grace of God, as we see in this comment of his:

> The human race whom Satan had endeavoured to destroy shall at length be victorious . . . Since a stronger one has come down from heaven to subdue him, the whole Church of God shall, under her Head, and like Him, be victorious.

E. W. von Hengstenberg, an extremely influential Christian writer on the Messianic prophecies in the Hebrew Bible, and someone who follows this line of thinking himself, defends a more general interpretation in this way:

---

[286] Genesis Rabbah 20:5.

Even according to this interpretation, the passage justly bears the name of the Protoevangelium . . . It is only in general terms, indeed, that the future victory of the kingdom of light over that of darkness is foretold, and not the person of the Redeemer who should lead in the warfare, and bestow the strength which should be necessary for maintaining it.[287]

The Messianic interpretation

According to this interpretation of the verse, it is also symbolic of the ultimate victory of good over evil, but specifically as an allusion to the coming of the Jewish Messiah. He will demonstrate an ultimate triumph over the devil, who took the form of a serpent in the Garden of Eden, or at least was the master of that serpent. This, as I say, became the dominant Christian view of the verse in the early generations of the growth of the Church. Jesus, it was believed, would suffer terrible injury at the hands of the devil, but he would triumph in the end, destroying the devil once and for all. Of course Christians will benefit from this as well, as per the insight of Paul in Romans 16:20, but its primary reference is to Jesus himself.

If I might be forgiven a rare lapse into national nepotism, I will cite, as one example of a confession from the Reformation period which expressly adopted this Messianic view of the verse, the Scots Confession of 1560. At the relevant section, it reads:

> For this we constantlie beleeve, that God, after the feirfull and horrible defectioun of man fra his obedience, did seek Adam againe, call upon him, rebuke his sinne, convict him of the same, and in the end made unto him ane most joyful promise, to wit, That the seed of the woman suld break down the serpents

---

[287] E. W. von Hegstenberg, *The Christology of the Old Testament*, vol 1 (Edinburgh, 1854), pp 19f.

head [Gen 3:15], that is, he suld destroy the works of the Devill.[288]

Several modern Christian translations of the Bible have also shown a commitment to this interpretation of the verse by the way in which they have rendered the ambiguous Hebrew pronoun for 'he/it' in the second half of the verse simply by the appropriate masculine pronoun for 'he' in the translation-language. In the first half of the verse we are told that God will put a strong hostility between the two 'seeds'. In the words which immediately follow, English usage, for instance, would normally demand the neuter pronoun to refer to the noun 'seed'. Indeed the 1611 King James Version translated it accordingly: 'it shall bruise thy head'. But versions like the Revised Standard Version and the New International Version translate it under the influence of their Messianic understanding of its meaning. In their decision to help Christians to interpret it in the same way, they translate it as: 'he will crush your head'. The 'he' to whom this is seen to refer is clearly Jesus.

As we shall see shortly, the oldest Jewish version, the LXX, also renders this Hebrew pronoun by the Greek equivalent for 'he', strongly suggesting that those translators also worked with a Messianic understanding of the verse. But we shall return to the LXX in a later context. Presumably the strength of the popularity of this Messianic view in the Christian world explains why the Jewish leadership shied away from it and tried to marginalise its earlier popularity in the Jewish community. Thankfully, though, we do know that early on there were some Messianic interpretations of the verse which were popular among certain Jewish groups at least. Of course these interpretations did not view *Jesus* as that Messiah, but nonetheless they held that Gen 3:15 was a

---

[288] *Scots Confession*, article iv; ed G. D. Henderson (1937), pp 46f.

reference to the Messiah's work of destroying the work of Satan. Here are some of the relevant comments:

> And they [the woman's sons] will make peace in the end of the days of King Messiah.[289]

> As the incarnation of evil, Satan is the arch-enemy of the Messiah . . . God showed Satan the Messiah, and when he saw him, he trembled, fell on his face, and cried, 'Truly this is the Messiah who will bruise me' . . . [290]

> The things which God created perfect, since mankind sinned, have become corrupt, and will not return to their proper condition until the son of Perez comes.[291]

In the Talmud itself there is a lovely phrase which speaks of 'the heels of the Messiah', referring to the coming of the Messiah in time of crisis for Israel. This poetic image may very well owe its origin to the Messianic interpretation of our verse.[292]

In the midrash Tanhuma there is a lovely and revealing homily on the significance of the teaching of the targums that there will be no peace for the serpent's descendants in the days of the Messiah. In its way, it testifies to the reality of the Messianic interpretation of this verse in the thinking of the Jewish people at that time:

> In the world to come, all those having blemishes will be healed, but the serpent will not be healed, as it is written: 'Cursed are you above all cattle', because everyone will be healed, but it will not be healed. Of man it is written: 'Then shall the lame man leap like a deer' and 'The eyes of the blind shall be opened'

---

[289] Targum Pseudo-Jonathan, op cit. See also Targum Neofiti and the so-called Fragmentary Targum.

[290] Pesikta Rabbati 3:6.

[291] Genesis Rabbah 12. 'Perez' is a name of the Messiah from Judah in rabbinic tradition, based on their interpretation of Gen 38:29 and Ruth 4:18ff.

[292] See Sotah 49b.

. . . likewise of beasts and cattle: 'The wolf and the lamb will feed together, and the lion will eat straw like the ox'. But as to the serpent, 'dust will be its food', since it will not be healed, because it brought all creatures down to the dust.

Lukyn Williams made the feasible suggestion that there could well have been an ancient belief in the region of the Near East along the lines that human nature is so irredeemably corrupt that there is no hope for humanity unless some figure comes to rescue us.[293] Already in the time of Abraham, one of the high gods of Babylon, Merodach, was worshipped as the one who slew the evil serpent, Tiamat. Lukyn Williams suggested that in Israel they believed that someone would have to come who was stronger than even Merodach, because the serpent was only the servant of the source of evil, and the world was in need of the destruction of the source of evil itself. He offered John 8:56 as words of Jesus which might allude to such a belief:

Your father Abraham rejoiced at the thought of seeing my day; he saw it and was glad.

When all is said and done, though, there is no hard evidence for such a belief.[294] Be this as it may, early Jewish literature shows that a Messianic interpretation of this verse was held by Jewish people in the days when the Church was in the throes of developing its self-identity and its strategies of evangelism. Satan, or the devil, as he came to be regarded in Christian thought, was considered to be behind the figure of the serpent, and so it was his humiliating punishment which was seen to be being portrayed in the verse.

Let us return to the text. It seems to me unmistakable that

---

[293] A. Lukyn Williams, *A Manual of Christian Evidences for Jewish People*, op cit, p 116.

[294] For Jewish references to the ultimate victory over the source of evil, related to this current context, see Genesis Rabbah 56 and Deuteronomy Rabbah 11. In the New Testament, we have Rom 16:20; Rev 12:9; 20:2.

what we have here is a context of *moral* conflict, and not simply natural hostilities, since the Hebrew word used for 'enmity' 'êvah is one used of morally responsible characters in the other biblical passages where it is found (Num 35:21–22; Ezek 25:15; 35:5). What is more, these other passages suggest that this term for conflict refers to a lasting, conscious hostility. Who, then, are the parties in conflict in our present passage? There are two possible contexts in which to try to answer that question.

a) A corporate view of the word ' seed'.　In other words, the reference is to godly people in conflict with ungodly people. This could either be taken in a universal sense, applicable to all cultures and religious groups, or related specifically to Israel. Many Jewish scholars, especially in the modern period, have tended to opt for this interpretation.

b) An individual view of the word ' seed'.　In other words, the reference is to a climaxing of this conflict (between those people trying to follow God's will and those rebellious people under the influence of the serpent) in the persons of the Messiah and the devil. This has become the consensus view within the Churches. In support of this interpretation Christians have cited the analogous way in which Paul interprets the same word, 'seed', in Gal 3:15–25. In this passage Paul takes the verses which speak of Abraham's promised seed as having their ultimate fulfilment in the individual person of the Messiah, namely Jesus. Interestingly, in Gal 4:4–5, he also refers to the birth of the Messiah, stressing it in such a way that it reminds me of our verse in Gen 3:15:

> But when the time had fully come, God sent his Son, born of a woman, born under law, to redeem those under law, that we might receive the full rights of sons.

It strikes me that the reference here to Jesus being 'born of a woman' could well be an allusion to the Gen 3:15 promise given to the 'seed of the woman'. Paul might easily have been reminded of the famous Gen 3:15 'seed' passage as he developed his thinking about his primary concern at that point, namely the various Abrahamic 'seed' passages.

We need to pause to ask ourselves at this juncture whether there is any clue in the word itself which will help us in our deliberation of the meaning of the 'seed' in our verse. Jewish sources argue that even though in the Hebrew Bible the word for 'seed' is singular in grammatical form, it is actually used of a person's descendants (plural). In other words, they say, it is a kind of collective singular for one's descendants, devoid of any theological import whatsoever.

Christians have been quick to counter that although this line of reasoning might make perfect sense in most contexts, since the Hebrew word for 'seed' is, naturally, only used with reference to a *man's* procreative descendants, 'seed' being his contribution to the creative process, there must be some theological significance in the fact that it is the *woman* who is said to be the originator of this seed in Gen 3:15, not the man. Jewish refutationists have often rejoined, without any real textual warrant, that at this point Adam is simply missing from the conversation, so that God, when speaking to the serpent, naturally refers to the seed as Eve's, she being the only person beside them both.[295] This image of God turning to speak to Adam but finding only Eve there to be the recipient of his gesture and words, is somewhat weak as arguments go.

But Jewish commentators also point, with considerably more merit, to the case of Gen 16:10, where the angel of the Lord says to Hagar, not to Abraham, that the angel is going to ensure that her 'seed' becomes too numerous to count. This verse certainly strengthens the claim that at least

---

[295] See Gerald Sigal, *The Jew and the Christian Missionary*, op cit, p 3.

in the earliest days of Israel's language the word 'seed' could be used metaphorically of women as well as maintaining its normal usage *vis-à-vis* men.

Nonetheless, many Christians, as we shall see later, suggest that we have here in Gen 3:15 a hint of the *priority* of the woman over the man, itself being a hint of the virgin birth, the doctrine that Jesus was certainly born of a woman but without the participation of a man or his 'seed'.

However, we need to say a little more about the 'seed' before we move on to that issue. The word is used some forty times in Genesis in a corporate sense (eg, 7:3; 15:5), but also nine times in an individual/corporate sense (eg, 4:25; 22:17f). The noun itself is singular in form, as we have noted, but we find it used with plural verbs and adjectives when it is used corporately (eg, 15:13–16; 17:7f), and with singular verbs when used in an individual/corporate sense (eg, 16:10). It is therefore entirely possible, speaking solely in terms of the way in which the word is used, that in Gen 3:15 we are dealing with a verse in which the correct understanding of the word 'seed' is to see it in an individual sense. The pronoun in that verse is certainly singular in form, emphasising that *he*, not they, will go on to crush the serpent's head.

Indeed, to return to a point made earlier, some scholars believe that the LXX, the Jewish version of the Hebrew Bible from the mid-third century BCE, provides circumstantial evidence that there was at one time, long before the rise and flourishing of Christianity, a *standard* Jewish interpretation of this verse which was Messianic. The LXX translators would seem to have broken the rules of Greek grammar in order to maintain a masculine singular reference for the seed. The Greek word used here for seed (*spermatos*), from which we get our English word 'sperm', is neuter, not masculine. However, the pronoun in the second half of the verse which refers to it, and which should also therefore be in a neuter form in accordance with the rules of Greek grammar, in order to agree with the noun, is actually given in a *masculine* form (*autos sou*). Many Christians take this to be a deliberate suspension of the rules of grammar in order to make a theological point, namely that this seed will be a specific male person, namely the Messiah. This may also be somewhat weak, as arguments go, but the text of the LXX is certainly a puzzle, if this is not the correct interpretation of its translation policy.

There does seem to be something going on in this early Jewish version, and a Messianic interpretation of the verse was certainly known in the Jewish tradition, even though some try to deny this today. In a midrash on Gen 4:1, we find the following comment:

> Rabbi Tanhuma said, 'Eve had respect to that seed which is coming from another place. And who is this? This is the Messiah, the King.'[296]

David Kimchi, one of the most important medieval Jewish commentators on the Bible, wrote the following in his commentary on this passage in Genesis:

> As you went forth for the salvation of your people by the hand of the Messiah, the son of David, who shall wound Satan, the head . . . of the house of the wicked.

These references are general enough to allow several various interpretations, of course, but at the very least we have solid grounds for affirming that the Christian view of this verse as a prophetic reference to the conflict between the Messiah and the forces opposed to God is not actually un-Jewish.

Now to return to the matter of the virgin birth. If this is a Messianic prophecy of sorts, is the linking of the Messianic 'seed' to the woman and not, as would be expected, to the man, an indication that the Messiah's birth would be particu-

---

[296] Genesis Rabbah 23. See also Genesis Rabbah 51 and Numbers Rabbah 2, 22.

larly associated with his mother, rather than with his father? The Vulgate, the official Roman Catholic translation of the Bible into Latin, translates this indication into certainty in its rendering of our verse. While there are some manuscripts which translate the third line of the verse as 'he shall crush your head', the Vulgate's translation reads as follows:

> I will put enmity between you and the woman,
> and between your seed and between her seed;
> she shall crush your head,
> and you shall lie in wait for his heel.

The feminine personal pronoun, 'she' (*ipsa*) is undoubtedly a reference to Mary, the mother of Jesus. Although, as I say, this is the Vulgate version as we have it, it does not represent the opinion or translation of Jerome. In another place altogether he refers to the Old Latin translation of this verse and to an emendation he would make to it in the light of his understanding of the Hebrew text, and in both cases he uses the Latin pronoun for 'he' (*ipse*).

Nonetheless, the fact remains that an interpretation which sees a reference to Mary here has become standard in the Roman Catholic Church. On 1st November 1950, the doctrine of the Assumption of Mary was defined in the Apostolic Constitution entitled *Munificentissimus Deus*. In that work, we find the following summary:

> We must remember especially that, since the second century, the Virgin Mary has been designated by the holy Fathers as the new Eve, who, although subject to the new Adam, is most intimately associated with Him in that struggle against the infernal foe which, as foretold in the protoevangelium, would finally result in that most complete victory over the sin and death which are always mentioned together in the writings of the Apostle of the Gentiles.[297]

---

[297] This is a translation of the Latin original. The Latin text can be found in *Acta Apostolicae Sedis*, 4th November 1950, p 68.

It is not only Roman Catholics, though, who see a prophetic reference to the Virgin Birth in this verse. Some other Christians cite Gen 4:1b, only a few verses further on, in support of such a view. Most of the translations of that half of that verse add some phrase to it, like that of the NIV, 'With the help of the LORD'. However, such a phrase does not exist in the Hebrew original. The Hebrew text simply has: 'I have acquired a man – the Lord' (qanîtî 'îsh 'et-YHWH).

It can be feasibly argued that the meaning of the phrase *must* be that with God's help Eve has given birth to another son. Many scholars believe that some such phrase as 'with the help of the Lord' has dropped out of what was the original text. The LXX has already supplied a preposition to give this understanding of the verse. In spite of this, certain schools of Christian thought hold that the absence of such a phrase is deliberate. It is taken to be a prophecy of the Messiah, who will be not only a man but also the Lord among us. They see the two texts of Gen 3:15 and 4:1 as belonging closely together in their ultimate meaning as well as in their locations within the book of Genesis.

It is also significant, in my view, that when Eve has her third child she does not say, as the translations have it, 'God has granted me another child in place of Abel'. The Hebrew text is quite clear. She says, 'God has granted me another "seed" (zera') in place of Abel'. The serpent's nemesis, this 'seed', will come through the line of Seth. It has even been suggested that Lamech (one of Seth's descendants) thought that his son, Noah, who of course is one of the most significant characters in the Bible, was directly related to the great person who was believed to be coming one day to reverse the curses of Genesis 3. This is based on the close relationship between Lamech's words about Noah in Gen 5:29, and the curse set out in Gen 3:17–19.

I often wonder whether the strange episode recounted in Gen 6:1–4 reflects the belief that the devil tried to spoil the seed of the woman, thus corrupting the Messianic line. If so, perhaps that is why God sent the terrible punishment of the flood, ridding humanity of that corrupt seed while saving humanity from extinction by preserving the lives of Noah and his family. Could this be the real significance of Noah? Many people have pointed out that humanity soon returned to a state of moral corruption after the flood, and have therefore seriously questioned the worth of this drastic action by God. What did such a wholesale killing of almost all of humanity accomplish, if the next generation simply returned to the old ways? But it may be that the corrupt seed which had to be rooted out was specifically related to the offspring, or seed, of these 'sons of the gods' and 'the daughters of human kind'. Perhaps it was simply not a moral issue at all!

Whatever the relative merits of all the above arguments and understandings, the fact remains that Jewish people reject the application of this verse to *Jesus'* life and work. Daily experience shows, they claim, that Jesus did not destroy the works of the devil when he came, so that even if this were held to be a Messianic text, it would not refer to Jesus. Not only is there quite ample evidence of sin in the world around us, but Christians themselves are far from immune to it. Jewish people smile ironically when Christians mention texts like 1 John 3:8–9, or Heb 2:14, both of which speak about the task of destroying the devil's work, while the Johannine passage also maintains that those who are 'born of God' will not 'continue in sin'.

Jewish refutationists also like to quote passages such as 1 Tim 1:15 and 1 John 1:8, where sin is acknowledged as a sorry reality in the lives of the apostles, setting these words over against what they see as the naïve triumphalism of exhortations such as we find in Rom 16:20. The words of Paul in 1 Thess 2:18 are quoted quite often by refutationists to further give the lie, as they see it, to the claim that Jesus was the Messiah who destroyed the power of the devil.[298]

In the following discussion I will sometimes refer to 'the Devil/Satan' in this fashion, using these two different names to indicate a fundamental area of difference between Jews and Christians. Jewish tradition does not interpret the passages in the Hebrew Bible which speak about 'Satan' in the same way as Christians traditionally speak of the 'Devil'. The figure of Satan which we see in the opening chapters of Job, for example, where he is referred to as 'the Satan', as if it is a title rather than a personal name, is seen as some type of legitimate servant of God. He has the task of being a tester or prosecutor, albeit entirely under the authority of God. This is a different image altogether from the Christian one in which the Devil has no redeeming feature or purpose whatsoever, and according to which he is in total opposition to God, not seeking to serve him at all. This makes a significant difference in the way in which several New Testament texts will be interpreted by Jews and Christians.

The whole concept of the origin and nature of Sin/sins is also totally different in Jewish tradition from that found in Christianity. Putting these two issues together, this means that the relationship between Satan/the Devil and Sin/sins is radically different in the two communities. We have here another case of the reality that when Jews and Christians use the same terminology, they can nevertheless be meaning quite different things by those terms. We cannot take the space here to discuss this issue, but by using the terms together in the way that I shall, I hope at least to keep the matter alive in my readers' minds.

What are we to say, then, in response to this charge that Jesus did not crush the head of the serpent or its master? This is a serious criticism which the Jewish community brings, and one which we must treat with a great deal of respect. It is

---

[298] One who does this is Beth Moshe, *Judaism's Truth Answers the Missionaries*, op cit, pp 173f.

not unrelated to the issue which we spent some time examining in an earlier chapter in Part One of this book, namely the problem of a patent lack of *shalom* in the life of the world and the Church. How, then, do Christians respond to this challenge that the continuing presence of sin in our lives, and the evident power of the Devil/Satan, invalidate the Messianic claims of Jesus? There are four major responses which I think are important and relevant.

- The eradication of sin is not solely tied up with the Devil/Satan, but is essentially a result of our own corrupt human nature. If the Devil/Satan were to be destroyed completely today, we would all still wake up tomorrow as sinners. He tempts and exploits, but he did not create sin. It is worth pointing out that in the three great chapters of Romans concerning sin and grace, chapters 6–8, not once is the Devil/Satan mentioned by Paul. The power of sin in our lives, he believes, goes on because of our own lack of commitment to God, and because of our own self-centredness, not because of any inadequacy in Jesus. And so the continuation of sin is not actually evidence that the dominion of the Devil/Satan over the world has not been broken.
- It is therefore not a life without sin, but a life freed from bondage to the *habitual practice of sin*, and a life radically sensitised to the need for constant repentance and spiritual/moral contrition, which is the lifestyle said in the New Testament to be characteristic of those who follow Jesus. This is what is being said in 1 John 3:9, since the form of the Greek verb there describes habitual, not sporadic, action. The New Testament is not trying to teach that Christians do not sin. So once again, it has to be said that the mere fact of sin in the lives of believers does not mean that the Devil/Satan still has control of the world.
- Whereas the Devil/Satan no longer controls the lives of believers, God does allow him to tempt them. One of the profound aspects of the teaching of the Bible in this

context is that in both the Hebrew and the Greek languages the same word is used for both 'tempting' and 'testing'. This means that every temptation which we face is also a test, if we can only see it that way. It is a test of our faithfulness to God and of our resolve to live according to his will. Resisting a temptation is like passing this test, and this kind of test of our faith, coupled with the other kinds of test which we meet in life, develops in us perseverance and maturity (see Jas 1:2–4). This arena of temptation and struggle with sin is therefore to be accepted in a positive, not a negative, light. It is not a disqualification of Jesus' Messiahship, but rather a proof of our discipleship.

- Jesus' resurrection holds the key to this mystery, because it is our assurance of deliverance from the temptations of the Devil/Satan and from the Devil/Satan's power of death. This is presented as the message of 1 Cor 15:50–57. When Jesus returns, he will destroy the Devil/Satan once and for all, as it says in Revelation 20, and thereafter there will be no more death or pain of any sort, as it says in Revelation 21. But until that time, although his dominance is broken, his residual power is still strong enough to be more powerful than any human effort or strength. We have returned, as we so often do, to the crucial doctrine of the Second Coming of the Messiah to give the final word in this matter.

Christians are not therefore backed into a theological corner with respect to the Messianic interpretation of this verse, from which there is no reasonable defence, as refutationists would like to claim. As we noted quite frequently throughout Part One of the book, though, there is no room for any simplistic triumphalism in this matter.

Let me close this discussion of the Messianic interpretation of Gen 3:15 with a rather stimulating comment by Franz Delitzsch. In his commentary with Keil, he noted what seemed to him to be a significant point. As you study Genesis 3, you notice that Adam does not name his wife until verse 20, that is, *after* the series of curses. One might have expected this to have taken place more naturally at 2:22–24, the passage which actually marks her creation. Although the precise derivation and meaning of her name is not known to us, it seems clear that it has something to do with 'life', and Delitzsch intuits a prophetic word of promise here. He suggests that the timing of her name-giving is intended to act as a prophetic promise of the victory of life over death and sin, of blessing over curse.

Not only that, but this prophetic sign is associated with the woman, not the man (perhaps another veiled allusion to the Virgin Birth?). Delitzsch also noted in this specific context that if we count Adam as the first generation, then the seventh generation through Seth (the number seven being considered symbolically as the perfect number in Scripture) is represented by Enoch. We might therefore expect something significant about his life, if there is some merit in Delitzsch's intuition, and indeed we find the teaching of Gen 5:24 that Enoch did not die! Delitzsch therefore sees Enoch's translation to heaven as 'a prophecy in act of the future end of death'.[299]

Therefore, although the Messianic interpretation of this verse is perhaps rather less obvious than that of many other more famous verses, it certainly repays the serious thought which we are obliged to give it in the light of its importance in the thinking of the Church. Whether or not Christians will rush to the defence of this verse in the contemporary disputes, at least it is perhaps not so difficult as many might have thought to appreciate why the early Church saw in this verse, Gen 3:15, 'the first Gospel message'.

---

[299] Keil and Delitzsch on Genesis, op cit, p 41.

14

Is 'Shiloh' the name of the Messiah? Genesis 49:10

This verse is one about which both Jews and Christians agree – at least to the extent of agreeing that it is a Messianic prophecy. Thereafter, there are strong differences, as might be expected, but here is a text which has captured the imagination of both communities down the generations:

> The sceptre will not depart from Judah,
> nor the ruler's staff from between his feet,
> until he comes to whom it belongs
> and the obedience of the nations is his.

A second reading of this verse shows us that in this translation there is no mention of 'Shiloh', or any other name for the Messiah. Therefore what is the point of my title? In the actual text of the NIV translation, given here without the NIV notes, a footnote is attached to the third line of the verse which offers the alternative translation: 'until Shiloh comes'. Who, then, is 'Shiloh', and why do many Christians see him as being of Messianic significance? Why do some translations not have a reference to Shiloh in their text? We shall need to become involved in a certain amount of historical and linguistic study to come to an intelligent decision about these matters.

But we begin, as always, with some words about the context of the verse. Gen 49:1–28 is the record of Jacob's blessings on his sons. An immediate issue of interpretation is whether these are meant to be seen as simple historical blessings, or whether they are somehow prophetic, referring to God's plans for the last days, the days of the Messiah. In the opening verse of the chapter we find the enigmatic phrase, 'in the last days', translated in different ways in the Bible versions. Traditionally, both Jewish and Christian commentators have seen this phrase as a kind of formula referring to the days of the Messianic era, the last days of life as we know it before the ultimate intervention by God into history. Rabbi David Kimchi spoke for this tradition when he said: 'Whenever it is said "in the last days", it means the days of the Messiah.'

Indeed, this verse is so commonly assumed within the Jewish community to be referring to the Messiah that a famous rabbinic authority, known as the Ba'al Ha-Turim, brought as one piece of corroborating evidence of this interpretation the fact that the numerical value of the Hebrew phrase 'Shiloh will come' (yavo' shîloh) is exactly equal to the numerical value of the Hebrew word for Messiah (mashîah).[300] Whatever one may think of the significance or otherwise of such 'sacred play' with the numbers, the real importance, as I say, of this *particular* piece of sacred play with numbers is that it demonstrates the confidence of the rabbinic community that our verse is a bona fide Messianic prophecy of some sort. Hence the reason for any interest in this chapter at all by those looking for prophecies concerning the Messiah. Notice that the Messianic line is being further defined here. Reuben (verses 3–4), the first-born, and there-

---

[300] The number in question here is 358. In Hebrew, the letters of the alphabet also function as the numbers, so that every letter is also a number. Hence every word or phrase can also be said to have a numerical value if you simply add up the individual letter-numbers. Several systems of interpretation of texts grew up around this phenomenon, and the general term used to refer to them is *gematria*. For those traditional Jewish people who take this seriously (and there are very many), equivalence in numerical value, such as we have here, is regarded as especially significant, somehow linking the different words themselves.

fore the one to be expected to have pre-eminence, loses the blessing of the first-born. There are two other sons who receive the greatest blessings from Jacob, Judah (verses 8–12), and Joseph (verses 22–26). Of these two, it is clear from the chapter that the responsibility of ruling over the tribes falls to Judah. The Messiah, then, will come from the tribe of Judah.

Two words of caution must be given at this stage, however. Firstly, the New Testament does not draw attention to this as a Messianic text, so that not all Christians feel bound to support it as a vitally important text. Secondly, there are also many Jewish people today who do not see this in a Messianic light. For instance, Rabbi W. Gunther Plaut, writing the commentary on Genesis in his immensely influential volume of the last decade, categorically states that Gen 49:1 is 'not a reference to messianic days, as older translations . . . suggest'.[301] Nevertheless, the fact remains that in both rabbinic and Christian traditions, this verse is an established prophetic reference to the Messianic Era.

The promise comes in the context of Jacob's words to his son, Judah. The very name Judah (yehûdah) seems to come from a Hebrew verbal root (yadah) meaning 'to praise' (see verse 8a). There is actually a pun on his name in Gen 29:35. Ibn Ezra, a prominent Jewish commentator, says that Judah will be praised because God is so much in evidence in his life, whereas David Kimhi and the Rashbam argue that Judah's brothers will concede the right of royal rule to him as they praise him.

In verse 8b of our chapter in Genesis there is a promise of military victories, related in Jewish tradition to the many successes of Judah's great descendant, King David (see, for example, 2 Sam 22:41). The Hebrew Bible clearly portrays the tribe of Judah's numerical supremacy (Num 2:4; 26:22);

---

[301] W. Gunther Plaut (ed), *The Torah. A Modern Commentary* (Union of American Hebrew Congregations, NY, 1981), p 308.

its prestigious place in the marching line-up of the tribes (Num 2:3; 10:13–14); and its consolidation as the bearer of the royal line (2 Sam 5:1–3; 1 Chron 28:4).

Judah is also described in verse 9 as a lion cub who will grow up to be a protective lion, guarding the other cubs in their home territory. This is a remarkable and potent image. It is not without significance that Jesus is hailed as 'the Lion of the tribe of Judah' in Rev 5:5. Then in verse 10, the one which we are particularly interested in, Judah is associated explicitly with royal imagery. Maimonides, Nachmanides and most of the medieval and later rabbinic authorities agree that this signifies that Israel's royal power will come to, and through, the tribe of Judah. The sceptre is a sure symbol of royal authority and of sovereignty,[302] and most commentators also see the staff as a symbol of ruling power, paralleling the sceptre. It is taken this way in the LXX and the Vulgate.[303] Rabbi David Kimchi also takes it this way in his commentary.

Some rabbis, however,[304] claim that the staff is more properly associated with the *law-giver's* role in Israel, that is, the office of scribe and scholar. The interpretation of the staff as somehow referring to scribal, as distinct from royal, authority, is based on the view that the Hebrew word for staff (meḥaqeq) derives from the same root which gives us the Hebrew term for a statutory law (ḥoq), a word which is regularly used in connection with the commandments of God. This understanding of the staff, supporting the ideology that after the fall of the royal house of David God gave leadership of Israel to the rabbinic authorities, is already found in Targum Neofiti to Genesis. In this early work, we

---

[302] See also Isa 14:5; Ezek 19:11, 14; Amos 1:5, 8; Ps 45:7 (verse 6 in the English translations).

[303] For the staff symbol elsewhere, see Num 21:18; Ps 60:9 (verse 7 in the English translations).

[304] See, for instance, Genesis Rabbah 98:13, and Ibn Ezra.

find the translation that not only will the *sceptre* not depart, but 'neither shall scribes teaching the Torah from his sons' sons'.

I note that the NIV actually chooses this 'lawgiving' line of interpretation for the Hebrew word in quite another biblical context. Here in our verse it translates the word as 'ruler's staff', though the word 'ruler' is not in the Hebrew text at all. By this addition of the word 'ruler', the impression is given that the NIV translators accept the more usual understanding of the word. However, in Isa 33:22, at which point the word is used of God himself, they translate it quite differently. It is the final word in the second line of their translation:

> For the LORD is our judge,
> the LORD is our *lawgiver*,
> the LORD is our king;
> it is he who will save us.

In Judg 5:14, where the same word is found, a verse which also contains the word translated as 'sceptre' in Gen 49:10, the NIV translators preferred the military connotations of the English word 'commander'. Did they have that military responsibility of the king in mind in their understanding of the Genesis verse? Whatever the answer to that question, it must be said that although such an interpretation of Gen 49:10 in terms of *scribal* or *rabbinic* authority might have suited the rabbinic community quite well, so much so that some Christians are thereby disposed to doubt its originality, we cannot actually rule out the possibility that this Hebrew word does indeed relate positively to the notion of moral/spiritual/scribal authority as well as to royal sovereignty. We should keep it in mind as we focus on the consensus view that it is simply another reference to a royal symbol.

The phrase 'between his feet' is undoubtedly a euphemism for the procreative organs,[305] signifying that this right to rule over Israel will be inherited by Judah's descendants after him. The LXX, the Targums and the Vulgate all take it to mean his progeny. The impression is clearly given that Judah will have pre-eminence in Israel. Further evidence of this may be inferred from the Hebrew word (yiqhat), found in the final part of the verse. Some translators take this word to mean something to do with a 'gathering together' ('and the nations will gather together to him'), whereas others, for example the NIV, render it by the term 'obedience' ('and the obedience of the nations is his'). The LXX, the Syriac, and the Vulgate seem to have read another Hebrew word altogether, one which means 'hope' (tiqvah), and my intuition is that they were deliberately injecting a Messianic interpretation into the text at that point. But whichever way is correct, the key image, that of Judah's central role, is clearly being expressed.[306]

How then, focusing on our own particular concern, do the refutationists respond to the claim that this is a Messianic prophecy? Let us begin with an actual example from an influential polemical book, *The Book of the Covenant*, written by Joseph Kimhi in the twelfth century. We have quoted him before, and have noted that in his terminology, the term *min* denotes the Jewish believer in Jesus, while the term *ma'amin* is used to refer to the faithful rabbinic Jew.

> The min said: What can you say of the passage in the Torah: *The scepter shall not be taken from Judah, nor the ruler from his thigh until he comes who is to be sent?* This is Jesus, for when he came, you lost your kingdom and you have neither sovereignty

---

[305] For other instances of this same euphemism for the genital organs and that general area, see Deut 28:57 and Isa 7:20.

[306] For possible references to this word meaning 'gathering together', see Gen 1:9; Jer 3:17. A text where the same word seems to be used in the context of 'obedience' is Prov 30:17.

nor king because of what you did to the Messiah.

The ma'amin said: Do you not know that this blessing is in the benediction with which Jacob blessed his sons! He blessed each one of them with his own blessing. In blessing Judah, he gave him the kingship, i.e. the king who would reign over Israel, along with his progeny, would come forth from him. This was David, the first king who ruled over Israel . . . Judah was told that dominion would not pass from his sons until David came to receive his kingship . . .

For more than four hundred years before the coming of Jesus, the kingship had passed from the house of David. The last king from the house of David was Zedekiah whom Nebuchadnezzar king of Babylon blinded and led into exile . . . How then can you say that the kingship of the house of David did not pass until Jesus came?[307]

There is no explicit denial that this is a Messianic prophecy, and in fact there is actually an implicit consent to this interpretation, in that rabbinic Judaism accepts that the Messiah will be descended from David and fulfil the service of that royal house. However, the focus is on David himself in this whole section and the conviction is certainly there that this Messianic text was not fulfilled by Jesus. The argument that the sceptre (ie, ruling power) had indeed departed from Judah with the removal of King Zedekiah (2 Kings 24:12–20; 25:1–11), so that the verse cannot refer to Jesus, is used by almost all of the refutationists.[308] Christians often respond by saying that if this is the case, then there can never be any fulfilment of this prophecy, but since both Jews and Christians refuse to believe that, then, they say, there must be a flaw in the argument. Some Jewish people have replied that God had his Messiah in mind before the time of the desola-

[307] Rabbi Joseph Kimhi, *Sefer Ha-Berit*, op cit, 24b–25b.
[308] In our day it has been used by Samuel Levine, *You Take Jesus, I'll Take God*, op cit, pp 62f.

tion of Jerusalem and the house of David, and that the Messiah was to have been Judah's King Hezekiah.

Some Jewish polemicists do concede that the point of the text is that no matter who happens to be ruling Israel at any given moment in history, the *right* to rule belongs only to Judah. This point was made forcefully by Nachmanides in his public dispute with Pablo Christiani in Barcelona in 1263. He insisted that no matter whether Judah lost sovereignty over the tribes of Israel for a vast amount of time in the exile from the land of Israel, when the time came for God to forgive and restore his people, kingship would be returned to Judah. There is actually a prayer of the High Priest presented in the Talmud in which he prays in this vein on Yom Kippur, the Day of Atonement.[309] Thus even the exile and degradation of Israel cannot affect this promised right of Judah's to rule in Israel on behalf of the Lord God.

I would certainly see it in this light. Judah's rule over the tribes may be interrupted, perhaps even for some considerable time, but it will never be ended or replaced. We can see an analogous situation if we compare the promise of God *vis-à-vis* the Davidic dynasty, itself a sub-unit within the dynasty of the tribe of Judah, of course. It is clear from 2 Sam 7:11b–16 (and from the poetic version of this found in Ps 89:31–38, verses 30–37 in the English translations) that God's covenant promise to David was that his dynasty would never be overthrown or replaced, and that the right of rule over Israel belonged securely to the House of David, even though individual kings in that dynasty might neglect the Torah of God and need to be punished and replaced. So it is in the case of Judah: God's promise is of the eternal right to rule, even if individual rulers prove unworthy of their position and there are set-backs due to war, secession, or whatever. And just as this Shiloh passage is speaking of the Messiah as the ultimate

---

[309] Yoma 53b.

ruler from the tribe of Judah, so too will the same Messiah be the ultimate fulfilment of the Davidic covenant.

A key issue in the specific discussion of this point, namely the historical dimension of the ruling of Judah, is the correct interpretation of the phrase 'until' in verse 10b ('ad kî). I do not accept the view of those who say that it means when Shiloh comes then the right to rule will be taken away from Judah, in the sense that one might say something like: 'You are only in charge until our real leader comes'. Rather, we should take it to mean that Judah will have the right to rule all the way to the time when the Messiah, himself from the tribe of Judah, comes to personalise and exemplify that rule. He will reign as the supreme son of David. In support of this interpretation I would cite other places in the Hebrew Bible where the same phrase, translated as 'until', is used in contexts which are expressing the idea of a building up to a climax, not an arrival at a cut-off point.[310]

Many Christian leaders, however, have determined to see the force of this phrase 'until' in terms of a complete break in Judah's right to rule. Martin Luther stamped his own authority on this interpretation when he wrote:

> This sceptre of Judah shall continue, and shall not be taken from him till the hero come: but when he comes, then the sceptre also shall depart. The kingdom, or sceptre, *has* fallen; the Jews are scattered throughout the whole world, and therefore the Messiah has certainly come; for, at His appearing, the sceptre should be taken from Judah.[311]

Jewish scholars have also puzzled over the correct interpretation of this phrase. It would be fair to say that Jewish *apologists* have tended to take one of the following two different approaches to this question of the coming of Shi-

---

[310] See Gen 26:13; 41:49; 2 Chron 26:15.

[311] For a fuller quotation, and some discussion, see E. Hengstenberg: *Christology of the Old Testament*, op cit, volume 1, p 62.

loh. Either they have claimed that whatever it is that is being spoken about, it has not happened yet (eg, Targum Onkelos), or they have proclaimed that it all happened a long time before Jesus came on the scene (eg, Rabbi Samuel ben Meir). The latter approach became the more dominant in the Middle Ages, and its popularity continues to this day.

Joseph Kimchi was of the opinion that when King David came, then the tribal dynasty of Judah did indeed come to an end, replaced by the specific Davidic dynasty. 'Until' therefore meant 'until, and no later'.[312] Rashi taught that when the line of David was ended by the exile of Judah in Babylon, then the rightful authority of spiritual and communal leadership which Jacob had entrusted to Judah, was given by God to the forerunners of the rabbis, and thereafter to the rabbis themselves.[313] Even though this has no scriptural warrant, not least because neither the Pharisees nor the rabbis were descended *en bloc* from Judah, it has become extremely popular among Orthodox Jews to this day. Nonetheless, as we shall see, the clear majority of the ancient authorities, and a significant number of later ones, understood the word 'until' to mean that Judah's rule would continue until it led to the day when Judah's great son, King David, came to the throne.

The question which remains unasked, but which cries out to be answered, is the obvious one: who is this Shiloh about whom there is so much fuss? The whole matter is compounded by the fact that not all translations of the text even have a reference to a Shiloh. The NIV translation, which I quoted at the head of the chapter, does not have it, though it includes, as I mentioned there, a footnote with an alternative translation which does refer to Shiloh. Today, one can find four main approaches to understanding the Hebrew

---

[312] Rabbi Joseph Kimchi: *Sefer Ha-Berit.* op cit.

[313] See the translation of Rashi's commentary on the Pentateuch by M. Rosenbaum and A. M. Silberman (Jerusalem, 1973), pp 245–247.

term which is rendered in simple transliteration as *Shiloh*
(shîloh) only one of which sees it as a reference to the name
of the Messiah.

Some take Shiloh to be a geographical location. There was
an important biblical site of that name to the north of
Jerusalem, as any biblical map will show clearly. The Jewish Publication Society has adopted this translation in its
English version of the Hebrew Bible, and a large number
of Jewish commentators have taken this same line. They
claim that this part of the prophecy was fulfilled, at least
partially, when the Israelites gathered at Shiloh, as recorded
in Josh 18:1 (the word in that verse for 'gathering' (qahal) is
not the same one as is found in our verse, however). The
commentator who is quoted more than any in this regard
nowadays is the highly influential Rabbi Samuel ben Meir,
known as the Rashbam, who in his commentary on Genesis
wrote of this verse that 'Shiloh that is written here is just the
name of a city'. He notes there that this interpretation
'constitutes a refutation of the heretics'.[314]

W. Gunther Plaut, whom I mentioned above as a particularly influential Progressive Rabbi, wrote in his 1981 commentary that although he favoured another interpretation of
the term *Shiloh* in this verse, the possibility was there that it
could have this geographical reference. The translation
would then have to be: 'Until Judah will come to worship
at Shiloh', signifying the momentous era when 'the northern
and southern kingdoms will be reunited'.[315]

Shiloh, an important pre-Jerusalem sanctuary in the territory of Ephraim, is mentioned as a town thirty-three times in
the Hebrew Bible, but there is no evidence that a town of that
name actually existed in the time of Jacob. It is never

---

[314] These quotations are taken from the translation of this commentary by
Martin I. Lockshin for the Edwin Mellen Press (1989), p 362.
[315] Op cit, p 309.

mentioned in the Pentateuch, and in fact Josh 18:1 is the first reference to it to be found in the Bible. It is quite possible that the place was given the name 'Shiloh' upon or after the occasion when the tribes set up the Tent of Meeting there. There is a Hebrew root (shalah), which means 'to rest', and if the term *Shiloh* (shîloh) is related to that root, then it is possible that Shiloh became the name of the place after Israel and the Tent of Meeting 'rested' there. Franz Delitzsch, a leading Christian commentator of the last century with great expertise in the whole area of Jewish–Christian relations, took this view (as have a certain number of other Christian commentators) that Shiloh signifies a place, rather than a person. He wrote:

> Jacob promises to Judah the leadership of the tribes of his people as an inalienable right, won through his lion-like courage, until, on his coming to Shiloh, his dominion of the tribes should be enlarged to a dominion over the world.[316]

---

[316] Franz Delitzsch, *Messianic Prophecies in Historical Succession*, No 9 (1891) p 50.

Of course there are some stubborn little facts which need to be taken into account: Judah's dominion over the tribes did not begin until long after the tribes reached Shiloh; elsewhere in the Hebrew Bible, the place known as Shiloh is spelled differently (shiloh not shîloh); the sceptre of Judah would also suggest royal power, not just tribal authority, and Josh 18:1 does not mention this at all. Moreover, David, the descendant of Judah who became the archetypal king of Israel, was crowned king in Hebron, not Shiloh (see 2 Sam 5:1–5).

There are therefore some difficult and important problems with interpreting Shiloh as a geographical reference in our verse. And of course this whole discussion *assumes* that if it is a place, then it is the famous Shiloh location mentioned in the book of Joshua.

Some take Shiloh to be the name of a person, most probably the Messiah. The consensus of Jewish scholarly opinion, and this was definitely the case in the ancient sources, favours this view, seeing 'Shiloh' as a reference to the person of the Messiah. For instance, at Qumran, one of the documents speaks of Shiloh's sceptre as being Messianic, and not only that, but in fact the very sceptre mentioned in Balaam's oracle given at Num 24:17, where he says:

> I see him, but not now;
> I behold him, but not near.
> A star will come out of Jacob;
> a sceptre will rise out of Israel.[317]

Another Qumran document takes this Genesis verse to be about the Messiah driving out the Gentiles in the great eschatalogical battle.[318] But most explicit of all is a small

---

[317] The same word for 'sceptre' (shevet) is used in both verses. This interpretation is found in CD 7:19f.
[318] 1QM 11:6.

fragment found at Qumran which includes in its text of our verse, after the word Shiloh, the phrase, 'the Messiah of Righteousness, the Shoot of David'.[319] What we have here at Qumran is very early evidence in the Jewish world of an interpretation of 'Shiloh' as being the Messiah.

The LXX has a complex translation of the whole verse, but it is clearly taking it in a Messianic perspective. It includes the phrase 'and he is the expectation (*prosdokia*) of nations', referring to the Shiloh figure as a Messianic hope for the world. It is very possible that this LXX expression concerning someone who is somehow 'expected' by the world comes from an attempt to make sense of the Hebrew word which we looked at above, usually translated by 'gathering' or 'obedience' (yiqhat). The LXX translators may have seen a connection with the Hebrew root for 'waiting/expecting' (qavah), and translated it accordingly.[320]

The Jewish Targums, those Aramaic translations of the Hebrew Bible with commentary interwoven into the translation, also reflect this old tradition that the text is in fact a prophecy of the Messiah. Targum Onkelos has at this point in the text:

> He who exercises dominion shall not pass away from the house of Judah, nor the scribe from his children's children forever, until Messiah shall come, whose is the kingdom, and whom the people shall obey.

Kings shall not cease from the house of Judah, nor scribes teaching the Torah from his children's children, until the time

---

[319] This small fragment is known as 4 Q Patriarchal Blessings.

[320] This could also explain the translation of the Vulgate, which has at this point, 'donec veniat qui mittendus est', *mittendus* deriving from the Latin verb, *mittere*. On the other hand, Rabbi Samuel ben Meir, who was aware of this Latin translation, presumed that it came from a mistaken association of the word Shiloh with another Hebrew word, *Shaliaḥ*, meaning a messenger. See Lockshin's translation of the rabbi's commentary on Genesis, op cit, p 313.

that the king Messiah shall come, whose is the kingdom, and to whom all the kingdoms of the earth shall be obedient.

Targum Neofiti reflects the same tradition of interpretation:

until the time King Messiah shall come, to whom the kingship belongs.

There is one other important point to note about these Targumic versions, but we shall come to it in the next section. In the great midrash on Genesis, we read concerning this verse:

The rulership abides with the tribe of Judah until the arrival of Shiloh, that is, the Messiah.[321]

In the Talmud there is actually a section where the rabbis ask the question:

What is the name of the Messiah? They of the school of Rav Shila said, 'His name is Shiloh, as it is said, "Until Shiloh comes".'[322]

At the turn of the sixth century CE the great collection of midrashic texts known as the Midrash Rabbah was compiled. In the Genesis collection there is a casual reference to Shiloh which is the more significant because it is so *casually* assumed that there will be no serious disagreement about it. The midrash says: 'Shiloh. This alludes to the Royal Messiah.' This is therefore a well-attested interpretation in Jewish tradition. Bernard Grossfeld, a leading Jewish specia-

---

[321] Genesis Rabbah 98:9, 13; 99:8. See also the later text, *Yalkut*, 160. The great source book of kabbalistic theology, the *Zohar*, also identifies Shiloh with the Messiah in 1:25b.

[322] Sanhedrin 98b. There is an obvious play on words here. The letters of the names Shila and Shiloh are almost the same in Hebrew (shîla' and shîloh), and they are pronounced the same way. A ninth-century CE midrash on the Book of Proverbs also gives Shiloh as one of the seven names of the Messiah, as does Rashi in his commentary on the verse.

list on the Targums, offers this summary in a recent translation of one of the Targums:

> The identification of 'Shiloh' with the Messiah in the Targum . . . as well as in the Midrash and the Talmud, would appear to have been universally accepted during the Talmudic age.[323]

But of course other Jewish thinkers have taken it to refer to a person other than the Messiah. Mendelssohn and Kurvz both saw here a possible reference to the decision of God recorded in 1 Kings 11:29–39, where Ahijah, 'the prophet of Shiloh', tells Jeroboam that God has decided to take part of the kingdom away from Solomon and give it to him. Ten of the tribes will break away from the Davidic dynasty and follow the lead of Jeroboam in the northern part of the land of Israel. It is, however, difficult to see in this punishment by God, this fragmentation of the twelve tribes, a worthy fulfilment of Jacob's blessing.

The only real link between the two contexts is the phrase which is used of the prophet, that he 'belongs to Shiloh' (ha-shîlonî), literally that he is 'a Shilonite'. The intention, then, is to say that in Gen 49:10 the meaning of the verse is that the sceptre will not depart 'until the Shilonite comes'. This description is then said to be a reference to the only other person called this in the Bible, namely Ahijah. As I said, the association with the 1 Kings passage is not convincing, nor does it explain why the Genesis verse does not have the same Hebrew term for 'a Shilonite', which it could so easily have done. Nonetheless, this application of the Shiloh reference to Ahijah has been preserved among many of the refutationists, perhaps mainly and simply to provide an alternative which will close off the Messianic view. In a recent commentary,

---

[323] *The Targum Onkelos to Genesis: Translated, with a Critical Introduction, Apparatus, and Notes,* by Bernard Grossfeld (Michael Glazier, Inc, Wilmington, Delaware, 1988), p 163.

however, a Jewish scholar has actually tried to revive it with some confidence:

> The present verse clearly states that the descendants of Judah will rule over the whole of Israel *until Shiloh comes* ... The verse indicates that the House of Judah will not rule the complete kingdom forever. The House of Judah did in fact lose its control over the whole when Ahijah came. Ahijah ... came from Shiloh, and *unto him there was a gathering of the people* who, by virtue of Ahijah's prophecy, gathered around king Jeroboam, the first rebel king of the North.[324]

This is not likely to persuade many though. The understanding of Shiloh as the name of the *Messiah* is invariably associated with the proposal that it comes from the root meaning 'to be safe/secure' (shalah). This means that the name serves as a symbol of the conviction that the Messiah is the guarantor of peace and security for his people.[325] Friedlander actually translates that part of our verse as 'till peace comes', taking the word *Shiloh* to be a poetic way of saying *Shalom*. This interpretation of the significance of the name would then harmonise well with certain other Messianic passages about the Messiah being the harbinger of Peace/*Shalom* (eg, Isa 9:6; Mic 5:1–5).

Not surprisingly, seeing this as a reference to the person of the Messiah has been the favoured Christian interpretation of the term *Shiloh* from the earliest times. We see this view argued, for instance, in major works by Justin Martyr and Clement of Alexandria.[326] From their day right up to our own, the Shiloh prophecy has been celebrated as one of the classic Messianic texts, and 'Shiloh' has been accepted as one of the titles of the Messiah, Jesus.

---

[324] Robert D. Sacks, *A Commentary on the Book of Genesis* (The Edwin Mellen Press, Lewiston, 1990), pp 416f.
[325] We are reminded here of the proclamation of Eph 2:14, referring to Jesus, that 'He himself is our peace'.
[326] See Justin's *Apology* 1, 32; Clement's *Paedagogus* 1, 5, 15.

I would like to conclude this sub-section of the chapter by referring to a different 'Messianic interpretation' given to the term *Shiloh* by a leading Christian commentator on the book of Genesis, Claus Westermann. He is not satisfied that the word in the text is original, and goes so far as to propose that in fact the original word was *mashaloh*. There are, as might well be anticipated, technical and theological problems with such an emendation of the Hebrew text, but his emendation would give the Hebrew expression for 'his ruler'. There is an Akkadian word, *shelu*, which means someone who rules others, and the Hebrew root mashal carries this same meaning of ruling.

But what strikes Westermann as particularly suggestive is the fact that in yet another significant Messianic prophecy, Mic 5:1 (verse 2 in the English), this very root for ruling over people (mashal) is used of the Messiah! After speaking about Bethlehem *in Judah* as the birthplace of the Messiah, Micah goes on to say:

out of you will come for me
one who will be ruler over Israel . . .

Westermann is convinced that this same verbal root for 'ruling' lies behind what he takes to be a definite Messianic reference in Gen 49:10. He therefore translates our verse as:

The scepter shall not pass from Judah,
nor the staff from between his feet,
until 'his ruler' comes,
and the nations are obedient to him.

He sees this as a reference to the coming Messiah, born into the tribe of Judah and climaxing God's delegation of the right to rule over Israel to Judah, but he does not see here any mention of the name of the Messiah.[327] Having said this, it must be pointed out that in fact Shiloh is not used as a title for the Messiah in the New Testament (nor in the Hebrew Bible, apart from this verse, if it is used in this way here). But, on the other hand, Immanuel is not used of the Messiah either, apart from the classic verse, Isa 7:14, so the non-use of the title would not necessarily disqualify it. In other words, Westermann's suggestion is perhaps not too radical for consideration by Christians.

Shiloh does appear as a name of the Messiah in the Talmud passage we looked at earlier, but even the rabbis do not make much of it. Of course this rabbinic non-use may in turn be a reaction against the constant reference to this verse by the Christian community!

In spite of the variety of positions, the fact remains that in Jewish as well as Christian theology, there is a long and honoured tradition of seeing Gen 49:10 as a Messianic prophecy which refers, in one way or another, to the Messiah himself. It is not un-Jewish to view it as a Messianic prophecy.

Some take Shiloh *to be an abbreviated form of a Hebrew phrase meaning, 'whose it is'.* For this option, I must mention some Hebrew grammatical constructions as well as biblical theology, but the technical presentation will be very brief. The claim is that the word transliterated as *Shiloh* in the text (shîloh) is actually a contraction of a fuller phrase which would mean, literally, 'which is to him' (asher lô).

Delitzsch, whom we have had cause to refer to before, rejects this as being 'foreign to the prose style of ancient Hebrew'.[328] It would certainly be very unusual to find the

---

[327] For all of this see Claus Westermann, *Genesis 37–50, A Commentary* (translated from the 1982 German original by John T. Scullion, Augsburg Publishing House, Minneapolis, 1986), pp 218, 231.

[328] Franz Delitzsch, op cit, p 53.

late particle for 'which' in an early Judean text. On a second, though related matter, Delitzsch objected that the phrase 'to him' is always lô in the Hebrew Bible, and not loh as it would have to be here. He did concede that in the Hebrew Bible one sometimes finds the form boh for the expected bô (eg, in Jer 17:24), but the form loh never appears for the expected lô. But such a variant would have to occur here if this interpretation were to be correct, and though this is not impossible, its unlikeliness is seen by some people as circumstantial evidence against this interpretation. The linguistic debate is very lively, and discussions abound in the commentaries. Is it *linguistically* possible that *Shiloh* could be a contracted form of this phrase? If not, then the whole interpretation falls apart.

The LXX, however, seems to follow this interpretation, albeit in an overall Messianic context, with its translation, 'for whom it is laid up'. The ancient Syriac version of the Hebrew Bible, the so-called Peshitta, also supports this rendering, with 'until he comes, whose it is'. If you look again at the two passages quoted from the Targum in the previous section of this discussion, you will see that they seem to combine a perception that this is a Messianic prophecy with an understanding that this word *Shiloh* also conveys the idea of possession: 'whose it is'. Justin Martyr and Origen discussed the value and probability of this understanding in their work,[329] and quite a few influential Jewish scholars in the Middle Ages preferred this interpretation, notably Sa'adia Gaon and Rashi. Interestingly, this is the interpretation which has been chosen by the translators of the NIV, as we saw in my initial quoting of the verse in this chapter. There is also evidence, say some, that the prophet Ezekiel understood the Genesis verse in this way, within a larger context of seeing it as a Messianic prophecy. The

---

[329] Justin Martyr, *Dialogue*, op cit, 1, 20; Origen, *Against Celsus* 1, 53.

relevant passage is Ezek 21:30–32 (found as verses 25–27 in translations), which a number of commentators, myself included, hold to be an exposition of Gen 49:10. The Ezekiel passage could actually be a rather powerful Messianic prophecy in itself. The relevant phrase there for our present purposes is the one translated in the NIV as 'until he comes to whom it rightfully belongs', referring, in this interpretation, to the Messiah. This is virtually identical, as a translation, to the NIV rendering of the word *Shiloh* in Genesis 49:10. More importantly, the Hebrew phrase so translated in the Ezekiel passage is the very one presupposed by many to lie behind the word *Shiloh*, namely, asher lô.

The Ezekiel passage is certainly suggestive, and may well lend support to this interpretation of *Shiloh*, namely that although the Messiah is being referred to in Gen 49:10, he is not named there but only referred to by the pronoun 'he'. However, the phrase 'to whom it belongs' would be stressing very pointedly that the sceptre, symbolising the right to rule over Israel, belongs to the Messiah, thus making it a very attractive option.[330]

Some take Shiloh *to have been originally two words, meaning ' a tribute to him'.* There is some precedent for this interpretation in the standard Jewish commentaries,[331] but it would certainly be true to say that this was the least favoured view of the text in the Jewish community until its very recent revival by the Jewish Publication Society in the USA. Because of the influence of this translation on English-speaking Jewish people the world over, this particular understanding of the text is now quite commonly found.

---

[330] This Messianic linking between Gen 49:10 and Ezek 21:30–32 is actually accepted by most Jewish commentators too. See, for example, the Soncino Press commentary on Ezekiel by Rabbi S. Fisch (London, 1950), p 141.
[331] For example, *The Yalkut* and *Lekah Tov*.

In the 1985 edition of this translation, the whole verse reads as follows:

> The scepter shall not depart from Judah,
> Nor the ruler's staff from between his feet;
> So that tribute shall come to him
> And the homage of peoples be his.

Shiloh is seen as a simple two-word Hebrew phrase (shai loh) meaning 'a tribute to him', which in some way became compressed into what *looked* like one longer word (shîloh). This, it is claimed, explains the difficulty which people have had trying to make sense of the present text.

Shai is a word meaning a gift, or a tribute. It is found in Isa 18:7; Ps 68:30 (verse 29 in the English translations), and Ps 76:12 (verse 11 in the English translations). There is the same technical difficulty which we noted in the previous section about proposing that the next Hebrew word serves as a form of the phrase, 'to him', since the final letter would normally be different (lô not loh). But, as the defenders of this view point out, the very same use of the same final letter in the same grammatical context is found twice in the next verse ('îroh and sûtoh).

This particular translation of the difficult word *Shiloh* also provides a textbook example of one of the classic features of Hebrew poetic style, namely the use of what is usually called 'parallelism'. Even readers of the Bible in translation are familiar with this poetic style, especially in the Psalms. Here is a typical example of such parallelism, in this case from the first verses of Psalm 19:

> The heavens declare the glory of God;
> the skies proclaim the work of his hands.
> Day after day they pour forth speech;
> night after night they display knowledge.

In each of these two verses, typical of the whole poetic genre, we see an idea in the first line being extended, modified, re-expressed in the following line. If you read again the translation of Gen 49:10 by the Jewish Publication Society, you will see that this interpretation of *Shiloh* gives two sets of lines characterised by parallelism. The proposed term, 'tribute', is paralleled by the term 'homage' in the following line. Although there is something attractive about this interpretation for those Jewish people today who do not wish to focus on Messianic realities, it seems to me that such a restructuring of the word *Shiloh*, relating it to Judah as these modern commentators do, dilutes the power of the verse considerably. 'Tribute' might be appropriate for any monarch (as might 'homage', the word used in the next line of this translation), but this verse is speaking about the climactic appearance of the Messianic King.

How, then, may we summarise this discussion of the text? There is certainly a traditional consensus among Jews and Christians that Gen 49:10 is a Messianic prophecy, although there is no agreement as to exactly how it is to be understood. The one thing which really unites the Jewish community is the conviction that whoever, or whatever, *Shiloh* is referring to, it is not referring to Jesus. Christians, on the other hand, value this verse as a major prophecy concerning Jesus, who was indeed descended from the tribe of Judah (Matt 1:2–3; Luke 3:33; Heb 7:14; Rev 5:5); who brought peace, and the possibility of peace, to the world; and to whom the throne of David rightfully belongs.

Thinking back to the opening chapter of this book, one can say that although there must be a genuine modesty about the presentation of the Messianic interpretation of this verse *vis-à-vis* Jesus, nevertheless, Christians can be confident that their reading of it has integrity and perhaps even probability.

15
Did Isaiah know the 'virgin'?
Isaiah 7:14

This verse is probably the most famous of all of the Messianic prophecies which the New Testament teaches were fulfilled in the life of Jesus. Handel would have been quite unable to leave this verse out of his famous *Messiah* oratorio, and indeed it is featured in Part One of that famous work. In order to do justice to the disputes which surround the interpretation of the verse, we shall need to become involved in some historical and some linguistic study in this chapter, seeking to ensure that our theological reflections are well founded. The verse itself is known to many who never even attend church services except at Christmas-time – when it is celebrated and expounded each year:

> Therefore the LORD himself will give you a sign: The virgin will be with child and will give birth to a son, and will call him Immanuel.

Background

What, then, was the historical context of this 'sign'? Ahaz was the king of Judah for some sixteen years (2 Kings 16:1–20; 2 Chron 28:1–27), but he was one of her worst rulers. This is especially significant, as we shall see, in the light of the fact that his son and heir Hezekiah was one of Judah's greatest kings, ruling for some twenty-nine years (2 Kings 18:1–8; 2 Chron 29:1–2). Ahaz led his people at a particularly difficult time in the history of the Middle Eastern region, and he adopted a broadly pro-Assyrian policy in his attempt to preserve Judah's independence. However, the rulers of his two neighbouring countries to the north and north-east, Israel and Syria, had other ideas, and Judah was about to be caught up in the power politics of the day. Both the rulers of these two countries (Rezin, the king of Syria, and Pekah, the king of Israel) feature in chapter 7 of Isaiah's book.

Keep in mind throughout the following discussion two facts which are very important, yet which are so often forgotten by Christians today:

a) After the death of King Solomon, *the kingdom of Israel divided into two distinct kingdoms*, each with its own king, army, priesthood, etc (see 1 Kings 12). What causes some confusion is the fact that the northern ten tribes were named the nation of 'Israel', in distinction from the southern tribes, who were known as the nation of 'Judah'. Therefore, when reading the Hebrew Bible it is imperative to be aware of which people the name 'Israel' is being applied to in any given passage. Is it the whole union of the twelve tribes, relating to an early period, or is it only the historic northern nation during the time of the divided kingdoms? In Isaiah 7, set in a time when the two nations were not only in existence, but actually in conflict, we are dealing with the separate but neighbouring kingdom of Israel, which at that stage is threatening the kingdom of Judah. The situation is one of a form of civil war between the two groups of tribes of Israel.

b) *Syria and Assyria are two quite distinct political units*, and must not be confused with one another. Syria, often referred to by its other name of Aram, was a nation to the north and north-east of Judah. Geographically, we may think of it as covering roughly the same area as the country of Syria today. Assyria, on the other hand, was a huge empire to the east of Judah. It was, to borrow a contemporary image, one of the 'super-powers' with whom both Israel and Judah had to deal during the biblical period. The heartland of the Assyrian empire lay in what we today know as Iraq, and it was this empire which was in due time overthrown by the Babylonians. At the time of the events related in Isaiah 7, the Assyrians were moving westwards in their desire to conquer all the territories leading to the Mediterranean Sea. Their rival super-power, of course, was the Egyptian empire, and it too regularly sought to extend its control to include the Fertile Crescent of the Middle East. The Jewish people in the region, then as well as now, lived in an arena of constant conflict over land and resources.

Some time before, Israel had become subject to Assyria, as had Syria before that, and now both these kingdoms had revolted and formed a breakaway league against the Assyrians. It was only a matter of time before the Assyrian army moved against them, and they desperately wanted Judah to join their coalition, not just because of the increased troops which this would give them, but also because of the strategic value of the wedge-shape which the three countries would form. The city of Jerusalem would also present a major strategic block to the advancing Assyrian forces. So the two kings duly tried to persuade Ahaz to join them in their revolt against the Assyrians, but he was too afraid of the Assyrian dominance in the region and so refused to become their partner. It is in this context that we must see the opening verses of our chapter in Isaiah.

Rezin and Pekah decided to march against Ahaz, take over his kingdom for themselves, and join it to their alliance under the leadership of their own puppet king. We learn from 2 Kings 16:7–9 that Ahaz eventually appealed directly to the Assyrian emperor, Tiglath-Pileser, for help against the two northern rebel states. His appeal was successful, but this in turn cost Judah a vast treasure in tribute and also involved her yet more deeply in compromise with the Assyrians.

Judah's security and prosperity did not lie in political associations with other peoples. The events of Isaiah 7, however, took place before Ahaz appealed to Assyria, at the time when the king was still in a state of shock and fear at the prospect of war with Israel and Syria.

Ahaz was in need of the very best counsel, which is why Isaiah came on to the scene at all. He was determined to advise Ahaz to trust God for Judah's security and prosperity, not to rely on treaties with other nations, even super-powers. Ahaz did not follow that advice.

We need to note here the mention of the 'house of David' in verse 2, since a major aspect of Isaiah's concern was the threat to the Davidic *dynasty*, this being much more significant than the fate of any given individual king. What we need to appreciate is that in verse 6 we learn about the plan of Rezin and Pekah to replace the rightful royal *house*, not just the current ruling king, with another royal house altogether. Why should this be so important to Isaiah? Because it is a threat to the covenant which God made with David and his house after him. This in turn means that the Messianic line is under threat, a situation which God will not allow to develop. And then, adding insult to injury, this very threat to the Messianic line is coming from the very brother tribes of Judah in the northern kingdom!

God told Isaiah to go to Ahaz, and to take his son She'ar Yashuv with him. This is an important development, not least because it involves a significant measure of ambiguity. Literally, the boy's name meant 'a remnant will return', but was his presence with Isaiah meant to signal to Ahaz a message of encouragement and hope, or a warning of severe judgement to come?

Should we translate the name as 'a remnant will return', or as '*only* a remnant will return'? In other words, does the name communicate the message 'Don't be despondent! This is not the end of Judah – a good number of faithful people will return to begin again' (see 6:13b)? Or is the message really: 'Enough is enough! God is at last going to punish his people with quite drastic measures and only a few faithful people will survive' (see 6:11–13a)?

Perhaps Ahaz began to reflect on these two possibilities of the Hebrew name when he looked up and saw that Isaiah's son was accompanying him. At any rate, the three characters met as the king was inspecting the city's water supply in anticipation of a coming siege. When Isaiah spoke, however, it was clearly a message of consolation and hope. Ahaz is not to fear the conspiracy against him because, compared with God's power, these two kings to the north are nothing but puny threats. They will sputter for a time and then burn themselves out, producing a lot of smoke but no serious fire.

There is another lovely play on the meaning of a name in verse 6, regarding the Syrian whom it is said will replace Ahaz on the throne of Judah. His name is Tabe'el, a name which could mean 'God is good' – this being the kind of pious rhetoric which the Israelites might employ to justify their action against the house of David. But on the other hand, it could be taken, and probably was taken by Isaiah to mean, 'good-for-nothing', reflecting the attitude of the Judaeans.[332] All these name-plays are important for us to note, since much of the significance of the Messianic prophecy in verse 14 concerns the meaning of the message of the name 'Immanuel', another name which can be read in more than one way.

Ahaz is offered a sign to help him make his decision to trust in God at this critical moment in Judah's history. This in itself is unusual and serves to highlight the importance of what is about to transpire. But what will it take to convince

---

[332] The Hebrew letters would be the same in either case, with one change in the vowels effecting the difference in meaning. 'God is good' would be pronounced '*tov el*', whereas the phrase 'good-for-nothing' would be pronounced '*tov al*'. Both would make sense of the Hebrew letters found here (ṭv'l). As a matter of interest, the Masoretic (ie, vocalised) text has '*tov al*' here in Isa 7:6, but it has '*tov el*' in Ezra 4:7.

the king? The word used for a 'sign' ('ot) generally refers to those occurrences which act as pledges of the certainty of other things to come.[333] Ahaz is told by God that he can ask for any sign he likes that will serve as such a pledge of God's protection in the future. Notice how daring Isaiah's theology becomes at this point. He is so aware of the import of the events which are taking place that he says that Ahaz can seek a sign of his own choosing, even if it verges on forbidden areas of knowledge. This is the significance of the two reference points given in verse 11.

We see there references to 'the deepest depths' and to 'the highest heights'. The Hebrew word translated as 'the deepest depths' is the word she'ol (she'ôl) referring to the shadowy place of existence which was believed to be the destination of the souls of all the dead. When King Saul persuaded the witch of Endor to raise Samuel's spirit from she'ol, he was, as he knew well, disobeying the command of God to shun such practices (see 1 Sam 28). God's people were not to try to use this method of finding out the secrets of life: rather, they were to trust God and listen to his prophets. In the same way, they were forbidden to have anything to do with the religious beliefs and practices of those who held that the stars and heavenly bodies were in reality supernatural powers who could influence one's destiny. The 'deepest depths' and the 'highest heights' are therefore in fact the areas or dimensions associated with contacting the spirit world and consulting astrologers. I do not believe that Ahaz was being directed to contradict God's commands and actually consult some of the forbidden mediums, but I do believe that he would have looked sharply at Isaiah when he heard those words. He would have seen from Isaiah's face that he was pressing home upon him the urgency of the matter, and that he, Ahaz, was really being urged to ask for the kind of sign it

---

[333] See, for example, Exod 4:8–9; 1 Sam 2:34; Isa 38:8; Ezek 4:8.

would take to convince him that God could be trusted in this matter.

However, in spite of the obvious message from God, Ahaz still refuses to name a sign. He is not acting out of piety, as if remembering the words of Deut 6:16 about not putting God to the test, but he is reacting from the kind of nervous fear that God will in fact convince him to trust in his power. Isaiah realises that Ahaz has not responded out of a sense of unworthiness or piety, and this is why he rebukes him. And now comes our verse, where Ahaz is told that *God himself* will initiate a sign in spite of Ahaz's reluctance and fear. This is where the interpretative difficulties begin, because there is no agreement as to the precise nature of the sign. There are three aspects of the context of the sign, however, about which there is a general consensus:

- It is an especially significant sign, since God so specifically initiates it.
- The sign is directed to the house of David, not just to Ahaz personally.
- The sign somehow involves the extraordinary birth of a boy. The very Hebrew phrase which we find here, which literally says, 'Behold . . . is pregnant . . . and will give birth', is almost a kind of formula for especially significant births. In the Hebrew Bible it is actually found again in Gen 16:11 and Judg 13:3, 5, 7. A variation of it is also found in Gen 17:19.

And so to the different ways of interpreting the heart of the sign. As we shall see, various aspects of this prophecy have exercised both faith-communities down the generations. Whereas it is one of the classic Christian Messianic texts, not all Jewish commentators have taken it as being a Messianic prophecy, and those who do have often dated its fulfilment long before the appearance of Jesus on the scene.

'Immanuel'

Although everyone, Jew and non-Jew alike, agrees in the assumption that the specific name of the boy is highly significant, for some people the name is the single most important aspect of the sign. The Hebrew name 'Immanuel' ('imanû 'el) means, as is well known, 'God is with us'. This is clearly a word of reassurance and hope, implying that with God fighting for you, it makes no difference who the opposition is! The same thinking lies behind Paul's words to the Roman church in Rom 8:31, when he exclaims: 'If God is for us, who can be against us?'

There have been scholars who have tried to find a double meaning in this name, as in some of the others in this section of Isaiah, but I think that it is unlikely. There certainly could be some ambiguity in the name, in the sense that if God is with you, then judgement cannot be far away either. To be in the presence of God is to be convicted of sin, after all. But in the light of the situation which the people were facing at that time, and specifically in the light of the context of Isa 8:10, I believe that the name Immanuel was to be heard as a message of reassurance. Ahaz's son, King Hezekiah, certainly took these words in this sense, and took them to heart when he himself faced the might of the Assyrian empire under the leadership of Tiglath-Pileser's successor, Sennacherib. In 2 Chron 32: 7–8 we hear Hezekiah speaking to his commanders in words that consciously echo the meaning of the name Immanuel:

> Be strong and courageous. Do not be afraid or discouraged because of the king of Assyria and the vast army with him, for there is a greater power with us than with him. With him is only the arm of flesh, but with us is the LORD our God to help us and to fight our battles. And the people gained confidence from what Hezekiah the king of Judah said.

There is no good reason to doubt that Ahaz heard this prophetic name in the same way. But is this, then, the full force of the sign? Whenever Ahaz is tempted to doubt the providential care of God for his people he need only remember this special boy to be reassured of God's active presence with them? Is the name itself the sign? This does not strike me as an adequate climax for such an extraordinary episode in Judah's life.

Nonetheless, the name is certainly an important part of the sign. A recurring theme among refutationists has been to declare that Jesus could not have been the Messiah because nowhere in the New Testament is he ever called by this Messianic name, Immanuel. Gerald Sigal follows Troki carefully here and makes this point somewhat triumphalistically. As a matter of fact, the refutationists say, even Matthew, who cites this verse from Isaiah in Matt 1:23, never uses it of Jesus. Indeed he immediately precedes his quotation from Isaiah with a verse in which he stresses that Jesus' name was deliberately chosen to be Jesus, not Immanuel (verse 21).

Christians have responded by saying that Immanuel was a symbolic throne name, a theological title, if you will, not intended as a personal name. Support for this is sought from the life of King Solomon, whom we learn from 2 Sam 12:24–25 was to be called 'Jedidiah', meaning 'loved by the Lord'. Although this is expressly said to have been God's choice of name for him, he is never called that in the Bible. In the same way, it is claimed, Jesus is Immanuel without being expressly called that in the New Testament. There is certainly merit in this argument, and I would agree that the non-use of this name/title in the New Testament does not invalidate the claim that Jesus is the Messiah. On the other hand, it is perhaps a little puzzling that not one of the New Testament writers dwell on this name and its significance.

As a matter of interest, we have evidence from the Middle Ages of Christians using this very same argument against the common Jewish view that the boy referred to here was a son of King Ahaz. In his *Book of the Covenant*, Joseph Kimchi puts forward this understanding of the verse as referring to one of Ahaz's sons. The text continues:

> The min said: If so, who was this Immanuel and what was the sign that he gave to Ahaz? I do not see that a male child, Immanuel, was born to him.

Kimchi has the Jewish polemicist reply that even though the name Immanuel is not used of one of Ahaz's sons in the biblical text, this boy was indeed Ahaz's son Hezekiah, whose life displayed for all to see that God was with his people once again.[334] Isaac Troki was also very sensitive to this counter-challenge by Christians. He says that this son, Isaiah's son, in his view, had three symbolic names, each corresponding to one of the three kings involved in the dispute between Judah and the kingdoms of Israel and Syria:

> Referring to the king of Judah he was named Emanuel (God is with us), to indicate that from the time of his birth peace would prevail in Judea. Alluding to the king of Israel, he was called Maher-Shalal, and in allusion to the king of Syria he received the name of Hash-Baz, pointing out by the two latter names that those monarchs, with all their possessions, would soon become the spoil of the Assyrian kings.[335]

Whether or not we are impressed by Troki's understanding of Isa 8:3 and the name(s) given there, the point I wish to make at the moment is that he was also trying to make sense of the function of this name, Immanuel, in the present context. So we see the same argument about the lack of evidence that any Messianic figure was known by this name used by each community against the other. How important do *you* find it that Jesus is not called Immanuel in the New Testament?

The next issue to look at is the attempt to identify the mother and the child. If we may begin with the work of

---

[334] Rabbi Joseph Kimchi, *The Book of the Covenant*, op cit, 29b, p 56.
[335] *Faith Strengthened*, op cit, pp 99f.

Sigal which I have quoted several times before, he asserts that this prophecy has nothing whatsoever to do with Mary and Jesus, but was 'fulfilled' in the life of Hezekiah, whose mother, Ahaz's wife, was the young woman. The assurance of God that there was nothing to fear from the aggressive northern alliance was actualised, he says, in the events recorded for us in 2 Kings 15:29–30, 16:9, where we read that the Assyrians solved Judah's problem for her. Isa 8:1–10 and 10:5–34 indicate that this was God's preferred way of doing things.

This is actually an ancient Jewish tradition about Hezekiah being the Immanuel of Isa 7:14, and indeed the promised Messiah himself. It probably remains the most commonly known view among Jewish people. It is seen in Justin Martyr's dialogue with Trypho, in the second century CE, and is expressed poignantly in the following two passages from the Talmud. In the first, Rabbi Yohanan ben Zakkai, a first-century rabbi, says to his disciples:

> Remove all vessels lest they be rendered unclean, and prepare a throne for Hezekiah, king of Judah, who is to come.[336]

In this second quote, Rabbi Hillel, again a first-century leader, speaks more clearly still:

> There shall be no Messiah for Israel, because they have already enjoyed him in the days of Hezekiah.[337]

In our generation, Beth Moshe is one of the refutationists who has championed Hezekiah as a viable pretender for the Messianic throne:

> It is possible it is King Ahaz's own son Hezekiah. Refer to Isaiah 9:6–7, 'The Mighty God,' . . . By miraculous intervention, God defeated the Assyrians who attacked Judah during King Hezekiah's rule. Certainly, he could be designated

---

[336] Berachot 28b.
[337] Sanhedrin 99a.

'Immanuel', because during his reign God was with us in helping the Jewish people.[338]

Of course there are major difficulties with trying to reconcile Hezekiah with this prophecy, not the least of which is the fact that he was already five or six years old when his father, Ahaz, received the prophecy. The historical threat came around 734 BCE. According to 2 Kings 18:2, Hezekiah was twenty-five years old when he came to the throne in 715 BCE. This means that he was born in 740 BCE, and hence was already a young boy when Isaiah said that Immanuel was to be born. The prophecy of a birth which was yet to happen cannot be referring to someone who had been born some years previously. Some important Jewish commentators, for example David Kimchi and Joseph Abarbanel, were determined to find Ahaz the father of this child, and therefore speculated that Immanuel was a *younger* son of the king by a *second* marriage.

A second important candidate in Jewish tradition for the mother of this child is Isaiah's own wife, who was, perhaps, the 'prophetess' mentioned in Isa 8:3, so that 'Immanuel' would have been one of the prophet's own sons. Confirmation is sought from the fact that we know that Isaiah did indeed give such symbolic names to his children. In 7:3 we meet She'ar Yashuv ('a remnant shall return'), and in 8:3 we meet Maher-Shalal-Hash-Baz ('quick to the plunder, swift to the spoil'). What more appropriate, then, goes the claim, than that this third boy in these few chapters should also be one of Isaiah's own? This view was championed by, among others, Rashi and Ibn Ezra.

An unsurmountable problem with this view, right at the outset, is the fact that the word used in this verse for the 'virgin' or 'young woman' is extremely unlikely to have ever been used of a married woman, especially one who already

---

[338] Beth Moshe, op cit, p 160.

had children. Although we are still to come to the whole dispute about the correct meaning of this word, it needs to be mentioned here. At the very least, it designates a girl who has reached marriageable age, whether a virgin or not, but another word is used for women who are actually married. We know that Isaiah's wife had already given birth to at least one son, since Isaiah took She'ar-Yashuv with him when he gave Ahaz the sign. So to repeat this point, the Hebrew term used for the young woman who will be the mother of this child is never used of women who are already mothers. For this reason there are Jewish commentators who speculate again that Isaiah took a *second* wife, and that it was she who bore him this child.

A third option which is held by a number of scholars is that the mother of this child was a young court singer or servant to whom Isaiah pointed as he said the words. Circumstantial evidence for this view is claimed to be found in Song of Songs 1:3; Ps 68:26 (verse 25 in the English translations); and possibly Ps 46:1 (the title verse in the English translations). In these verses we find references (at least in the first two of them) to what appear to be court maidens. It is one of these, singled out by Isaiah and now known to both men, who shall give birth to the child.

Before Christians dismiss these attempts at identifying the mother and child too unthinkingly, let me point out that what these commentators are trying to do is to provide a scenario which will make sense of the immediacy of Ahaz's plight, and his need for a short-term solution. Christians also need to be able to provide a credible context in which to see this prophecy as meeting King Ahaz's need. As the refutationists say, what good would it be for Ahaz to be told that in several centuries time a young boy would be born![339] He needed to know what to do in the coming days and months.

---

[339] For instance, see Joseph Kimchi's *Sefer Ha-Berit*, op cit, 29a, p 55.

The fact that this is seen as a prophetic word for Ahaz's generation does seem to receive some confirmation from the words which immediately follow our verse. In verses 15–17, though there is some debate as to whether the reference to 'curds and honey' is intended to suggest a life of ease and wealth, or a life of sparse subsistence (in other words, the same debate as whether She'ar-Yashuv is a message of comfort or a warning of hard times ahead), it does appear that the child in question will still be young when the danger is passed. This therefore cannot be referring to the birth of Jesus. See also the symbolic name of Isaiah's son which we are given in 8:1–4. Before that boy is old enough to call out '*Abba*' or '*Ima*' the danger will be past. So the historical context strongly suggests that God certainly intended to give Ahaz a sign which would be of *immediate* relevance.

Not only that, but the grammatical structure of the announcement in Isa 7:14 suggests to some people that the birth is imminent. The verb which is translated by 'will give birth' can legitimately be considered to relate to the future. However, the verb translated as 'will be with child' is actually a present participle in Hebrew, and might be better translated by 'is with child'. In other words, this woman is already pregnant, although the actual delivery of the baby is still to come. The LXX translates this participle as if the conception itself is still to happen in the future, but the most natural way to take the verbs in this sentence is to translate them as referring to a woman who 'is pregnant, and is about to give birth'. The whole grammatical issue is complicated by the use of the Hebrew word 'behold' in front of the participle for being pregnant. Some people think that this was a kind of formula construction relating to future events. Support for the interpretation that the woman is already pregnant, or that the pregnancy is at least imminent, is found in the other passages where this 'formula', if it is a formula, refers to *imminent* births (Gen 16:11–16; 17:19–21; Judges 13).

There is a strong case to be made, then, for an understanding of the prophecy which keeps it relevant to Ahaz's generation.[340] Some English translations (eg, the Authorised Version) adopt this view that the woman is already pregnant, while others (eg, the NIV) move the whole event into the future. Jewish commentators, as can be appreciated, favour the present tense for the conception of this child, thus distancing it altogether from the story of Jesus, while many Christians try to suggest that the whole thing is in Isaiah's future, relating it solely to the birth of Jesus. It becomes the prophecy of Jesus' virgin birth, his mother being Mary, the betrothed wife of Joseph (Matt 1:22–25).

Certain Christians, unhappy at the seeming lack of relevance of this prophecy to Ahaz's situation and yet determined to restrict the prophecy to Jesus' birth, have sought to explain the apparent dilemma by suggesting that verses 15–17 of this chapter do not refer to Immanuel at all. Instead, they relate them to the young boy, She'ar-Yashuv, who was there with Isaiah and Ahaz. Why else would Isaiah have been instructed to take him along, they argue? Assuming that the age of moral responsibility for boys alluded to in verses 15–17 was then thirteen years, as of course we know it was at a later stage, then She'ar-Yashuv would have been about nine or ten years old when this conversation between Ahaz and his father took place, and that is certainly possible.

The difficulty, of course, is that a normal reading of the text does not suggest this interpretation. We have to imagine the boy standing beside his father, the prophet. Isaiah turns to the king and utters the words of verses 13–14 about a remarkable boy who is to be born at some point in the future; then he turns to his son, She'ar-Yashuv, puts his

---

[340] The suggestion that a promise of the birth of the Messiah some hundreds of years in the future could have served as a real comfort to Ahaz, after the fashion of Exod 3:12 and Isa 37:30, where future events are held to be guarantors of a safe journey through the future until the time of those events, is, I think, a little stretched here.

hands on his shoulders, and says the words of verses 15–17 to the king about *him*. It is not impossible, but it is a forced reading of the text, in my opinion.

We need to look a little more carefully at the verses which follow verse 14. Three different interpretations of the 'curds and honey' are to be found among the commentators, Jewish and Christian. Some relate it to ancient Near Eastern texts which speak of this as the food of gods. This in turn suggests to them that we have some clue here as to the birth of a divine being. Others see here an allusion to the famous phrase about the Promised Land, that it would be flowing with 'milk and honey' (see Exod 3:8; Num 13:27; 16:13; Deut 11:9). In other words it is a promise of a time of plenty and security to come. Yet others are of the opinion that this is an image of desolation, portraying a country where there is neither meat nor vegetables/fruit for its population to eat.

Perhaps the ambiguity is deliberate, as it so often seems to be in the Bible? If Ahaz trusts God, then 'Immanuel' will mean that God will be with them to deliver them from the northern alliance and from the Assyrians as well. However, if Ahaz turns to the Assyrians for protection (as he in fact did), then God will allow the Assyrians to destroy the alliance and then desolate Judah by exacting dreadful tribute from her (see Isa 8:1–8 for this same scenario).

Of course the choice of 'right and wrong' in these verses may not be referring to moral maturity at all, but simply to the ability to recognise safe or good food from harmful food. If this is the case, then it might be referring to the age of around two years old. Isaiah might then be saying that in about two years and nine months time, the alliance will be history. This would turn out to be quite a good option, since this prophecy is believed to have been given in about 734 BCE, and Syria and a large part of Israel were taken by the Assyrians in about 732 BCE. This interpretation maintains the integrity of the whole passage in Isaiah 7, and is to be preferred over the attempt to artificially break the verses into two sections, each one referring to a different child.[341]

Another type of possibility altogether also exists, however, one which is favoured by many Christians. Put simply, it is this: some prophecies, of which this would be an example, have two levels of fulfilment. On the one hand, there is the immediate, or near-immediate, level of fulfilment. God speaks to the fears and concerns of the person or the generation which receives the prophecy. But on the other hand, there is the deeper level of fulfilment, one which will not be realised until the days of the Messiah. One might include here the prophecies of Israel's restoration to God and to the land of Israel which are found in many of the biblical prophets. In one sense they were fulfilled when the tribes returned from the Babylonian exile, but in a more profound sense altogether, they are to be fulfilled when the days of the Messiah come.

Therefore it is possible to view a 'double fulfilment' of this prophecy. Yes, there was an application to Ahaz's generation, concerning the specific trauma of the Israelite–Syrian conspiracy to overthrow the Davidic dynasty. But the full realisation of God's commitment to be with his people would only be seen at the birth of the Messiah – 'Immanuel'. One problem which could be seen with this interpretation is that Christians often speak as if the virgin birth of Jesus was a unique event in history, itself a miracle restricted to Mary and Jesus. Would this interpretation necessitate the occurrence of two virgin births? Anticipating the debate which we shall be examining shortly as to whether the mother is called a 'virgin' or simply a 'young woman', perhaps once more we have a deliberate case of ambiguity? If the word used by Isaiah can have either of these two meanings, then maybe the

---

[341] Having said this, it must be conceded that several important Christian figures have adopted the view that two children are being referred to here. John Calvin, for instance, saw verses 14 and 15 as referring to Jesus, but verses 16 and 17 as referring to someone in Ahaz's day.

first fulfilment of the prophecy was to involve a young woman, while the second, *climactic* fulfilment was to involve a virgin?

I am sure that this line of thinking, that we are dealing with a kind of 'double fulfilment' prophecy, is the correct way to interpret the Immanuel promise. The Church, then, can certainly defend with theological integrity her claim that this is a prophecy about the birth of Jesus. But, as I have stressed several times already, such a defence must be made with due modesty. It is not self-evidently true simply from reading the text in Isa 7:14. In a moment we must turn to the thorny issue as to whether it is actually a *virgin* birth which is being spoken about here. But before we do that, I would like to mention the view of one influential Jewish believer in Jesus who suggests that the vagueness of the wording of the prophecy, at least in one respect, is quite deliberate.

Arthur Kac has offered an imaginative interpretation of the fact that the mother of this child is left unnamed in the prophecy. He suggests, in direct and I think deliberate contrast to the Roman Catholic and Orthodox Christian traditions, that the mother is in fact *theologically* unimportant. He compares her role in Jesus' life with that of the town of his birth, Bethlehem. Both were very important in their own right, of course, and Kac does not devalue either Mary as a person or her role in bringing Jesus up in the love of God. However, for him the really significant theological aspect of Jesus' birth was its anonymity, its lack of pomp and circumstance, its seeming insignificance. He relates this point to both the geographical and physical place of Jesus' birth, and to the lack of personal involvement of his mother in conceiving him. He puts it like this:

Messiah's mother will not be, as she would have been had the Davidic dynasty remained faithful, a queen residing in the royal palace; instead she will be just an 'almah', some unnamed and insignificant maiden . . . The Bethlehem prophecy of Micah and the Immanuel prophecy of Isaiah combined to stress the element of humiliation associated with Messiah's birth, as part of the working out of God's judgement upon Israel – the nation and its Davidic dynasty.[342]

There may well be some truth in Kac's reading of the texts, and it is certainly an interpretation which will prove attractive to many Protestant Christians. Interestingly enough, quite a number of commentators have wondered whether the following verse in Micah, after the reference to Bethlehem, might itself be an inner-biblical commentary on Isa 7:14. Mic 5:2 (verse 3 in the English translations) reads:

> Therefore Israel will be abandoned
> until the time when she who is in labour gives birth
> and the rest of his brothers return to join the Israelites.

However, whether this is a reference to Isa 7:14 or not, Kac's suggestion does lead us nicely into the next section of our discussion about the exact nature of this Isaianic prophecy. We need to try to ascertain just how anonymous this woman was. Was she unknown to Isaiah and Ahaz, or only to us? This question forms part of the major discussion which we must now undertake.

'A virgin'

For most people, the most serious dimension of the controversy is the question whether the 'young woman' is also a 'virgin'. Traditionally, Jewish people and Christians part company here. The Church has consistently proclaimed, in the light of Matt 1:22–25, that this is a prophecy of a virgin birth; the Jewish community, on the other hand, has insisted that the Hebrew term used by Isaiah is simply one which means a young woman of marriageable age, whether or not a

---

[342] Arthur Kac, *The Messianic Hope*, op cit, pp 140f.

virgin. For instance, the new Jewish Publication Society translation renders the verse:

> Look, the young woman is with child and about to give birth to a son. Let her name him Immanuel.

It is also a fact that certain modern 'Christian' translations of the Bible prefer to speak in terms of 'a young woman' here, so it has become vital that we look at the word which has caused all this debate. Isaiah uses the Hebrew term *'almah* ('almah), this being one of the two Hebrew terms which he could have used in this context. As we shall see, the Church has traditionally said that this is the very word which we would expect him to use if he intended to speak about a virgin. The Jewish community has responded that, on the contrary, the other Hebrew word, *betulah* (betûlah), is the one which he would have chosen had he wished to convey this sense of virginity.

Jewish refutationists frequently blame Jerome, the Roman Catholic scholar who translated the Bible into Latin for the western Church, for mistranslating the Hebrew term and thus giving rise to the controversy. It is certainly not as easy as that, but it is still being said, nonetheless. Joseph Kimchi, again, is often quoted. He dealt with this matter almost casually in his attempt to dismiss the Christian interpretation:

> I shall say a few words concerning the way in which those who have explained this passage have strayed from the path of reason. They did not perceive clearly that the passage to which you referred is not in Scripture. Rather, Jerome your translator is the one who led you astray and caused you to err. May he rest in the congregation of the shades (Prov 21:16). You said, *the virgin shall conceive*, but Scripture says, *the young woman shall conceive*.[343]

Not content to leave it at that, however, he goes on to say that

---

[343] Rabbi Joseph Kimchi, *Sefer Ha-Berit*, op cit, 28b, pp 53f.

although there was a good basic text for Jerome to work from, and although he did indeed use this as a basic text, he also ignored it when it suited him, as for example when it came to our text. Kimchi says this about Jerome's use of the text:

> Jerome the translator relied upon it, translated from it, and trusted it, with the exception of a few words which he did not understand or which were contrary to his belief and which he altered, changing the root of the faith to wormwood.[344]

Few charges would prove to be more serious than this one in any attempt to discredit an interpretation which did not appear acceptable to the religious authorities. This mutual accusation of deliberate tampering with the text is one which has reared its ugly head several times in the history of Jewish–Christian relations – sometimes, it must be said, with some justification. We looked at this issue in an earlier chapter of this book. However, we must postpone our discussion of the translations of our text by the old, important versions of the Bible until we have looked more closely at the Hebrew text itself.

Already in the mid-second century CE we see the teaching of the virgin birth of Jesus being ridiculed by the Jewish community:

> Among the tales of those whom we call Greeks, it is said that Perseus had been born of Danaë, still a virgin, by him that they entitle Zeus, flowing down upon her in the form of gold. And in fact you ought to be ashamed of saying the same sort of things as they, and should rather say that this Jesus was a man of human origin . . . [345]

This looks for all the world like a Jewish rejection, *in principle*, of the very notion of a virgin birth, but Lasker

---

[344] Ibid.

[345] Justin Martyr, *Dialogue*, op cit, 67. See also 43, 68, 71, 77.

makes the point that this is not exactly true. It may well be that there were Jewish polemicists who chose to adopt the position that virgin births were impossible, by definition, but that did not become the standard Jewish position. This is something which is extremely important for us to realise. Lasker states plainly that the real issue was not that of the possibility or otherwise of God ordaining and effecting a virgin birth, but rather the question of whether God himself would become human by this means. He writes:

> The doctrine of the virgin conception was not attacked *per se*. The possibility . . . is conceded in the Talmud [Hagigah 14b–15a]. Nevertheless, the Jewish polemicists rejected the notion that God could become incarnate by impregnating a virgin and fathering an offspring who was, according to Christian doctrine, God Himself.[346]

We may listen to the words of one of these Jewish refutationists as he makes this very point:

> We cannot deny the possibility that God, blessed be He, could create a creation in a virgin, even one whom no man has known, for He created everything out of nothing. Rather, we deny that there was a need for incarnation.[347]

It is obviously important for Christians to understand that the *essential* Jewish difficulty concerns the whole concept of the incarnation of God in Jesus, rather than the claim that Isaiah is speaking about a virgin birth. It means, among other things, that the interpretation of Isa 7:14 as involving a virgin birth is not in itself anti-Jewish, even though some contemporary refutationists wish to make it appear so.

Of course there also exists another strategy altogether whereby refutationists set out to discredit this New Testament teaching about Jesus being born of a virgin in fulfilment

---

[346] Abraham Farissol, *Magen Avraham* (c 1500 CE), ch 11, fol 14b–15a.

[347] Abraham Farissol, *Magen Avraham* (c 1500 CE), ch 11, fol 14b–15a.

of the prophecy of Isaiah. It is simply this: those who wish to discredit Jesus and his family state that the account of his virgin, and hence miraculous, birth was merely an attempt to cover up the fact of his illegitimacy. This very strategy is found in the Mishnah, where we have the following claim made concerning Jesus, though he is actually unnamed in the Mishnah passage:

> Rabbi Simeon ben Azzai said: I found a family register in Jerusalem, and in it was written, *'You-Know-Who* is a bastard through (a transgression of the law of) your neighbour's wife.'[348]

Jewish family registers were kept in the temple precincts in Jerusalem, but when the temple was destroyed in 70 CE these records were lost. Rabbi Simeon ben Azzai is said to have seen the records before they were lost, and thereby is able to discredit Jesus. The point is not, as some Christians have tried to have it, whether or not any person did or did not see those records of Jesus' family. The point is that the rabbis were intent on convincing their people that in principle someone would have been able to discover this record of Jesus' illegitimacy, because they were *already* sure in their own minds that Jesus had been born out of wedlock.

This has certainly become the classic Jewish critique of the Christian doctrine of the virgin birth of Jesus. A thirteenth-century rabbi voiced this particular challenge in very urbane terms in his rather patronising critique.

> I agree with your saying, *the virgin shall conceive and bear a son*, for there are found many such women. There are many former virgins who have been found pregnant, but when they

---

[348] Yebamot 4:13. The translation 'You-Know-Who' I have borrowed from some contemporary refutationists, who refer to Jesus in this way. The usual translation of the text is something like, 'Such a one', or 'That man'. The point is that everyone knew who was being referred to, without his name having to be written or spoken aloud.

are pregnant, they are not virgins, and when they are virgins, they are not pregnant.[349]

He makes his point bluntly, and it is by now the standard Jewish understanding of the case.[350]

But let us return to the text. The first thing one notices is that the Hebrew word under discussion is defined by the definite article. Isaiah says that *the* virgin/young woman is pregnant. Some translations omit the definite article and make the whole event seem very vague: 'A young woman is pregnant . . .' This would hardly merit being called a sign! No, the Hebrew is unambiguous. It is not a woman, but *the* woman who is being referred to. This might well suggest that a specific person was in Isaiah's mind. Indeed it could be taken to mean that this person was known to both Isaiah and Ahaz. And as we have seen, two commonly-suggested women who would have been known to them in this way are the wives of Ahaz and Isaiah. The natural question to ask after the intimation of the coming sign as that of 'The virgin/young woman', would be: '*What* virgin/young woman?'

Some Christians have suggested that the reason for the definite article is that it is the reader who is supposed to know who this particular person is, and hence supply the name. This is part of the interpretation that Mary and Jesus are the two people involved, so that Christians who read this Isaiah verse know that the ultimate virgin is Mary. It is certainly likely that we see this kind of use of the definite article in the Hebrew text 1 Kings 18:4, which states that Obadiah hid the prophets 'in the cave'. Which cave? We must suppose that the reader was presumed to know the tradition of the cave. However, some of the ancient versions

---

[349] Rabbi Isaac Halevi, who was probably the author of the work entitled *Pa'aneah Raza*, written in the late thirteenth century CE. See O. S. Rankin: *Jewish Religious Polemic*, op cit, for discussion of this point.

[350] See Beth Moshe, *Judaism's Truth Answers the Missionaries*, op cit, p 159.

did not know which cave was being spoken about, and so we find them providing a different text, 'in two caves'. The NIV follows the alternative reading from the Hebrew.

It may be, then, that someone definite was in Isaiah's mind, at least for the first dimension of the fulfilment of the prophecy. Arnold Fruchtenbaum, who is a Jewish believer in Jesus and a highly influential theological writer among Messianic Jews, stretches this point too far, though, when he tries to restrict the fulfilment of the prophecy to Jesus alone. He has to resort to saying that since the presence of the definite article suggests that the reader should know who is being spoken about, but since, on the other hand, there is no obvious woman in the context, we need to retrace the steps of the Messianic prophecies until we come to the nearest appropriate reference to such a remarkable woman. He proceeds to claim that the only real possibility is the reference to Eve in Gen 3:15, a verse we have already looked at!

For Fruchtenbaum, our Isaianic verse actually supplies a further commentary on Gen 3:15 to the effect that this 'seed' of the woman (the Messiah) who will destroy the 'seed' of the serpent (the devil), will be born of a woman who is herself a virgin. This is very strained exegesis indeed to my way of thinking. More likely to me is the concept of a double fulfilment. But I quite agree that the presence of the definite article means that someone definite was in Isaiah's mind.

What, then, of the Hebrew term itself? The word *'almah* comes from a root ('alam) which means 'to be sexually mature', though not necessarily sexually experienced. The feminine noun which Isaiah uses here ('almah) is found nine times in the Hebrew Bible, but never, significantly, in any clear context of a woman who is *not* a virgin. It certainly seems impossible to establish that any of the uses of the word could involve a non-virgin. The term is one which presupposes virginity in any young woman who is described by it, reflecting the assumption of the culture which used the term. The assumption would certainly be that any unmarried, sexually mature woman would be a virgin.

Significantly, there is a cognate term (*glmt*) in Ugaritic (a Canaanite language closely related to Hebrew), a term which is also never used of a married woman or goddess. C. H. Gordon wrote a famous article on this term, '*almah*, concentrating on its use in our verse in Isaiah, but utilising in the process an important Ugaritic wedding text as well.[351] At the end of his study, reflecting on Matthew's translation of the term by the Greek word for a 'virgin', he wrote:

> Therefore the New Testament rendering of 'almah' as 'virgin' for Isaiah 7:14 rests on the older Jewish interpretation, which in turn is now borne out for precisely this annunciation formula by a text that is not only pre-Isaianic but is pre-Mosaic in the form that we now have it on a clay tablet.[352]

Coming from a distinguished *Jewish* scholar, this is an important article and conclusion for Christians to note. In these same ancient texts from Canaan researched by Gordon there is a lady known by the name of Hry. Although she is referred to as a '*glmt*' *before* her marriage to a man named Keret, she is never so described afterwards. In Hebrew legal documents and contracts this memory of '*almah* meaning a virgin is retained in the fact that the term '*almah* is never used of married women. This is all circumstantial evidence, I agree, but it is very strong and consistent circumstantial evidence. If we cannot find any places in the Hebrew Bible where this term is used of non-virgins, then we have a very strong case for arguing that indeed a virgin birth is being

---

[351] The Ugaritic text is called *The Wedding of Nikkal and Yarih*, and the cognate term, *glmt*, is used at 77:57.

[352] Cyrus H. Gordon, 'Almah in Isaiah 7:14', *Journal of Bible and Religion*, vol 21, no 2 (April 1953), p 106.

prophesied by Isaiah. Let us look at the other occurrences of the term in the Hebrew Bible:

Genesis 24:43. This verse is speaking about Rebekah, Isaac's future wife. Troki insisted that the use of the word *'almah* here only showed her stage of life and was not a necessary indication of virginity. Sigal adopts that position too, in his refutationist book. However, in verse 16 of the same chapter, Rebekah is explicitly called a virgin. The term used in verse 16, in this context of establishing her virginity, is the other Hebrew word which is important to this debate. It is the word *betulah* (betûlah), which is the term which Jewish polemicists say is the only *unambiguous* Hebrew word to denote a virgin. Two important points may be made here:

a) If *betulah* does clearly mean a virgin, then this means that *'almah* is also an acceptable term for a virgin, since *'almah* is the term used in verse 43.

b) More importantly, in verse 16, after the word *betulah*, we find the Hebrew phrase, 'and no man had known her'. *This*, in point of fact, is the only really unambiguous way to say in Hebrew that someone is a virgin. It is a phrase used several times in the Bible to make virginity quite explicit. It certainly suggests that the use of the term *betulah* in verse 16 was *not* in itself sufficient to denote virginity. This in turn suggests that *'almah* is as good a term as *betulah*!

Exodus 2:8. It is true, as the refutationists say, that Miriam is simply being referred to here as a young woman. But it is also true to say that the *presumption* is of virginity, unless we are shown otherwise. The circumstantial evidence of this verse, such as it is, supports the notion of virginity rather than challenging it.

Psalms 46:1; 68:25 (verse 26 in the English translations). The title of Psalm 46 (actually the first verse in the Hebrew text) may be a musical direction of some form, but if it is relevant to our discussion at all, then it speaks of a choir of young women in the temple service, and again the *presumption* must be that they are virgins fit for this service. The verse in Psalm 68 is speaking either of a procession of virgins or honourably-married women, and the former is the more likely.

Song of Songs 1:3; 6:8.   The context of the second of these two occurrences of the word '*almah* in the Song of Songs convinces us that in both verses the word is best translated by 'virgins'.

Proverbs 30:19.   Berger and Wyschogrod claim in their book that the point of this quite enigmatic teaching has to do with the fact that no trace of the encounter is left when the subject moves on and is gone. They take this interpretation because it suits their case against '*almah* meaning a virgin. Assuming that their interpretation is correct for the Proverbs riddle, they say that, had '*almah* meant a virgin, there would be a trace left when the man moved on, namely that the young woman would no longer be a virgin! But there is no agreement among scholars that this is the correct interpretation of the riddle. It is going beyond the evidence of the text to conclude that the proverb is speaking here about a liaison which results in sexual intercourse. This would not have been the assumption of the culture at all! Indeed the contrast in the next verse, verse 20, might suggest that perhaps a sexually-innocent girl is intended here in verse 19.

It seems to me that the common denominator in verse 19 is the unpredictable nature of the subjects involved from the perspective of the observer. Who can tell what a hovering eagle, a slithering snake, or a sailing ship will do next? They are free to take the best course which seems open to them, since there are no set paths for them. It is important to remember that in those days there were no shipping 'lanes' to obey. And in the same way, who can predict what the outcome will be when a man and a woman meet? Will they be attracted to one another or not? The combination of innocence, nervousness and desire to find a partner leads different people in different ways. There are many possible interpretations of this verse which would not in the least rule out the possibility of the '*almah* being a virgin.

The evidence from these other instances of the word '*almah* is all circumstantial, and this must be admitted by both Jewish and Christian commentators. Sadly, as I have pointed out before, the desire to score points against the opposition has often led people on both sides to claim that texts prove their own case beyond any possible doubt or ambiguity. This is rarely, if ever, true. However, even accepting the rule of modesty, Christians can certainly defend their conviction and teaching that Isaiah's use of the word '*almah* in 7:14 is consistent with the meaning of that term as 'virgin'. I personally believe that Isaiah intended to denote a virgin in this passage.

At this point we would do well to turn to the LXX to see whether it can help us. The LXX translates the word by the Greek term, *parthenos*, a word which is usually restricted in meaning to refer to 'a virgin'. It is the very word used in Matthew's Gospel when he quotes this verse from Isaiah, whether he quotes directly from the LXX or translates the Hebrew term for himself, and hence Christians have invariably held this LXX witness to the meaning of '*almah* as 'a virgin' to be substantial proof that Matthew was right. The LXX text certainly is an important witness, and the term *parthenos* is indeed very regularly used to denote virginity. However, say the refutationists, it is clear that even this Greek word does not *always* denote virginity, as we can see in the LXX translation of Gen 34:3, where it is used of Dinah, who has just been raped. Her virginity was certainly wrenched from her, but nonetheless she was no longer a virgin. The word *parthenos*, they say, must then be another general word for a young woman. The point is well made, and must be taken seriously.

When looked at carefully, however, it does seem to me that verse 3 is actually speaking about Shechem's desire (love?) for Dinah *before* the awful incident of the rape. He spoke tenderly to her and sought to win her love, even though the families were not likely to be pleased with his intention. In a context of frustration, he raped her. The rape is mentioned before his longing to marry her (see verse 8) in order to highlight the offence. Would Shechem have been so keen to marry her had she not been a virgin when he met her? Presumably not, in the context of that culture.

Therefore I take verse 3 to be an editorial word, as it were, seeking to explain that this was not just a random and violent rape, expressing that corrupt type of male desire for dominance over women, but rather a crime of passion, tragically ruining the life of a young virgin and without any possibility of justification, but also tragically involving a man who perhaps genuinely loved her. I believe that even within the full context of these verses, *parthenos* can still credibly be seen to refer to a virgin.

On another level altogether, if this verse is held to discredit *parthenos* as a word meaning a virgin, then it also serves to damage the credibility of the Hebrew term *betulah* as a word for a virgin, since *parthenos* is regularly used by the LXX to translate *betulah*. But as I say, I do not think that *parthenos* is discredited. In any case, we should note especially that it is only used to translate '*almah* in two places in the Bible: Gen 24:43, where we know it *is* being used of a virgin, and Isa 7:14.

Again I would say that the circumstantial evidence is on the side of *'almah*.[353]

It should be mentioned that there are several places where the word *betulah* is also used in contexts which might connote virginity (eg, Lev 21:3; Joel 1:8), again subjecting us to circumstantial evidence for our conclusions. However, there does seem to be one text where the presumption must be that the women concerned are *not* virgins, even although they are clearly described as *betulot* (the plural of *betulah*). This text is Esther 2:17, where the context of verses 14–17 suggests that the women in the king's harem were not virgins. Having a text where *betulah* seems clearly to mean a woman who is not a virgin serves to weigh the probability in favour of *'almah* being the one word, if indeed there was one, which always connoted a virgin.

Two final pieces of circumstantial evidence which seem to argue against *betulah* being the Hebrew language's best term for a virgin come from related semitic languages. In the Ugaritic texts which we looked at previously there is a cognate term for *betulah*, namely, *btlt*, and this term is used constantly of the highly promiscuous goddess, Anath. She is not at all a virgin! Then again we also have an Aramaic text where the corresponding term, *betulat* is used to refer to a woman who is having difficulty bearing her first child.[354] Of some interest is the fact that Rashi translated this term *'almah* by 'young woman' in Isa 7:14, but by 'virgin' in the Song of Songs 1:3; 6:8. This would seem to be a matter of

---

[353] It is true, however, that the Greek term (*parthenos*), and the Latin term, *virgo*, so often declared by Christians to be unambiguously words meaning virgin, are not quite so clear-cut. For the evidence on this matter, see H. G. Liddell and R. Scott, *A Greek–English Lexicon* (revised edition by H. S. Jones and R. McKenzie, Oxford, 1961), p 1339b, s.v. *parthenos*; C. T. Lewis and C. Short, *A Latin Dictionary* (Oxford, 1907), s.v. *virgo*.

[354] See J. A. Montgomery, *Aramaic Incantation Texts from Nippur*, text 13:9, p 178.

expedience rather than exegetical integrity! He admits in his comments, though, that even in his day (eleventh century CE) there were rabbis who privately reckoned that Isa 7:14 was also referring to a virgin.

It would seem, then, that the *'almah* in Isaiah's prophecy is in all likelihood a virgin and not just a young woman. The semantic and grammatical issues may not be clear-cut or self-evident, and in fact they are not, but the Christian ground is firm enough to be held with integrity. The historic understanding of the Church that Jesus' birth from Mary's womb was not the result of a sexual union between Mary and Joseph (or any other man), based on Matthew's account and the faith of the early Church, is not undermined by the homework undertaken in the light of the specific challenges of the Jewish refutationists.

This prophetic word given by Isaiah to the house of David was always going to be a Messianic promise, in the sense that even in Isaiah's day a threat to the Davidic line was automatically a threat to the Messianic line. The Messiah was to be the Son of David. This sign was a pledge from God that not only would the tiny kingdom of Judah survive the alliance of Syria with Israel, but that the Messianic line would remain intact.

Modest confidence, rather than inappropriate and insensitive triumphalism, is called for in these linguistic and historical matters, but such a confidence in the Christian interpretation can be all the stronger for the sense of integrity which accompanies it. I am sure that Isaiah knew the person he was speaking about when he gave this prophetic word to Ahaz, but I am also sure that he could have had only a vague understanding of the greater fulfilment that was to come in the birth of the Messiah himself.

16

Jesus and the throne-names of the Messiah
Isaiah 9:5

In this chapter we turn our attention to one of the other most famous Messianic prophecies in the Hebrew Bible. This is another text which is celebrated at every Christmas season in churches throughout the world, and which is also loved by many people because of its central place in Part One of Handel's *Messiah* oratorio. The Hebrew text is verse 5 of this chapter in Isaiah, but note that English translations, following the verse ordering of the LXX here, have it as verse 6. Here are the words of this exquisite prophecy:

> For to us a child is born,
> to us a son is given,
> and the government will be on his shoulders.
> And he will be called
> Wonderful Counsellor, Mighty God,
> Everlasting Father, Prince of Peace.

Like chapter 7 of Isaiah's book, this chapter was written in the shadow of the approaching Assyrian empire. The threat from the Israelite/Syrian alliance has been dealt with, God having promised to take care of that, but because of Israel's persistent rebellion against him, God is going to allow the Assyrians to come and inflict severe punishment on her. However, this is not to be seen as the end of Israel, since it is a serious *disciplining* of the people whom God loves, not an abandoning of them as if they were his enemies. The 'darkness' brought about by their sin (8:22) will eventually be removed by the grace of God's initiative for salvation.

The Galilee region will be the first to see God's light dawning on the dark land (9:1–2). We may note in passing that in the *Zohar*, the late medieval source book of Jewish kabbalah, an interpretation is given that this passage means that the Messiah will reveal himself first in Galilee! Christians, of course, are in happy agreement with this interpretation, relating it not to Jesus' birth, which was in Judaea, but to the inauguration of his actual ministry (Matt 4:12–17). Isaiah goes on to say that when this great Messianic day comes, there will be freedom from oppression (verse 4) and from war (verse 5). The key to this is the gift from God of a boy-child (verse 6) who will rule over God's people (verses 6–7).

Jews and Christians have agreed that this is referring to a real person, but have differed greatly over the correct interpretation of his names, character, and purpose. It is the names themselves which provide the insight into the person's identity and life, as was the common case in that culture, and we shall be devoting most of our attention to them. However, we note first of all that no mention is made here of the parents of this child. In Isa 7:14 we had the famous reference to the 'virgin' who, while unnamed, was at least mentioned. Here there is nothing at all. But we are justified, I believe, in understanding this to be the son of the royal house of David, the Messiah. In verse 7 it is said that the boy will 'reign on David's throne' as the Messiah, the son of David, was to do.

One other thing to be highlighted at this point is the issue of the correct understanding of the tenses of the verbs which are used. Essentially, we are looking at the issue of whether Isaiah is to be understood as saying that the reign of this new ruler is still in the future, or already in process. Note that the NIV, as with most non-Jewish translations, has given a future orientation, whereas, as we shall see, the Jewish Publication

Society, as with many Jewish commentators, has placed the event in the past. This is a highly technical area, since Hebrew does not have a verbal conjugation system based on *tenses*. There are rules governing the use and meaning of verbs, of course, but not strictly in relation to time-orientation. The context must dictate the time-frame. In the narrative portions of the Bible this is sometimes quite straightforward to analyse, but in poetic and prophetic passages like the present one it is rarely, if ever, clear-cut. This is therefore a factor in the interpretation of our verse, as we shall see.

A tendency to be over-dogmatic, found in too many Christian and Jewish polemicists, will prove as unhelpful in this matter of verbal tenses as in other matters. Sigal is quite out of order when he says in his challenge to the Christian:

> Christians incorrectly translate the verbs in verse 5 in the future tense, instead of the past, as the Hebrew original reads.[355]

It is by no means as simple as that. According to the context, which alone will have the casting vote in this matter of the tense of these verbs, the child may very well be someone who is yet to be born.

How, then, do the Jewish commentators interpret the meaning and significance of these grand names for the Davidic ruler? Is it acknowledged that they are the titles of the coming Messiah, or are they seen as being related to other kings? There are essentially three different interpretations given to these names in the Jewish traditions.

Some say that all the titles refer to God himself, not to the boy.   The point they wish to make is that although the boy is given a wonderful name, it is really God who is celebrated as

---

[355] Gerald Sigal, *The Jew and the Christian Missionary*, op cit, p 31.

being wonderful, not the boy. His name will simply serve to point to God and will carry no implications for his own nature or power. This is hardly a reasonable interpretation of the way that the verse is presented in the text, but it was advocated by some commentators and polemicists, presumably in an attempt to deflect attention completely away from speculation about whether or not Jesus lived up to the names. Having said that, however, this view has had a quite disproportionate influence on English-speaking Jewish people, because it was taken up by the Jewish Publication Society in their original translation:

> Wonderful in counsel is God the mighty,
> the everlasting Father, the Ruler of Peace.

The new version of this translation, which I have already cited several times with respect to other verses, is faithful to this basic understanding of the text, while differing in some specific terms. Here is the full context concerning the names in the new version:

> For a child has been born to us,
> A son has been given us,
> And authority has settled on his shoulders.
> He has been named
> 'The Mighty God is planning grace;
> The Eternal Father, a peaceable ruler'.

In justification of this translation, or at least a part of it, the translators refer us in a footnote to Isa 25:1, which they translate in the following way:

> O LORD, You are my God;
> I will extol You, I will praise Your name.
> For You planned graciousness of old,
> Counsels of steadfast faithfulness.

The last two lines of this verse are obviously relevant to the first two names of the Messiah in the view of these Jewish scholars. Many Jewish people have been influenced in their understanding of these names by this approach. To recapitulate, then, this view of the text sees the names as being only symbolic, as regards the boy. They are not to be taken as implying that the boy himself is anything other than a human being. The situation with regard to these names is exactly the same as it is with so many of the names of biblical characters, these translators claim. To have a wonderful name which refers to God does not mean that you are any more than a human being. This future ruler of Israel, then, whether the Messiah or not, will be simply a human being. Of course God may, and presumably will, endow the Messiah with special gifts and abilities, but these will in no way reflect his inner nature.

Gerald Sigal, keen to remove all thought of a supernatural Messiah, states this case as well as anyone in his polemical book:

> The words of this name form a sentence expressive of God's greatness which will become manifest in the benefits to be bestowed upon the future king in his lifetime. Thus, the name, though borne by the king, serves, in reality, as a testimonial to God.[356]

The LXX seems to be trying to convey something of this same understanding in its idiosyncratic translation of the verse. The divine power to act which is implied by these names is reserved for God alone in the LXX, in keeping with this general interpretation, but the names themselves have become quite garbled in the attempt of the LXX translators to see the boy as a mere messenger of God, akin to the prophets perhaps. The LXX presents God as speaking, and reads as follows:

> and his name is called the 'messenger of great counsel', for I will bring peace upon the princes and health to him.

---

[356] Gerald Sigal, op cit, p 29.

The point is being made here, albeit in a very different way from the translation of the JPS, that the boy is simply a human being who rules by God's choice and enabling. The basic message of this interpretation is that the names, while given to the boy, refer to God, and to his nature and power.

Some say that the first three names refer to God, but that the fourth one refers to this special person.   For instance, Rashi states in his commentary on this passage:

> The Holy One, blessed be He, who is wonderful in counsel, a mighty God, and eternal Father, called Hezekiah 'prince of peace'.

Joseph Kimchi, following Rashi, says that Jerome is again responsible for misleading Christians by mistranslating the verse, which should be translated:

> the Wonderful Counsellor, Mighty God, Everlasting Father shall call his name the prince of peace.[357]

Isaac Troki tried to insist that this was really the only normal way to read the text, but it is certainly *not* the 'natural' understanding of the word order in the verse. This interpretation of the names was developed to provide a rendering which refers the three most 'controversial' names to God, leaving the relatively unobtrusive fourth name for the boy himself.[358]

What is more, this interpretation raises a technical question about the correct way to read the verb used here for 'calling' the person by these names. The same Hebrew letters which are used here (vyqr') can be read, with two different sets of vowels added, as either conveying an active meaning ('he/it will call') or a passive meaning ('he/it will be called')

[357] Rabbi Joseph Kimchi, *Sefer Ha-Berit*, op cit, 19b, p 29.
[358] *Faith Strengthened*, op cit, p 105.

of the verb. It should be noted that the LXX, the Syriac version and the Vulgate all took this in the passive sense.

If it was meant to be an active meaning of the verb, with the first three sets of names acting as the subject of the verb and the object of the sentence being 'his name the prince of peace', then we would not expect the phrase 'his name' to come after the verb and before the subject, which is what in fact we do find here. We would expect the word order to be: first the verb, then the subject, and finally the object. Nor would we expect the phrase 'his name' to be separated from its companion phrase 'the prince of peace' by the subject. But this is precisely what we do find. It is in fact much more 'natural' to take the verb in a passive mode, as, for example, the NIV does, with all the names then being equally part of the extended object and in the order we would expect them.

This interpretation looks again like anti-Christian polemic, designed to distance the concept of the Messiah from any notion of divinity or supernatural nature. We shall look at a further interpretation, namely that Isaiah was referring to King Hezekiah, after the next section.

The older commentaries, and even some of the medieval masters, were of the opinion that the names all refer to this special person, namely the Messiah. Targum Jonathan has this:

> And there was called his name from of old, Wonderful Counsellor, Mighty God, He who lives for ever, the Messiah, in whose days peace shall reign upon us.[359]

Ibn Ezra, acknowledged by the Jewish community as one of the greatest biblical commentators, knew that many of his contemporaries, following many of their teachers before them, preferred to remove this passage from any Messianic

---

[359] See also Deuteronomy Rabbah 1, on Gen 43:14; and Numbers Rabbah 11.

speculation. But he himself was not prepared to turn his back on what he considered to be the true meaning of the passage. He wrote:

> There are some interpreters who say that 'wonderful counsellor, mighty God, everlasting Father' are the names of God, and only 'prince of peace' is the name of the child. But according to my view, the right interpretation is that they are all the names of the child.

This is the Christian understanding too, of course. We shall shortly need to look at the actual meanings of these names and the implications which they are believed to present about the nature of the Messiah, since the Jewish and Christian communities view this matter quite differently. However, it is important to note that before the days of the medieval Jewish commentators and polemicists, a fully Messianic interpretation of these names was quite acceptable. It was once again a question of later anti-Christian polemic which led to the attempted rejection of a Messianic option.

When we looked at the dispute over Isa 7:14 in the last chapter, we noted that one of the Jewish objections offered against Jesus being the 'Immanuel' spoken of there was that he was never called by this name in the New Testament. The very same objection is raised with regard to the names given here in Isa 9:5. Jesus is not called by these names by anyone in the New Testament, nor does he refer to himself by them. The very same response must be given here as was offered previously. The mere fact that the names are not employed in the New Testament is not really important, since these are *titles* for the Messiah, not personal names.[360]

On this matter of titles, it may well be that we have in this

---

[360] Having said this, there are Christians who do believe that we have a veiled allusion to these titles in Luke 1:32–33, but I am far from convinced of this.

verse a series of symbolic throne-names for the future royal Messianic ruler of Israel. The giving of such honorific titles (either at the birth of the heir-apparent to the throne, or at the enthronement of the new ruler) was certainly the custom in the Egyptian and Assyrian empires, both of which exercised an immense influence on Israel. In Egypt the ruler was given five titles, whereas in Assyria he received only four. If we are right in seeing some significance in this context, then presumably these 'throne-titles' for the Messiah would serve as a polemic against the gods and kings of those empires. Isaiah would be saying that none of them could compare with the King of kings who was to come!

Some scholars have tried to find five throne-titles here in our verse, because they would prefer an Egyptian context, but several factors argue against this: attempts to make a fifth title out of the words which open the next verse are all strained; the three other symbolic names which we find in this section of Isaiah are all balanced in pairs (She'ar Yashuv, in 7:3; Immanu-El, in 7:14; Maher-Shalal-Hash-Baz, in 8:1); the Assyrian kings were especially noted for their boasting about their wisdom and power, so that we have an excellent context for the polemic of these titles; it was in fact the Assyrian empire which was uppermost in Isaiah's and Ahaz's minds at the time.

We may very well have here, then, a deliberate naming of the throne-titles of the Messiah, celebrating the future coming to power of the great King-Messiah. Jesus, in that case, would not be called these titles by his family, but will be acknowledged by them all upon his return. Of course those Jewish refutationists who are prepared to admit that this verse is speaking about the Messiah but who claim that the real Messiah is still to come, say that when he does come, he will be given these names, as well as the name Immanuel. Interestingly, although many of the Jewish traditions relate this verse to King Hezekiah, as for instance we saw in Rashi's commentary, they do not find it strange that *he* is never called by these names either! However, let us look now at the way in which those who do advocate that Hezekiah was the person in mind, relate these titles to his life and character.

Wonderful Counsellor is said to relate to God's marvellous plan and purpose for his people, a plan which would be forever linked to the name of Hezekiah (see Isa 14:24–27; 37:5–20).

Mighty God is said to speak of God miraculously protecting Judah against its far more powerful enemies, a promise from God which Hezekiah trusted (see Isa 37:33–35).

Eternal Father is said to refer to the fact that God, who alone controls time and eternity, super-naturally and graciously added time on to Hezekiah's lifespan (see Isa 38:5; 2 Kings 20:6).

Prince of Peace is said to speak of the wonderful peace which God gave to Judah under the kingship of Hezekiah (see Isa 39:8).

Looking at the whole of this verse, and not just the names, Beth Moshe presents what she sees as a cogent apologetic for Hezekiah being the one who fulfilled the role of this person:

> With expanded imagination, the names could be made to suit Hezekiah, but never the unborn Jesus. Hezekiah did have a government. He was a wonderful religious leader. He could be likened to displaying the mighty power of God which destroyed the enemies miraculously. As a religious purifier, he assisted God's everlasting watchfulness. And his reign did have peace after the enemies were defeated. The peace could be described as abundant, therefore with no end in the Biblical sense. Even though this explanation is not smoothly fitted, you can see that it has all the elements to be considered correct. Christianity's explanation lacks all the elements necessary.[361]

---

[361] Beth Moshe, *Judaism's Truth Answers the Missionaries*, op cit, p 149.

We see here how it is possible for different groups of people to find texts and arguments to justify their own particular theological points of view even when they are working from the same basic sources. Christians will not be impressed by this claim for Hezekiah, just as Jewish people are just not impressed by the claim for Jesus. As it turns out, there is little doubt that the claim that Hezekiah was the Messiah (had Israel only recognised this fact) was initiated, and has been developed, in response to two major factors. On the one hand, it came about as the result of a deliberate policy among many of the rabbis to play down all Messianic speculation among the Jewish people. There were a number of false Messiahs who rose and fell in Israel's history, each one leaving his own legacy of bitter disappointment among the people and sometimes a certain amount of antisemitic reaction from the host society as well. Therefore it seemed to many of the leaders of the Jewish people that a past Messiah was preferable, at least in the foreseeable future, to an anticipated one.

Secondly, of course, there was a more specific reaction against the claims of believers in Jesus that he alone fulfilled this prophecy. Rather than expose the general Jewish public to involved disputes with Jewish believers and other Christians about the nature and mission of the coming Messiah, etc, it was easier to settle for a policy which stated that the Messiah had come already but Israel had not been ready or worthy to accept him. The attempt to create this mindset among Jewish people was largely successful, as we see from the fact that even today many Jewish people have no interest at all in debate about the Messiah, being content to state that the rabbis teach that he was probably Hezekiah. This does not, of course, represent the view of all Jewish people today, but there are still many who do dismiss the whole issue in this fashion. The strategy was created as a means to dismiss debate, and it still serves the same purpose for all those who so desire to use it!

Now what about Jesus? Why does the Jewish community believe that he could not possibly be the person who fulfilled the message of these names in Isa 9:5? The same *specific* charges are made by all the contemporary refutationists, and I shall list them here. The refutationists argue that:

- This person will be called *Wonderful Counsellor*, BUT . . . We see from passages like Matt 21:18–22 that Jesus cannot always be trusted to give wonderful counsel. Jesus' own selfishness is exposed here, just as we see him seeking to win people over to himself by promising them the power to indulge themselves.

  How would *you* answer this argument?

- This person will be called *Mighty God*, BUT . . . We learn from passages like Luke 2:5–6 and Heb 5:8 that Jesus had to develop and mature, even learning to live in obedience to others; we learn from passages like John 5:30 and 14:28 that Jesus did not experience the full might and sovereignty of God in his life.

  How would *you* answer this argument?

- This person will be called *Everlasting Father*, BUT . . . We learn from passages like John 1:18, 3:16, and a host of other verses, that Jesus saw and knew himself, and was known by his followers, as a *son*, not a Father.

  How would *you* answer this charge?

- This person will be called *Prince of Peace*, BUT . . . We learn from passages like Matt 10:34–36 that Jesus did not come to bring peace, but rather strife and difficulty.

  We have met this issue before, in the first part of this book, but the question remains: How would *you* answer this argument?

By the use and abuse of such New Testament texts, the refutationists try to demonstrate that Jesus is simply unworthy of consideration as the Messianic figure of Isa 9:5. Let us look, then, at the significance of these names, and the way in which Christians see them fulfilled in the person and work of Jesus of Nazareth.

Wonderful Counsellor. First of all, we shall take a look at these two words separately.

Wonderful (pele'): This Hebrew term, and the root which lies behind it, is one which is consistently used in the Hebrew Bible to describe the amazing work of God himself. For example, it is used of God in Israel's celebration after the Exodus from Egypt (Exod 15:11); God uses it of himself in Isa 29:14 to proclaim that he is going to completely astound people with what he is about to do (see also Isa 25:1); and then, in a very significant passage, the same two roots which are used side-by-side in our verse for 'wonderful counsellor' are used of God in Isa 28:29. That verse is worth quoting here for its importance to our context:

> All this also comes from the LORD Almighty,
> wonderful in counsel and magnificent in wisdom.

It is not going too far, therefore, to state that this term is uniquely associated with God himself. The person who is called by this name, as Christians see it, will partake of the nature of divinity. He will be able to do the same wonderful things that only God can do, because he himself will be divine in nature. This is related to the life and miracles of Jesus as we see him and them in the gospels. The Jewish people knew that Jesus was quite different from any other prophets or holy men they had encountered, because he was able to do such wonders (see, for example, John 9:32; Mark 2:12b).

Counsellor (yô'ets): This Hebrew term refers to an adviser in the matter of guidance for one's plans in life, rather than a pastoral psychologist or the like. Having said this, such advisers did have to try to make sense of what concerned the life of the people they were advising, and to help them to live an integrated life. Unlike Hezekiah or any other leader or indeed person, who all need such counsellors to help them in their decision-making (see Isa 41:28–29), this person will be like God, who needs no counsel from others but rather acts as a counsellor for them (see Isa 40:13). There is surely some significance in the fact that one of the themes of Isaiah's whole ministry was the failure of the people's counsellors and wise men (see Isa 1:26, 3:3, 5:21, 19:11–15, 28:7–10, 29:9–14, 30:1–2, 31:1–3, 47:10–13).

Since this word is used in conjunction with the previous one, then perhaps we are being told that it is in the holding of a perfect plan for our lives that we will experience the true wonder of this Messiah.[362] He will make sense of our lives and set us on the way that leads to life with God. Again, Christians point to the New Testament for evidence that this was people's experience with Jesus (see, for example, John 4:29, 2:45–51; Mark 12:28–34).

Mighty God ('el gibôr). While it is undoubtedly true that there are many people in the Hebrew Bible whose names have been formed from a combination of this word for 'God' ('el = *el*), along with a second word (eg, Eliab, 'elîab, meaning 'God is Father'; Elijah, 'elîyahû, meaning 'The Lord is God'), Christians have always pointed out that this is not the case with the name found in Isa 9:5. These other names were just expressions of a valued relationship with God, implying nothing about any unique nature or character for the person with the name. However, in our present verse we have the two words written distinctly, each one standing with its own integrity. This is not just another example of a compound name. In support for the interpretation that this name is more than simply a reference to God and in fact implies a sharing in the nature of God, Christians point out

---

[362] The accentuation of the Masoretic Text supports the reading of these two words as one unit, as does the circumstantial evidence of Isa 25:1, 28:29, and 29:14.

that this very name is used for God himself in the Hebrew Bible (see Deut 10:17; Neh 9:32; Jer 32:18). It may be that the most significant of all these passages which speak of God as this 'Mighty God' is one which occurs in the very next chapter of Isaiah (10:21). It is highly unlikely that any Jewish person reading the book would fail to be struck by the fact that unlike all the names with '*el*' in them, this is a name which actually belongs to God himself! It is, in short, a divine title.[363]

In closing, I should mention that in Isaiah 11, recognised by both Jewish and Christian communities as a Messianic passage, and only two chapters away from our present verse, this quality of 'might', using the same root as we have here, is said to be one of the characteristics of the Messiah.

Everlasting Father ('avî 'ad). This is the name which causes the real problem for many Christians. It is such a commonplace of Christian theology, based fully upon the text of the New Testament, that Jesus is the *Son* of the Father, and not the Father, that it seems contradictory to refer to him here as being himself the Father. And yet Christians are convinced that this is as much one of the titles of the Messiah as any other. Is there a way to solve this dilemma without losing any sense of credibility or integrity?

The Hebrew words, as they are usually interpreted, convey literally that this person will be 'father of eternity', or 'father of eternal life'. There are several legitimate possibilities for the interpretation of this phrase. The traditional Christian interpretation, followed, as a rule, in the Bible translations and immortalised for our century by Handel's chorus in his *Messiah*, is to say that this phrase means that the Messiah

---

[363] It is also significant to note that in Ps 24:8 God is called by the name, 'mighty Lord', using the very same construction but based on the actual name of God (YHWH gibôr).

will indeed be called 'Everlasting Father'. Hence the problem for Christians, and the focus of the ridicule of the refutationists.

A number of Christian commentators, unhappy with this traditional interpretation, opt for an interpretation which means that the Messiah will provide for his people *like* a father (or, like his Father) would. In this fashion, Eliakim, the son of Hilkiah, is said to be 'a father to those who live in Jerusalem' (see Isa 22:21), and Job describes himself as someone who was 'a father to the needy' (Job 29:16). God himself is called 'a father to the fatherless' in Ps 68:6 (verse 5 in the English translations). Putting it another way, this understanding of the text presents the Messiah as one who will be a 'Son' *vis-à-vis* God, the Father, but a 'father' *vis-à-vis* his people. Martin Luther, for example, was one who favoured this interpretation. In his comments on this name he took it to mean that Jesus is a messiah

> Who at all times feeds His Kingdom and Church; in whom there is a fatherly love without end.

While one can appreciate the line of thought which lies behind this attempt to rescue the traditional rendering of the Hebrew word 'av by the English word 'Father', it seems to flounder on the fact that Jesus has not replaced the Father in Christian experience or theology! God the Father is very much alive and well, and he is our Father in heaven, caring and providing for his people as he always did before the birth of Jesus. Our Father is the father of the fatherless, the creator and provider God; Jesus, the Son, is the mediator, the redeemer, the elder brother, etc. I think that this interpretation of the name as speaking of the Messiah as a father-figure is altogether well-intentioned, but nonetheless leading in the wrong direction.

One other interpretation, which I think has missed the point altogether, is being considered by some modern commentators. In this view, the word traditionally translated as 'eternity' ('ad) is taken, rather, to be the word, spelt identically, for 'booty' or 'prey'. This word is actually found in Gen 49:27; Isa 33:23; and Zeph 3:8. In our verse it is taken to mean that, in the custom of the Near Eastern cultures, the King-Messiah would have sole authority over the spoils of the final war. All the glory, in other words, would be due to him. We meet this theology in the biblical concept of the *herem*, the 'forbidden things', meaning the spoils of war. These were to belong to God alone, as a symbol of his complete lordship and also as an acknowledgement that victory in battle was really due to his intervention (see, for example, Josh 7).

The reason that I think that this understanding is wrong is my conviction that the Hebrew word 'ad does in fact mean 'eternal life' in this context. It is the *other* word which I believe needs to be reinterpreted.

This other possibility depends on the fact that semitic languages, of which Hebrew is one, have two idiomatic expressions which use the relationships of father and son in quite metaphorical ways. Readers of the Bible are familiar with the Hebrew idiom 'son of . . .', which is often used metaphorically to mean that something or someone is a member of a characteristic group or class, etc. When Amos says that he is neither a prophet nor the 'son of a prophet' (Amos 7:14), he means that he has had no tradition at all of prophetic training or of being associated with other prophets. He is saying that he is not a member of a prophetic group or class. He does not mean to say that his biological father was not a prophet either. The very same idiom about being of the class or group of prophets is found in 1 Kings 20:35.

In Num 17:25 (verse 10 in the English translations) the phrase translated as 'the rebellious' is literally, 'the sons of rebellion', showing clearly the use of the phrase 'son of . . .' to designate that the person or thing belongs to a certain category or type. Throughout the book of Ezekiel, the prophet is referred to by God as 'son of man' (eg, Ezek

2:1). This is a way of expressing his human frailty and his limitations, in contradistinction to God; it is not simply a 'poetic' way of saying 'man'. The New English Bible translators caught this well by translating it as 'mere mortal'.

Therefore to say 'son of . . .' is a well-established way of saying that someone or something belongs to a certain type or category, etc. However, there is also a semitic idiom, 'father of . . .', which is common, for example, in Arabic. It is not found very frequently in Hebrew, but nevertheless it is found, and this could well be an example of it. This particular idiom means that the person being described as the 'father of something' possesses, or has authority over, or is the origin of, the object mentioned. It does not mean literally being a father. We have a good instance of it, for example, in Gen 4:20f., where its use means that the arche-types or originators of the skills of livestock farming and music were Jabal and Jubal. If we have a case of that idiom here, then it means that the Messiah is the one who has authority over eternity. An appropriate translation would then be 'Ruler of Eternity', 'Eternal One', or the like. By this I do not simply mean, as others suggest, that the title promises eternal life for the Messiah (cf 2 Sam 7:16; Ps 72:5, 17). My own conviction is that we are being told here that the Messiah is eternal and has the authority to mediate this eternal life for *others*. Perhaps the words of Jesus in Rev 1:8 are to be seen in this light?

> I am the Alpha and the Omega . . . who is, and who was, and who is to come, the Almighty.

This same sentiment is expressed in Heb 13:8, where we find the proclamation that

> Jesus Christ is the same yesterday and today and for ever.

Similar in result to this interpretation is another one which, in my opinion, deserves much more attention than it usually receives. In later Hebrew, though granted not in the Hebrew

Bible itself unless this is an occurrence in our verse, the word translated as 'father (' av) is also used in a metaphorical way to express the meaning 'source or origin'.[364] In other words, this title could mean that the Messiah was not being described as a 'father' at all, but as the *source* of eternal life for his people. An appropriate translation might therefore be 'Giver of Eternal Life'. This would certainly reflect a great deal of the teaching of the New Testament, especially in John's Gospel, concerning Jesus' mission.

To offer some examples, there is the famous word of Jesus in John 3:16, proclaiming that to believe in Jesus is to have eternal life. Or, using the symbol of water to represent life, Jesus says to the Samaritan woman that he has the power to offer the 'living water' of life. This water which Jesus can give will become 'a spring of water' in each person (see John 4:7–15). In John 5:21 Jesus says that he 'gives life' to his own. It is in John's Gospel that we hear Jesus saying that unless you share his life you have no real life in you. But anyone who shares in Jesus' life 'has eternal life' (see John 6:53–58).

In Revelation 21:6, the risen Jesus actually says the following words:

> I am the Alpha and the Omega, the Beginning and the End. To him who is thirsty I will give to drink without cost from the spring of the water of life.

Most suggestive of all, perhaps, as support for this interpretation of the name in Isa 9:5 is the fact that a title of precisely this sort is used of Jesus in Heb 5:9, where it says:

> he became *the source of eternal salvation* for all who obey him . . .

---

[364] A good account of this usage, with examples from rabbinic sources, is given by M. Jastrow in his standard reference work, *A Dictionary of the Targumim, the Talmud Bavli and Yerushalmi, and the Midrashic Literature*, 2 vols (Luzac & Co, London, 1903), ad loc.

Therefore 'Giver of Eternal Life' would be my understanding and suggested translation of this great title for the Messiah, a title which is actualised in the life and mission of Jesus.

Prince of Peace (sar shalôm). This great title speaks directly of the vocation of the Messiah in at last making *shalom* possible for people. It is precisely this task which the Jewish traditions deny has been accomplished since the coming of Jesus. However, we have already dealt with this issue of the peace which Jesus brought to Israel and to the world in a previous chapter in the first part of this book, and there is no need to rehearse that whole debate again here. To repeat what was said there: in spite of the fierce insistence to the contrary by refutationists, it is still a fully tenable position for Christians to claim that Jesus did fulfil the mandate of this title by making real peace, real *shalom*, possible for us. In the light of the fact that one of the other titles here is 'Mighty God', where the word used for the concept of 'might' is the same as the word used to describe valiant warriors, we should beware of any naïve assumptions that the Messiah will have only lovely peaceful activities to concern himself with when he comes! There will be whole-sale and massive resistance to the Messiah, and the forces which represent this resistance will initiate war. This is highly relevant to the discussion about conflict in the days of the Messiah which we dealt with in that earlier chapter of this book.

A final comment, in the light of our discussion about the Messiah not being the same person as the Father God, is to wonder whether there is any significance in the fact that the Messiah is not called here the 'King of Peace'. The Hebrew term for 'king' (melekh), which is commonly used for God in the Hebrew Bible, is not used here. Instead we have the term for a 'prince' (sar). Is this another way of saying that the Messiah, while being a full partner in the Godhead, is not the Father, but, in some relational way, under the authority of the

Father? This would certainly reflect the consensus of Christian theology, which teaches that although equally God, the three Persons of the Triune God are distinct Persons, in a distinct relationship.

Looking back on these four Messianic titles, it is interesting to note that other leaders in Israel's life were known as 'counsellors' (see Isa 1:26), 'warriors' (see Isa 3:2), 'city fathers' (see Isa 22:21), and 'princes' (see Isa 1:23), using part of the vocabulary of these titles. The people of Israel knew the kind of help they needed from God. Isaiah knew what they needed from the Messiah. But no one else ever personified the particular nature of these four unique titles. At the end of the chapter, I think that we can legitimately conclude by saying that Christians can have every confidence in seeing this verse as a prophecy about the person and work of the Messiah; and moreover, that they can be secure in their conviction that the titles point unerringly to Jesus of Nazareth, the true Son of David.

Did the psalmist prophesy about the crucifixion? Psalm 22:17

The most celebrated portion of the Hebrew Bible which is held by Christians to speak about the suffering and death of Jesus for the sake of the world is undoubtedly Isa 52:13–53:12. After that will come Psalm 22, the psalm which is the focus of our attention in this chapter. In particular, we shall be examining verse 17 (which is verse 16 in the English translations) to test the claim that it is speaking about the manner of the death of the Messiah, namely by being nailed to a wooden post in an act of crucifixion. The relevant part of the verse, at least as it is usually translated in most Christian Bibles, reads:

> they have pierced my hands and my feet.

Such a great deal is held to hang on the correct translation of these few words (only three words in Hebrew: k'ry ydy wrgly), that we shall find ourselves necessarily involved once more in linguistic arguments as well as theological debate. I must repeat that while technical material will be kept to a minimum, the technical issues themselves cannot be ignored, since they are part and parcel of the viability of the various interpretations of Scripture.

There is no solid evidence that this psalm was interpreted as an important Messianic prophecy before Jesus and the early believers presented it as such. But since the time of Jesus, the psalm has been regarded as a central Messianic text by Christians. No more traumatic cry can be found in the

New Testament, or the whole Bible, for that matter, than Jesus' words as he hung dying: 'My God, my God, why have you forsaken me?' These words transport us immediately to the opening of Psalm 22, and Jesus' use of them on that occasion served to immortalise the psalm in the Christian community (see Matt 27:46). In the Middle Ages we do have one Jewish text which makes a reference to Ps 22:8 (verse 7 in the English translations) in connection with the supposed second Messiah, known as the son of Joseph, being humiliated and mocked before his death.[365] However, there is precious little material in the Jewish traditions, and none of it is early.

In verses 7–9 (verses 6–8 in the English translations) the psalmist is described as being despised by the nation, thus paralleling what is said of the Suffering Servant in Isaiah 52:13–53:12. We may note here that in the very same way that that famous Isaianic song ends in triumph for the Suffering Servant, so our psalm moves to a climax of praise and positive testimony to God's goodness. A further parallel is that the Jewish community interprets this psalm as speaking of the experience of the whole people of Israel in the world, just as the general Jewish view of the Isaianic passage is that it too is painting the picture of Israel's destiny in history.

Christians have traditionally interpreted the reference to 'people' in verse 7 as referring not to the nations of the world, as Jewish commentators have taken it, but as meaning the people of Israel. In this case, if those who are mocking the psalmist are the Israelites, then the central character represented by the psalmist cannot also be the Israelites. Verses 11–12 (10–11) are regarded as being more applicable to a person than to a nation, and verses 23 and 26 (22 and 25) certainly seem to make more sense when

---

[365] *Yalqut* on Isaiah 30. This is a tenth-century text.

seen in the context of a person giving testimony to the whole people. So, in the light of Jesus' reference to the opening line of the psalm while he hung on the cross, the Church has seen the psalm as centred on the life, death and resurrection of the Messiah.

This very issue of how to make most sense of the dramatic nature of the passage, by asking which characters are speaking in which verses, lies at the heart of the problem of interpreting Isa 52:13–53:12 as well. Indeed this issue is the central exegetical bone of contention which divides the Jewish and Christian traditions regarding the Isaianic song. It is also a basic issue here in Psalm 22.

In the New Testament, verses 15–19 (14–18) are related specifically to the manner of Jesus' death by crucifixion, and to the callous attitude of the Roman soldiers for whom this was just another execution in a day's work. These terrible words of the psalmist are taken to refer to the profuse sweating, the dislocation of bones, the rupturing of the heart, the excessive thirst and the hammering of nails into the hands and feet of someone who is experiencing crucifixion. They also describe the awful aloneness of Jesus when both Roman soldiers and Jewish crowds dismissed the significance of his life. For references to these aspects of Jesus' death we can read Luke 23:34–39, and John 19:23–24, 28–30.

When you read through the whole of this psalm you realise the strength and confidence of its conclusion, and therefore many Christians, this writer included, believe that Jesus had the whole psalm in mind, not just its opening words, while he hung on the cross. He would certainly have known the whole of the psalm by heart, as would the Jewish people who heard him utter the words. At least those who realised he was quoting the psalm would have appreciated the full context of the words (see Matt 27:47). This is perfectly reasonable, of course, since Christians today would also have in mind the whole psalm if someone offered only the first line. If you were to quote simply the line 'The Lord's my Shepherd' to even a moderately committed Christian or Jewish person, the chances are that they would immediately be aware of the entire content of Psalm 23 without having to consciously work their way through it.

If you do not believe that Jesus was thinking about the whole context of Psalm 22 when he cited it, then his cry on the cross takes on something of the feel of defeat rather than confidence in God. This requires that we believe that Jesus led his hearers into the opening of a psalm with no thought as to the context of his words, and with no intention that those who heard him should recognise the psalm and go on to connect the words to their context. This is hard to believe. But of course it is the interpretation which suits the refutationists. Some demand to know why Jesus would cry out in utter dereliction at the very moment of what Christians regard as his greatest triumph, unless the truth was that Jesus suddenly realised that he was going to die and was not going to see God miraculously intervene to save him from death on the cross.

The point is, however, that although Jesus suffered the agony of bearing the weight of the sin of the world on the cross, and although it looked to the world as if he had died defeated and abandoned, this death was actually the costliest stage of his service to humanity, a stage which would in turn be followed by victory over sin and death. The words of dereliction must not be taken out of their context![366]

Others point out what they see as a contradiction within the gospel records. Matthew and Mark give this defeated word of Jesus, whereas Luke 23:46 gives the confident and

---

[366] In the Midrash Tehillim, various interpretations and applications are offered for this verse of dereliction at the start of Psalm 22. For instance, it is said by one to have been cried by the Israelites at the Sea of Reeds just before the Lord parted the waters for them to cross safely. Another says that it was uttered by Esther in the throes of trying to make up her mind whether to accept Mordecai's challenge to help the Jewish people.

peaceful words which Jesus quoted from Ps 31:6 (verse 5 in the English translations). How can we trust the accounts of those who contradict one another, they ask? Again, the point is that in the context of the whole of Psalm 22 they do not contradict one another. It is well known that the four gospels do not all record the same events and conversations, etc, although there is a large measure of overlap. But each has preserved something of the trust of Jesus in his Father even at his time of death. It is not at all unreasonable to assume that Jesus moved through the experience of Psalm 22 before resting in the security of Psalm 31. It is quite possible that Jesus cited both psalms on the cross.

However, our focus in this chapter is not on the opening of the psalm, nor its overall context of confidence, but on the phrase which Christians claim speaks directly of the method of Jesus' death, namely crucifixion, by which his hands and feet were pierced by large nails, thus pinning him to a cross-shaped execution stake. He was left to die there as a circle of people stood by and watched.

Whereas the traditional Christian understanding and translation has been 'they have pierced my hands and feet', the traditional Jewish translation, whether as a genuine understanding of the text or as a counter-measure to the Christian interpretation, has been the one followed in the recent Jewish Publication Society version:

> Dogs surround me;
> a pack of evil ones closes in on me,
> like lions [they maul] my hands and feet.

The third line is obviously the crucial one. The phrase, 'my hands and feet' is agreed by both traditions. But in place of what Christians maintain is the final part of the jigsaw of that line, namely, 'they have pierced', we find the quite different phrase, 'like lions [they maul]'. The verb in parentheses is supplied, along with the parentheses, in the Jewish translation, because there is no such verb in the text. What it all means is that there is a Hebrew word in the text which Christians and Jews translate differently: Christians take it as a verb meaning 'to pierce', while Jewish tradition takes it as a phrase meaning 'like lions'. However, this leaves the Jewish tradition with no verb with which to make sense of the whole line, and so the commentators are forced to speculate that a verb must have dropped out of the text at this point. They then supply this supposed verb, either 'to maul', as in this translation, or some such verb.

Interestingly, the Jewish translation referred to above gives a footnote to this line of text. It states simply that the translators are here following the tradition: 'With Rashi; cf Isa. 38:13'. Their translation of that verse in Isaiah reads as follows:

> Then it was as though a lion
> Were breaking all my bones;
> I cried out until morning.

Their intention is to give the impression that this verse is simply another poetic description of the anguish of a person's soul when he or she is under the kind of oppression that the psalmist and others experience.

This certainly makes sense, and if it had been spelt out that way, then there would never have been any controversy. But it is not spelt out that way. The lack of a verb in this Jewish reading is a very serious flaw. Rashi knew this difficulty, but proceeded to translate the phrase this way:

> As if crushed by the mouth of a lion are my hands and my feet.[367]

---

[367] There is a strong tradition of reading the text in this way in the Jewish community, although there is also a variety of ways in which the reference to a lion is understood. Perhaps the least faithful to the intention of the psalmist is the interpretation of Malbim, who has: 'my hands and my feet are like those of a lion in that they are able to stand up to the enemy' !

The Masoretic Text, which forms the basis of the translations of the Hebrew Bible for both Jews and Christians, has a set of vowels which make it read as if it were a phrase meaning 'like the lion', even though it is always taken as 'like a lion', or 'like lions', in the translations. The real question is whether this was the *original* reading of the word. The particular technical issue here concerns the fact that in Hebrew, vowels and consonants are quite distinct, so that adults are expected to be able to read and write without the presence of vowels in a text. It is still this way today in modern Hebrew books, newspapers, etc. The original scrolls of the Hebrew Bible did not have the vowels included, and the scrolls of the Torah in synagogues to this day keep up this ancient tradition: there are no vowels included in them either. Printed editions of the Hebrew text of the Bible have vowels included, because they are directed specifically towards people who have either lost, or never had, mastery of the Hebrew language, which is to say most modern Jews and Christians. But it is most important that readers appreciate the fact that it is only when vowels are added to letters, whether physically on a page or in the mind of the reader, that specific words are formed. Until vowels and letters are combined, a Hebrew 'word' could mean several things. By way of analogy, I could write the following combination of English letters without any vowels and ask the reader to list as many words as possible that would satisfy the letters: BRD.[368] It is clear, then, that it is of the utmost importance to ask whether the Masoretic text faithfully preserves the original vowels for this difficult word.

The Masoretic text was completed in the eighth to tenth centuries CE, close to a millenium after the time of Jesus and the rise of the Church. The final and authoritative decision as to the correct way to read the text was not made, therefore,

---

[368] I can immediately think of the following possibilities: bird, bard, board, bored, bread, beard, bride. There are others, too.

until the Middle Ages. Of course the community had been reading the text as if the vowels were there because they knew what the words meant. But had all the Jewish communities read the word in our verse as if it were the phrase 'like the lion'? Or did the Masoretes change the vowel tradition to bring it in line with their own thinking, thereby dissociating the psalm from any connection with the death of Jesus? Were the vowels which turn these Hebrew letters into the phrase 'like the lion' actually the original ones?

Now I realise that this very discussion may sound quite disturbing to many Christians who have been unaware of this issue of letters and vowels in the Hebrew manuscripts. Perhaps it sounds as if I am dabbling with unacceptable matters. But lest some might think that I am moving into dangerous territory just for my own purposes, let me quote three relevant sentences from the Preface of the New International Version of the Bible:

> Sometimes vowel letters and vowel signs did not, in the judgement of the translators, represent the correct vowels for the original consonant text. Accordingly, some words were read with a different set of vowels. These instances are usually not indicated by footnotes.[369]

In other words, this debate about the original text of the Hebrew Bible, focusing on the matter of the vowels associated with the letters, is a live issue at the heart of Bible translation work. To return to our current text, it is highly significant that the LXX, itself a Jewish translation made 250 years or so before the birth of Jesus, did not translate the word in the fashion of the Masoretes. The LXX gives us the translation, 'they pierced/dug at my hands and feet' (using the Greek word *oruxan*). Clearly the Jewish translators understood the key word to be a verb, not a noun-phrase,

---

[369] *The Holy Bible. New International Version* (International Bible Society, East Brunswick, NJ, 1984), p viii.

and moreover, the specific verb 'to pierce' or 'to dig'. The Vulgate followed this LXX tradition (using the Latin verb, *foderunt*), and most Christians, living in this tradition, will have been quite unaware of any controversy over the word. These translations would seem to presuppose one of the following Hebrew verb forms: k'rû, krû or kôrû.

It will be worthwhile to pause at this point to ask the question whether a reference to lions is even appropriate in this verse. There has been a reference to lions some verses before, but the metaphor has now changed to that of a pack of wild scavenging dogs forcing the poor man into a corner.[370] It does seem that a mention of 'the lion' would be inappropriate here.[371]

This difficult word, about which Christians and Jews differ so greatly, will now have to occupy our attention. The Hebrew text has k'ry at the crucial point, and it is the correct way to read this word which lies at the heart of the problem. At one level, Christians point out that the word for a lion which the Jewish traditions say is being used here is in fact never found in the psalms as a word for a lion. The word which is used in the psalms is slightly different, namely 'ryh not 'ry. In other words, the traditional Jewish interpretation of this word has certain textual problems, as does the

---

[370] For references to dogs as symbolising those who prowl at night to prey on the vulnerable, see 2 Kings 9:35–36; Psalms 59:7, 15 (verses 6 and 14 in the English); 68:24 (verse 23 in the English); and Jeremiah 15:3.

[371] In fact the Masoretes themselves saw the problem here, as we can see from the marginal comment they made to the effect that this word only occurs twice in the Bible in this form, and that it has a different meaning in each case. In the other case, namely Isa 38:13, it must mean 'like a lion', so that they saw it as meaning something else here. For a full discussion of this technical point see C. F. Keil and F. Delitzsch, *Commentary on the Old Testament*, vol 5 (Eerdmans edition, Grand Rapids, MI, 1976), pp 317–20.

traditional Christian interpretation.[372]

But at a more serious level altogether, Christians claim that the original Hebrew word was in the form of a verb, even although the Masoretic text presents it as being a preposition followed by a definite noun. In other words, Christians have said that the text was deliberately altered by the rabbis and the scribes to express an anti-Christian polemic.

The commonest suggestion made by Christian commentators is that the original Hebrew text used a root krh, meaning 'to dig' or 'to bore'. Jewish critics make two objections to the standard Christian interpretation: on the one hand, if this were the original verbal root, they say, then it could not have resulted in the word found in the text; and on the other hand, this verb never means 'to pierce' in the Hebrew Bible.

The specific criticism of the first point is that a root krh could not produce a verb where the first three letters would be kr', which is what we have in our verse. We shall return to this point shortly. With respect to the second criticism, Jewish commentators state that this particular verb is found in the Hebrew Bible meaning 'to dig', but not 'to pierce'. Some examples of passages where the verb is used in this sense are Gen 26:25; Exod 21:33; Num 21:18; Ps 7:16; 57:7 (verses 15 and 6 in the English translations). Some refutationists actually proceed to offer advice to Christians who wish to find a suitable verb for their desired result! In Exod 21:6 the verb for 'piercing' is rts'; in Isaiah 13:15 it is dqr; and in 2 Kings 18:21 it is nkr.

This criticism sounds very serious for the Christian position. Can a legitimate connection really be made between the letters of the Hebrew text and the translation of the LXX and the Christian community? The Hebrew verb can and does mean 'to dig', and so it seems to me that in the context of the

---

[372] For this word in the psalms, see Ps 7:3 (verse 2 in the English), 10:9, 17:12 and, especially, verse 13 (verse 14 in the English) in this very Psalm 22.

verse we can arrive at an acceptable translation along the lines of 'they dig into my hands and my feet'. This could portray the image of dogs gnawing at the man's bones just as they would gnaw at any other bones. The particular issue is that many Christians are set on establishing the specific translation 'pierce', rather than 'dig', so that they can achieve a reference to the crucifixion, when Jesus' hands and feet were pierced by the nails.

Some prefer to derive the verbal form of 'piercing' from another root than the one mentioned above. They see the present Hebrew word as a damaged or altered form of the plural participle (k'rîm) of the root kôr, meaning 'to bore through, to pierce'. The verse then reads that dogs/evil men have surrounded the psalmist, 'piercing my hands and feet'. Those who object that the root kôr could not give a form k'ry with the appearance of the glottal stop ('), need to realise that precisely this type of irregularity is found elsewhere in the Hebrew Bible.[373] The biblical Hebrew language was a living language and, like all languages, it had its range of dialectical and other irregularities which went into its creation and development.

Delitzsch noted that this word in Psalm 22 occurs in one other place in the Hebrew Bible, in a verse which we mentioned earlier, Isa 38:13,[374] but he was sure that in the Isaianic text a *verbal* form was undoubtedly called for. His suggestion that we read the word in the psalm exactly as the word in Isaiah has the merit of keeping the letters as we now have them, without requiring the reinstatement of any letter which may have dropped out of the text. Only the vowels need to be emended, according to his suggestion. In place of the present form, ka'arî, meaning 'like the lion', Delitzsch

---

[373] For example, in Hos 10:14 we find q'm for the usual qm; in Ezek 28:24, 26 we find sh'ṭîm for the expected shṭîm.

[374] C. F. Keil and F. Delitzsch, *Commentary on the Old Testament*, vol 5, on Ps 22:16, pp 317f.

held that the original form was ko'arê, a participle meaning 'piercing'. Some Hebrew manuscripts actually have this or another verbal form here, as Delitzsch also noted.

Delitzsch was happy to presume that it was the verb kôr which lay behind this verbal form, citing as analogous irregular forms of such verbs the form of the verb 'to be high' in Zech 14:10, and the form of the verb 'to stand' in Dan 7:16.[375]

In short, the issue involves highly technical considerations of the grammar and semantic roots of the Hebrew language. The truth is that neither Jewish nor Christian commentators can claim the certainty which they wish to claim. Each community is making assumptions about what is or is not possible concerning the Hebrew language of First Temple Israel. Once again, I counsel Christian readers against being either linguistically or theologically dogmatic. However, the LXX understanding of the text, followed by Christian scholarship down the centuries, is perfectly defensible, and Christians can certainly retain their confidence in their interpretation.

The rabbis may well claim that the LXX was altered by the Christian churches which preserved it, so as to provide a text which suited them, and Christian leaders may well respond by saying that it was the rabbis, specifically the Masoretes, who altered the text in order to cripple a powerful Messianic prophecy about the death of the Messiah. Did the psalmist see a crucifixion in his own mind's eye, or just the sight of a man being stabbed by the spears of his persecutors? Was he perhaps simply using metaphorical language, imagining the man's suffering as being like that of someone who is surrounded by wild dogs? We cannot bring any proof to establish an answer to that question, but the appropriateness of the psalm to the figure of Jesus hanging on the cross is clear for

---

[375] In Zech 14:10 we find r'mh, and in Dan 7:16 we find q'my'.

every Christian to see. There is no real reason to doubt that Jesus saw in the whole of Psalm 22 a profound reference to his own death and to his resurrected witness to God. The whole psalm was an indispensable part of Jesus' own commentary on what was happening at his death, and the difficult verse which we have focused on plays its full part.

POSTSCRIPT

'In quietness and trust is
your strength'

These words from Isa 30:15, spoken in another context originally, also speak to me in the context of responding to Jewish refutationists. Right at the beginning of this book I made a point of emphasising two attitudes which I believe are not only appropriate from believers in Jesus, but also effective in sharing with Jewish people the Good News of Jesus' Messiahship: confidence and modesty. Isaiah's words are translated by 'trust' and 'quietness', but they are emphasising the same attitudes.

The whole Bible, from Genesis to Revelation, is a wonderfully integrated revelation from God, and, in spite of the attacks of its detractors, it does reveal God's plan for Israel and the world. The Messianic prophecies which are found in the pages of the Hebrew Bible, the first part of the biblical revelation, are clearly fulfilled in the life and ministry of Jesus of Nazareth – at least it is clear for those who have discovered for themselves that Jesus is the Messiah. However, for all those Jewish people (and others) who have not made this great discovery, it is far from clear that these words on the pages of the Hebrew Bible refer to Jesus.

What is more, for those whose vision is limited to the evils of life which we see around us every day, it is far from evident that there is a God in heaven, the God of Israel, who is in control of life, let alone that the Messiah has already come to his people.

Sometimes I meet Christians who characterise Jewish people who actually *deny* that Jesus is the promised Messiah as enemies of the Gospel, but I do not think that this is fair or helpful. In one sense, we might want to say that any denial of Jesus' Messiahship is an expression of antagonism towards him, but so few Jewish people, in my judgement, are really enemies of Jesus in the commonly understood meaning of that term that I doubt whether it is right to speak like this. I think that the various specifically Jewish objections to Jesus are legitimate objections, as far as the Jewish community is concerned. And they need to be taken seriously, considered fairly and responded to in a serious manner.

In this book we have looked at the basic Jewish objections to the Gospel, and have even spent a little time examining a few of the most important Messianic texts which are related to Jesus. I hope that I have succeeded in convincing my readers of what I see as the two pillars of any appropriate and effective sharing of the Good News of Jesus with today's Jewish community:

- *Confidence in the truth of Jesus' Messiahship.* There is no need for Christians to fear any honest and rigorous exegesis of the Messianic prophecies. At the end of the examination, the application of the prophecies to Jesus will be intact, even if there are also other applications which are technically possible. What is impossible is the attempt by some to disconnect the lines which connect Jesus to the prophecies. In spite of all the efforts to disqualify Jesus from being the promised Messiah, he remains the only true candidate, looking back over the past two millennia. Those who wish to argue that the Messiah is yet to come must realise that the burden of persuasion lies on them.
- *Personal modesty in our presentation and representation of Jesus.* This is not at all because of any doubt about Jesus in the mind of the community of believers, but out of respect for the Jewish community's reluctance to trust Christians and Jewish people who have become believers in Jesus. That reluctance is based on centuries of negative

experience in which the Churches' antisemitic actions spoke so very much louder than their words and interpretations.

The testimony of your life is the best testimony to the Messiahship of Jesus which you can offer any Jewish person. It is only when the Spirit of God himself touches any person's heart that the biblical evidences really become persuasive. This is not in any way to denigrate Scripture, or to devalue the power of the Word of God, but it is to put things in their right perspective. Jesus, the Word of God incarnate, is the central revelation of God among us, and he is the one who makes Scripture live for us.

May the Holy Spirit bless us with real love for the Jewish people, with genuine respect for their calling, with repentant hearts for what was done to them in the name of Jesus, and with a transforming vision of the loving purpose of God for them!

May the Holy Spirit bless us with the excitement and commitment which Paul knew, and may we also be inspired by the knowledge that

> If their rejection is the reconciliation of the world, what will their acceptance be but life from the dead?

May the Holy Spirit bless us as we seek, humbly but joyfully and confidently, to introduce Jesus, the Messiah, the Son of David, to those of the Jewish community who, for various reasons and in a variety of ways, deny that he is the Messiah!

Notes on persons and sources

Jewish historical figures of note mentioned in the text

NB The use of the historical–geographical–political terms
'Palestine' and 'Palestinian' in these biographical sketches
is not at all a reflection of my attitude to the issues of modern
Zionism or the like. The Jewish community itself uses the
two designations 'Babylonian' and 'Palestinian' to differentiate between the two regions of spiritual and political
authority in the Jewish world in those early and formative
centuries.

Abbahu (*c* 279–320 CE) One of the Palestinian Amoraim who
lived and worked in Caesarea, which was at that time the
centre of Roman administration for the region. It was also the
intellectual centre of Palestinian Christianity, and he was
involved in many polemic debates with Christians.

Abraham Ben Mordecai Farissol (*c* 1451–*c* 1526 CE) This
noted geographer, biblical exegete and polemicist spent his
life in Italy. He was chosen by the Jewish community of
Ferrara to represent Judaism before the Duke of Ferrara in a
public disputation with two Dominican monks. His fame as a
polemicist rests now on his work, *Magen Avraham* (*The
Shield of Abraham*), which attacks Christianity but also has
a chapter attacking Islam.

Abraham Ibn Ezra (1089–1164 CE) Born in Spain, he lived
there until 1140, amassing his depth of scholarship until he
became a true polymath. His areas of expertise covered
poetry, medicine, philosophy, Hebrew grammar, astronomy

and biblical exegesis. In 1140 he became a wandering scholar, and most of his creative work comes from this period. He insisted that the plain meaning of the biblical text is what determines all correct exegesis, and his commentaries are still highly valued in the Jewish community.

Akiva (c 50–135 CE) One of the most prominent and influential of all the Tannaim, making a decisive mark on the development of *halakhah*. Although he began life as an uneducated shepherd and became a 'mature student' in his adult life, few scholars equal his place in the tradition. He died as a martyr for Judaism.

Amoraim This is the title given to the rabbinic scholars who were active from c 200 CE, when the Mishnah is thought to have been completed, till the time when the two Talmuds were completed (mid to late sixth century CE). It is their deliberations and decisions which form the bulk of the Talmuds.

Bahya Ben Joseph Ibn Pakuda (c 1050–c 1120 CE) This great moral philosopher, ethicist and composer of liturgical poetry lived in Muslim Spain. His major work, written in Arabic, is known in English as *The Duties of the Hearts*, and has had a massive impact on all subsequent Jewish pietistic and moral literature and thought.

Bar Kappara (early third century CE) One of the Palestinian scholars who lived in the period linking the Tannaim and the Amoraim. He lived around Caesarea, possibly at Lydda, and was regarded as an outstanding authority by his peers. He specialised in teaching by means of fables and parables. He was known for his disputes with Christians.

Bar Kochba (died 135 CE) Little is known of this man, whose real name seems to have been Shim'on Bar Koseva. However, he became the leader of the Second Jewish Revolt against the Romans, in 132–5 CE, and was killed at the end of that revolt. He was reputedly of Davidic descent and must have possessed a charismatic personality as well as great military skill. In fact we are told in the Jerusalem Talmud that Rabbi Akiva considered him to be the Messiah. He is known by his nickname Bar Kochba, meaning 'Son of the Star', which is derived from the use of this word for a star in Num 24:17, a passage regarded as Messianic by many Jewish people.

David Kimhi (*c* 1160–*c* 1235 CE) This famous son of a famous father (Joseph Kimhi) came from Narbonne, in Provence. He is an acclaimed grammarian and biblical exegete, and is often referred to by the acronym Radak (standing for Rabbi David Kimhi). He was a champion of the plain rational sense of the Scripture and was involved in anti-Christian polemics, taking pains to charge Christians with having a corrupt text of the Hebrew Bible, and with using irrational interpretations of Scripture.

Essenes This is the name given to an intense Jewish brotherhood (sect) which flourished in the second half of the Second Temple period, from the second century BCE to the end of the first century CE. It was a strictly religious, quasi-monastic movement centred, in Jesus' time, on the NW shore of the Dead Sea. They lived by their own farming skills and the selling of crafts and other things which they prepared in their community. There were possibly never more than 5,000 of them at any time. They gave immense emphasis to ritual and moral purity, requiring a three-year initiation period before new initiates could join their movement. They had their own religious calendar and spiritual leader, attacking the Jerusalem priesthood as corrupt in all its duties and responsibilities, and they devoted themselves to painstaking study of the Scriptures. Some scholars believe that they had an influence on John the Baptist.

Franz Rosenzweig (1886–1929) An influential German theologian and philosopher who nearly went through a 'cultural conversion' to Christianity early in his life, but balked at the hypocrisy of it. Some years later, however, under the clear influence of a distant relative, Eugen Rosenstock-Huessy, he decided once more to convert, but this time as a way to somehow 'complete' his Jewishness in a philosophically-responsible Christianity. So in 1913 he attended what he thought would be his last Yom Kippur service before his conversion, but instead was so inspired by the service that he resolutely rejected Christianity as being in any sense a fulfilment of Judaism, and devoted his work thereafter to a defence of the Jewish faith. He is very well known for his 1921 classic, translated into English in 1971 as *The Star of Redemption.*

Ge'onim This is the term used to designate the formal heads of the two Babylonian rabbinic academies from the end of the sixth to the mid eleventh centuries CE. The singular, *ga'on*, is a word meaning 'eminence' or the like. These men were the highest authorities in world Jewry throughout those generations.

Hillel the Elder (end of first and start of second centuries CE) Perhaps the greatest of the Second Temple period rabbinic scholars, he was born in Babylon but later lived for a while in Jerusalem. He was appointed as the Nasi, or head, of the rabbinic assembly in his day and became the founder of a whole school of thought and practice which gradually became the dominant one in rabbinic tradition. He is famous, among other reasons, for giving his name to the seven systematic principles of hermeneutics for determining the *halakhah*.

Hoshaiah (third century CE) A Palestinian *amora* who lived in Caesarea, though he was actually born in Babylon. Deeply respected, above all for his piety and humility, he was known simply as 'The Great'. He was closely associated with refutations of Christianity.

Isaac Ben Judah Abrabanel (1437–1508 CE) Born in Lisbon to a Spanish family, after the expulsion of 1492 he moved to Naples and then finally to Venice. He became a statesman, philosopher and biblical exegete of note, well versed in renaissance humanistic philosophy as well as Jewish philosophy. He wrote expositional commentaries on all the prophetic books, paying especial attention to the Messianic prophecies. He also interacted to a great degree with Christian expositions of these passages.

Isaac Mayer Wise (1819–1900) Born in Bohemia to an Orthodox family, he studied in Prague and Vienna before emigrating to America in 1846. He served as an Orthodox rabbi in a couple of congregations in America, but began to introduce reforms in them, such as mixed seating, the use of the organ in music and confirmation ceremonies for the youth. He continued along this path of pioneering Reform Judaism and was known as 'the father of Reform Judaism in the USA'. He also became a fierce opponent of any concept of mission to Jewish people, both speaking and writing against it with barb and determination.

Jacob Ben Asher (*c* 1270–1343) A great halakhic authority of the Middle Ages, he was born in Germany, but left there to study and work in Spain. He is best known for his seminal codification of the *halakhah* which is called the *Arba'ah Turim* (*The Four Rows*). In this work he organised the legal aspects of Jewish religious life into four major sections. From this work he gained his common nickname, the Ba'al Turim.

Jacob Frank (1726–91) One of the Jewry's most famous false messiahs, he was born in Poland but travelled extensively. He was intensely ambitious and also became fascinated by Jewish mysticism. Both of these factors came to the fore in his career as self-styled successor of the infamous false messiah, Shabbetai Tzvi. He formed his sect around the embers of Shabbetai Tzvi's movement, starting as a regional leader and authority within the movement and then claiming to be the inheritor of his mantle. A rabbinical assembly excommunicated them in 1756. Fearing persecution, Frank appealed for protection to the Catholic bishop. This suited the Church, which dreamed of a mass conversion to Christianity, and Frank played them off very skilfully, pretending to believe in the Trinity yet seeing himself, not Jesus, in the role of Messiah. He took part in several disputations with rabbis at the request of the bishop, notably in 1757 and 1759, and actually led many of his followers through the rite of baptism in 1759.

Joseph Albo (*c* 1380–*c* 1440) A Spanish Jewish philosopher, most famous for his deeply influential book of philosophical theology, the *Sefer Ha-Ikkarim* (*Book of Principles*), completed in 1425. He was one of the major Jewish participants in the Tortosa Disputation of 1413–14.

Joseph Kimhi (*c* 1105–*c* 1170) A noted grammarian, biblical exegete and polemicist, he was born in Spain but fled persecutions there to Narbonne, in Provence. He was a fervent champion of the need to work from the literal meaning of the text. He published an anti-Christian polemical treatise, the *Sefer Ha-Brit* (*Book of the Covenant*), which was one of the first such works written in Europe and exercised a vast influence on subsequent works in this genre.

Joshua Ben Levi (early third century CE) A Palestinian *amora* in the transition period from the Tannaim, and one of its leading figures. He served the Jewish community in diplomatic relations with the Romans. He was also noted for his disputations with Christians, the sources associating him especially with concern for the coming of the Messiah.

Judah Bar Shalom (fourth century CE) A Palestinian *amora* especially associated in the traditions with anti-Christian polemics. He stressed the significance of the Oral Torah in his many dealings with Jewish believers in Jesus.

Judah Halevi (*c* 1075–1141 CE) One of the greatest of all Hebrew poets and philosophers, he was a physician by profession. Born in Spain, he always had a desire to emigrate to Palestine to await the coming of the Messiah. Eventually he made the journey there, via Egypt, but died on the final stage of his voyage from Egypt to Palestine. His most famous philosophical work is known in English as *The Book of the Khazars*, an apologetic for Judaism in the face of the threat from Aristotelian philosophy, Christianity and

Islam. The book purports to be an account of the conversion to Judaism of the king of the Khazar kingdom, after he had heard representatives from the vying philosophies, and reflects Halevi's conviction that Judaism is The Religion *par excellence*.

Leo Baeck (1873–1956 CE) A German-born rabbi and a leader of Progressive Judaism into the twentieth century. He has proven very influential in the Christian world too, acting as a mediator of Jewish perspectives and insights for Christians. One of his most famous works, called in English *The Essence of Judaism*, was published in 1905 as a response to the equally-famous liberal Protestant book of Adolph Harnack, entitled in English, *The Essence of Christianity*. Baeck argued that Christianity was a typical 'romantic' religion, unconcerned with the here and now of life and its struggles, whereas Judaism was the archetypal 'classical' religion, committed to action and involvement in the world.

Martin Buber (1878–1965 CE) Born in Vienna, he became one of this century's most important Jewish philosophers, religious or otherwise. He became an authority on the Hasidic movement and a profoundly influential leader within the Zionist movement. The wider world knows him best for his seminal work published in 1925, *Ich und Du*, translated into English under the title *I and Thou*. This book represents one expression of his pioneering work in the philosophy of dialogue.

Me'ir Ben Shim'on Ha-Me'ili (first half of the thirteenth century CE) Born in Provence, he later became the head of its Jewish community, basing himself in Narbonne. He frequently engaged in disputes with Christian clergy, and his most important work, *Milhemet Mitzvah*, from around 1245, is an account of one such disputation with the Bishop of Narbonne.

Me'ir Loeb Ben Yehiel Michael (= *Malbim*) (1809–79 CE) Born to a Polish family, he became a very popular and important biblical exegete and preacher. He was appointed

Chief Rabbi of Rumania. His commentary on the Hebrew Bible quickly became one of the most influential in the Jewish community. His emphasis was on the literal meaning of the text as the only sure foundation for any true exegesis. Working from the text of Daniel, he actually speculated at one point that the Messianic Age would begin somewhere between 1913 and 1928.

Moses Ben Maimon (= *Maimonides* = *Rambam*) (1135–1204 CE) One of Judaism's great giants of scholarship. A physician by profession, he was also a magisterial philosopher and halakhist in the Jewish community. Born in Cordova, Spain, he moved in 1160, with his family, to settle in Fez, Morocco. His codification of Jewish laws, his commentary on the Mishnah and his celebrated book for Jewish people whose faith was being shaken by developments in philosophy (known in English as *Guide for the Perplexed*) have guaranteed that no one person has had as much impact on the development of Judaism since his time. He had a strong influence on Christian scholastic thought as well.

Moses Ben Nachman (= *Nachmanides* = *Ramban*) (1194–c 1270 CE) A Spanish talmudist, biblical exegete, kabbalist and physician who became another of Judaism's most influential religious authorities. Many non-Jews also came to value his counsel, including King James I of Aragon. In 1263 he was forced into his famous disputation with Pablo Christiani at Barcelona. He easily 'won' the debate, and thereby also won the bitter hatred of the Dominicans and the Franciscans who were there. After he published his account of the disputation, an action which further outraged the church authorities, he was forced into exile from Spain. In 1267 he arrived at Acre, later travelled to Jerusalem for a while and finally returned to live and work in Acre.

Moses Mendelssohn (1729–86 CE) A celebrated German Jewish philosopher of the Enlightenment, in its pre-Kantian period. He became a spiritual leader of German Jewry, and was one of the intellectual leaders of his age, within the larger Christian society as well. He strongly emphasised the priority of human reason as the only true arbiter of truth. He was most certainly not a confrontationist personality, and when he finally gave way and responded to the challenges of a Swiss pastor, Johann Kaspar Lavater, his public response avoided any attack on Christianity. He was, however, vigorously opposed to missionary activity of any kind directed towards the Jewish people, and saw Christianity as based on dogmas opposed to reason and natural religion.

Nathan Ben Joseph Official (thirteenth century CE) One of the leading polemicists of Franco-German Jewry and a passionate apologist for Judaism. He often debated with church officials and Jewish converts, and wrote an account of the 1240 Paris Disputation, since Rabbi Yehiel Ben Joseph of Paris, the main Jewish respondent, was his teacher. He also wrote accounts of various disputes in an influential work which he entitled *Yosef Ha-Mekanne* (*Joseph the Zealot*). This is a polemical commentary on the Bible, focusing on christological passages and refuting their christological interpretation verse by verse. It also contains a criticism of Jesus' life as depicted in the gospels.

Profiat Duran (died *c* 1414 CE) A Spanish Jewish physician and biblical exegete, and a fierce opponent of claims that Jesus was the Messiah. He wrote two polemical tracts against Christianity, especially denouncing the christological interpretation of the Messianic prophecies and the irrational nature of Christian doctrines. It seems that he had been coerced into outward Christian conversion at the time of the 1391 persecutions in Spain, only returning to an open Jewish life when he managed to escape into southern France. This must be the context for understanding his bitter opposition to Christianity.

Rabbi The title of 'rabbi' is derived from a Hebrew root meaning 'great'. In this noun form it came to mean 'master' and was developed as a title for the sages. Literally, it means 'My Master'. However, this development only took place in Palestine, in the tannaitic period after the destruction of the temple in 70 CE. In Babylonia they used the related term *rav*. These rabbis (in Babylonia as well as Palestine) were the spiritual and community leaders who inherited the mantle of the Pharisees of the period before the destruction of the temple. Their function was not as pastors or priests, but as teachers and arbiters in matters of *halakhah*. However, it was not considered fitting to make one's living from the teaching of the Torah, and so they almost all had professions or jobs from which they made the money necessary for daily life (cf Paul's profession as a tent-maker – Acts 18:3).

Savoraim This is the name given to the rabbinic sages who flourished between the ages of the *Amoraim* and the *Ge'onim*, that is, roughly from the end of the fifth to the end of the seventh centuries CE. The term *savora* is an Aramaic one used to denote a scholar with authority to render halakhic decisions.

Shabbetai Tzvi (1626–76) The most (in)famous of Jewry's false messiahs, he was born in Smyrna but his movement spread throughout the Jewish world. His movement fed on the awful misery of the Jewish communities of that time, most especially in the wake of the traumatic Chmielnicki massacres of 1648. But the other (and obviously related) major catalyst was the growth in interest in the Messianic and kabbalistic interpretations of history which was then prevalent. These two factors came together in the fervour with which Tzvi, who must have had a remarkable personality, was acclaimed by so many Jewish people. Even after he converted to Islam in 1666 to save his life, most of his devotees remained loyal to him, and even after his death many believed he would return to consummate his Messianic work.

Shlomo Yits'aki (= *Rashi*) (1040–1105 CE) Another of the great giants of Jewish scholarship and community leadership, he was established as the key commentator on the Hebrew

Bible and the Talmud. He was born in Troyes, France, and lived his life there, founding a centre of rabbinic study in *c* 1070. He was primarily concerned to establish the literal meaning of biblical texts, but also championed the rightful use, as he saw it, of midrashic interpretations when they really elucidated the text. He has had an enormous impact on Christian scholarship also, particularly via Nicholas de Lyra, who was himself such an influence on Martin Luther.

Shmuel Ben Me'ir (= *Rashbam*) (*c* 1085–*c* 1174 CE) A noted commentator on the Hebrew Bible and the Talmud from northern France. He was the grandson (and a student) of the great Rashi in Troyes. He adopted an extremely literal interpretation of the biblical text, and took part in several disputes with Christians, particularly attacking their use of typology and allegory.

Tannaim This is the term used to describe the sages from the time of Hillel the Elder to the final compilation of the Mishnah, *c* 200 CE. In other words, these are the scholars of the first two centuries CE, and represent the named teachers in the Mishnah. The word itself comes from an Aramaic root meaning to study/teach.

Yehiel Ben Joseph (died *c* 1265 CE) In 1224, this noted French Talmud scholar became the head of the Paris talmudical academy. He was admired by Jews and non-Jews alike for his intellectual and moral integrity. In 1240 he was chosen to be the chief Jewish representative at the Paris Disputation. About 1260, he emigrated to Palestine, and established a *yeshivah* at Acre, where he died a few years later.

Yohanan Ben Zakkai (died *c* 80 CE) This Palestinian *tanna* was the leading Pharisee and sage of his generation, and one of the great giants of Jewish tradition. He frequently engaged in open disputes with the Sadducees. After the destruction of the temple in 70 CE he was responsible for establishing what became the centre of rabbinic learning and the home of the Sanhedrin, in Yavneh.

Yom Tov Lipmann Muhlhausen (fourteenth to fifteenth centuries CE) A Bohemian rabbi who was mostly active in the city of Prague itself, he was an important biblical exegete, kabbalist and very active polemicist. He became so influential in the Jewish community that several Christians took it upon themselves to respond to his anti-Christian refutations. In 1390 he published what was to become an extremely popular compilation of disputation material under the generic title *Sefer Ha-Nizzahon* (*Book of Victory*).

Yose Ben Halafta (mid second century CE) A Galilean *tanna* from the city of Sepphoris, where he established one of the finest rabbinic centres in Palestine. He was a leader in the period after the traumatic defeat of the Bar Kochba Revolt. He is also known to have been regularly involved in disputes with Galilean Christians.

Christian historical figures of note mentioned in the text

NB Those people whose names are listed within square brackets [ ], are Jewish people who then 'converted' to Christianity.

Anselm (*c* 1033–1109) Born in Italy, he left for France in 1056, and then in 1059 entered the monastic school at Bec in Normandy. In 1063 he became prior there; in 1078 he rose to the position of abbot; and his outstanding intellectual ability and spiritual depth were acknowledged when he was consecrated as Archbishop of Canterbury in 1093. He championed the defence of the Christian faith by the use of reason, and is associated with the development of the tradition of establishing rational 'proofs of the existence of God'. In this he was influenced by, and influenced, leading Jewish philosophers.

Augustine of Hippo (= Aurelius Augustinus) (354–430) This Latin Father of the Church was born in North Africa to a pagan father and a Christian mother. After much soul-searching and teaching in the various philosophical schools of thought, he realised that it was moral, not intellectual, factors which were preventing him from a full commitment to Christianity. The year 386 saw this turning point in his life. He was baptised in 387, became a priest in 391, and in 396 became bishop of the see of Hippo. He led the Church's battle against what it saw as the major heresies (Manicheism, Donatism and Pelagianism) and few theologians have equalled his authority and influence in the Western Church to this day. He was the chief architect of what became one of the Church's basic policies *vis-à-vis* the Jewish people, namely that they should not be destroyed or banished from Christian lands but tolerated as a kind of visual sermon. Their pitiful status and condition was to be enforced upon them so that Christians could look at them and be reminded of what would befall anyone who rejected the ways of God. This policy probably saved Jewish lives, but contributed greatly to the tradition of teaching contempt for the Jewish people.

Calvin, *John* (1509–64) A French reformer and theologian who gave his name to a family of Churches in the Protestant tradition. After being brought up in the Roman Catholic Church and also studying theology in Paris for five years, he broke with that Church in 1533. Fearing persecution, he fled to Basle in 1535, and one year later began work in Geneva, organising the Reformation community there. He was a firm believer in the ongoing value of the civil law sections of the Hebrew Bible, and devoted himself to producing a theocratic government in Geneva along the lines laid down in the Hebrew Bible. His commentaries on the books of the Hebrew Bible have proved very influential in Reformed circles.

[*Christiani*, *Pablo*] (died 1274) A Jewish man from southern France who then converted to Christianity and thereafter became a fervent anti-Jewish polemicist. He joined the Dominican Order and began a special campaign of preaching to Jews in Provence. Finding no success there he moved to Aragon, becoming known for his leading role in the famous 1263 disputation at Barcelona. He was convinced that one could prove the truth of Christianity from the text of the Talmud itself. In 1269 he persuaded Louis IX of France to force Jewish people to listen to his sermons and to wear the Jewish badge.

Chrysostom, John (c 347–407) This Greek Father studied law and rhetoric before turning to theology. Early on in his life he felt called to a monastic lifestyle, and he lived this austere life for some eight years. He was ordained as a priest in Antioch in 386, being commissioned to devote himself to a preaching ministry. He was eventually elected Bishop of Constantinople. He was particularly gifted in public communication, and indeed his name is the Greek term for 'goldenmouthed'. His series of homilies on nine biblical books, delivered between 386 and 398, are regarded as the cream of the expositions of his age.

On the other hand, he was also one of the most virulently antisemitic preachers of all time. In the course of his first two years as a priest in Antioch he delivered eight homilies against the Jews. These were written down, copied and widely distributed, becoming immensely influential in poisoning people's minds against the Jewish people. We know that in large measure his bitterness was caused by the fact that many Christians were deeply impressed by the reverence and purity of Jewish worship and the wisdom of the counsel given by rabbis, and so were frequenting synagogues and the homes of rabbis.

Church Fathers This general term is used to designate the spiritual and intellectual/doctrinal authorities in the first centuries of Christianity. There are two groups of such Fathers, those in the Latin-speaking Western Church and those in the Greek-speaking Eastern Church.

Clement of Alexandria (c 150–c 215) A most important Greek Father, probably born in Athens, but finally settling in Alexandria in 180. He went there as a student at its famous Catechetical School, and eventually became its head in 190. In the year 202 he was forced to flee due to persecution.

Known for his determination to harmonise the best of Greek philosophy with the scriptural faith, he became a celebrated controversialist, especially against the Gnostics.

Crispin, *Gilbert* (*c* 1046–1117) A disciple of Anselm of Canterbury who later became Abbot of Westminster. He is important for his account of his religious debates with an unnamed Jewish merchant from Mainz, around 1095. This account is remarkable for its frank presentation of the good points made by his Jewish acquaintance, its generally respectful tone and the relatively high intellectual level of the debate.

Delitzsch, *Franz* (1813–90) An outstanding German Protestant scholar of Hebrew and Semitic languages, the Bible and Judaica. He became renowned as an expert in study of the Talmud and medieval Jewish religious sources. He was also a passionate champion of sensitive and informed mission to Jewish people. In 1880 he founded the famous Institutum Judaicum expressly for the training of Jewish and non-Jewish missionaries to Jewish people. He was also a fierce and tireless opponent of antisemitism.

[*Donin*, *Nicolas*] A thirteenth-century French Jew who became a pupil of the renowned Rabbi Yehiel Ben Joseph of Paris. However, he was eventually excommunicated for certain heretical views which he was said to hold. Later he converted to Christianity, joined the Franciscan Order and became a bitter opponent of his former co-religionists, especially his old teacher. He compiled a list of thirty-five accusations against the Talmud, calling for its public burning as a source of heresy and blasphemy. He was the prime mover in the decision to hold the 1240 Paris Disputation, in which Rabbi Yehiel was called as one of the four Jewish authorities to defend the Talmud. Shortly after this disputation was over, twenty-four wagonloads of Talmuds were confiscated and burned in Paris. It is worth pointing out that he was eventually condemned in 1287 by the General of the Franciscans, for his attacks on the Order.

Epiphanius (*c* 315–403) Born in Palestine, he was himself probably a Jewish believer in Jesus. He supported the monastic movement, and *c* 355 established a monastery near his home in the Judaean hills. The measure of the respect given to him is shown in the fact that he was elected as Bishop of Salamis. He is especially known as an impassioned opponent of all heresies, and his importance has been guaranteed by the preservation of his *Panarion* (Greek for 'Breadbasket'), a work attacking all the heresies known to him.

Irenaeus (*c* 130–*c* 200) Born probably in Smyrna, this Latin Father went to Gaul to live and serve, following a period of study in Rome. He was elected as Bishop of Lyons. He is acknowledged to be the first great Catholic theologian, linking the best of the Eastern and Western scholarship of his day. His chief work is known in English as *Against Heresies*. Above all he was a key person in the development of the Church's understanding of the two natures of Jesus.

Jerome (= Eusebius Sophronius Hieronymus) (*c* 342–420) The celebrated Christian scholar who produced the Vulgate Bible at the close of the fourth century CE. He first began to learn Hebrew in the period of three or four years when he lived as a hermit in the Syrian desert. His teacher was a Jewish believer in Jesus whom he met there.

Justin Martyr (*c* 100–*c* 165) One of the great early Christian apologists. He came from a pagan family and was born in Nablus (the biblical Shechem). After a long search in the various philosophies of his day he became a Christian around 130. He taught for a while at Ephesus, traditionally held to be the place of his famous dialogue with the Jewish person whom he refers to as Trypho. Later on he established a Christian school in Rome, and was eventually martyred there. He is best known for the account of his dialogue, a document which has proved considerably influential in the Church, whether it is actually based on a series of personal encounters or is simply an apologetic work presented in that fashion.

Lavater, *Johann Kaspar* (1741–1801) This Swiss pastor was also a mystic and a spiritual counsellor whose admirers included Goethe and William Blake. He challenged Moses Mendelssohn to defend Judaism as a worthy religion for eighteenth-century Europe, being keen to see the Jewish people convert and integrate as Christians into the new Christian society of Europe. His model of this new Christian Europe was typically one which endeavoured to integrate traditional Christian faith and the rational/cultural insights of the Enlightenment. The ongoing debate he had with Mendelssohn proved to be very significant at the close of the eighteenth century.

[**Lorki**, *Joshua*] (= Geronimo de Santa Fe) (died *c* 1419) Born to a Spanish Jewish family in the mid fourteenth century, his thoughts were directed to the Christian faith by the conversion of his teacher. Later on, these thoughts were galvanised and encouraged by the famous Dominican preacher, Vincent Ferrer. In 1412 he formally converted to Christianity, taking the baptismal name Geronimo de Santa Fe. He became a bitter opponent of Judaism and organised the Tortosa Disputation of 1413–14. He also wrote two anti-Jewish polemics. The Jewish community nicknamed him Megaddef, which means 'The Blasphemer', based on the initial letters of Maestre Geronimo de Fe.

Luther, *Martin* (1483–1546) This German Roman Catholic became a priest in 1507, and one year later was appointed as a lecturer in moral philosophy at the University of Wittenburg. In 1512 he became a Doctor of Theology and a Professor of Scripture, but he also became increasingly worried and distressed at the tension which he saw within himself and the Church over the relationship of life and righteousness to the unmerited grace of God. He came to believe that the traditional doctrines and practices had become unacceptably unbalanced, and in 1517 he pinned his famous Ninety-Five Theses to the door of the Schloss-kirche in Wittenburg. The German Reformation had begun.

In his early ministry he condemned the oppression of Jewish people, the burning of the Talmud, etc, and urged a new spirit of real brotherhood with them. He clearly believed that the Jewish people had been held back from seeing the truth of the Gospel by the attitude and behaviour of the Church, and was convinced that they would realise the Messiahship of Jesus when provoked to jealousy by a Church which treated them properly. Many Jewish leaders looked with hope and relief on this reformation movement, but there were no wholesale conversions to Christianity.

Whether this fact alone embittered Luther, or whether there was some specific catalyst, we do not know, but he certainly changed in his attitude to the Jewish people in his later ministry. He uttered some of the most virulently anti-semitic statements made by any Christian, and even went so far as to recommend the burning of rabbinic literature and the banishment of Jewish communities.

Martini, *Raymond* (*c* 1220–85) A Spanish Dominican friar who, although involved in some important anti-Muslim disputes, devoted himself to anti-Jewish polemics. He became an expert in Hebrew and in rabbinic texts, and took an active part in the 1263 Barcelona Disputation as a supporter of Pablo Christiani. In 1264 he became a member of the first Commission for censoring Jewish literature, looking for passages which they would judge to be offensive to Christianity. His most famous work has become one of the classics of the genre. It is entitled *Pugio Fidei* (*The Dagger of Faith*), dates from around 1280, and uses rabbinic litera-ture as well as biblical texts to prove his theological and christological claims.

Origen (= Origenes Adamantius) (*c* 185–*c* 254) Born to a Christian family in Alexandria, this Greek Father became one of the Church's most influential biblical exegetes and theologians. He was ordained as a priest in 230, and one year later founded his own important Christian school at Cae-sarea. In the persecutions of 250 he was imprisoned and tortured, dying from his traumatic condition a few years later. He is famous for his collection and presentation of six versions of the Hebrew Bible in a work known as the *Hexapla* (Greek for 'sixfold'), his successful opposition to the major heresy of Marcionism and his development of the Christian understanding of three levels of interpretation of the biblical text. In his exegetical and expositional work he talks about the three levels being the literal, the moral and the allegorical. He strongly favoured the last of these as the best.

Classic Jewish and Christian religious sources mentioned in the text

Apocrypha This term, meaning 'the hidden things' in Greek, is the name given to those books which were part of the Greek canon of the Jewish Bible, but never part of the Hebrew canon. They range in date from *c* 300 BCE to *c* 100 CE, from which we note that they all pre-date the final parting of the ways between Judaism and Christianity. They are of inestimable value in helping to create our picture of Jewish history and life in the intertestamental period. In the first four centuries of the Church, both in the East and the West, many leading authorities quoted from the Apocrypha as freely as they did from the Hebrew canon. The apocryphal books continue to hold a deutero-canonical status in the Roman Catholic Church. The Protestant Churches have, however, been quite ambivalent towards them, appreciating their worth and yet not willing to associate them with the level of inspiration of Scripture. Martin Luther, for example, included most of the Apocrypha as an appendix to his 1534 translation of the Bible into German.

Dead Sea Scrolls This is the name given to thousands of scrolls and fragments of documents found in the years from 1947 in the region of the Qumran community by the shore of the Dead Sea. A whole community lived there, and they seem to have been related to the group known as the Essenes. These documents provide the earliest copies of Hebrew biblical text by centuries and are thus priceless witnesses for the study of the text of the Hebrew Bible. Also found there were fragments from some apocryphal and pseudepigraphal texts, and many pieces produced by the members of the community. Their significance for the life of Jesus and the early Church is still a matter of scholarly controversy and speculation.

Kabbalah This is a Hebrew word which simply means 'tradition', but it has come to be used in a special sense for the Jewish mystical traditions. There always was such a mystical stream within the religious fabric of Judaism, but from the twelfth century CE the term kabbalah really became almost a technical term for what its adherents saw as a continuous tradition of spiritual searching for a vital, intense contact with God and the supernatural realm. Jewish scholars began to specialise openly in this esoteric teaching and lifestyle, which was deeply influenced by gnostic and neo-platonic philosophies. The most famous and influential of the several schools of kabbalistic thought is that of Isaac Luria, in sixteenth-century CE Safed.

Midrash Coming from a Hebrew root meaning 'to seek, to enquire', this term is used to refer to that method of interpretation which seeks to find other meanings than the literal in a biblical text. But there is real discipline involved in this exercise: it is not simply eisegesis. There are rules of interpretation which are to be strictly followed when working with a text, and the whole enterprise is grounded in a profound love for, and desire to be obedient to, the text. Discrete examples of this kind of interpretation are called midrashim, and whole collections of such interpretations are also called midrashim. The most famous and influential of these collections is one which deals with the Pentateuch and the Five Scrolls of the Jewish festivals. It is simply called *Midrash Rabbah* (*The Great Midrash*).

Other important midrashim mentioned in this book are the *Lekah Tov*, from the late eleventh century CE, affected by the First Crusade of 1096; the *Tanhuma*, utilising materials from the late fourth century CE onwards but completed in the ninth or even tenth century CE; and the *Yalkut*, compiled in Germany in the thirteenth century CE.

Mishnah Coming from a Hebrew root meaning 'to repeat, to teach', this term refers to those teachings of the rabbinic sages whose deliberations and decisions about the laws for the Jewish community became the authoritative foundation of rabbinic Judaism. These teachings and sayings, which were originally transmitted orally, were finally compiled in the form we have now by Rabbi Judah Ha-Nasi in around 200 CE. A discrete portion of teaching is also called a mishnah, as is the whole collection. The Mishnah forms the basis of the Talmud.

Peshitta This Syriac word meaning 'simple' is the name given to the official Syriac version of the Bible used by Syriac-speaking Christians, both orthodox and heterodox, in the region we now associate with Syria, Iraq and Iran. The translation of the Hebrew Bible shows affinities with the Targums at times and, generally speaking, it is believed that this part of the Peshitta was prepared by Jews, or at least with the active assistance of Jews.

Pesikta Rabbati This is the name given to an eclectic collection of midrashim put together in Palestine, probably in the seventh century CE. It is presented as homilies for the Jewish festivals and special Sabbaths. *Pesikta* is an Aramaic word which simply means a 'section, portion', and the full name of this Midrash, '*The Greater Pesikta*', serves to distinguish it from others of the same name and to highlight its importance.

Pseudepigrapha This term, which means 'false writings' in Greek, refers to an extremely important collection of religious books, and derives its name from the fact that one of the characteristics of the books is a deliberate policy of giving as the purported author an authoritative figure from

Jewish history. These books overlap to a great degree with those of the Apocrypha, but were never included even in the Greek canon. They are particularly concerned with the resolution of the conflict between good and evil and God's final intervention in history to vindicate himself and his people.

Septuagint (= LXX) This Greek version of the Hebrew Bible derives its name from the Latin term for seventy, hence the symbol often employed for it. According to the *Letter of Aristeas*, Ptolemy Philadelphus (285–246 BCE) commissioned this translation so that he could have a copy of the famous Jewish Scriptures for his celebrated library in Alexandria. Its name derives from the legend that seventy (or seventy-two, in another version) Jewish scholars undertook to translate it independently of one another, and yet all came up with exactly the same Greek text. As a matter of fact, there exist several different text traditions of the LXX, probably reflecting its actual origin as a collection of oral translations for the Alexandrian congregations. It is the oldest of all of the ancient versions and is therefore extremely important.

Sometimes it seems to have used a Hebrew text different from the Masoretic Text, while at other times we appear to have cases of deliberately chosen (mis)translations, and even misunderstandings of the Hebrew original. It includes those books not found in the Hebrew canon, known as the Apocrypha; it organises its books in a different order from the Masoretic Text; and there are some significant differences in the actual texts of 1 Kings, Jeremiah and Job. The New Testament uses it frequently, and it became the Bible of the early Greek-speaking Church.

Talmud Coming from a Hebrew root meaning 'to learn, to teach', this is the name given to the two great compilations of scholarly deliberations and decisions of the rabbinic sages in the generations after the completion of the Mishnah. The Jerusalem Talmud was completed in Palestine *c* 400 CE, while the Babylonian Talmud was completed over a century later. Of the two, the Babylonian Talmud is considerably longer but, more importantly, it has achieved by far the greater authority. Each of them consists of the Mishnah together with commentaries and supplements to it, and this second layer of material is said to 'complete' the Mishnaic tradition. The term for this second, completing layer, is Gemara, and both together are technically the Talmud, though many people misuse the word Talmud to signify simply the Gemara.

Targum This is an Aramaic word for 'interpretation, translation'. It is used for the Aramaic interpretative translations of the Hebrew Bible which derived from the tradition of having special interpreters translate the biblical texts orally in synagogues for the congregation members who were no longer fluent in biblical Hebrew. The Talmud says that this translation tradition goes back to the days of Ezra (Neh 8:8). Over many generations, these translators added more and more explanations and interpretations in their 'translations', creating a whole genre of sophisticated oral literature. Eventually these oral traditions were collected and committed to writing, and they have a great deal of authority in the Jewish community to this day. The three important targums to the Pentateuch are known as the Onkelos, the Pseudo-Jonathan, and the Palestinian targums.

Torah This profound Hebrew term is poorly served by the translation 'Law'. It encompasses much more than laws, although they are certainly part of it. The Hebrew root has something to do with firing something at a target, and it involves the whole of the dimensions of life. At its most narrow, the term Torah refers to the Pentateuch, but it is also used to denote the whole of the Hebrew Bible. It is clear that apart from laws of various types, this corpus includes poetry, historical models, wisdom sayings, visions, prophetic words, etc. Consequently, other English translations are preferred by many scholars (eg, Teaching, Instruction, Revelation).

I use the term 'Direction'. This word not only keeps alive something of the root meaning of the Hebrew original, showing that the Torah is the Direction of God for our lives, but also carries with it the idea of authority, being from the same root as the words Director, or directive.

In Jewish tradition the Hebrew Bible is called the *Written Torah*. But there is also a second stream of Torah in Jewish tradition, known as the *Oral Torah*. From long before the time of Jesus there evolved an oral tradition of interpretations and applications of the biblical text, especially the Pentateuch. Over the generations this community teaching became so integrated with the written text that it was believed that the text could not be understood and applied without it. Indeed the Pharisees and rabbis taught that one should not even try to separate the two. In time this significance of the traditions was expressed in the teaching that God gave this Oral Torah to Moses on Mount Sinai at the same time as he gave him the biblical revelation. After Moses, the rabbis taught, there was a kind of 'apostolic succession' of authority within the Oral Torah, being passed on through Joshua, the prophets, and those regarded as sound guardians of the tradition by the rabbis. Consequently, the Oral Torah is held by Orthodox Jewish people to have exactly the same authority as the Written Torah. The Talmud is a massively important part of this Oral Torah.

Tosefta This is a supplement to the Mishnah, and is held in high esteem as a halakhic source. Some of its sections provide alternative traditions and teachings to their Mishnaic equivalents, but usually it is simply a case of supplementary or complementary material.

Vulgate Before the end of the second century CE we know that there were translations of the Bible in Latin for those citizens of the Roman Empire who were not expert enough in Greek to use the LXX or other Greek versions. Essentially, this meant in the regions of southern Gaul and North Africa. In Rome itself there was no similar pressure until well into the third century CE. However, there were several versions of these translations, all of which are known by the title of Old Latin Versions, and all of which were based on the LXX. In the last part of the fourth century CE, Pope Damasus commissioned a biblical scholar, Jerome, to prepare a new Latin translation, in order to produce a single authoritative text for the Western Church.

After arriving in Palestine in 385 CE, Jerome realised that such an authoritative work would need to be based on the Hebrew original, not on the LXX, and he set about preparing just such a translation. He worked on it at his monastic centre in Bethlehem from 390–405 CE, but it was probably not until the sixth century CE that the whole Church accepted it in the form which we now know as the Vulgate. Its name comes from a Latin root meaning that it was the people's Bible. It is one of the great scholarly achievements of the Western Church, and was the official Bible of the Western Church until the Reformation, though even then it continued to have this role in the Roman Catholic Church until the 1940s.

Zohar This Hebrew word for 'brightness' is used as a title for what has become the most famous and influential of all of the Jewish kabbalistic works. It ascribes itself to the *tanna* Shim'on Ben Yohai, and to his circle of scholars and practitioners of the mystical traditions, but it is really a medieval Spanish work from the late thirteenth-century CE kabbalist, Moses de Leon. However, it undoubtedly does contain material which goes back centuries before his time. It takes the form of a type of commentary on parts of the Pentateuch.

Select bibliography

General Background

Cohen, Martin A., and Helga Croner. *Christian Mission – Jewish Mission* (Paulist Press, NY, 1982).

Greenstone, Julius H. *The Messiah Idea in Jewish History* (JPSA, Philadelphia, 1948).

Patai, Raphael. *The Messiah Texts* (Wayne State University Press, Detroit, 1979).

Riggans, Walter. *The Covenant with the Jews* (Monarch Publications, Tunbridge Wells, 1992).

Jesus Ben Joseph. An Introduction to Jesus the Jew (Monarch Publications, Tunbridge Wells, 1993).

Schochet, Jacob Immanuel. *Mashiach. The Principle of Mashiach and the Messianic Era in Jewish Law and Tradition* (SIE, NY, 1991).

Silver, Abba Hillel. *A History of Messianic Speculation in Israel* (revised edition, Beacon Press, Boston, 1959).

Classic and Pre-modern Jewish Refutations

Berger, David. *The Jewish–Christian Debate in the High Middle Ages* (JPSA, Philadelphia, 1979).

Chazan, Robert. *Daggers of Faith. Thirteenth-Century Christian Missionizing and Jewish Response* (University of California Press, Los Angeles, 1989).

Crool, R. Joseph. *The Restoration of Israel* (London, 1812).

Herford, Travers R. *Christianity in Talmud and Midrash* (Ktav, NY, 1903).

Lasker, Daniel J. *Jewish Philosophical Polemics against Christianity in the Middle Ages* (Ktav, NY, 1977).

Rankin, O. S. *Jewish Religious Polemic* (Edinburgh University Press, 1956).

Talmage, Frank. *The Book of the Covenant of Joseph Kimhi* (The Pontifical Institute of Mediaeval Studies, Toronto, 1979).

Troki, Isaac. *Faith Strengthened* (Hermon Press edition, NY, 1970).

Wise, Isaac Mayer. *A Defense of Judaism versus Proselytizing Christianity* (The Bloch Publishing & Printing Company, Chicago, 1889).

Contemporary Jewish Refutations

Alfandari, Mordecai. *Is Jesus Coming Again?* (Private publication, Jerusalem, 1980s).

Arkush, Shmuel. *Operation Judaism. Fact Pack* (Operation Judaism, Birmingham, 1986).
Target: Jews. A Case for Concern (video, Operation Judaism, Birmingham, 1988).

Berger, David, and Michael Wyschogrod. *Jews and 'Jewish Christianity'* (Ktav, NY, 1978).

Charing, Douglas S. *What You and Every Missionary to the Jews Should Know* (JLS Publications, London, 1971).

Fisch, Dov Aharoni. *Jews for Nothing* (Feldheim, NY, 1984).

Golding, Shmuel. *A Counsellor's Guide* (Vikuach Ve Dusiach, Jerusalem, 1985).

Levine, Samuel. *You Take Jesus, I'll Take God* (Hamoroh Press, Los Angeles, 1980).

Moshe, Beth. *Judaism's Truth Answers the Missionaries* (Bloch Publication Co, NY, 1987).

Schochet, Jacob Immanuel. *Square Circles* (tape of a public lecture, London, 1992).

Segal, Benjamin J. *The Missionary at the Door – Our Uniqueness* (Youth Commission, United Synagogue of America, NY, 1972).

Sigal, Gerald. *The Jew and the Christian Missionary* (Ktav, NY, 1981).

Singer, Tovia. *The Jewish Response to Missionaries* (Nine-part audio tape series with full Study Guide, Jews for Judaism, NY, 1994).

Sobel, B. Z. *Hebrew Christianity. The Thirteenth Tribe* (John Wiley & Sons, NY, 1974).

Christian and Messianic Jewish Responses

Fruchtenbaum, Arnold. *Jesus was a Jew* (Broadman Press, Nashville, 1974).

Jocz, Jacob. *The Jewish People and Jesus Christ* (3rd edition, Baker Book House, Grand Rapids, MI 1979).
The Jewish People and Jesus Christ after Auschwitz (Baker Book House, Grand Rapids, MI, 1981).

Justin Martyr. *Dialogue with Trypho the Jew* (ed A. Lukyn Williams, SPCK, London, 1930).

Kac, Arthur W. *The Messiahship of Jesus* (Moody Press, Chicago, 1980).

McCaul, Alexander. *The Old Paths* (London Societies House, London, 1837).

Williams, A. Lukyn. *A Manual of Christian Evidences for Jewish People* (2 volumes, SPCK, London, 1919).

The Covenant with the Jews

Walter Riggans

God once made a covenant with the Jews. Has he abandoned his promises—in favour of the Church? The Church has a shameful history of anti-semitism: is this because Christians think of themselves as the inheritors of God's favour? Are the Messianic Jesws, who remain culturally Jewish but accept Jesus as their Messiah, the key to the situation?

In answering these questions, the author motivtes us to explore our heritage more deeply. 'Evangelicals must learn to appreciate the insights of Judaism,' suggests Walter Riggans. 'They need to come to the point of genuine repentance for Christian anti-semitism. At the same time we must never lose sight of the fact that Jesus is Israel's one and only Messiah, and that our biblical mandate is to share this truth with the Jewish people.'

The Rev Dr Walter Riggans lived in Israel for nine years, and spent three of them as Director of the Church's Ministry among the Jews in Tel Aviv. He is now a tutor at All Nations Christian College in Ware, Hertfordshire.

ISBN 1 85424 188 5

Monarch
Publications

Messianic Jews:
The Search For Identity

John Fieldsend

One of the most significant phenomena of the church today must be the growth of the Messianic Jewish movement—Jewish people who have come to realise that Jesus of Nazareth really is the Messiah of Israel and the Son of God.

Of course there have always been such Jewish people in our churches, but today we are seeing the commitment of many of them to develop their own congregations and lifestyle, based on their Jewishness as well as their New Testament faith. Is this dangerous, or exciting and appropriate?

In this important and very readable book John Fieldsend, himself a British Messianic Jewish leader, helps us to explore the beliefs and practices of Messianic Jews today. He covers the nature of contemporary Judaism, the objections for both Jews and Christians, the chief characteristics of Messianic Judaism, and the part it can play in shaping the future development of the Body of Christ.

Co-published with Olive Press.

ISBN 1 85424 228 8

Monarch
Publications